# THE MARINES,
# COUNTERINSURGENCY,
# AND STRATEGIC CULTURE

# THE MARINES, COUNTERINSURGENCY, AND STRATEGIC CULTURE

## Lessons Learned and Lost in America's Wars

### JEANNIE L. JOHNSON

Foreword by Gen. Jim Mattis, US Marines (Ret.)

Georgetown University Press / Washington, DC

The publisher is not responsible for third-party websites or their content. URL links were active at time of publication.

Library of Congress Cataloging-in-Publication Data

Names: Johnson, Jeannie L., author. | Mattis, James N., 1950– writer of foreword.
Title: The marines, counterinsurgency, and strategic culture : lessons learned and lost in America's wars / Jeannie L. Johnson ; foreword by Gen. Jim Mattis, US Marines (ret.).
Description: Washington, DC : Georgetown University Press, 2018. | Includes bibliographical references and index.
Identifiers: LCCN 2017046605| ISBN 9781626165557 (hardcover) | ISBN 9781626165564 (pbk.) | ISBN 9781626165571 (ebook)
Subjects: LCSH: Counterinsurgency. | Strategic culture. | United States. Marine Corps. | Low-intensity conflicts (Military science) | United States—History, Military—20th century. | United States—History, Military—21st century.
Classification: LCC U241 .J635 2018 | DDC 359.9/6480973—dc23
LC record available at https://lccn.loc.gov/2017046605

19 18     9 8 7 6 5 4 3 2   First printing

Cover design by Jeremy John Parker.

Cover image courtesy of the Defense Visual Information Center.

*This book is dedicated to Steve, Benjamin, Sam, and Jess for their wonderful support and significant sacrifice across the many years necessary to complete this research.*

# CONTENTS

# FOREWORD

The last dozen years of war can be examined from many perspectives, but two points are clear: First, absent a historical framework, we cannot comprehend the implications of the type of wars we have fought inconclusively during the opening years of this century. Second, if we wisely anticipate that future enemies will move against our perceived weaknesses, then it is critical that we learn the enduring lessons of counterinsurgency.

In this focused monograph, Jeannie L. Johnson provides a researched and defined appraisal of the Marine Corps's institutional incorporation of the "lessons learned" in its twentieth- and twenty-first-century counterinsurgency operations. Bringing forward a fresh assessment and an occasionally controversial perspective, she has made a valuable contribution to understanding military innovation in a complex world. Ours is a world in which we are not permitted to fight only the wars for which our nation's forces are best suited. With competing missions and varied roles, the Marines have adapted to the nation's needs to defeat enemies "in every clime and place"—from shipboard detachments and landing parties with the US fleet to counterinsurgency in Central America, from trench warfare in France to amphibious shock assaults across the Pacific, from extended operations ashore when grossly outnumbered to counterguerrilla battles in Korea's mountains, from counterinsurgency against the Viet Cong to fighting main force North Vietnamese regular army units, from evacuation of embassies to humanitarian operations, and from mechanized operations across Middle East deserts to an amphibious assault over 350 miles into Afghanistan. So, as we embrace Dr. Colin Gray's advice to have the fewest big regrets when the next crises strike, only an open discussion incorporating perspectives that Dr. Johnson draws together will help us to fight well when the enemy next moves against our perceived weakness.

America's history is, of course, rife with counterinsurgency warfare. Professor Johnson's focus on the Marines' role is an appropriate topic through which the American experience can be examined. This is not the history one would expect. Her weaving together threads from various conflicts into a tapestry showing patterns permits a detached and arguably objective assessment of our country and, in particular, the Marine Corps's ability to build on a body of knowledge gained at great cost in treasure, lives, and moral authority. As such, it is unique in its efforts to examine a subject that will remain operant as we come to grips with a world in which the state system is under attack. Thoughtful yet revisionist, researched with historical references yet leavened with input from those who have fought, her analysis presents a picture that can serve as catalyst for change in the American approach to counterinsurgency.

Writing with insight and probing deeply into the US Marine Corps's counterinsurgency campaigns, Professor Johnson reminds us that even a Corps lacking any institutional confusion about its role being to fight well in every circumstance must learn—*really learn*—from its experiences. Charles Darwin, of course, being adamant on the alternative to adaptation, makes this imperative clear. Accordingly, to remain relevant as a naval expeditionary force-in-readiness, the Corps must appropriately incorporate war's lessons learned to stay in tune with warfare's changing requirements. If America's experiment in democracy is to thrive and pass on its freedoms intact to the next generation, its Marines must pass on and incorporate the lessons learned by the "soldiers of the sea" who preceded them in these complex "wars among the people." Professor Johnson's contributions are worthy in carrying out this endeavor.

Gen. Jim Mattis, USMC (Ret.)
Hoover Institution
Stanford University
Stanford, California
December 2016

# ACKNOWLEDGMENTS

I owe an enormous debt to Beatrice Heuser for her contributions, advice, and steering throughout my research process. I must also extend thanks to Kerry Kartchner for setting me on the path of strategic culture and Jeff Larsen for corralling these efforts into our first book. As they well know, this changed the course of my academic life, and I have appreciated their continued support throughout. The scholar who sealed my devotion to the topic of strategic culture was, without equal, Colin S. Gray. He may be thanked for inspiring my current career track and for continuing to surprise and delight me with strategic insights.

Generating the foundational methodology of this work, cultural topography, was only possible through the determined and enthusiastic support of Matthew T. Berrett in the Office of Near East and South Asian Analysis at the Central Intelligence Agency. His ability to clear a pioneering pathway for experimentation with a cultural method and his genius in arranging its original architecture are the reasons it is currently in play today. My academic department heads in the Political Science Department at Utah State University have been exceptionally supportive. In this vein I would like to thank Randy T. Simmons, Roberta Herzberg, Michael Lyons, and Tony Peacock, as well as my dean, John Allen.

The United States Marine Corps is an inexhaustibly fascinating topic, made all the more interesting by the insights, timely advice, and contributions from many of its members. In particular I would like to thank all of the Marines who patiently answered my questions and generously dedicated their time and thoughts to this product. The Marines of the Combined Action Platoon (CAP) program stand apart as an exceptional group and have my thanks both for their national service and for their gracious hosting of an academic in their midst. Their generously supplied oral histories and interviews will register as treasures in our national research repositories. CAP Marine Tim Duffie, with a heart of gold, will forever stand out as one of my heroes. I would also like to make special mention of Roch Thornton for his insights and thoughtful analysis of his own service. I am deeply indebted to retired general Jim Mattis for his patient and always thorough responses to my lists of never-ending questions and to Lt. Col. William Curtis for providing a sound scrubbing of the manuscript in its first drafts. Jeffery Davis, Jason Spitaletta, Joseph Mariani, Jake Falcon, and Ivan Cherry deserve special thanks, not only for their always valuable insights on Marine Corps culture, but also for making me smile every time they delivered them. Indispensable resources were generously supplied by Randy Shepard from J. Walter Thompson, Joan Thomas and Vickie Stuart-Hill from the National Museum of the Marine Corps, and Beth Crumley and Greg Cina from the USMC Historic Division.

Thanks to those who were willing to review and critique sections of this thesis even in its very rough first drafts. The reviewers who supplied their critical feedback through Georgetown University's publication process have set the gold standard as far as I am concerned. Their suggestions on both content and additional resources were invaluable and are much appreciated. Theo Farrell supplied critical adjustments to this research midstream and boosted confidence in the value of the work. Terry Terriff proved an expert guide on all things Marine, and Frank Hoffman has gifted me both his critical analysis and access to his vast knowledge of primary and secondary sources. I am greatly in his debt.

Blagovest Tashev shared his wisdom on Marine Corps service culture, and Kerry Fosher kept me honest regarding the state of cultural study within the Corps. Ben Connable, one of the most talented analysts across the Corps, made sure my assumptions did not go off the rails. Kael Weston is a valued friend and national hero who has provided service above and beyond the call of duty in Iraq and Afghanistan and offered me firsthand insight on the operations of the Corps across seven years of serving alongside Marines.

I leaned on Briana Bowen more often than should be morally permissible for her excellent editing and wordsmithing skills. She is an incredibly gifted writer, and I benefited much from her pen on my work. Research assistants Tyler Thomas and Lauren Roberts supplied valuable help in the research and editing process. I am so grateful for Ms. Roberts's attention to detail! Carlie Morrison kept me going through her sheer enthusiasm for the US Marine Corps and provided a critical assist by transcribing hours' and hours' worth of oral interviews with CAP veterans. Thanks also to Christine Leah, Steve Sharp, and Peter Crosby for their editing feedback and valued friendship.

Most of all, a heartfelt bow to my parents, Lynn and Cheryl Humphreys, who inspired in me a love of country, truth, and problem-solving and laid the foundation necessary for the confidence and skill set to pursue this work. And to my husband, Steve, thanks is too small a word for the gratitude I feel for the sacrifices he made and unremitting support he provided to see this through. He and our children, Benjamin, Sam, and Jess, never ceased to cheer on my efforts no matter how difficult it became. They are remarkable. This work is dedicated to them.

# INTRODUCTION

*Learning Counterinsurgency*

America's search for a counterinsurgency formula that will defeat insurgent foes and produce political stability will continue to stumble if not guided by sound understanding of the role its own strategic culture plays in the "lessons learned" process. The merits of a particular counterinsurgency practice and its historically successful track record are insufficient to inspire effective implementation. To be adopted and consistently applied, best practices must gain traction within the constructs of national- and service-level cultures. If the best of counterinsurgency lessons learned pose too great a challenge to cherished aspects of national- and service-level cultures, they will be resisted in implementation and may disappear altogether. Nations and the service institutions within their strategic communities are not dispassionate and unencumbered actors. Rather, the humans within these enterprises are wedded to modes of belief and behavior that shape the lessons they are willing to consider and determine which are adopted into accepted practice. Investigating the phenomenon of "strategic culture" forces us to reexamine our assumptions about rational learning and come to terms with the identities, norms, values, and perceptions that shape our preparation for future warfare.

This is not a comfortable notion. Far more comfortable are traditional assumptions that imply clear cause and effect for military learning. Typical of this school of thought is Chris Twomey's assertion that disadvantageous tactics and strategies "will have great and direct costs in blood and treasure" and that therefore any operational approach or policy that has been "selected for predominantly cultural reasons" will be condemned by the clear-cut outcome of the conflict.[1] As attractive as this cost-benefit paradigm may be, its formula presumes a clarity in battle that is often inconsistent with reality. Given the complexity of warfare strategy and the friction it encounters on the ground, the feedback loop on any particular maneuver is far from "clear-cut."[2] Strategists have a wide repertoire of battlespace contingencies from which to choose when assigning blame for setbacks or defeats. When cultural predispositions are deeply embedded, institutions that generate or execute policy are perfectly capable of ignoring evidence that contradicts their preset beliefs about best practices or seems to indict the performance of a favored tactic. Pointing to the example of the Vietnam War, Colin Gray notes that American strategic "culture simply did not register the unwanted Vietnam experience. Cultures, including strategic cultures, are capable of ignoring what they wish to ignore."[3]

Another common assumption concerning military memory and lessons learned is that consistent historical practice with one type of warfare or another translates into military culture, military preferences, and therefore key military competencies. Lessons learned and implemented would most plausibly be derived from the most regular form of practice. Although an intuitive proposition, historical experience appears to be far from determinative in shaping aptitude and preferences in military culture. The United States has a long record of experience in counterinsurgency practice and chooses to ignore most of it in favor of its infrequent but highly popular past engagements in conventional war.

If not regular practice, perhaps it is national victories that settle firmly into military psyche and are stitched together to form the basis of preferred memory. William Kincade argues as much concerning American national style and strategic culture. Core to his claim is the assumption that "cultures tend to be formed by the images of their triumphs and successes more than by their failures or departures from national ideals."[4] This assertion certainly has merit but cannot bear the full weight of explanation when selective memory and the learning process are concerned. The US Army's historic experience is instructive. As Robert Cassidy notes, despite its admirable victory in the Philippine Insurrection (1899–1902), the Army "virtually erased" this experience from its institutional memory and was bereft of its lessons in the run-up to the Vietnam War.[5]

Research on the Marine Corps's counterinsurgency experience, starting with its solo forays in the Caribbean in 1915, running across the bumpy terrain of Vietnam, and stretching into this century's invasion of Iraq, indicates that the selective memory that informs the lessons learned by a military service is heavily influenced by cultural constraints within organizational, military, and national cultural communities. The bulk of scholarship within the field of strategic culture tends to focus on one particular level of culture—typically national or military culture—when examining cultural influences on security policy and behavior.[6] While a number of these studies have yielded useful insights, this sort of unidimensional approach may fail to anticipate the negotiated outcome of competing or, conversely, compounding layers of culture in the creation of security policy and may lead to flawed projections of future security behavior.

The tightly constructed brotherhood of the US Marine Corps and its experience with counterinsurgency across a century represents a particularly compelling case for examining the multidimensional impact of cultural influences on security policy outcomes. The Corps's twentieth-century experience with counterinsurgency was characterized by operations guided by service instinct rather than codified doctrine, a combination that represents a best-case scenario for examining the impact, and limits, of service-culture influence on irregular warfighting practices. The results indicate that even a service culture as self-aware and dedicated to innovation as the Marine Corps is significantly constrained in the lessons-learned process by preferences endemic to the larger cultural contexts within which it operates: US military culture and American national culture. Across its small-wars history, strategically advantageous innovations distinct to the Marine Corps often fit within its own organizational culture but ultimately became "lessons lost" rather than institutionalized and learned owing to their misfit with traditional US military preferences or the demands of American national culture. In other cases, the influence of Marine cultural preferences on counterinsurgency practice was powerfully reinforced by matching preferences within national public culture and the cultures of its sister services.[7] When compounded in this fashion, some culturally preferred operational practices persisted even when they proved a dysfunctional fit with the security environment. In a few important areas, some counterinsurgency innovations have survived and represent the ways in which Marine Corps service culture offers a distinctive instrument for small-wars practice apart from the Army. The resultant package of Marine counterinsurgency instincts, therefore, is not easily reducible to service culture but is, rather, a negotiated outcome that has survived the collisions and constraints of multiple cultural layers.

As the United States considers additional engagements in peripheral wars of sometimes steep consequence, it would be well served to understand its own predispositions and habits of practice in irregular battlespace.[8] Most counterinsurgency theorists who recite Sun Tzu's admonition to "know thyself and know thy enemy" do so solely with the "enemy" bit in mind.[9] This book makes plain chronic deficits in the "know thyself" component and argues the necessity of strategic introspection as a prerequisite to planning. Recognition of which aspects of comprehensive counterinsurgency warfare the US military is able and willing to perform, and perform well, and which have persisted as national shortcomings must feature in any future decision to fight irregular war.

This volume engages three distinct veins of scholarship. From a methods standpoint, it offers a fresh approach to strategic culture studies, applying an analytic tool proven within intelligence circles—the Cultural Topography Framework—to an introspective study of the US strategic community.[10] The Cultural Topography Framework is grounded in an interpretive approach that requires deep immersion in multiple sources of data in order to identify patterns in identity, norms, values, and perceptual lens for the group under study. The emergent patterns within each of these four categories are coded into distinct cultural traits and are cast in a dialectic with the particular issue in question—in this case, counterinsurgency—in order to assess relevance.

The cultural components that emerge from this process as both robust and relevant are situated within the larger cultural outlay experienced by members of this group. For Marines this includes their own service culture as well as components of US military and US national cultures. This cultural mapping process illuminates the importance of exploring tensions between layers of culture existing simultaneously within a strategic community and examining the dynamic relationship between them, exploring why one yields to the other and in which circumstances it does so. The results offer insights concerning which cultural predilections are likely to "win out" when placed under stress. The importance of this complex dynamic in projecting security behavior, while implicit in other works, is made explicit here.

This text also contributes to scholarship examining counterinsurgency history, principles, and practice. Counterinsurgency scholarship includes volumes on doctrine, comparative texts looking at lessons drawn from diverse conflicts across history, in-depth texts looking at the experience of the US military across time or within one particular counterinsurgency theater, and John Nagl's work looking specifically at the learning experience of the Army in the counterinsurgency context of Vietnam.[11] The assumption that underpins most counterinsurgency scholarship to date is a reasonable and admirably optimistic one: that there is a right formula for counterinsurgency that may be discovered and trained into new doctrine by one nation studying and learning vicariously from the successes and mistakes of others. The research presented here is seeking not to restructure or add significantly to the debate concerning sound counterinsurgency practice but rather to pose serious questions about the character of a nation's learning curve: its ability to learn from another's experience or even from its own. By examining organizational and national cultures as organic "goods"—supplying identity, sense of place, and cherished modes of behavior to its members—this research allows a weightier role for cultural goods in human decision making than is typically assumed within realist and neorealist modeling. The analysis offered within this volume examines the Marine Corps brotherhood—the identity, norms, values, and perceptual lens that make up its ties, as well as its relationship with the nation that sends it abroad—providing a new lens on historical lessons learned and lost, as well as a cautionary tale concerning future irregular engagements in which the United States may be involved.

The analysis of Marine Corps culture leads to engagement with a third body of literature—that which seeks to understand the compelling and vibrant brotherhood of America's Spartans. Most of this work is constructed as a stand-alone portrait, meant to acquaint the reader with the ins and outs of Marine life in order to prepare for entry into its ranks,[12] to glean lessons from its leadership structure for commercial endeavors,[13] or simply to satisfy native martial interest.[14] Very little of this literature is written by scholars outside Marine active or retired ranks, although serious endeavors by Marine scholars tend to be very good.[15] No particular volume within this body of literature has, as yet, tackled the subject of a cultural dialectic with small wars, a curious omission given the Marines' colorful history in this mode and a deficiency meant to be remedied here.[16]

In today's force posture, the Marine Corps presents a particularly intriguing paradox. As an institution, the Corps has a long relationship with counterinsurgency—a history more extensive by far than its record with conventional combat. Marines engaged in three separate counterinsurgency fights across the "Banana Wars" era: the occupation of Haiti (1915–34), the intervention in the Dominican Republic (1916–24), and the suppression of rebels in Nicaragua (1927–33). Deploying the Army would have constituted an act of war, thus it was left to the Marines to land ashore and deliver lethal effects somewhere beneath the "war" threshold. Out of these experiences the Marine Corps became the first US institution to assemble and codify doctrine on small wars, in its *Small Wars Manual*. Today Marines continue to claim a role as America's "First to Fight" force and as such are often positioned to capitalize on, or lose, the early "golden hour" of counterinsurgency operations. Forward-looking surveys conducted by the Marines' own advertising agency, J. Walter Thompson, indicate that the youth pool from which future Marine recruits will be drawn are eager to engage in the sort of multiple tasks modern counterinsurgency offers: hunting down belligerents while building schools and roads for local villagers.[17] This century's fights in Iraq and Afghanistan have produced a generation of Marines with over a decade and a half of hard-won counterinsurgency experience. Perhaps most important, whether one consults historic patterns or current trends, it is clear that the country they serve—the United States of America—will fight as counterinsurgents again. And again.[18] Despite this, the Marine Corps is reluctant to become the nation's institution of professional small-wars warriors. Rather, it yearns to turn back to what are perceived to be its traditional conventional roles and "amphibious roots."[19]

An evaluation of Marine Corps service culture and its interplay with counterinsurgency operations is most appropriately begun at the beginning—with the Marines' first solo forays into counterinsurgency battlespace. The Banana Wars each provide a window into the Corps's learning curve in advance of any counterinsurgency doctrine. Despite their proximity in time and location, the interventions in the Caribbean unfolded with surprisingly limited cross-fertilization in terms of best practices or lessons learned—this was to come with hindsight—and thus offer evidence of Marine Corps instinct (rather than doctrine or training) across three nearly contemporaneous but distinct test cases.[20] This unusual and fortuitous historical happenstance adds an additional layer of robustness to the findings. If, after learning the hard reality of a lesson in three theaters, identifying and discussing this lesson (with hindsight) across multiple articles within its service journal, and choosing to codify this lesson as doctrine within the *Small Wars*

*Manual*, the Corps still failed to institutionalize it into practice for the next round, one must assume that something beyond a purely rational approach to the lessons-learned process is at work.

The next round of serious counterinsurgency fighting for the Corps came in the thick of Vietnam. While most operations were dictated to Marines by Army command in this war, a few of the Corps's most obstinate carved out space to run a Marines-only counterinsurgency experiment. The Combined Action Platoon (CAP) program in Vietnam was the result. Although the program was relatively small—of the eighty thousand Marines deployed to Vietnam, only some twenty-five hundred served in the CAP program at any point in time[21]—the contrast it provides with concurrent "big Army" behavior supplies a particularly rich source of Marine-specific cultural data and a test case for service lessons learned—as well as blind spots—carried over from the Caribbean.

Together, the Banana Wars era and the CAP program in Vietnam provided a small-wars heritage from which Marines could draw when thrust into the next century's irregular battlespace. Which lessons they drew on when Operation Iraqi Freedom birthed an insurgent foe and which they did not remained a negotiated product of default preferences, the joint culture of the US services, and their compelling need to meet national expectations.

The experiences of Marines across their counterinsurgency history will be examined in three principal categories. Those operational approaches that were recognized as best practices and were accepted and internalized into service culture may be properly termed *lessons learned*. These may or may not have been codified into formal doctrine, but persistence of the practice (or mind-set) through informal mechanisms is enough to merit the lessons-learned category. A lesson that was recognized as valuable during (or immediately after) the era in which it was employed but failed to be institutionalized into long-term practice constitutes the second category: *lessons lost*. These lessons may have, at some point, merited recognition in formal doctrine but were largely ignored or dysfunctionally implemented in future endeavors. The third major category of concern is cultural *blind spots*. These come in negative and positive form. Negative blind spots are those malpractices or misperceptions that persisted unaddressed across episodes for lack of recognition as a problem. These are the thorniest of counterproductive practices, very often the most deeply embedded, and the least likely to be expunged. Unfortunately, they are also of potentially enormous strategic significance. Cultural blind spots may cause warfighting institutions to disregard or underweigh the negative backlash produced by aspects of their own behavior. Blind spots may cause security organizations to prioritize some efforts over others (e.g., civic action over providing security) in ways that are a mismatch for the local security environment. Cultural blind spots may mean employing a skewed measuring stick in assessing "success" or simply asking the wrong questions about an adversary.

Positive blind spots represent opportunities lost. These are often make-do innovations of the moment that yield strategic benefits not fully recognized by those pursuing them. These potential lessons learned remain blind spots for the service culture—lessons unrecognized and not carried forward—not only because of lack of identification, but often because of strong cultural preferences or habituation toward a more traditional course of action.

The research conducted here examines aspects of Marine identity, norms, values, and perceptual lens as part of a larger cultural context that helps explain the Corps's counterinsurgency footprint: the lessons it has learned and incorporated, those it has lost, and those to which it remains blind. Within the Cultural Topography Framework, *identity* is defined as the distinguishing traits a group claims for itself and the role and reputation it pursues. *Norms* are accepted, expected, and preferred modes of behavior (as well as taboos). *Values* are identified as admired goods that may be ideational (such as key features of honorable character) or material (an excellent rifle) but are designated as values owing to their power to increase one's status within the group. The group's *perceptual lens* is the filter through which this group views the world and the specific actors in it. It is colored by default assumptions about how the world works, the nature of human beings, and the motivations of specific others. These four dimensions of culture do not represent an exhaustive list of important cultural factors but do represent core features within the cultural constructs that groups fashion for themselves. For research purposes, each of the four angles is distinct enough to inspire a separate set of research questions but elastic enough to accommodate a wide range of often overlapping data. It is the overlap between categories—a cultural trait manifesting itself in multiple ways, as both an aspect of identity and an attendant norm, for instance—that acts as a signal of robustness and helps the researcher narrow down the most salient traits for examination.

For the purposes of identifying relevant patterns across Marine identity, norms, values, and perceptual lens, the research that informs this book is of a "deep immersion" sort. In keeping with the analytic design of the Cultural Topography Framework, I examined a host of diversely arrayed data sources. My multisource approach includes a compilation of published memoirs of boot camp by both drill instructors and the recruits who became Marines; systematically reviewed submissions from the two primary Marine Corps publications, *Leatherneck* and the *Marine Corps Gazette*, during periods of counterinsurgency engagement (1916–34, 1965–72, and 2002–5); a close read of key speeches by Marine Corps commandants, submitted to the *Gazette* or *Leatherneck* across the time frame of concern (1916–75); content analysis of three key doctrinal publications, the *Small Wars Manual*, MCPD-1 *Warfighting*, and the contemporary *Small-Unit Leaders' Guide to Counterinsurgency*; a complete survey of Marine recruitment posters from 1913 to 1974 and television commercials from 1970 to 2003;[22] visits to local recruiting offices, the National Museum of the Marine Corps, and the Marine Corps Historical Division; insight derived from Marine "classics" on the commandant's reading list; and a wider net cast in the spirit of Geertzian "thick description" that includes documentaries, Marine blogs, published humor, YouTube videos, and scores of conversations with both officers and enlisted personnel across the Corps.[23] The research also included content analysis of the Marines' most celebrated narratives—those that have found their way into material culture and are stenciled on mugs, clothing, vehicle decals, and other overtly displayed identity markers.

Marines do not shy from opportunities to talk about their Corps and the life it provides. The result is a rich supply of oral histories and interviews from active-duty Marines. Forty-five contemporary oral histories were provided through the Veterans History Project sponsored by the American Folklife Center within the Library of Congress. This collection captures the military experiences of Marine Corps veterans of Iraq and Afghanistan. These men and women are of diverse regional US origins, rank, time in the Corps, and military specialties. A second set of over one hundred oral histories recorded in audio form and in real time before departure from Vietnam from 1966 to 1968 was provided by the Marine Corps Archives and Special Collections division and subsequently transcribed for ease of comparative analysis.[24] In addition, twenty-one veterans of the CAP program supplied contemporary interviews for this research in order to provide hindsight views on their service.[25]

## PLAN OF THE BOOK

The chapters that follow are divided into two parts. Part I offers insight into the various cultural layers that affect Marine behavior. Chapter 1 leads by introducing the strategic culture paradigm, some of the useful strides it has made over the years, the various pitfalls to effective analysis and forecasting that remain, and the remedies to such offered by the Cultural Topography Framework. Chapter 2 provides a look at the key cultural factors within American public culture and military culture that surfaced across research as pivotal in understanding Marine choices and behavior in counterinsurgency theaters across time. This chapter becomes especially critical as subsequent analysis highlights instances when the Marine Corps stepped out on its own—sometimes through brutal practices and sometimes in productively innovative fashion—during irregular conflicts. In several cases the institutionalization or abandonment of these practices had less to do with Marine Corps organizational culture and more to do with receptive fit with notions of "Americanness" held by the American public.

Chapter 3 starts an engaging journey through Marine Corps identity formation and role conception. The transformative process of becoming a

Marine is tracked from the Corps's early years to recruitment calls within the modern era. The Marine Corps presents a unique case where role conception is concerned. Because its institutional role has shifted so significantly across time, the Marine brand has been established on a state of "being"— who they are—to a far higher degree than on a well-defined role—what they do. This flexibility of role—a willingness to "do windows"—means that Marines are better positioned than their sister services to adapt to the often shifting demands of counterinsurgency and nation-building. That said, the prizing of the Corps's historical role of amphibious assault poses significant challenges to institutional commitments toward small-wars training and professionalism. Those effects are examined across the Banana Wars years, Vietnam, and the carryover into modern theaters.

Chapters 4 and 5 tackle the tall order of assembling and analyzing the colorful combination of practices, values, and perceptions that have come to characterize the modern Marine Corps. These are treated in compounding form, demonstrating how an established value underpins key norms and may cultivate service perceptions that validate both. One of the key contributions of these chapters is transparency into a research approach that does not treat norms and values in mutually exclusive fashion but rather as layering elements within a shared cultural context—strengthening, or alternatively, competing with one another. Highly regarded norms and values celebrated by the Corps are not always compatible with an immediate mission or with each other. These tensions form critical decision points for Marines, who must prioritize competing cultural mores and take action. Cultural collisions of this sort expose to view the often subconscious ranking of complex cultural sets. Although Marines may claim loyalty and adherence to the complete set of taught values, when these are juxtaposed in critical decision frames it is often informal culture—the sort more difficult to capture—that guides Marine decisions on which principles to sacrifice and which to pursue.

Part II applies the cultural data amassed in part I to the question of counterinsurgency practice. Chapter 6 sets the stage by providing a snapshot of the campaigns in Haiti, the Dominican Republic, and Nicaragua and of the CAP program in Vietnam. Then it introduces features of the American cultural mind-set that shaped outcomes in each encounter. American naïveté concerning the ease of changing indigenous cultural patterns, of providing sustainable infrastructure, and of incurring the gratitude of locals by offering material largesse is a long-standing tradition. The history examined here makes clear that current criticisms of this sort levied against America's efforts in Iraq and Afghanistan were equally applicable in earlier eras.

Another theme treated in depth is the impact of ethnocentrism, sometimes manifest as biting racism, on operations abroad. Material gifts to the state in the form of improved sanitation and infrastructure did not make up for the Marines' rude and sometimes lethally abusive treatment of darker-skinned locals on Hispaniola. The overtly racist behavior of the Banana Wars era contrasts markedly with what were often warm and respectful relations between Marines and Vietnamese villagers in the CAP. Given the vulnerable position of CAP personnel, what often began as instrumentally inspired good behavior resulted, for some, in heartfelt and gratifying relationships over time. Lessons from the CAP program were drawn on and reinforced by top Marine leaders as they sent their enlisted warriors forward in Iraq. The treatment of locals there, however, remained uneven—a product of the tension between the "first, do no harm" expectation set by leadership and the combat default settings bred into America's action-oriented shock troops.

Chapter 7 explores functional themes across the Marine Corps' counterinsurgency experience, including a special focus on the repercussions of the Marines' martially inspired values when applied to nation-building. Marines in the Caribbean embraced their tasks of governing and training national constabularies in very typical military fashion: by prioritizing order and efficiency. This approach served to establish the infrastructure and material health of the state with often unprecedented speed but also modeled—in ways Marines did not clearly foresee—authoritarian rather than democratic rule.

The Caribbean efforts are contrasted with the limited state-building activity within the CAP program—a happy accident of resource deprivation rather than conscious choice—in which the relative poverty of Marines and their much closer association with villagers yielded a selection of strategic advantages that had eluded Caribbean forebears. The fate of this potential lesson learned—the operational benefits of frugal civic action—within the CAP is examined through the lens of American strategic culture, one bent on measuring success through quantifiable achievements and notable changes to infrastructure.

Chapter 8 examines the impact on counterinsurgency readiness effected by the strong preference within US forces to prepare for and fight conventional conflicts. The first part of the chapter examines the effect of this preference on small-wars doctrine and follows by tracking the trajectory of a few key Marine innovations, including the Marines' small-unit force structure and penchant for constant patrolling. The chapter ends with a focus on the Marine Corps's decentralized leadership patterns. This lesson, already a part of Marine training and conscious practice by the end of the Banana Wars era, received a boost from the Corps's CAP experience in Vietnam and remained a signature feature of Marine practice in its post-9/11 counterinsurgency fights.

Chapter 9 concludes part II by examining the Marine experience across the Iraq War in order to identify which of the lessons learned through the Marines' formative counterinsurgency experiences persisted into the modern era. The range of lessons learned, as well as lessons lost and persistent blind spots, is cast against the multilayered context of Marine Corps culture, US military culture, and American public culture in order to extract explanation and project future trends. Operational cultural narratives that persisted across counterinsurgency eras are captured in the book's conclusion. These combine elements of national culture, US military culture, and the distinctive culture of the US Marine Corps. The result is a cautionary tale for even the best suited of the American services in its counterinsurgency adventures abroad.

## NOTES

1. Twomey, "Lacunae in the Study of Culture," 352.
2. Gray, *Modern Strategy*.
3. Gray, "British and American Strategic Cultures," 47.
4. Kincade, "American National Style," 12.
5. Cassidy, *Peacekeeping in the Abyss*, 84.
6. For examples of scholarship treating strategic culture at the national level, see Johnston, *Cultural Realism*; Heuser, *Nuclear Mentalities?*; Mead, *Special Providence*; Longhurst, "Why Aren't the Germans?"; Glenn, Howlett, and Poore, *Neorealism versus Strategic Culture*; Gray, "British and American Strategic Cultures," 47; Johnson, Kartchner, and Larsen, *Strategic Culture and Weapons*. For examples of strategic culture scholarship focusing on military culture, see Builder, *Masks of War*; Klein, "Theory of Strategic Culture"; Kier, "Culture and Military Doctrine"; Legro, "Which Norms Matter?"; Nagl, *Learning to Eat Soup*; Terriff, "Innovate or Die"; and Barnett, *Navy Strategic Culture*.
7. Throughout this work, references to "Marine" will be capitalized in deference to Marine culture, as documented by the late Brig. Gen. Edwin H. Simmons, USMC (Ret.), director emeritus of Marine Corps History and Museums: "Marines believe in their Corps. They also believe that they are the best. They insist that the 'M' in 'Marine' be capitalized. The highest accolade they can bestow on a member of another service is 'He would make a good Marine.'" Simmons, foreword to Alexander, *Fellowship of Valor*, xi.
8. Perhaps the most excellent work on this is Gray's "Irregular Enemies."
9. Sun Tzu Wu, *Art of War*, 51.
10. The Cultural Topography Framework approach, including the Cultural Mapping method, was designed by the author with Matthew T. Berrett during his tenure as the Near East and South Asia Office director at the Central Intelligence Agency. See Johnson and Berrett, "Cultural Topography."
11. Highlights from this field include Haycock, *Regular Armies and Insurgency*; Beckett, *Roots of Counterinsurgency*; Marston and Malkasian, *Counterinsurgency in Modern Warfare*; Collins, *America's Small Wars*; Boot, *Savage Wars of Peace*; and Nagl, *Learning to Eat Soup*.
12. Krulak, *First to Fight*; Price, *Devil Dog Diary*; Sturkey, *Warrior Culture of the U.S. Marines*.
13. Freedman, *Corps Business*; Dye, *Backbone*.

14. Ricks, *Making the Corps*.
15. See, for instance, O'Connell, *Underdogs*.
16. However, Cameron examines the First Marine Division across World War II and the Korean War in *American Samurai*.
17. PowerPoint presentation supplied to the author by J. Walter Thompson senior advertising executive Randy Shepard, November 3, 2011.
18. Acknowledged in the first pages of the Army's new *Field Manual on Stability Operations* and detailed in the following sources: Boot, *Savage Wars of Peace*; Yates, *US Military's Experience*; and Collins, *America's Small Wars*. The Marines' own *Marine Corps Vision and Strategy 2025* also reflects this assumption.
19. See Eliason, "Interview with James F. Amos"; "Interview with James T. Conway"; Arthur P. Brill Jr., "Out Call with the Commandant," *Leatherneck* (September 2010).
20. Bickel, *Mars Learning*.
21. Hemingway, *Our War Was Different*, 177; Peterson, *Combined Action Platoons*, 123.
22. A special thanks to the US Marine Corps Historic Division and the National Museum of the Marine Corps for allowing photographs of their own exhaustive supply of recruitment posters and an additional thanks for their careful documentation of accurate dates and use. A comprehensive collection of television commercials was provided to the author by J. Walter Thompson, longstanding USMC advertising agency.
23. Clifford Geertz popularized Gilbert Ryle's notion of "thick description" by arguing that this approach represents the aim of ethnography: to use a wide range of contextual cues drawn from multiple data sources in order to determine the significance and meaning of words and actions across a shared culture. Geertz, *Interpretation of Cultures*, 5–10. In addition to the text-based sources listed as resources in this research, the author has had the opportunity since 2009 to interact with Marines in a training capacity within the Marine Corps Intelligence Activity (MCIA) branch, Information Operations Center (MCIOC), and Center for Advanced Operation Culture Learning (CAOCL), as well as a variety of other offices and branches at Quantico.
24. Forty-five contemporary oral histories were transcribed and supplied as hard copy from the Library of Congress's Veterans History Project through its American Folklife Center in Washington, DC. More than a hundred Vietnam-era oral histories were supplied in audio form through the United States Marine Corps Vietnam War Oral History Collection, Marine Corps Archives and Special Collections, Gray Research Center, Quantico, VA.
25. Interviews conducted at the CAP Reunion in Branson, Missouri, November 9, 2013.

# PART I

# THE STRATEGIC CULTURES OF AMERICANS, THE US MILITARY, AND MARINES

# CHAPTER 1

# KNOW THYSELF

*Turning the Strategic Culture Tool Inward*

The idea that warring groups often behave according to distinctive practices is not a new one. Classical writers took note of particular "ways of war" practiced by Scythians, Persians, Huns, Saracens, and Turks, among others.[1] Theories that draw linkages between the peculiarities of a particular ethnonational group and its resultant way of war are not novel to this century or the last one. So it may be with some ignorance of the past that most strategic culture literature has accepted the late 1970s as the concept's starting point. It was in 1977 that the term "strategic culture" was coined by Jack Snyder and defined as "the sum total of ideas, conditioned emotional responses and patterns of habitual behavior that members of a national strategic community have acquired through instruction or imitation with each other with regard to nuclear strategy."[2]

Despite the multiplication of definitions that have emerged since Snyder's writing, a slight adjustment to his original nuclear-oriented definition—replacing "nuclear strategy" with "national security"—manages to capture the essence of most strategic culture literature today. Snyder was part of the first generation of strategic culture theorists who devised this concept as a supplement to, or amelioration of, the shortcomings of prominent theoretical constructs such as realism and neorealism.[3] Snyder's peer, Ken Booth, championed Snyder's concept of strategic culture to a greater degree than Snyder did himself, insisting that neorealism's rational-actor model and use of game theory were "unhistorical approaches."[4] At a baseline, Booth and other first-generation scholars rejected the "black box" theory espoused by neorealism: the assumption that the behavior of states on the world stage may be predicted according to a metric of universally understood rationality that supersedes and therefore renders internal state dynamics irrelevant.

According to these theories, states (and by assumption their internal-security communities) that may find themselves in similar security contexts would pursue similar strategies since all could be counted on to exercise the universal mechanism of cost-benefit analysis in pursuit of the same ends: advancing relative security and power.[5] If the dangers inherent in this type of mirror-imaging analysis are not sufficiently clear, Booth works hard to point them out. Forging his premise during the Cold War, Booth insisted that "there have been and are distinctively American and Soviet ways of thinking and behaving" and these "are not explicable simply in terms of rational actor models, comparative advantage, technological imperatives and so on."[6] Colin Gray's comments on the subject are a touch more colorful. Acknowledging that the cultural approach is certainly experiencing some growing pains, he maintains that "the sins of the would-be cultural theorists pale by comparison with the nonsense we know as neorealism. . . . The neorealist proposition that strategic history, past, present, and future, can be explained strictly by reference to the relations among political entities, with no regard paid to their domestic processes, is, frankly, preposterous."[7]

Not all strategic culture scholars are as dismissive as Gray in their assessments of neorealism's virtues, and even Gray is careful to preserve a place for realpolitik and the original tenets of realism. He notes that his version of strategic culture is not at odds with the idea that actors act rationally in pursuit of their ends. It is neorealism's assumptions about the content of those ends and about "rational" behavior that strategic culture scholars take to task. Actors in all forms—individuals, subnational groups, nonstate actors, and national polities—are likely "rational" in the sense that they pursue their own interests rather than someone else's. Rationality, however, is culturally encoded. The factors included in a cost-benefit analysis for one actor and the values assigned to those variables may be quite different from another. Tactics included in the strategic arsenal of one actor may not be acceptable or even considered by another. Motives for beginning wars, incentives for ending them, and identities that determine how one fights are often culturally derived. The lessons a military force chooses to learn and those cast to the side are also heavily influenced by culturally derived preferences. To understand the rational calculus of actors within an organization, we must understand the identities, mind-sets, traditions, and habits that provide context.

No serious scholar of strategic culture argues that the strategic culture component of security policy is the only, or perhaps even primary, predictive element of strategic outcome. Readily acknowledged in the field is that strategy is a heavily contested enterprise in which a number of weighty players collide. One might sum up the security policy process as "the negotiated result of elite (usually civilian) agendas processed through national culture, the national policy process, and security related organizational cultures, constrained by material capabilities, and inhibited or advanced by external actors."[8] Strategic culture theorists have made their mark in the security studies field by demonstrating the value of examining a critical and under-studied aspect of this formula: the impact of national and organizational cultures on security policy.

Given the complex subject matter, it is unsurprising that diverse inter-pretations abound concerning the appropriate approach to studying strategic culture. A number of attempts have been made to capture into useful categories the wide variety of scholarship strands within the body of strategic culture scholarship.[9] Concurrently, sharp criticism has been directed at the field for not achieving some level of methodological consensus.[10] David Haglund acknowledges such criticism but points out that this is likely representative of the growing pains of any big idea. In his essay "What Good Is Strategic Culture?" he compares the concept of strategic culture to equally amorphous and contested concepts such as "power" and "wealth." Despite eluding precise definition, these foundational concepts remain essential to discussions of security policy.[11]

A few consistent threads across the strategic culture literature are worthy of note, especially as they pertain to the design of the Cultural Topography Framework. Strategic culture remains a largely state-based method of analysis.[12] Few attempts have been made to apply it to nonstate actors, a deficit that has always been problematic but is perhaps most obviously so in light of twenty-first-century security concerns.[13] If a core purpose of pursuing cultural study is to win advantage against adversaries, then any analytic concept fit for that purpose must be flexible enough to deal with both traditional state-based threats and threats that operate independently of the Westphalian structure.

Although early work on strategic culture tended to resort to somewhat static profiles of state strategic cultures—a national personality of sorts—later work has emphasized cultural dynamism and complexity—a topic that naturally prompts questions about the causes of cultural shift over time. Positions on this topic range the spectrum from Patrick Porter's portrayal of cultural influences as menus of choice, undergoing constant morphing on the battlefield,[14] to Gray's insistence that cultural variables that merit inclusion under the strategic culture label be robust to the point of semipermanent status, traits "not easily amended, let alone overturned, by acts of will."[15]

Semistatic portraits of national strategic culture have drawn criticism from a range of scholars, including historians who point out that in some historical episodes states exhibit the behavior expected from the assembled portrait of their strategic culture and that in others they do not. Any fore-casting tool that assesses the influence of cultural variables must do a better job of explaining *when* this will occur and *why*.[16] The literature that comes closest to tackling this thorny problem is the scholarship dedicated to examining strategic culture and change. Most tends to focus on strong external shock as the primary impetus for change,[17] either in the form of

battlefield defeat or exposure to extreme logical fallacy.[18] Here again, however, change is examined within the parameters of a state as the unit of
analysis. Strategic culture is characterized as a package of robust variables,
born out of national circumstance and experience, that tend to shape the
state response to security threats. Change is explained as a significant shift
in key variables, dispensing with some and adding others, within the core
package of a state's strategic culture, rather than the circumstantial flexing
of a complicated and perhaps internally inconsistent set of strategic culture
preferences.

My experience applying the strategic culture approach in the forecasting
world of defense and intelligence analysis has made clear that state-based strategic culture profiles are invaluable repositories of background information
but provide little by way of actionable intelligence. As has been effectively
argued by Christopher Twomey, security studies that attempt to draw predictive power from the comprehensive portrait of an amorphous and often
internally contradictory national "strategic culture" often suffer follies of
overgeneralization and static analysis and reach, as a consequence, question-
able conclusions about the sources of security policy.[19] After years of writing
on the subject, first-generation scholar Gray does not disagree. His recent
work on strategy and culture argues that scholarship that attempts grand profiles often sweeps "away complexity in the interest of an elegant and potent
economy and simplicity that usually pays too high a price for its virtues."[20]

The more complicated truth is that strategic culture should rarely be
referenced in the singular for any particular regime. There is not, typically,
one internal variety. Walter Russell Mead identifies four distinct narratives
within US strategic culture and posits that our various foreign policies are
formed from the "collisions and debates" they inspire.[21] The idea of composite cultures is not restricted to analysis of the United States, of course.
Authors writing on the United Kingdom, France, and Germany,[22] China,[23]
India,[24] and Iran,[25] to name a few, all note the internal conflict of competing
security narratives within these regimes. Both Oliver Lee and Alan Bloomfield have worked to develop the idea of competing national subcultures and
their contested influence on security policy outcomes.[26] As Gray notes, however, "the relations between what should be sub-cultures within a supposedly
simply national cultural domain, and between those sub-cultures and the
much grander national level of culture (public and strategic), remains poorly
governed intellectual space."[27] It is this neglected intellectual space that the
cultural mapping exercise within the Cultural Topography Framework is
designed to address. The cultural mapping exercise prompts researchers to
move beyond simple acknowledgment of the variety of subcultures within
any particular regime and toward rigorous analysis of their interplay. The
aim is to determine which of the layered and perhaps competing internal
cultural narratives is dominating discourse and action—acting as the operational cultural narrative—on a particular issue.[28]

Applied and refined over the last ten years, the cultural topography approach has proved a useful and illuminating tool for intelligence analysts. It is being exercised here for the purposes of the strategist: Rather than studying alien cultures, its lens is being trained on our own. A strategist interested in ascertaining organizational "fitness" for counterinsurgency within his service ranks would employ the cultural topography method in its most robust form, conducting individual cultural mapping exercises across services (Army, Navy, Air Force, and Marine Corps) bound to the issue of counterinsurgency practice and assessed across time. The pooled result would deliver a textured topography of service orientations—areas of common ground, likely sources of resistance, individual strengths, and potentially debilitating cleavages—within the service community on this issue. This book represents the first iteration within that process.

Strategists may use the insights derived from cultural mapping exercises for a variety of purposes: anticipating organizational resistance to norm changes, improving messaging strategies, smoothing interservice tensions, or guiding the immediate task of matching service organizations to the operational set for which they are best suited. When pooled cultural topography results indicate that a strong service match is not possible, the informed strategist can plan for the friction he is likely to encounter when mission tasks run counter to service culture. Sometimes the key finding from a cultural mapping exercise is that the organizational culture in question has no clear script for action on the issue selected. If discovered early, this undetermined cultural space may be used to advantage by strategic planners in forging interservice consensus on best practices. If discovered late—when operations are already under way—it may be flagged by planners as an area of uncertainty likely to be characterized by diverse performance.

The insights derived from employing the analytic tools of the Cultural Topography Framework aim for practical utility—namely, to supply the strategist with a range of probable behaviors in order to enhance efforts at planning, creating doctrine, manipulating the context in which security policy is forged, and possibly highlighting strategic deficiencies that need to be addressed. Understanding cultural preferences should provide opportunity to exploit the strategic habits of adversaries, to plan toward smoother relations with encultured allies, and to hedge against habitual vulnerabilities in oneself.

## THE CULTURAL MAPPING EXERCISE

A cultural mapping exercise represents one iteration of the Cultural Topography Framework's analytic process. A single group is selected from among the constellation of actors relevant to an issue of policy concern and is targeted for study through the framework's analytic method. The patterned data that emerges from this process allows the researcher to identify the operational cultural narrative driving perceptions and action on this issue for this group. Repeated across actors, multiple mapping exercises create a "cultural topography"—demonstrating for the researcher where the same operational cultural narrative stretches across groups relevant to this issue, where it breaks down, and why. Analysis highlights which aspects of the narrative are particularly robust and widely shared and which are thinly distributed or contested. Equipped with this information, the researcher is better able to anticipate responses from the groups studied when shifts to the policy issue occur. The following subsections offer an explanation of each analytic step within the cultural mapping exercise.

| | |
|---|---|
| **Step 1:** | Identify an Issue of Strategic Interest |
| **Step 2:** | Select an Actor for Focused Study |
| **Step 3:** | Amass a Range of Potentially Significant Cultural Influences |
| **Step 4:** | Pursue Research through Four Perspectives: Identity, Norms, Values, and Perceptual Lens |
| **Step 5:** | Hone Data to Critical Cultural Factors (CCFs) |
| **Step 6:** | Map the Scope of CCFs across Cultural Influences |
| **Step 7:** | Assess Results |

FIGURE 1.1. Core Components of the Cultural Mapping Exercise

## Identify an Issue of Strategic Interest

Lessons learned across both academic and policy-based endeavors to capture cultural data in ways useful to strategic planning have made clear that tightly targeted cultural analyses are of far more utility than sweeping national profiles. To provide actionable insights to policymakers, the cultural mapping exercise must be conducted in response to a particular issue of policy concern. Rather than seeking to understand the primary or dominant cultural tendencies of a group across time, the mapping exercise aims to isolate the aspects of group identity, norms, values, and perceptual lens likely to weigh in for *this group* on *this issue*. Therefore, the initial choice of issue is paramount.

As noted earlier in the chapter, any culture of substantial complexity possesses internal contradictions, multiple narratives, and sometimes an evolutionary history stretching over centuries. Assessing which aspects of that cultural heritage matter now for this particular context on this particular issue requires, first, a clear delineation of the issue itself. Cultural profiles built without the focus of a particular security question are of limited utility to operational planners.

A researcher need not remain married to the initial issue generated. As she wades into the data collected, she may find that her framing of the initial strategic issue needs narrowing (or widening). She may find that a far more compelling question emerges. Looping back to refine and restructure the initial problem set is not only welcome—it is recommended. The subject matter of this book underwent just such a journey. The topic initially selected for consideration was the character and success of stability operations—those nonkinetic, state-building tasks often wrapped into counterinsurgency operations—when performed by the US military. Stability operations had captured the conscious attention of US defense planners, and the result was unprecedented and exclusive treatment of the subject in doctrinal form: Joint Doctrine JP 3-0, the Army's new *Stability Operations Field Manual: FM 3-07*.[29] This seemed to beg investigation. As research progressed, however, it became increasingly clear that segregating stability operations from the larger realm of counterinsurgency operations would be an artificial distinction performed by the author and not a defensible match with practice as it was performed by Marines across their history of small-wars endeavors. Perhaps more important, historical research revealed intriguing misfires between the strategic intentions of nation-building efforts pursued by Marines alongside kinetic activity and actual results. The interplay of Marine efforts on both fronts—captured in the far more inclusive subject of comprehensive counterinsurgency operations—provides a more compelling story than treating either kinetic efforts or stability operations exclusively.

## Select an Actor for Focused Study

If forecasting is improved by narrowing the focus to a particular issue, it is further improved by narrowing analysis to a particular actor. Rather than defaulting to the state-based approach favored by most authors writing within the strategic culture paradigm, the mapping exercise assumes that the actor selected for study ought to be determined by the players relevant to the policy issue selected. The substate actor likely to have most impact may shift considerably depending on the particular policy issue in question. Most strategic culture work privileges elites as the key actor set (whether at the national or organizational level) regardless of the issue at hand, arguing with Anja Dalgaard-Nielsen that while public opinion may influence which of the various narratives within a policy compete for prominence, "it is arguably the elite—owing to its role as gatekeeper, its expert knowledge and its privileged access to means of communication—that ultimately decides which way security policy goes."[30] This logic breaks down when one is assessing the impact of cultural influences within the context of counterinsurgency and stability operations. Given the pivotal role of local popular opinion and the historically unscripted role of diverse military services in this type of military engagement, understanding public culture and the cultures of the distinctive services, the insurgent group(s), and significant substate groups becomes paramount. Thus, the level of culture studied and specific actor selected should be intimately tied to the policy issue in question.

After exploring and evaluating the various actors that may influence decision making on the issue selected, an analyst selects one of these for focused study. The choice may stem from any number of needs. The strategist may assess that the selected organization or actor set is a "wild card" in need of scrutiny, an organization that is likely to take the lead in determining policy outcome, or a member of his strategic community that is being asked to fulfill a novel role (a frequent occurrence for the Marine Corps). Sound intelligence practice advises assumption checks on even the most dearly held notions about long-standing adversaries; the same logic ought to be applied to an understanding of one's own internal organizations.

The looping process recommended for issue selection applies to actor selection as well. An actor selected at the outset of research may be benched in favor of one that looms larger in importance as the research progresses. Alternatively, the same actor may be retained but disaggregated into component parts that are treated individually. Researchers reared on a positivist skill set need to be reminded: The objective of the cultural mapping method is not to run a streamlined "test" of a particular hypothesis, but rather to serve the needs of the strategist by unearthing policy-relevant cultural data on a security issue of interest. If reforming the security question or actor set enhances utility, the analyst is encouraged to loop back and do it.

The first round of research for this book underwent just such a process. Initial research focused on the "US military" as the primary actor for examination. This approach fit well with the literature. Much of the work (nearly all) on strategic culture assumes a set of shared preferences across a nation's military instrument rather than disaggregated strategic culture along service lines.[31] An investigation into America's counterinsurgency history, however, revealed some rather striking differences in counterinsurgency practice between the two ground forces that wage it: the Army and the Marines. As America's "First to Fight" force, the Marines are often the first in and therefore the first to capitalize on or lose the "golden hour" of counterinsurgency operations. Owing to this critical initial role, a historical small-wars identity, their sometimes innovative counterinsurgency practices, and perplexing current posture (a return to amphibious roots), the Marine Corps surfaced as the most compelling case for focused study.

## Amass a Range of Potentially Significant Cultural Influences

In the spirit of Kevin Avruch's pithy "for any individual, culture always comes in the plural,"[32] the third step of the cultural mapping exercise prompts the researcher to gather data on the array of various cultural narratives that may weigh in on decision making for members of the actor set selected. Anthropological literature is replete with the demonstrated influences of national, ethnic, religious, socioeconomic, generational, and gendered cultural narratives on actor behavior. Some influences are not as well understood. For instance, one enterprising young scholar investigated the influence of cultural norms cultivated across social media as accelerants to the process of radicalization.[33] Those employing the cultural mapping tool are encouraged to research widely and unconventionally for cultural influences that may be providing context for actor behavior.

The various cultural narratives amassed in this step represent the spectrum of possible sources—the cultural repertoire—from which members of the actor set may draw their identity, norms, values, and perceptual lens. Behavior on one aspect of the security question need not be inspired by the same cultural influence as a separate aspect. For instance, the success of individual Marines in connecting positively with Vietnamese villagers during the Combined Action Platoon (CAP) program may have had less to do with their institutional training in the Marine Corps and more to do with family culture, religious culture, or socioeconomic class. Conversely, the ability to conduct effective night patrols may have had very little to do with the cultures new recruits brought with them to boot camp and much to do with norms instilled during USMC infantry training. Both modes of behavior—good relations with villagers and effective prosecution of night patrols—were necessary for success in the CAP program but stemmed from diverse cultural roots.

It is a very regular feature of human behavior to shift back and forth between diverse cultural layers when determining codes for action. Which norms are deemed appropriate may be determined by situational context (a person behaves differently as a student in the classroom than a student at a party) or role (a Marine will behave differently in his role as drill instructor than in his role as base sergeant major) even if, over time, both put him in contact with the same Marines.[34] It is this movement between contextually driven normative sets that make the issue-dependent nature of cultural research so critical. For any particular activity, it must be assumed that actors are free to move between the many and varied cultural domains they inhabit and that the cultural narrative that appears most pronounced in day-to-day interactions may not be the narrative that will inspire behavior *on this issue*. Forecasting ability requires a method that can unearth the operational cultural narrative for a particular issue—the combination of key features of identity, understood norms, relevant values, and aspects of worldview or perceptual lens drawn on by members of the actor set in response to the security issue at hand.[35] The process of narrowing the range of possible cultural factors down to those that feature in the operational cultural narrative starts with a general survey of the diverse cultural narratives likely to be experienced by members of the actor set. Chapter 2 of this book offers key insights that emerged from this step, exploring two powerful sources of cultural narrative for members of the Marine Corps: American public culture and US military culture and the ways in which these influenced counterinsurgency practice over time.

## Pursue Research through Four Perspectives: Identity, Norms, Values, and Perceptual Lens

The four analytic categories that lie at the heart of the cultural mapping method—identity, norms, values, and perceptual lens—represent common themes around which much of the cultural literature swirls. This is so because each is a powerful cultural locus and represents a reoccurring common ground experienced by members of shared cultures. Those employing the cultural mapping method are invited to employ these four as a starting point and, as their research progresses, subdivide them or incorporate new categories as the data may inspire. As noted in the introductory chapter, the four key categories are defined as follows:

- Identity: the character traits this group assigns to itself, the reputation it pursues, and individual roles and statuses it designates to members
- Norms: accepted, expected, and preferred modes of behavior and shared understandings concerning taboos
- Values: material or ideational goods that are honored and confer increased status to members
- Perceptual lens: the filter through which this group views the world, the default assumptions that inform its opinions and ideas about specific others

A rich multidisciplinary literature contributes to our understanding of each of these cultural categories and the ways in which they might be employed.

## Identity

Identity is a group's self-assessment—its view of group character, its strengths and weakness, and its intended role, now and in the future. In sharp contrast to the assumption posited by neorealism—that actors proceed according to their relative position in global power configurations and will respond similarly to similar external stimuli—the cultural mapping exercise is founded in the strategic culture assumption that actors have diverse goals based on a normative understanding of who they are and the role they *should be* playing.[36] Theo Farrell draws the link to military organizations: "Culture, as both professional norms and national traditions, shapes preference formation by military organizations by telling organizational members *who they are* and what is possible, and thereby suggesting what they should do. In this way, culture explains why military organizations choose the structures and strategies they do, and thus how states generate military power."[37]

Service cultures possess distinct identities sought after and then defended by the human agents who claim them. Services do not just provide occupations—they provide particular personas and identities to those who rate membership. Thomas Mahnken makes the key point that "people join the Army, Navy, Air Force, and Marine Corps, not 'the military' in the abstract. . . . They join because they identify—or want to identify—with a service's values and its culture. It is therefore not surprising that two decades after the passage of the Goldwater-Nichols Act, which sought to promote jointness, an officer's service affiliation remains the most important determinant of his views, more than rank, age or combat experience."[38]

Writing more than three decades ago, Carl Builder argued much the same and pointed out that the personal "identity goods" derived from service culture are an inhibiting factor for organizational change: "Many who choose a particular military institution and dedicate their lives to it make their choice because there is something about the service—who it is or what it is about—that appeals to them. They see something in that service attractive or admirable and make an implicit contract with that service to serve in exchange for the associative benefit they perceive." Preset expectations and the self-selection process are part of what keeps organizational culture robust from one generation to the next: "If impending changes in their service then threaten that which [members] found attractive, they will exert a restoring or stabilizing pressure. With tens or hundreds of thousands of such implicit contracts outstanding, the potential for voluntarily changing the institution is very small."[39] If successful change to the institution comes, it must be within an acceptable identity package.[40] At the end of the day all bright strategic ideas, from whatever source, will be lost on a service that finds them anathema to its own identity orientation.

Jim Smith notes that the same cultural bonding that gives an organization its sense of mission, identity, and commitment can inspire unproductive responses to nontraditional mission sets. Should identity territory be intruded on or role conceptions come under threat, service organizations will push back: "Organizations fight hardest when they feel that their core mission is being challenged. The organization will favor policies that promoted the core mission, it will fight for autonomy in performing that core mission, and it will seek to defeat any challenges to those functions that it associates with its core." Perhaps most important, "it will be largely indifferent to functions it sees as peripheral to its core, even if those functions are part of its assigned purpose. . . . It will try to push out, or reject accepting, non-core missions as possible detractions from its core focus."[41] Identifying identity strands within a military institution may clarify why some strategically important tasks are pursued with enthusiasm and others left to neglect.

## Norms

The term "norms" encompasses a wide range of cultural practice. Authors from a variety of disciplines have struggled with the concept of norms as it seems to embody both a set of practices and the world of beliefs that inform those practices. Theo Farrell focuses on the power of ideas when he defines his use of the term: "Norms are intersubjective beliefs about the social and natural world that define actors, their situations, and the possibilities of action."[42] Peter Katzenstein, in his seminal volume *The Culture of National Security*, favors a slightly more behavior-oriented approach. Norms are "collective expectations for the proper behavior of actors with a given identity."[43]

In the final analysis, a strategist cares more about how organizations and nations *behave* than any other aspect of the cultural package. The definition employed here, therefore, captures both ideas and practice: Norms are accepted, expected, and preferred modes of behavior and shared understandings concerning taboos. Implicit in this definition is an assumption that beliefs of varying strength and quality inform these norms. Both beliefs and the behaviors they inspire are subject for consideration.

In his defining essay on military culture, James Burk points out that although military and service norms are, in the main, born of an aspiration toward warfighting and often influence when and what sort of wars are fought, this does not render them inherently instrumental. Military traditions may not always enhance warfighting capability.[44] Beatrice Heuser sums up the general tendencies of military establishments regarding preferred norms of behavior: The proclivity of armed forces is to fight wars "not in ways that are most appropriate to reach the desired end state with regard to the adversary. Given any say in the matter, they prefer to fight the wars they have prepared for, for which they have acquired equipment, for which they have configured and which they want to play out in reality."[45] This does not mean that services asked to pursue battlefield practices contrary to their preferred tactics will refuse, but it may mean that service members tend to view the battlefield through a lens that focuses on opportunities to engage in preferred practices at the expense of more effective but less familiar tactics.

Jack Snyder's addenda to realist thinking argue for the weight of bureaucratic habit as a companion to, and perhaps infringer on, "rational" thinking. In his words, "once a distinctive approach to strategy takes hold, it tends to persist despite changes in the circumstances that gave rise to it, through processes of socialization and institutionalization and through the role of strategic concepts in legitimating these social arrangements."[46] Kerry Longhurst calls this "path dependency"—a label she uses to describe the cultural inertia of policies that made sense at one point in time but, owing to heavy initial investment (both intellectual and material), tend to bias their makers toward continued investment, even after that path becomes insensible because of changed strategic realities.[47]

Her research, alongside others', indicates that humans may not, in fact, weigh each decision separately and project its long-term consequences but may very often rely on habit as the locus of behavior.[48] Valerie Hudson argues that national habits of this sort might be termed "foreign policy action templates" that represent "a repertoire or palette of adaptive responses from which members build off-the-shelf strategies of action."[49] Even if habitual solutions are somewhat suboptimal, they may be less "expensive" in terms of time and energy costs than pausing before each decision to carefully weigh options. This approach to rationality goes some distance in explaining "cultural inertia" or bureaucratic practices that seem to have limited fit with current security realities.[50]

Habitual solutions might be considered a service's "default settings." These organizational norms may take a beating when applied to the battlefront, especially in those conflicts for which they are not a good fit, but may reappear in surprisingly robust form in the next go-round. The battlefield, and wars generally, offers an opportunity for the rational cleansing of unfit practices, but services are perfectly capable of ignoring the diagnosis. As John Nagl noted in his rigorous study of the US Army in the Vietnam War context, the pressures for change exerted by an ongoing military conflict may be insufficient: "A strong organizational culture can prohibit learning the lessons of the present and can even prevent the organization's acknowledging that its current policies are anything other than completely successful."[51]

Sometimes the norms of the general public intervene to shape or inhibit military action. Greg Giles explores the power of national norms on security policy in a number of places in his work on Israel. One particularly poignant example focuses on the conclusions drawn by the Israel Defense Forces (IDF) when responding to the 1987 Intifada. The IDF concluded that it could not eliminate the Intifada without violating social norms. There was, therefore, no military solution acceptable to the Israeli population. The situation would have to be resolved politically.[52]

Whether stemming from a national culture or service culture source, Kevin Avruch supplies a useful caution concerning the study of norms. He notes that norms are not internalized evenly across a population. Some may have very shallow roots, "the equivalent of cultural clichés," while others are deeply embedded and "invested with emotion or affect."[53] It is here that values are usefully overlapped with norms. Norms that are intimately wedded to specific values exist at the "internalization" rather than "compliance" level of behavior. One might think of cultural practices as falling along a spectrum. At the deep end are norms informed by dearly held, profoundly invested beliefs. These norms are internalized and will persist without supervision and despite more "logical" recommendations. At the shallow end are those practices that are widely observed socially but fit Avruch's notion of "cultural clichés." These may be practices mandated by those in authority—complied with by underlings but quickly abandoned as soon as the supervising power is removed. Cultural clichés may also be something as simple as habit carried forward by social inertia, long severed from its original raison d'être or any sincere belief system.

Mariano Grondona marks a useful differentiation between norms born of intrinsic or instrumental values. The first are "those we uphold regardless of the benefits or costs" and are synonymous with "internalization." Those he deems "instrumental" are pursued because they yield direct benefit to the actor. The salience of Grondona's point for our purposes is that the attractiveness of norms attached to intrinsic values for members of a particular target group is "inexhaustible" since the norms are valued for their own sake rather than as a means to an end. Combat action registers in this category for Marines. Instrumental norms, on the other hand, are pursued only until the end is accomplished; they are far less deeply rooted, existing primarily at the "compliance" level.[54] Nearly all paperwork and processing falls into this category for Marines. Understanding the difference allows strategists to discern between those norms that are likely to shift easily if members of the organization are presented with a "better way" to pursue traditional ends. Instrumental norms will yield to such logic. Intrinsic norms, however, are valued for their own sake rather than the ends they achieve and are thus profoundly resistant to change. When a norm achieves both instrumental utility (a proven track record for achieving intended ends) and intrinsic value (it fulfills emotional or moral needs created by the group), it may be regarded as particularly robust.[55]

### Values

The concept of "values" explored here comprises character traits and material goods that elevate one's status in the relevant society. Proposed changes to military or other structures that run counter to core value sets are unlikely to meet with success. The norms tethered to those values will be instinctively defended. Gray points out that "traditional beliefs and behaviors frequently are more than merely habitual; their persistence is likely to be recorded in, and possibly policed by, an ethical code that expresses cultural attitudes towards right and wrong that may well reflect assumptions long unchallenged and therefore unexamined."[56]

Deeply held prejudices and pervasive racism may lead one society to value the humans of another at a significantly degraded level and thereby reduce the threshold for inhumane treatment. Beatrice Heuser notes that a pattern of engaging in operational restraint against some groups and not against others has remained a consistent feature of human practice since antiquity.[57]

The weapons selected for use are a further value-laden category.[58] John Lynn traces the marriage of weapons choice and cultural values as far back as the Greek hoplites. Though one was far more likely to lose life and limb wielding a spear than a bow, the bow was considered cowardly, and Greek conventions on war mandated that its use be limited.[59] Jeffrey Legro argues that the value-laden nature of weapons assessment has not changed much since the Hellenic era. Organizations continue to channel resources toward those weapons that are a match with its culture. Those that are well suited will be perceived as more feasible and more attractive than those incompatible with organizational culture and will subsequently receive the organization's attention and funding.[60]

The values the Marine Corps holds dear may be amplified or, conversely, threatened by irregular warfare. Identifying which are likely to feature in the operational cultural narrative for the Corps as it responds to counterinsurgency tasks will require an examination of professed Marine Corps values, as well as those found at the grassroots level in symbols, ritual, icons, and legends. What sorts of warfare practices do Marines deem honorable? Does counterinsurgency fit this bill? Are hero stories told of counterinsurgency episodes? What actions or characteristics are valued in the tale? Are these sufficient to inspire competency in counterinsurgency warfare, or do competing and more privileged values come under threat should the Corps move this direction? The results of this assessment will offer strategists some idea of Marine Corps trajectory and of counterinsurgency practices that are likely to find a sound fit in Devil Dog quarters.

### Perceptual Lens

As encultured beings, humans interpret events through biased cognitive filters: a perceptual lens. Beliefs (accurate or misinformed) and experiences (or the lack of experience) color the way the world is viewed. As is widely understood, behavior is based on the perception of reality, not reality itself. Perceptions of "fact," concerning our own histories, our image abroad, what motivates others, the capabilities of our leadership, the utility of our national resources, and other security-related ideas all play a strong role in forming what each regime believes to be rational foreign policy. Alastair Iain Johnston sums up the role of perceptual lens quite nicely: "Ahistorical or 'objective' variables such as technology, capabilities, levels of threat, and organizational structures are all of secondary importance: it is the interpretive lens of strategic culture that gives meaning to these variables."[61]

There are a number of ways that a perceptual lens colors thinking and influences behavior. Elizabeth Kier notes that the consciously cultivated culture of an organization "shapes its members' perceptions and affects what they notice and how they interpret it: it screens out some parts of reality while magnifying others."[62] A particular mind-set is easily identified when organizational beliefs and the habits they inspire seem out of step with battlefield realities. Kier demonstrates this by examining the French defense posture after World War I. The French perceptual lens before World War I assumed conscript armies were incapable of waging offensive war. This belief led the French military to disregard its own intelligence reports, which indicated that the Germans planned to attack with young conscript forces. In Kier's estimation, the French perceptual lens led to a significant underestimation of the strength of the German offensive.[63] Most remarkable about this is that, despite being proved wrong, the French maintained their belief about conscripts into the future. During the interwar years, the political Left won France's internal debate on the structure of the military, restricting its ranks to one-year conscriptions. Given this restriction, the French military elite believed they were forced to resign themselves to a defense posture. Kier explains the establishment of a defense posture as a result of the continuing (albeit disproved) organizational mind-set concerning the capabilities of conscripts: "Other militaries would not [necessarily] respond similarly; constrained within an organization that has powerful assimilating mechanisms, the officer corps 'sees' only certain doctrinal options."[64]

Mind-sets imbued with strong biases regarding what is possible in foreign policy and what therefore ought to be achieved can often outlive repeated experiences that seem to falsify those notions. Americans persist in their belief that, if taught and mentored properly, their form of democracy can be implanted within other nations within a reasonably short period. Foundational mind-sets about how the world works, what forces control it, and what humans are meant to do about it are called a "cosmology."[65]

Perceptions of self add another layer to perceptual lens. Given that remembered history is the operative history, one must assess how the group in question characterizes and perceives its own past.[66] Gray notes that while "objective realities certainly matter, there are assumed realities and narratives that people choose to believe."[67] When unpacking "remembered history," it may be useful to ask: Which events are highlighted? Which are omitted? What does this group's history tell them about "dangerous" behaviors?

Perhaps one of the most fascinating areas of study concerning perceptual lens is in the area most would contest as uncontestable: determinations of victory and defeat. Victor Hanson is nearly lyrical in his portrayal of the bloody exactness of the battlefield: "There is an inherent truth in battle. It is hard to disguise the verdict of the battlefield, and nearly impossible to explain away the dead, or to suggest that abject defeat is somehow victory."[68] He is wrong. Victory and defeat are human perceptions that may or may not coincide with the mathematics of the dead. Societal myths, national ambitions, or historically inherited criteria may define for a military or a society the standards of victory and defeat. Material outcomes—the territorial-, technological-, and casualty-based victories measured by outsiders—may not, in fact, be the primary determinants of success in the minds of the relevant contenders. Dominic Johnson and Dominic Tierney investigate the phenomenon of nations perceiving victory in defeat and vice versa by examining a number of case studies in which an objective observer would have come to an opposite conclusion than the adversaries did themselves. One of these, the 1973 Yom Kippur War, was a substantial military victory for Israel over Egypt and Syria by any material standard. Israel took out Arab tanks, aircraft, and troops in ratios of nearly five to one and demonstrated that its tactical skills were far superior to those of its adversaries. And it held more territory than ever before by the end of the war. Despite all of this, the war was seen in Israel as a distressing defeat, "a failure [just] short of a catastrophe," and became the source of "enormous disillusionment" in the country.[69] The success of Arab forces in surprising Israel's military establishment and achieving initial victories was a near fatal blow to the credibility of the country's entire security apparatus. In sharp contrast, despite material losses, Egypt's Anwar Sadat was able to claim "the most glorious days in our history" for his nation.[70] He had restored Arab honor by achieving the impossible: a surprise attack that involved crossing the Suez Canal and establishing a beachhead on the other side, losing only 208 soldiers in the process. Egypt's bold move had, in the eyes of Egyptians and many Arabs across the region, redeemed the shame of the 1967 loss with a firm belief that Arab states were "capable of fighting, capable of victory."[71] In this case, it was not the end of the war that defined victory but the beginning, not material consequences but perceptions.

When dispatching its Marines, the cosmological perceptions held by the American polity as regards what is *possible* and *right-headed* in the foreign policy arena have had significant impact on the types of counterinsurgency tasks the force has been asked to pursue. The Marine Corps's own perceptual lens has complemented more often than competed with general American notions regarding nation-building and effective strategies for winning states as friends. Patronizing perceptions about the capabilities and motives of the indigenous noncombatants with whom Marines interacted in counterinsurgency tasks and the insurgents they pursued colored the approach to these two populations.

## Hone Data to Critical Cultural Factors

The gathering of data in each of the four aforementioned categories is pursued within the spirit of interpretivist research and Grounded Theory: seeking an "insider" understanding of a particular group through the collection of "rich data." Data collection and analysis occur simultaneously in order to code cultural traits and assemble them into consistent patterns. Categories become "saturated" when newly gathered data from multiple sources no longer offer surprises or fresh insights.[72] Once saturation is achieved to satisfaction, cultural data is evaluated for *relevance* (for the issue selected), *robustness*—an evaluation of the level to which a particular trait has been internalized by a critical component of the population—and, perhaps most important, the likelihood of a cultural factor or trait to provoke a *response* (cooperative or conflictual) when the strategist engages this group on this issue. Those cultural traits that consistently surfaced across multiple data sets and passed relevance, robustness, and likelihood to provoke a response tests are deemed "critical cultural factors" and are assessed as key components of a group's operational cultural narrative.

## Map the Scope of Critical Cultural Factors across Cultural Influences and Assess Results

Critical cultural factors that surfaced across research and are assessed as key components of the group's operational cultural narrative on this issue in this era are tracked back to their source—the cultural domain from which they are primarily derived (ethnic, organizational, national, religious)—in order to determine scope (which portion of the larger population is likely to espouse the same cultural narrative) and to aid strategists in crafting tailored operations engaging this group on this issue. If the strategist is looking internally at his own security forces, this portion of the exercise allows him to assess which of the cultural factors deemed "advantageous" to the security policy in question stem from peculiarities within a service organization and which are simply products of being reared within a particular nation, ethnic group, region, or other cultural setting. If the advantageous cultural factors are *absent* from organizational or service culture but do not run *counter to it* and can be emphasized during training in ways genuinely internalized by new recruits (the principal purpose of boot camp), then leadership has the opportunity to change training in order to strengthen what had been an organizational deficit. When short-term training is unlikely to instill the desired factors (perhaps the desired factors are the product of a deep-seated worldview or value set particular to a socioeconomic class or region of the country), strategists will have to become far more serious about tailored recruiting strategies and screening applicants for key leadership positions.[73]

The cultural mapping method also holds promise for improving efforts toward jointness. When the mapping exercise is repeated across services, creating an analytic view of the joint cultural topography, a strategist is provided a keen sense of where the services are likely to cooperate and where their distinctive service cultures will cause rifts. Applied to combined contexts—with allies and regional partners—the same utility applies.

Researchers must bear in mind the uncomfortable fact that any "cultural analysis is intrinsically incomplete."[74] The "soundness" of the insights derived from this method is assessed by their ability to be further validated rather than undermined by the continued consumption of data.[75] In the real world of the strategist, there is often a sharper test: direct application to the field. The cultural inferences generated will be put into operational play and will either prove insightful or fall flat. One of the beauties of creating forecasting mechanisms for the policy sphere is that one does not need to wait the length of a career to see if the offered method is valid and useful. The "proof," so to speak, is usually measured in rather immediate time frames.

With this in mind, the following chapters attempt to offer some measure of utility to the strategist on one targeted front: what cultural analysis has to tell us about the US Marine Corps's relationship with counterinsurgency and its likely practice in the future. The critical cultural factors that emerged as significant across research for this study were mapped across three key cultural domains: American public culture, US military culture, and the distinctive culture of the Marine Corps. Chapter 2 will examine key inputs from the first two.

## NOTES

Portions of this chapter previously appeared in Jeannie L. Johnson and Matthew T. Berrett, "Cultural Topography: A New Research Tool for Intelligence," *Studies in Intelligence* 55, no. 2 (June 2011): 1–22.

1. Heuser, *Evolution of Strategy*, 19.
2. Snyder, *Soviet Strategic Culture*, 8.
3. The tenets of realism championed by Hans J. Morgenthau can be found in Morgenthau, "Six Principles of Political Realism," 7–14. Criticism of realism and neorealism from second- and third-generation strategic culture scholars may be found in Katzenstein, *Culture of National Security*, and Glenn, Howlett, and Poore, *Neorealism versus Strategic Culture*.

4. Booth, "Concept of Strategic Culture," 123. A quintessential example of the rational-actor paradigm is provided in Mearsheimer, "Anarchy and the Struggle for Power," 50–60.
5. See Waltz, "Anarchic Structure of World Politics," 29–49.
6. Booth, "Concept of Strategic Culture," 123.
7. Gray, "Out of the Wilderness," 227.
8. Johnson, "Conclusion: Toward a Standard," 243.
9. Johnston, "Thinking about Strategic Culture," 32–64; Glenn, "Realism versus Strategic Culture"; Greathouse, "Examining the Role."
10. Bloomfield, "Time to Move On"; Greathouse, "Examining the Role."
11. Haglund, "What Good Is Strategic Culture?"
12. An exception is Meyer's work on the European Union as a superstate structure: "Purpose and Pitfalls," 669–90; "European Strategic Culture?," 523–49.
13. A nice exception is Long, "Al Qaeda Strategic Culture?"
14. Porter, Military Orientalism.
15. Gray, "British and American Strategic Cultures," 37. See also Gray, "Irregular Enemies."
16. Bloomfield, "Time to Move On."
17. Berger, "Norms, Identity, and National Security," 317–56; Berger, Cultures of Antimilitarism; Legro, "Whence American Internationalism." Theo Farrell agrees that external shocks are one likely source of change but argues that "norms entrepreneurs" must be present and prepared to take advantage of the mood for change in order for lasting shifts in doctrine to occur. Farrell, Norms of War, 12–15.
18. Schivelbusch, Culture of Defeat; Eisenstadt and Pollack, "Armies of Snow," 549–78; Dalgaard-Nielsen, "Test of Strategic Culture," 347.
19. Twomey, "Lacunae in the Study of Culture," 338–57.
20. Gray, Perspectives on Strategy, 98.
21. Mead, Special Providence, xvii.
22. Heuser, Nuclear Mentalities?
23. Feng, "Dragon on Defense," 171–88.
24. Jones, "India's Strategic Culture," 117–36.
25. Molavi, Soul of Iran.
26. Lee, "Geopolitics of America's Strategic Culture."
27. Gray, Perspectives on Strategy, 98.
28. Johnson and Berrett, "Cultural Topography," 2.
29. United States Army, Field Manual on Stability Operations, vi.
30. Dalgaard-Nielsen, "Test of Strategic Culture," 342.
31. Thomas Mahnken's work is a nice exception: "U.S. Strategic and Organizational Subcultures."
32. Avruch, Culture and Conflict Resolution, 15.
33. Michael Burnham, "Anonymity Catalyzes Radicalization among Internet Community," paper prepared for "PS: 4890 Strategic Culture," Utah State University, with the support of the Cultural Intelligence Institute, May 2011.

34. Hall, *Beyond Culture*, 99–100; Eriksen, *Small Places, Large Issues*, 51.
35. A thank you to David Newcomb for contributing to the "operational cultural narrative" label.
36. Writing in a constructivist vein, Theo Farrell makes the same argument: *Norms of War*, 1. For an interpretivist explanation, see Moon, "Logic of Political Inquiry," 180.
37. Farrell, "Culture and Military Power," 416 (italics added).
38. Mahnken, "U.S. Strategic and Organizational Subcultures," 76.
39. Builder, *Masks of War*, 39.
40. For an example of successful organizational change via savvy manipulation of organizational identity, see Terriff, "Warriors and Innovators."
41. Smith, *USAF Culture and Cohesion*, 8.
42. Farrell, "Constructivist Security Studies," 49.
43. Katzenstein, *Culture of National Security*, 5.
44. Burk, "Military Culture," 448.
45. Heuser, *Evolution of Strategy*, 494.
46. Snyder, "Concept of Strategic Culture," 4.
47. Longhurst, "Why Aren't the Germans," 147–65.
48. Eriksen, *Small Places, Large Issues*, 91; Swidler, "Culture in Action"; Hudson, "Cultural Expectations."
49. Hudson, "Cultural Expectations," 768.
50. Alastair Iain Johnston approaches the subject of historical inertia from a slightly different angle. His explanation focuses on the durability of heuristics. Early, formative experiences craft interpretive lenses that are slow to change, "lagging behind changes in 'objective' conditions." Johnston, *Cultural Realism*, 1.
51. Nagl, *Learning to Eat*, 217.
52. Giles, "Continuity and Change," 109.
53. Avruch, *Culture and Conflict Resolution*, 19.
54. Grondona, "Cultural Typology," 45.
55. Legro offers up additional mechanisms for measuring norm strength. See *Cooperation under Fire*; Legro, "Which Norms Matter?"; Kowert and Legro, "Norms, Identity and Their Limits," 451–97.
56. Gray, *Perspectives on Strategy*, 104–5.
57. Heuser, *Evolution of Strategy*, 72.
58. For interesting looks at nuclear choices, see Heuser, *NATO, Britain, France and the FRG*, and Heuser, *Nuclear Mentalities?*
59. Lynn, *Battle*, 5–7.
60. Legro, "Which Norms Matter?," 36.
61. Johnston, *Cultural Realism*, 1.
62. Kier, "Culture and Military Doctrine," 69. See also Fisher, *Mindsets*.
63. Kier, "Culture and Military Doctrine," 82.
64. Ibid., 68.
65. Keesing and Strathern, *Cultural Anthropology*, 505.
66. Fisher, *Mindsets*, 4.

67. Gray, *Perspectives on Strategy*, 90.

68. Hanson, *Carnage and Culture*, 7.

69. Johnson and Tierney, *Failing to Win*, 176–77, 164–68.

70. Ibid., 170.

71. Ibid., 171, 193–94.

72. Peter Wilson's article captures the research philosophy and data-extraction process pursued within a cultural mapping exercise and offers a strong argument for attention to the interpretivist method, Grounded Theory, and the English School for future analysis in international relations: "English School Meets Chicago School," 567–90.

73. Mark Moyar dedicates an entire book to this topic as it concerns competent counterinsurgency leadership at company and squad levels, *A Question of Command*.

74. Geertz, *Interpretation of Cultures*, 29.

75. Glaser and Strauss, *Discovery of Grounded Theory*.

# CHAPTER 2

# BOUNDING THE POSSIBLE

*The Impact of US National and Military Cultures on Counterinsurgency Practice*

The cultural traits examined across this chapter represent aspects of identity, norms, values, and perceptual lens within American public and military cultures that surfaced across research as critical cultural factors in understanding US Marine activity in irregular war. Given the time frame covered in this study—a century-long stretch—these may also qualify within the "semi-permanent" standard that Colin Gray insists on for strategic culture traits. This is not to say that each factor mentioned has weighed in equally across all time and spaces, but rather that each has existed with some consistency, perhaps surging and receding, within the way of life we know as "American." Contextualizing these factors across the three specific counterinsurgency eras, the task undertaken in part II of this book, provides insight into which critical cultural factors have been drawn together to create remarkably consistent operational cultural narratives for American counterinsurgency practice across time.

The interplay of cultural layers in influencing security policy can be observed in the behavior of the most granular units of security policy: those wearing boots on the ground. Before crossing the threshold into service ranks, each military recruit has been molded by national, regional, ethnic, religious, and various organizational cultures and carries many of these pre-existing norms and values with him or her throughout a military career. Commenting on our small-wars subject matter in particular, Sam Sarkesian makes what is perhaps an obvious, but nonetheless critical, point: Counterinsurgency strategy and practice are constrained by American national norms. This is not only an unconscious, natural process—it is also an overt expectation: "The American people expect their military men to behave in general accord with the norms of society. Thus, society's values must be reflected in military professional ethics and behavior, even on the battle-field." Sarkesian is careful to point out that this general rule may be bent on occasion—sometimes for expediency and sometimes because, where coun-terinsurgencies are concerned, "the conflict touches such a small segment of the American people" that they simply fail to notice.[1]

It must be noted that despite the heavy cultural interconnectedness between a nation and its armed forces, the military services see as part of their purpose the crafting of new men and new women—an honorable war-rior breed fit for engagement in the business of war. This process, by design, includes a breaking down of former civilian identities and habits and a transformative rebuilding of a capable military class in its place. The Marine Corps prides itself on a transformation more complete than that of any of the other services. The result is a distinctive subculture that runs counter to some aspects of national culture, including, in some cases, the strategic culture preferred by the public as a whole.[2] The following sections capture in brief form particularly salient aspects of American national culture and US military culture when assessing impact on counterinsurgency practice.

## AMERICAN NATIONAL CULTURE

The US military is its own cultural incubator—the individual services even more so—but with members drawn from an already heavily encultured national population: one reared in a democratic setting that prizes individ-ual worth, justice, and fair play and celebrates the American exceptionalism captured within the American dream—individualism, equal opportunity, and the right to pursue happiness.[3] These laudable American traits come packaged with others, some that have potential to serve well in small-wars engagements and others that do not.

Jeffrey Record argues that there are two key weaknesses in American culture where waging successful counterinsurgency is concerned. The first is "the American tendency to separate war and politics—to view military victory as an end in itself, ignoring war's function as an instrument of policy." The second is a flat-out aversion to counterinsurgency.[4] This aver-sion is not wholly attributable to the type of fighting itself but is due, at least in part, to a lack of confidence in the fights selected. James Warren points out that many thoughtful Americans are aware of US counterinsur-gency successes but doubt the judgment of policymakers in steering the effective application of military force. Worried about mission creep and "the pursuit of lofty generalities such as 'the expansion of democracy and freedom'" in places that seem inhospitable to it, Americans "recoil from the deployment of ground forces far more than they do the use of air or sea-launched cruise missiles."[5]

History has given Americans good reason to believe that well-meaning political administrations may lack an informed foundation on the risks, possible humiliation, and other large-scale costs of irregular wars. From the Philippines to the Banana Wars to Vietnam and then Afghanistan and Iraq, US policymakers did not foresee the protracted nature of the counterinsurgency and nation-building enterprises on which they were embarking and therefore supplied little by way of direction or advanced planning to the military forces sent to engage in them.

The frustrations born of poorly executed counterinsurgencies have historically led to denial. The event of the Vietnam War, for instance, was perceived by both the military and the nation as an aberration and, like other irregular conflicts, "outside the scope of American political-military policy."[6] Denial has consequences. Eliot Cohen argues that Americans compound their own counterinsurgency conundrum by "simply refusing to believe that they will again send soldiers into obscure corners of the world to fight for limited political objectives against a hostile non-European power." The consequence of this mind-set is a state of chronic underpreparedness when faced with the next round.[7]

A number of factors may explain Americans' aversion to, failure to plan for, and at least initial stumbling within counterinsurgency settings. One that nearly ensures costly and repeated mistakes is "a cultivated ignorance of other nations,"[8] combined with a debilitating proclivity for ahistoricism.[9] Samuel Huntington argued in 1957 that American indifference to international affairs was a natural repercussion of American-style liberalism, which had deeply and homogeneously rooted itself in the nation. Liberalism in America did not incorporate any coherent philosophy vis-à-vis foreign affairs, leaving Americans only domestic solutions for international problems.[10] Oliver Lee argues that this trend has continued, undiminished, in the decades since Huntington wrote. American insularity is a repercussion of an "extraordinary degree of individualism" in American culture, which compels the American people to focus "their concerns and energies upon advancing the interests of the individual and his or her family and perhaps their local community, and to some extent of the nationwide community, but [demonstrate] little interest in or concern about the wide world beyond...."[11] This knowledge gap about the outside world, however, does not inhibit Americans from possessing strong opinions about it.[12] Unsurprisingly, this often leads to offensive behavior, born more of ignorance than malice.[13]

American leadership is not required by its public to demonstrate a significantly more refined grasp of the world. Civilian policymakers and elected officials are rarely punished for manifesting a limited sense of history or analytic capability.[14] A premium is placed on experience-based common sense and forward-looking ambition.[15] Revered American icon Henry Ford is reported to have said, "History is more or less bunk. It's tradition. We don't want tradition. We want to live in the present and the only history

that is worth a tinker's dam [*sic*] is the history we made today."[16] Writing in
1944, D. W. Brogan, a British observer of American culture, attributed the
American habit of disparaging the past to a necessary pioneer temperament.
The forward-looking attitude required in the "making" of America took
"extraordinary energies" and, he observed, bred a peculiarly American attitude that refrains from looking back.[17] Writing twenty years later, Stanley
Hoffman made the point more sharply, claiming that Americans' faith in
progress has led them to not simply improve on history, but to shed it completely—"historical virginity."[18]

The dismissive ahistoricism rooted in the frontier era continues to permeate the American general public and the institutions that serve it. Even
the intelligentsia of American society often suffer from serious deficits of
historical knowledge. Walter Russell Mead points out:

> The deep lack of interest in the history of American foreign pol-
> icy is not confined to high officials. The overwhelming majority of
> their talented and hardworking colleagues in think tanks, univer-
> sities, the national media, and government departments that are
> concerned with developing, carrying out, reporting, and reflecting
> on the foreign policy of the United States do not know very much
> about the history of American foreign policy before World War II,
> do not particularly want to learn more than they already know, and
> cannot think what practical purpose a deeper knowledge of Ameri-
> can foreign policy history might serve.[19]

Research conducted by Edward C. Stewart and Milton J. Bennett, authors
of the seminal classic *American Cultural Patterns*, underscores the point
that Americans know little of other lands, tending toward biases in favor
of mutual similarity and gross oversimplifications.[20] Both Edward T. Hall
and Gary Althen argue that the result is an ethnocentric tendency toward
viewing others as "underdeveloped Americans."[21] Rather than owning up
to a clear-eyed recognition that their projected policies are often an attempt
to change indigenous cultural patterns at a fundamental level, Americans
perceive their efforts as hastening "progress," "democratization," and the
spread of Western values and tend to believe sincerely that education and
training, combined with sufficient resources, will rather quickly produce
desired and lasting changes in behavior. Surveying the extensive work on
American culture within his field, anthropologist Leonard Mason provides
a consistent finding: Accustomed to a history of success in mastering their
physical environment, Americans "are equally confident that undesirable
social conditions can be remedied just as easily and are confused when such
proves not to be the case."[22]

Hubris regarding the social and cultural projects it undertakes can create pitfalls for American foreign policy. Matthew T. Berrett provides the

optic of an intelligence officer with three decades of experience serving the
Oval Office:

> As I witnessed ... decisionmakers in action ... I came to con-
> clude that the "inertia of culture" was often underrated in their
> assessments of opportunities and obstacles. ... America's cultural
> view features the notion that Americans can achieve anything, any-
> where—including going to the moon—if they just invest enough
> resources. This notion is understandable but perhaps hazardous. ...
> I have rarely seen American policymakers ask "Will our desired for-
> eign policy outcome require change over there at the cultural level?
> Over what period and with what resources is such cultural change
> achievable?"[23]

A number of explanations exist for why the United States, despite its
global-power status and consistent reach into other lands, maintains an acul-
tural and ahistorical predisposition. Aculturalism may be due, in part, to
the home population's enthusiastic veneration of America's own culture and
political system. Early twentieth-century Americans had more reservations
than their descendants about the portability of American-style democracy.
Europeans were viewed as "not yet ready" for the American pattern, and
Central and South Americans were regarded as not sufficiently civilized.[24]
Perhaps buoyed by the obvious success of the American system, later generations came to perceive the predetermined path for nations as one inevitably moving toward democracy and international stability—an aspect of
perceptual lens that suffered disappointment from time to time but tended
to reemerge in rather robust form.[25] Moved by this perceived eventuality, it
became part of American fiber to proselytize the American model at every
opportunity in an effort to hasten progress on the world stage.[26] Gray notes
that even in the heat of its wars, modern America "is not content, indeed
culturally it cannot be content, simply to discipline wrongdoers. Instead, the
United States must seek to remake in some variant of its own image those
parts of the world where its soldiers' boots crush the dust."[27] This often results
in a tension between irrepressible messianic urges and unrealistic impatience
when the US applies its democratic model to little-understood cultures.
    Americans are also prone to believe that the generosity of their inten-
tions will supersede any potential cultural missteps. Americans have, since
the beginning, regarded their nation as exceptional in the rightness of its
motives toward other nations and have expected their efforts to be regarded
by foreign populations in that light.[28] As self-identified defenders of the
underdog, Americans tend to believe that common people around the world
are naturally disposed to like them.[29] Rather than learn about local values and culture, US forces lean on American generosity to forge relationships. American impulses across time are a consistent pattern of attempts

to win over indigenous populations by defaulting to material gifts: dispensing goods and building up infrastructure. In this, anthropologists Edward and Mildred Hall claim that American generosity is "matched by no other country we know."[30] As a result, America's typically well-meaning citizens become confused and disillusioned when these efforts do not produce the strategic friendship sought and become deeply resentful if the "beneficiary" population seems ungrateful.[31] Americans have a pronounced desire to be liked and react strongly when they perceive they are "not wanted."[32] When indigenous populations demonstrate resentment toward American military presence and actively call for troops to be drawn home, US citizens and service members alike tend to sour on the worth of counterinsurgency efforts. These sentiments are easily exploited by political opponents in America's home sphere, who tend to push for reduced troop levels, restrained financial investment, and an early termination to the occupation.[33]

American ahistoricism may be derived, in part, from the nation's penchant for valuing novelty over tradition and its dedication to forward thinking.[34] Visitors to the United States are often presented with "change" in local environments as markers of positive progress.[35] Forward-leaning views that celebrate change are undergirded by a belief in the steady march of progress, that the natural state of things is advancement toward a better life for an expanding percentage of people.[36] Observers of American culture across the nation's history have repeatedly noted the American zeal in problem-solving. Humans, in the American mind, are meant to be active and enthusiastic agents of change. Some years ago a Russian student in one of my university classrooms stood to give a comparative presentation on Russian and American culture. She started by saying, "Americans are not human beings." This captured immediate attention. "Americans," she went on, "are human *do*-ings. They don't know how to *be*." Chroniclers of American culture across time agree. Americans are incessantly on the move.[37] "*Doing* is the dominant form of activity for Americans," and this American "bias for action," to borrow Marine parlance, means trial and error is acceptable as a learning method, overreaction is more easily forgiven than inaction, and heroes resemble the action-oriented, "rugged individualist" of the frontier past.[38] Patience, restraint, and caution in the employment of kinetic effects do not come naturally to Americans. Not only is deliberate action the preferred state of activity—it is also the basis for identity. For Americans "one *is* what one *does*."[39] Because status is dispensed in American society on an individual basis and according to an achievement-oriented measuring stick, Americans are prone to make mistakes abroad when their achievement orientation underrates the influence of nonproductive individuals who wield significant influence in ascriptive, relationship-based societies.[40]

The American penchant to *do* is harnessed to a nearly unsinkable optimism that it can be *done*. Brogan tracks American optimism back to the continent's earliest settlers: Intrepid enough to brave life in the New World, they exhibited an optimism that became a national brand. Within the "religions of economic and political optimism," he observed, "dissent, especially continuous pessimistic crabbing," was "near to treason."[41] Writing in 1955, Cora du Bois observed American optimism undiminished; she highlighted "effort optimism" as a focal value of American culture—a trait that continues to be emphasized by scholars of American culture today.[42] Applying these findings to the subject of warfare, Gray notes that "it is quintessentially American to be optimistic and to believe that all problems can be solved, if not today, then tomorrow, and most probably by technology."[43] America's optimism informs its expectations about economics, politics, and foreign relations. Expectations for success permeate US national security documents.[44] The historical result, Gray cautions, is an American way of war that is not easily discouraged once invoked: "The problem-solving faith, the penchant for the engineering fix, has the inevitable consequence of leading US policy, including its use of armed force, to attempt the impossible."[45] Consequent failures, however, tend to be explained in the American mind as products of insufficient resources or insufficient human will, *not* as a result of attempting the impossible.[46]

As dedicated problem-solvers, Americans expect to be able to shape the "foreseeable future."[47] The future is perceived as foreseeable because, as linear thinkers dedicated to causal chains, Americans tend to see the world as a set of isolated, solvable problems rather than a complex web of historical relationships.[48] This comfortable fiction allows Americans a stronger sense of control over their own world and a sense of independence from the decisions and actions of others, a sometimes strategically fatal perceptual lens when applied to counterinsurgency contexts.[49] The result in counterinsurgency operations has tended to be an American cognitive and planning pattern that focuses on host government institutions as *items to be built* or *problems to be solved*, with little acknowledgment of the potential limits of a foreign entity in doing so. A premium is placed on an infusion of resources and proper training as a panacea to the ills of indigenous institutions. When host institutions fail to perform adequately, American problem-solving agents dressed in military uniforms begin to step in and do it for them. Unsurprisingly, economic, material, and political transformations made during these eras of hands-on military administration often meet with quick reversal once US troops are withdrawn.

A decided problem-solving approach, combined with an action orientation emphasizing efficiency, means that Americans are repelled by time-consuming or sociohistorically complex diagnoses of problem sets and may be more likely than others to fall prey to single-solution concepts.[50] Americans possess a near obsessive regard for deadlines as a means for increasing efficiency and accelerating progress and expect the same veneration of deadlines from others.[51] Life orchestrated to a fast tempo ("hurry sickness") is not a new aspect of American culture; de Tocqueville noted excessive working and rushing in American life in the 1830s.[52] The "hurry" experienced across the American timeline is inspired by "a race for success," a race that is won by the acquisition of material goods.[53] Brogan tracks the American obsession with material success back to ideas inspired in the Protestant Reformation and then amplified within American religious circles, resulting in a conflation of prosperity and virtue.[54] Progress and prosperity became synonymous in the New World, and very early on Americans established a persistent pattern of measuring achievement by way of material outcomes.[55] This mentality fueled the economic growth that propelled the United States into superpower status and remains the key to the nation's unparalleled logistical excellence and success in conventional war. When applied to counterinsurgency theaters, however, America's traditionally successful formula threatens to become a handicap. The American captivation with controllable, efficient, streamlined solutions and quantifiable metrics for success produces an impatient public that demands "quick, conclusive results" of a sort rarely achieved in counterinsurgency theaters.[56] Insistence on efficiency and measurable results has, as the following case studies will demonstrate, led to an obsession with quantifiable operational methods that often lose sight of, or run counter to, strategic ends.[57]

The analysis of American culture thus far may pose a striking resemblance to what one might assume of US military culture as well. For all the similarities that may be drawn between American culture generally and the manifestations of it found in the armed services, a British Army brigadier serving alongside US forces made a surprising claim (at least for this American) about the gulf between American public and military culture. In speaking of the US Army, he said, "The US Army's habits and customs, whilst in some respects very obviously products of American society, are also strikingly distinct, much more so than most militaries, to the extent that some individuals almost seem like military caricatures, so great is their intent on banishing all traces of the civilian within. US Army soldiers are not citizen soldiers: they are unquestionably American in origin, but equally unquestionably divorced from their roots."[58]

Eliot Cohen points out that one aspect of American culture its military members would be well advised to reject is the overarching aversion to limited war. Cohen insists that in order to succeed, the military must reconcile its craving for popular support as "at once understandable and unacceptable for a country that must fight small wars."[59] It may be the case, however, that in embracing limited war the military would not be rejecting American public culture only—it would be rejecting the core preferences of its own culture as well. American "roots" in this category at least may not be so rooted out after all.

## US MILITARY CULTURE

Robert Cassidy defines military culture as "a set of beliefs, attitudes and values within the military establishment that shape collective (shared) preferences of how and when military means should be used to accomplish strategic aims." He submits that these are "derived or developed as a result of historical experience, geography, and political culture."[60] Cassidy's focus on these three components is valid, but they are best thought of as ingredients that are then internally processed and digested, with some aspects absorbed and some rejected by the body of military culture. The US military's development of strong conventional preferences even while engaged in irregular conflicts is an interesting case in point.

The US military posture across time may be explained in good measure by a mechanism that fixates on those conflicts (lived or foreseen) that edify a preferred identity and largely dismisses those that do not. Cassidy argues that mission sets close to core identity will be emphasized and pursued at the expense of perhaps equally important mission sets that pose challenges to a military's self-concept.[61] As a case in point, an American army that was engaged for years in frontier fighting failed to cultivate doctrine, training, or any level of professional literature on how to effectively engage the adversary of the day—Indians it deemed "master[s] of guerrilla warfare."[62] Battle with various Native tribes never registered in the American military mind as genuine Army business.[63]

The youthful American forces yearned for an identity elevated above frontier fighting—a conventional profile that would place them on peer status with European forces.[64] They measured their status in terms of potential success in future gentlemen's battles, not present success in internal guerrilla wars. Thus, Deborah Avant claims, the US military used the advantage of relative isolation from congressional oversight to develop along its preferred identity lines: a force prepared for Prussian-style big war based on classic military principles. Any use of the Army for internal policing-like duties was considered "beneath the soldiers' vocation."[65]

Once identity notions of this sort take hold, they are very difficult to eradicate, even in situations of pressing need. One particularly distressing repercussion is the impediment organizational culture may pose to military innovation when new ways of warfare lie outside the organization's core role.[66]

To understand how the identity, norms, and values embedded within America's conventional force influence its ability to wage counterinsurgency, it is useful to take a closer look at the collection of preferences that combine to form America's preferred way of war. The bulk of current literature typifies American strategic norms as favoring wars of annihilation against conventional enemies,[67] accomplished in short time frames and with sophisticated technology,[68] rather than sophisticated strategy (or any strategy at all).[69] The notion of annihilation as the preferred way of

American war was chronicled and launched into popular consciousness by Russell F. Weigley.[70] Victor Davis Hanson concurred and defined it as "head-to-head battle that destroys the enemy."[71] Brian Linn, among others, has challenged this characterization of the American way of war, pointing to the vast amount of experience that the US military has had with limited attritional wars.[72] Although Linn is correct in noting the preponderance of limited wars across US history, the logic that this experience naturally translates into a national way of war is flawed. Thomas Mahnken provides the necessary correction by acknowledging US historical experience with small wars but maintaining that a military profession's strategic culture is founded on its *preferences* and *aspirations* far more than actual practice.[73] In this, Antulio J. Echevarria II would argue that the American preference remains "'taking down' an opponent quickly," rather than engaging in the lengthy, complex, and political experience of irregular or limited wars.[74] Gray emphasizes the American short-term mentality, noting that "the mindset needed to combat an enemy who is playing a long game is not one that comes naturally to the American soldier or, for that matter, to the American public."[75] Conventional war, in the American mind, is successful in short time frames by combining "lavish firepower,"[76] "mobility, and an aggressive hunt for the main body of the foe."[77]

The American partiality for a conventional war extends not just to the preferred mode of destroying the enemy forces, but to a preferred division of labor perceived as available in conventional contexts. The American military machine yearns to focus on the waging of war and on delivering expert warfare, rather than shaping its activities toward political consequence: building an advantageous peace.[78] Whether true or not, American military professionals see conventional conflicts as arenas that allow for military and political experts to operate successfully within their separate spheres to a much higher degree than do unconventional engagements. When the United States is forced into limited war contexts, Echevarria argues that the bifurcation between American diplomatic political centers and military sources of power leads to an "American way of war [that] tends to shy away from thinking about the complicated process of turning military triumphs, whether on the scale of major campaigns or small-unit actions, into strategic successes." The result is an American armed force that is geared to "fight wars as if they were battles and, thus, confuses the winning of campaigns or small-scale actions with the winning of wars."[79]

The successful coordination of military might in the service of political aims is the essence of strategy. Unfortunately, according to Gray, "American understanding of strategy, and sound practice of it, is almost desperately rare. Strategic thinking and behavior worthy of the name are endangered activities in this country."[80] Strategic dysfunction may stem, in part, from the decentralized nature of America's foreign policy and security machinery.[81] It may also stem from a preference for technological over strategic sophistication. Williamson Murray cautions that "the greatest danger for the United States in the coming century is that the American military will possess self-satisfied, intellectually stagnant cultures that believe they have found the technological lodestone."[82] Rather than strategic excellence, Yankee-style military expertise boasts strengths of largesse,[83] technical superiority,[84] and logistical dominance.[85] These may enjoy full play in a conventional arena but are rendered problematic in a counterinsurgency context in which "irregular enemies pose problems of a kind where technology typically offers few real advantages."[86] Counterinsurgency is manpower intensive and relies heavily on special skills, most of these people- and relationship-oriented: building intelligence networks within the population, conducting civil affairs, building and training police forces, improving public health, and information operations.[87] Nearly all of these require skill in local languages and do not fall within America's big-war competencies. As Cohen quips, the American valuing of technical expertise over regional knowledge, cultural understanding, or linguistic depth means the "American proficiency at imparting technical skills is matched only by American insensitivity to local conditions."[88]

Cultural insensitivity has repercussions beyond treatment of locals in counterinsurgency theaters—it affects relations with allies and inhibits a proper evaluation of oneself. Gray warns that "for a state that now accepts, indeed insists upon, a global mandate to act as sheriff, [a] lack of cultural empathy, including a lack of sufficiently critical self-knowledge, is most serious."[89] Murray agrees. Writing presciently in advance of the US miring in Iraq and Afghanistan, he notes, "Above all, the [US] services need to practice some profound introspection, for unless they understand themselves and how different their world views are from those of the country's opponents in the next century, the United States is headed for a major crack-up that could prove even more disastrous than the Vietnam War."[90]

Naiveté on both home and foreign fronts very likely explains the American dearth of what Eliot Cohen cryptically characterizes as "skills of manipulation." He notes, rightly, that military and political problems are complexly intertwined in small wars. Skills of manipulation are needed on this front, as well as in the backrooms of waging coalition warfare. He claims that the skills of this type are scarce and "in some measure anathema to the American military."[91] William Kincade sees this as a natural outgrowth of American national culture: Americans remain suspicious of international politics and diplomacy. The belief persists that the US cannot play the game in the cynical manner of other nations and that Americans are often cheated at the bargaining table. Impatient with the complexity or ambiguity of international diplomacy and the amoral compromises it often produces, Americans tend to prefer "bargaining from strength" or a radical, principled style of diplomacy in which the US holds the high cards or high moral ground.[92]

The most remarkable historical bit may be that the United States, with a style that seems to run so counter to counterinsurgency success, has waged counterinsurgency at all or has ever been good at it. To that point, Robert Cassidy's historical study of the US peacekeeping and counterinsurgency experience reveals a distressing competency reversal, a historic degradation in capabilities: "America as a fledgling state started off doing unconventional operations well but as it moved toward and achieved great power status, it started doing these operations poorly."[93] Cassidy expresses some frustration at the small-wars competencies that were jettisoned in favor of loftier conventional aims: "It is somewhat ironic, revealing, and disquieting that an institution with more history and experience fighting irregular conflicts of limited intensity than total wars without limits, would have its core culture so profoundly influenced by Sherman, Upton, and the World War II experience."[94]

John Nagl offers some rationale for this phenomenon by voicing a sentiment shared by many across the armed services. He acknowledges a trade-off: developing small-wars expertise may degrade conventional readiness. In the revised preface to his counterinsurgency classic *Learning to Eat Soup with a Knife*, Nagl notes that when he wrote his book he "underestimated the challenge of adapting an army for the purposes of defeating an insurgency while simultaneously maintaining the army's ability to fight a conventional war."[95] Whether the trade-off is genuine or not, it is certainly perceived as such among those in uniform. The extent to which Marines share these sentiments and fall in line with the strategic culture package often attributed to the US military will be examined in the next three chapters.

## NOTES

1. Sarkesian, *America's Forgotten Wars*, 9–10.
2. Lee, "Geopolitics of American's Strategic Culture," 273–78.
3. Sarkesian, *America's Forgotten Wars*, 14–15; Lotz, "Myth and NAFTA," 81.
4. Record, "American Way of War." This theme is also developed by Robert M. Cassidy, who contrasts the civil-military disconnect in the American armed forces with the integrated civil-military approach of the British in *Peacekeeping in the Abyss*.
5. Warren, "Small Wars and Military Culture," 59. See also Lee, "Geopolitics of American's Strategic Culture," 273–78.
6. Sarkesian, *America's Forgotten Wars*, 4.
7. Cohen, "Constraints on America's Conduct," 181.
8. Kincade, "American National Style," 13; Stewart and Bennett, *American Cultural Patterns*, 11.
9. Murray, "Anglo-American Strategic Culture?," 157. Interestingly, Murray beats the British about the ears for the same ahistorical failings. In another work he claims that this trait is nearly universal: "There are few military organizations

that possess a culture that encourages the study of even the recent past with any thoroughness." Murray, "Does Military Culture Matter?," 140.

10. Huntington, *Soldier and the State*, 149.
11. Lee, "Geopolitics of American's Strategic Culture," 276.
12. Lotz, "Myth and NAFTA," 84.
13. Hall, *Silent Language*, 9.
14. Sarkesian, *America's Forgotten Wars*, xii.
15. Stewart and Bennett, *American Cultural Patterns*, 158; Lotz, "Myth and NAFTA," 80.
16. Henry Ford interview in the *Chicago Tribune*, May 24, 1916, Quotations Page, http://www.quotationspage.com/quote/24950.html.
17. Brogan, *American Character*, 5.
18. Hoffman, *Gulliver's Troubles*, 110. See also Williams, "Values and Modern Education," 66, and Althen, *American Ways*, 10–11.
19. Mead, *Special Providence*, 7.
20. Stewart and Bennett, *American Cultural Patterns*, 11.
21. Hall, *Silent Language*, 9; Althen, *American Ways*, xvi.
22. Mason, "Characterization of American Culture," 1269. See also Datesman, Crandall, and Kearny, *American Ways*, 135.
23. Johnson and Berrett, "Cultural Topography," 1–2.
24. Cunliffe, "Formative Events," 9.
25. Hoffman, *Gulliver's Troubles*, 111.
26. Mahnken, "U.S. Strategic and Organizational Subcultures," 71; Meilinger, "American Military Culture," 81; Heald, "Foreign Relations, American Style," 197–98. Phillip Meilinger notes this trend as it applies to Mexico in 1847, Cuba and the Philippines in 1898, Europe in 1918, and Germany and Japan after World War II, as well as Korea, Vietnam, Iraq, and Afghanistan. Theo Farrell takes the supposition of democratizing as a general US foreign policy trend to task in his article "America's Misguided Mission," 3.
27. Gray, "British and American Strategic Cultures," 41.
28. Brogan, *American Character*, 63–66; Heald, "Foreign Relations, American Style," 204.
29. Stewart and Bennett, *American Cultural Patterns*, 108.
30. Hall and Hall, *Understanding Cultural Differences*, 153.
31. Stewart and Bennett, *American Cultural Patterns*, 108; Hoffman, *Gulliver's Troubles*, 101–2.
32. Hall and Hall, *Understanding Cultural Differences*, 152.
33. Pei, Amin, and Garz, "Building Nations," 68. See also Lee, "America's Strategic Culture," 280.
34. Brogan, *American Character*, 136; Du Bois, "Dominant Value Profile," 1233; Lotz, "Myth and NAFTA," 79; Datesman, Crandall, and Kearny, *American Ways*, 105.
35. Stewart and Bennett, *American Cultural Patterns*, 142–43; Williams, "Values and Modern Education," 66.

36. Brogan, *American Character*, 65.
37. Du Bois, "Dominant Value Profile," 1234; Mason, "Characterization of American Culture," 1268–69.
38. Stewart and Bennett, *American Cultural Patterns*, 69, 155; Datesman, Crandall, and Kearny, *American Ways*, 85–86.
39. Stewart and Bennett, *American Cultural Patterns*, 76 (italics added).
40. Adamsky, *Culture of Military Innovation*, 75.
41. Brogan, *American Character*, 32–34, 74.
42. Du Bois, "Dominant Value Profile"; Datesman, Crandall, and Kearny, *American Ways*, 85–86.
43. Gray, "British and American Strategic Cultures," 45.
44. Moore, "Strategic Culture."
45. Gray, "Irregular Enemies," 33.
46. Stewart and Bennett, *American Cultural Patterns*, 75.
47. Brogan, *American Character*, 148; Williams, "Values and Modern Education," 65–66; Stewart and Bennett, *American Cultural Patterns*, 36; Hall and Hall, *Understanding Cultural Differences*, 148; Kincade, "American National Style," 12–13; Althen, *American Ways*, 11.
48. Hoffman, *Gulliver's Troubles*, 111. Linear thinking is a cognitive style exhibited by much of the Western Hemisphere; see Lam et al., "Cultural Differences," 1296–1309. For an intensive examination of American cognitive style, see Adamsky, *Culture of Military Innovation*.
49. Stewart and Bennett, *American Cultural Patterns*, 69. Claude S. Fischer cites a Pew poll from 2002–3 that collected data from across forty-four nations: "At a ratio of two to one, Americans were the most likely . . . to *reject* the proposition that 'success in life is pretty much determined by forces outside our control.'" *Made in America*, 210.
50. Mason, "Characterization of American Culture," 1268; Stewart and Bennett, *American Cultural Patterns*, 30–31; Datesman, Crandall, and Kearny, *American Ways*, 106; Gray, "Out of the Wilderness," 224.
51. Mason, "Characterization of American Culture," 1268; Stewart and Bennett, *American Cultural Patterns*, 74; Hall and Hall, *Understanding Cultural Differences*, 140–41;
52. Datesman, Crandall, and Kearny, *American Ways*, 106.
53. Ibid., 34–35, 103.
54. Brogan, *American Character*, 67.
55. Du Bois, "Dominant Value Profile," 1235.
56. Gray, "Irregular Enemies," 44.
57. Williams, "Values and Modern Education," 65–66.
58. Aylwin-Foster, "Changing the Army," 35. Thomas Ricks notes the same disdain for, and attempts at complete divorcement from, civilian culture in the Marine Corps. Ricks, *Making the Corps*. An energetic defense of the culture gap between US military and civilian society is provided by Hillen, "Must U.S. Military Culture Reform?"

59. Cohen, "Constraints on America's Conduct," 168.

60. Cassidy, *Peacekeeping in the Abyss*, 7.

61. Ibid., 6.

62. Ibid., 93.

63. Nagl, *Learning to Eat Soup*, 44.

64. Ibid., 46.

65. Avant, "Institutional Sources," 415.

66. Cassidy, "Back to the Street without Joy," 14. See also Murray, "Does Military Culture Matter?," 134.

67. Cassidy notes that as late as 2002, "the National Training Center (NTC), the U.S. Army's premier desert collective training opportunity, still focused exclusively on conventional battles with linear boundaries and phase lines." He later cites a Rand Corporation study asserting that the "small wars the U.S. Army engaged in during the Cold War . . . may have only strengthened the big-war preference." Cassidy, *Counterinsurgency and Global War on Terror*, 103, 115. James Kurth, writing on the US engagement in Iraq, notes the persistence of this notion. Kurth, "Iraq."

68. Gray, "British and American Strategic Cultures," 49; Farrell, "Strategic Culture and American Empire," 8; Sondhaus, *Strategic Culture*, 60–61; Mahnken, "U.S. Strategic and Organizational Subcultures," 74; Sarkesian, *America's Forgotten Wars*, 5.

69. Numerous American-culture theorists have made this argument but perhaps none so convincingly as Gray in "National Style," 33, and "Irregular Enemies."

70. Weigley, *American Way of War*.

71. Hanson, *Carnage and Culture*, 22. Both Hanson and Echevarria acknowledge that a preference for annihilation is shared across a number of Western nations. This characteristic is not attributable to the United States alone. Echevarria, *Toward an American Way of War*, 2.

72. Linn and Weigley, "American Way of War Revisited," 501–33. Boot adds meat to this argument in his volume *Savage Wars of Peace*.

73. Mahnken, "U.S. Strategic and Organizational Subcultures," 73.

74. Echevarria, *Toward an American Way of War*, 16. See also Morgan, "Evolving View of Warfare," 147–69.

75. Gray, "Irregular Enemies," 27.

76. Mahnken, "U.S. Strategic and Organizational Subcultures," 74. See also Gray, "Irregular Enemies," 11. Maj. Russell A. Moore counters this notion in a thesis prepared for the Marine Corps. His assessment of the then-current national security doctrine revealed an emphasis on precision rather than mass firepower. Moore, "Strategic Culture."

77. Gray, "Irregular Enemies," 11.

78. Ibid., 30.

79. Echevarria, *Toward an American Way of War*, 7, 10.

80. Gray, "Irregular Enemies," 3–4.

81. Melton, "Conceptualizing Victory Anew."

82. Murray, "Does Military Culture Matter?," 151.

83. Meilinger, "American Military Culture," 81.

84. Record, "American Way of War," 5.

85. Gray, "Irregular Enemies," 46. Murray calls this "projecting military power" and credits Britain with the same superior capability. Murray, "Anglo-American Strategic Culture?," 152.

86. Gray, "Irregular Enemies," 36.

87. Record, "American Way of War," 6.

88. Cohen, "Constraints on America's Conduct," 169. Gray would add that the insensitivity in question extends to dangerous ahistoricism as well. Gray, "Irregular Enemies," 32.

89. Gray, "Irregular Enemies," 34.

90. Murray, "Does Military Culture Matter?," 151.

91. Cohen, "Constraints on America's Conduct," 170.

92. Kincade, "American National Style," 27.

93. Cassidy, *Peacekeeping in the Abyss*, 36.

94. Ibid., 98.

95. Nagl, *Learning to Eat Soup*, xiv.

# CHAPTER 3

# LIFE IN THE SEAMS

## Establishing Marine Corps Identity and Role

Although an observer of the Marine Corps today might see Marines as possessed of an obvious and clearly defined sense of identity apart from soldiers, sailors, and airmen, it has not always been so. A review of the discourse penned by Marine officers in their earliest published journals reveals a service struggling between two service identities—Army and Navy—and still searching for ground to call its own.[1] Marines in the first decades of the twentieth century most often referred to themselves as "soldiers" (a label for which even well-meaning civilians will be reprimanded for applying to them today) and confessed that although they bunked on ships, they had far more in common with a French infantryman than an American sailor.[2] Marines speak in a lexicon born of the Navy (doors are "hatches," walls are "bulkheads," beds are "racks") but early on drew manuals, doctrine, rank structure, and training from the Army. Thus, the historical influence of these two sister services (much more so than the Air Force) cannot be dismissed as formative in the evolution of today's Marine Corps. "Marines fight like soldiers, talk like sailors, and think like both."[3]

Most of the work done on Marine culture is by Marines for Marines. Tom Ricks is perhaps the best-known outsider to have conducted systematic observations of culture within the Corps. He defines service "culture" in succinct fashion: how members treat each other and how they fight.[4] Ricks notes Carl Builder's omission of the Marine Corps in his classic work *Masks of War*, which details US service cultures.[5] Builder profiled the cultural characteristics of the Army, Navy, and Air Force and their projected strategic impact on warfighting but dismissed the Marine Corps and the Coast Guard as "colorful" institutions with limited strategic voice in military force planning.[6]

According to Ricks, Builder thought better of it by 1994 and offered a lecture on Marine Corps culture at the US Army War College. He noted that the other services tended to measure themselves in numbers: the Navy by counting its ships, the Army its troops, and the Air Force the performance quality and number of its aircraft. The Marines, by contrast, focused on their internal culture: their ability to preserve an independent identity apart from the other services and remain self-sufficient, "taking more pride in who they are," Builder argued, "than what they own."[7] Ricks agrees: "The Air Force has its planes, the Navy its ships, the Army its obsessively written and obeyed 'doctrine' that dictates how to act. Culture—that is, the values and assumptions that shape its members—is all the Marines have. It is what holds them together. . . . Theirs is the richest culture: formalistic, insular, elitist, with a deep anchor in their own history and mythology."[8] Marines, in a measure significantly above the other services, recognize the essential nature of fostering allegiance to their own traditions and history and have made the practice a part of their doctrine. The handbook for noncommissioned officers (NCOs) emphasizes that "these traditions give the Marine Corps its spirit. . . . As our traditions, our institutions, and even our eccentricities—like live coral—develop and toughen, so the Corps itself develops and toughens."[9]

The examination of Marine Corps culture that follows explores identity and role within the Corps, with an eye toward understanding the implications for the full spectrum of counterinsurgency tasks. Understanding core components of Marine Corps culture and comparing them to operational practice across counterinsurgency campaigns may shed light on why some lessons have been learned and integrated over time and others lost to history. Identity is an appropriate starting point. Of the four aspects of culture examined across these chapters, it carries disproportionate weight, often acting as the deep anchor to which norms, values, and perceptions are bound.

## IDENTITY

Marine Corps identity indoctrination starts well in advance of boot camp. Recruitment media, Hollywood films portraying Marines, Marine legends that permeate the national consciousness, family ties to former Marines, and exposure to Marine material culture (bumper stickers, T-shirts, decals, tattoos) are all part of the presetting of American notions about what it is to be a Marine.

Those identity narratives that are consciously cultivated by the Corps, specifically through recruitment posters and commercials, capture the narrative the Corps *intends* to send, the image it means to cultivate, and the sort of young person it hopes to draw in. A systematic review of Marine advertising since the early years of the twentieth century reveals a set of mixed narratives—some of which would be anathema to the Marine Corps of today—threaded together with a few constant themes. To understand how surprising some of these narratives might be to today's Marine Corps recruiters, it might be useful to paint a clear portrait of a standard visit to a recruiter's office in the contemporary setting.

The "transformation" of a civilian into a Marine takes place over a series of stages—an art form the Corps has consciously and studiously cultivated over the years. In the words of Commandant Charles Krulak: "Our Corps' survival depends upon the transformation."[10] Popular images of warrior swagger that draw a civilian to a Marine recruiter's door are only reinforced by the exchange that happens once he walks in. It is made clear to any new walk-in that joining the Corps is a privilege. The Marine behind the desk may be "recruiting," but it is the civilian who is being measured in the exchange.[11] Interested parties stepping into the office in search of scholarships, a stable livelihood, or travel may be invited to step out and visit the Army's office next door.[12] One Marine recounts:

> I was thinking about going in to the Army because they offered more money for college. I first went into the Marine recruiter's office and asked what they could give me. They told me I should be happy just to join the Marine Corps. He also told me that if all I wanted was money for college I should get out of his office and go join the Army. I left and wondered why they did that. Shortly after, I returned to the Marine recruiter's office and asked him if I could join the Marines.[13]

Recruiters are looking for a particular type of young person: one who emphasizes the "intangible" rather than "tangible" rewards of joining. Recruiters make their own assessment of the young person in front of them, sometimes as soon as he or she walks in the door, but they add evidence to their initial impression, both for themselves and for the potential recruit, by throwing a collection of eleven plastic tags on the table. Each is inscribed with a different attribute: Pride of Belonging; Courage, Poise, and Self-Confidence; Challenge; Leadership and Management Skills; Self-Reliance, Self-Direction, and Self-Discipline; Physical Fitness; Professional Development; Financial Security, Advancements and Benefits; Educational Opportunities; Technical Skills; Travel and Adventure. The civilian youth is asked to select from the stack the five that are most important to him. Recruiters are looking for those young people who lean toward the "intangibles" such as challenge, leadership, and self-reliance, reflecting an attributes orientation (*becoming* a Marine), rather than a benefits orientation (*what will I get* from the Marines?). Those youth seeking membership in the Corps who select in favor of "intangibles"—and also have a high school degree, lack tattoos in visible spaces (forearms, neck, face), and have potential to perform at the level of the Marines' fitness standard—are encouraged to apply. Recruiters today must own their recommendations. They will write to and keep track of a recruit all through his boot camp training. A failure at boot camp is a black mark on a recruiter's record.[14]

In some offices a list hangs above a recruiter's computer warning that the individuals named on it are not to be allowed into "Our Beloved Corps." They have, in some way, shown themselves unworthy to join this coveted brotherhood but act as pests, trying one recruiter after another. Marine recruiters recognize that their modern image is that of the elite, the toughest of the branches, and they flex this to full effect. Gallup polling taken from 2001–11 indicates that across the first decade of the twenty-first century, the American public consistently viewed the Marine Corps as its most prestigious branch.[15] It must be noted, however, that this trend stands in sharp contrast to previous eras. In a national opinion survey conducted just before Pearl Harbor (November 1941), young men of fighting age, as well as their parents, ranked the Corps as the *least* attractive American military service because of its members' "rowdiness and hard living."[16]

Marines have learned to use their hard-core reputation to advantage. Their perception is that the young people drawn to their door want to be pushed, want to be screamed at by an ungodly drill instructor (DI), and want to get into the mud. One might make this assertion solely owing to the self-selection that occurs in response to Marine Corps ads. The Corps went a bit further, however, and in 1994 hired a team of psychologists to tell them what the youth of Generation X "wanted." Their conclusions: "Generation X does not want to be babied. These young Americans are looking for a real challenge. They desperately want to be part of a winning team; they crave the stature associated with being one of the best."[17] Oral histories of contemporary-era Marines seem to confirm that this trend continues. When asked why they picked the Marine Corps, Marines' typical answers include "'Cause it was the hardest one"; "I was always interested in the Marine Corps, like the difficulty of it, of course I wanted to do the hardest . . . which would be the Marine Corps"; "I wanted to go to the toughest training"; "It was definitely a challenge and that's exactly what I was looking for"; "I picked the Marine Corps because they are the best. I don't just say that because I am a Marine. We back it up. The Marine Corps is the hardest branch of the service, and the Proudest. I always had an interest in the military. But when it came down to it, if I was going to be in any branch, I didn't want to know that there was someone out there in another service that is working harder than me."[18]

Half of the walk-ins to a Marine recruiting office have already decided that they want to join the infantry. This hard-hitting, frontline image is the one the modern Corps projects and the one most often in the minds of those who want to join. Today's Marines join the Marines because they want to be "forged" into hard steel, they want a challenge, and they want to be part of an elite.[19] It is becoming a Marine, above all, that is the lure.

Against that modern portrait flow historical narratives and images of a sometimes very different sort. A look at the recruitment posters of the early Banana Wars era (1913–16) reveals a Marine Corps whose selling tag is "good pay, foreign travel, and congenial employment"—the very tangibles that Marine Corps recruiters treat with contempt today. This is not yet the Marine Corps that can exist on its brand. Poster images in the pre–World War I era depict Marines rushing to "colonial" duty in tropic scenes. Two themes dear to modern Devil Dogs and already emergent here are "first" and "fighting." Marine posters brag: "First to Hoist Old Glory on Foreign Soil" and "For Fighting . . . Join the Marines."

"First" and "fighting" persist as two of the Corps's most salient identity themes. "First to Fight!" is still a quintessentially Marine slogan (and title of the Corps's most recommended book, authored by Marine leadership legend Victor "Brute" Krulak)[20] and is reflected in a number of identity labels, including "shock troops" and "the nation's 911 force."[21] Combat readiness is an essential feature of this Marine Corps role.[22] Given the significant overlap in Marine Corps function with the other services, *readiness*, or the ability to immediately sprint into action, provides a distinguishing trait, one essential to modern security and one that the Corps seeks to protect. Thus, the dispatch of US Army Special Forces as America's first entry force into Afghanistan in 2001 and their domination, alongside Central Intelligence Agency operatives, of the early phase of the war, supplied a painful shock to Marine identity. In an award-winning essay published in a 2003 edition of the *Marine Corps Gazette*, Capt. Owen West laments, "No service was better prepared to fight the war on terror than the Marine Corps, yet it was relegated to the periphery. Has the Nation's premiere small unit infantry been replaced by the joint Special Operations Command?"[23] Although Marines led in the 2003 invasion of Iraq, worries over retaining their premier status as a first-response crisis force continue to prick at the Corps.

World War I marked a dramatic shift in Marine Corps identity and recruitment calls. Unsurprisingly, posters of that era are loaded with scenes of the war front. Perhaps more surprisingly, many of the Marines depicted are aboard ship. Although the Marines of World War I were already claiming far more in common with infantrymen than sailors, the Corps was reluctant to give up its naval image.[24] Most posters of this era bridge the gap between services by touting Marines as "soldiers of the sea." Neither contemporary Marines nor their predecessors ever called themselves "sailors"—despite the fact that the Corps's departmental affiliation lies with the Navy. The explanation is partly bound up with the Marines' earliest origins as guard detachments aboard ships.[25] One of their primary responsibilities was keeping potentially unruly sailors from engaging in mutiny or any other nefarious deeds. To call oneself a "sailor" would be to stoop to the level of those policed. Even today, sailors far more than soldiers are the butt of Marine jokes when the ire is directed at other services.[26] The second, and perhaps more compelling explanation, is that the Marines' occupation is soldiering. Their resistance to being referenced as a "soldier" today is not genuinely definitional but roots in the instinctive need to forge an identity separate from the US Army's.

The identity tension of a service inhabiting a somewhat shifting middle ground between formidable sister services has not disappeared in the modern era. Worries at the turn of the twentieth century about where exactly the Corps fit could be the blueprint for discussions of a similar sort, both within and outside the Corps, across its institutional history and into the modern day.[27] When asked with which service they most identify, today's Marines will, with nearly knee-jerk instinct, respond "the Navy." Marines tend to be very competitive with the Navy ("Yes, we are Department of the Navy, the *Men's* Department") but are far more resistant on an institutional level to being seen as "a second land army," a resistance that borders on paranoia.[28] Although their nautical heritage is woven into a Marine's everyday language (even duffels are called a "sea bag"), many Marines will never step aboard a ship.[29] Those same Marines, however, will spend their service career performing tasks nearly identical those of the Army (but quicker and better!). Marines' instinctive institutional reach to the Navy, therefore, has less to do with competence at sea (Marines perform almost no ship-related functions while transiting with sailors) and more to do with a deeply forged attachment to the role that brought them glory and institutional claim as an essential and distinctive service: amphibious assault.

Before those heady days, however, the Corps was to make a name for itself in rather Army-like duty, albeit with flare. At the breakout of World War I, recruitment posters boasted the Corps as the first to change from "the Old Campaign Hat" to "the Modern Helmet" of a world war. The Marine Corps commandant at the time, Maj. Gen. George Barnett, understood instinctively that despite a naval heritage, his Marines must be involved in the ground fighting in France. In testimony before the House Committee on Naval Affairs, he made a case for significantly increased personnel among Marine ranks (from 37,564 to 49,133) and an increase to the battlefield beyond the ground brigade of 11,000 Marines already in France. He saw their participation there as "absolutely essential for the morale of the Corps." Their "high professional standard and morale" depended on "taking an active part at the front in the greatest war known to history."[30]

Their "active part" was to become Marine Corps legend in Belleau Wood. The June 1918 eponymous battle boasts its own shrine within the Marine Corps Museum and "is known by all who have worn the uniform of the U.S. Marine Corps as the battle that established the base identity for Marines to this day."[31] In the first two days of the month-long action, Marines lost 60 percent of the infantry sent into the fray—a thousand officers and men—a number of casualties that exceeded the sum of all others up to that point in its history. "Rifles and raw courage" faced down experienced Germans wielding machine guns.[32] Hard-charging hero figures such as Dan Daly made their mark tearing across enemy lines and into legend: "Come on, you sons of bitches! Do you want to live forever?"[33] Marines fell by the hundreds as they swarmed across open fields toward the Germans but would not relent. Their mettle and audacity captured the heart of the American press and won praise from the very soldiers they were trying to kill. Internal German reports noted the "bravery and dash" of the young Marines and predicted their future as formidable adversaries.[34]

Craig Cameron marks Belleau Wood as the Marine Corps's "rite of passage to maturity": "A respected foe had granted recognition of the marines' institutional distinctiveness that perforce made them a representative of the United States, separate from the Army. Never before had the Marine Corps been so clearly set apart from other American soldiers, and to this day, marines take great pride in the sobriquet 'devil dogs' (*Teufelhunden*) bestowed on them in their first major battle."[35] Affectionately and often applied, the nickname "Devil Dog" reigns supreme as the first bit of history Marines are required to learn and memorize from the *United States Marine Guidebook of Essential Subjects* (known to Marines simply as *Knowledge*). Of "Devil Dog" it reads: "The term 'Devil Dog' came into use during World War I, and is said to have originated as follows: During interrogation, a captured German soldier was asked his opinion of U.S. Marines in the bitter fighting in Belleau Wood during June, 1918. He replied that the Marines fought like teufel hunden, legendary wild, devil dogs that at one time roamed the forest of northern Germany."[36]

Unfortunately for Marine legend, not only is this an improper rendering of the German word (it should read *Teufelshunde*), but there seems to be no evidence of the *Teufelhunden* story in any form in German records.[37] The lack of evidence in history, however, has failed to diminish Marine affection for the term. Marine newborns are often referenced as "devil pups," and Corps enthusiasts continue reproducing the vintage *Teufelhunden* poster and its modern variants on decals, coffee mugs, T-shirts, tattoos, and nearly every other printable surface. Incidentally, the nickname "leatherneck"—stemming from an earlier era in which black leather stock collars were worn—is also included in *Knowledge* as a term of affection bantered about by Marines. "Jarhead," however, is noticeably absent. Marines are less inclined toward this term, which stems from disputed origins, the most popular of which is as a reference to Marines' "high and tight" haircuts.

The early years of World War I represent a stronger effort than had been previously applied at branding awareness for the Corps. One poster boasts the eagle, globe, and anchor of the Marine Corps emblem and says simply, "This device on hat or helmet means U.S. Marines." The eagle, globe, and anchor, or EGA, has become a deeply internalized and beloved symbol for the Corps. Its official description in the *United States Marine Guidebook of Essential Subjects* is appropriately historical: "The emblem . . . of the Marine

Corps consists of the eagle, globe, and anchor. The globe and anchor signify worldwide service and sea traditions. The spread eagle is a symbol of the nation itself. The emblem was adopted by Brigadier General Jacob Zeilin, 7th Commandant, in 1868."[38] Far more colorful, and indicative of Marine culture, is the leatherneck-favored explanation penned by an unknown poet and often posted in Marine Corps barracks and offices: "We stole the eagle from the Air Force, the anchor from the Navy, and the rope from the Army. On the 7th day, while God rested, we over-ran his perimeter and stole the globe, and we've been running the show ever since."[39]

The cockiness manifest in this rollicking depiction of the Corps's emblem is signature Devil Dog fare. Some in the modern Corps term their brethren a "pack of alpha males"[40]—self-selected because of their exposure to the bare-chested Marine image. Male virility is explicitly tied to the warrior ethos in most Marine advertising across time. What the Corps is offering is raw, brazen, male toughness. Typical fare for the mid-1990s involved brawny young men running gauntlets of deadly obstacles in ancient tombs, slaying something very close to Tolkien's Balrog in a Roman-like stadium, or playing the part of an action hero in a summer blockbuster. Each is rewarded at the successful culmination of his impossible feat with the ultimate honor: physical transformation into a full-fledged Marine in dress blues. Commercials in the last five years remain dominated by action hero combat scenes but have also featured a peppering in of nation-building and humanitarian tasks and a focus on racial and gender diversity. Although many within the Corps now mock the "slay the dragon" advertising that drew them to the recruiter's door (especially after experiencing repetitive "field days"—cleaning every surface in sight—that are part and parcel of genuine Marine Corps life), they are also admitting that the image was effective. Of the recruits he studied, Ricks notes that many came seeking a new identity, "the straightforward and simple definition of manhood offered by the Marines."[41] Nathaniel Fick, in his insightful memoir, notes that this mentality explains his draw to the Marine officer corps as well: "I wanted something . . . transformative. Something that might kill me—or leave me better, stronger, more capable."[42]

A favorite Devil Dog "truth"—rather difficult to test—is that US Marine Corps boot camp is the toughest recruit training in the world. Excerpts drawn from Larry Smith's collection of DI oral histories provide windows into this collective narrative: "By emphasizing tradition, unit cohesiveness, harder discipline, being harder on them physically and psychologically, we're able to mold them quicker." Of their training methods: "A lot of people thought we were extremists but, yeah, we have to be, because we're gonna be the guys who are killing the bad guys," and "After a while you'd take pride in training in misery."[43]

Extremist methods came under serious scrutiny after the 1956 Ribbon Creek incident in which six Marines drowned in a late night punitive march through a swamp. Methods up to that era "had grown seriously out of hand," including "'thumping,' punching recruits in the stomach, burning recruits with cigarettes, forcing them to eat the butts, stacking them in trash bins, and making them run a 'belt line,' which was a gauntlet of belt-swinging fellow recruits."[44] One DI mused on the changes that descended on boot camp training after Ribbon Creek, including kinder, gentler standards that encourage DIs to train by example and persuasion and to do so without using profanity: "They say this is the roughest boot camp there is. Well, I'll be honest with you: It's not really that rough. I've seen other boot camps in the Army that are a little bit more intense in certain areas than we are, but we have that mystique, that thing that says you're a Marine."[45]

Allan Millett has compiled the most exhaustive published history on the Corps to date and notes that the Marine elitist image began early on, founded in the concept that every Marine is a volunteer. Elitist notions fostered across the early years of the twentieth century were based in the Marine mind on military appearance (an attribute still conspicuously emphasized today), strict obedience to orders, and disciplined behavior. These were burnished in an effort to differentiate Marines from the officers and sailors of the US Navy.[46] Interestingly, Millett's own account does not seem to bear out "strict obedience to orders" as an attribute of behavior for the same period. This is not entirely unusual. Discrepancies in identity standards and actual behavior are not uncommon within culture groups but can provoke defensive reactions from the group in question when deviations from the identity ideal are raised to public view. Cameron claims that the higher standards espoused by the Marines started out as an abstract concept, a standard of behavior "so high that it was intended to compensate for the marines' sense of inferiority"— an insecurity stemming from the Marines' lack of statutory protection as a separate organization and its obsession with forging a distinct and elite identity during the interwar years.[47] Cameron may be right about standards, but Marine bravado and sense of elitism easily predate the interwar identity crisis and have only gained momentum in their move forward in history.[48]

A detailed study of Marine Corps boot camp unlocks some of the mystery regarding this institution's intensive brotherhood and esprit de corps. For the recruit, boot camp itself is less about military training and more about "earning" the title of Marine. For the DIs responsible for them, it is about "making Marines." The Marine handbook *Sustaining the Transformation* (US Marine Corps MCRP 6-11D) reminds mentors: "Our Corps does two things for America: we make Marines and we win our nation's battles."[49] Victor Krulak of *First to Fight* fame sees "making Marines" as an expectation of, and obligation to, the nation. One of the things the American people believe about the Marines, he writes, "is that our Corps is downright good for the manhood of our country; that the Marines are masters of a form of unfailing alchemy which converts unoriented youths into proud, self-reliant stable citizens—citizens into whose hands the nation's affairs may safely be entrusted."[50]

"Making Marines" at the boot camp stage is more form than function. Civilian identity is stripped and replaced with Marine posture, reflexes, priorities, and attitude. Disciplined courtesy, strict codes of appearance, tightly orchestrated movement, and respectful language are drilled into recruits as Marine codes of conduct.[51] The harshest punitive measures are not meted out for failures of martial skill but rather for breaches of Marine cultural protocol.[52] The Corps is overt about this core feature of initial training. In its seminal doctrine, *Warfighting*, Corps general officers state, "All officers and enlisted Marines undergo similar entry-level training which is, in effect, a socialization process. This training provides all Marines a common experience, a proud heritage, a set of values, and a common bond of comradeship. It is the essential first step in the making of a Marine."[53]

Essential to that transformation is the stripping of individuality in favor of the team. When "boots" first arrive at Parris Island, Ricks observes, they are positioned on yellow footprints so closely aligned that "newcomers can't be seen as individuals. Standing nearly heel to toe in the dark night their faces are hardly visible, and their bodies become one mass. The effect is intentional: Marine Corps culture is the culture of the group, made up of members who are anonymous."[54] Fick notes that officers are socialized the same way. Being called an "individual" is a profound insult, spat out as if it were a "synonym for child molester."[55] In both enlisted and officer training, it is repeatedly emphasized to would-be Marines that they have left a culture of self-gratification, the "me" society, for one of self-discipline and a focus on the group. Drill serves the same function, to build unit cohesion and discipline.[56]

Enlisted recruits are required to adopt a submissive posture by addressing themselves in low-ranking third person ("This recruit requests permission to . . ."). Only if they successfully endure the physical and mental tests imposed on them will they have the privilege of calling themselves "Marines." Slips of address are harshly reprimanded. E. B. Sledge remembers his World War II–era DI booming, "Your soul may belong to Jesus, but your ass belongs to the Marines. You people are *recruits*. You're *not* Marines. You may not have what it takes to be Marines."[57] Young men and women who successfully run this gauntlet are preconditioned by Marine Corps advertising ("Maybe *you* can be one of us!"[58]) and their American sense of Marine Corps elitism for the emotional peak of the transformative moment. In 1976 the *Gazette* selected an essay among the many submitted to "represent what we believe many Marines feel on the 201st anniversary" of the Corps. In it, Gy.Sgt. John H. Lofland III captures familiar Marine sentiments at the conclusion of boot camp:

> My esprit de corps, superciliousness, if you prefer, began at "boot camp," or Marine recruit training. There I was treated with contempt, marched a thousand miles, put through a million drilled

acts of obedience, taunted with the fact that I volunteered, taught to take aim on a twelve inch diameter target five hundred yards away—and hit it. Then at the end of all of this it was hesitatingly admitted that I just might make a Marine. To say I was seething with pride at the successful accomplishment of "boot camp" would be an understatement.[59]

Becoming part of the Corps includes embracing, and being able to reproduce, Marine Corps history. James Burk notes that "a diffuse but still important, influence on military culture is the collective memory or imagination of past war that is widely shared among members of the military and is frequently relied on as a normative guide for behavior in the present." He cautions that "collective memories are not histories, characterized by concern for detail and accuracy; they are symbolic constructions condensing events to communicate their essential meaning simply and powerfully."[60] Although T. R. Fehrenbach's *U.S. Marines in Action* admits to being less fact and more fable, he makes some rather good points about the utility of studying legend in order to understand culture: "The story of the first century of the United States Marines is as much composed of legend as of fact. To say this is to do the Corps no disservice, for legend is as important to a fighting organization as ever any fact. . . . Legends give them a code to live by, a standard to measure up to."[61] Terry Terriff agrees: "The history of a military organization, whether of the organization itself or of specific historical individual members, furnishes the primary source material that informs understandings of self-identity. The narratives that constitute cultural identity, however, are not always composed solely of history per se, for they may mix historical fact with the apocryphal and the mythical."[62]

Marines take this to heart. Their "history" is their religion.[63] History is not only taught in the classroom—it is woven into the discourse and formal construction of all recruit training. For instance, each major requirement of the "Crucible"—the brutal culminating event of recruit training—is dedicated to, and framed around, a well-known Marine Corps Medal of Honor recipient.[64] Marines of all ranks are consciously aware that members of their Corps know and promote both service and unit history in a depth that shames their sister services.[65] Some are even rather clear about why:

During [the boot camp] process, we all acquired a number of illusions, all valuable. We all firmly believed that in its history, the Marine Corps had never failed at anything, and that upon our shoulders rested the awesome responsibility of upholding the most spectacular military tradition known to man. This overall esprit de corps may suffer in translation over the years, but the basic concept remains the same: for all of us in the Marine Corps, attitude is a weapon.[66]

New recruits are bound to this legacy during their training in boot camp and forever thereafter. Marine heroes are set up as mentors of sorts—men continually watching their Corps from beyond the grave. Woe betide any newly minted Marine who lets them down.[67] Writing in 1944, Col. Charles A. Wynn tried to capture the mythical transformation from recruit to Marine and the uncanny ownership of the Corps that takes place in the souls of young men in such a short period. Part of this is a "gifting" of history, legends, places gone, bandits fought, and valor won from one generation to the next: "The oldtime drill master can . . . convince the rookie that he is an integral member of each of those units in which the preceding one is contained, right up to and including the Corps itself, to such an extent that the rookie, almost from the beginning, regards the Corps as his personal property, for whose honor he will fight anybody else to the death."[68] Ricks validates that this trend continues in Marine boot camps today. DIs make first-person ownership references of the sort the recruit is aspiring to, using phrases such as "my bus," "my island" (for Parris Island), and "my Corps."[69] Fick acknowledges the impact of this internalization. Once he owns the Corps, and the Corps owns him, a young Marine draws "inspiration to face danger, and reassurance that death in battle isn't consignment to oblivion. His buddies and all future Marines will keep the faith."[70]

For all its attention to history, the Corps has been selective in the history exploited and learned. Despite its long history with small wars, the Corps of today focuses almost exclusively on heroic acts in conventional conflicts. Before Belleau Wood or Mount Suribachi, Marines successfully wrested pride from their small-wars exploits. In 1917 the *Gazette* ran a piece titled "The Marines Have Landed," which lauded the Corps as "a veteran body of seasoned officers and men to whom the seizing of coast towns, the razing of supposedly impregnable native strongholds, and the secrets of bush fighting and street fighting in tropical countries became an open book."[71] For the modern Corps, however, any valor won in those conflicts is trumped by the legends forged in conventional war.

For the Marines, selective memory may be explained in terms more complex than preferred modes of war. The premium here may be the opportunity provided by conventional conflicts for favorable comparison with the other armed forces. For instance, although World War I and the early years of the Banana Wars were prosecuted simultaneously, one might explain the dearth of attention paid to the Marines who fought in the Caribbean as being, in part, a result of having no US Army there to provide a competitive contrast. In "the Great War," the Corps fought with and beside other armies, enabling comparisons of fighting spirit and valor. Within American ranks "there was . . . a fierce rivalry between the Marines and the [Army] infantry," and fortune smiled on the Marines—offering them the opportunity to demonstrate their training, discipline, and skill in an epic battle that "lifted [them] briefly from the anonymity of [the] war." [72] Belleau Wood's heroics caught the romantic heart of the American press, and the resultant reporting meant the Marine contribution outshone, in disproportionate measure, the efforts of the US Army in headlines back home.

If Belleau Wood provided the Corps with happy notoriety, World War II was "the conflict that did more than any other to elevate the Corps from a naval police force into a legitimate fighting force that could stand as an alternative to the US Army."[73] The iconic symbol of the stuff Marines are made of is the Iwo Jima flag-raising. Iwo Jima has been referenced as the "signature battle" of the Corps and is commemorated in the official Marine Corps monument, as well as in the physical profile of the National Museum of the Marine Corps.[74] Marines relish the idea (whether still true or not) that their lifting of the flag is the most recognized and most reproduced image in the history of photography.[75] As proud moments for the Corps go, the lodestar is Iwo Jima. One sergeant major quipped that, for a Marine, a trip to Mount Suribachi "would be like a Muslim going to Mecca."[76]

A paradoxical side effect of the Corps's heroic action in World War II was a loss of, or at least significant lull in, many of its saltier traditions. Historian Col. R. D. Heinl claims that "World War II . . . dislocated the Marine Corps." This was due to "the twenty-five fold expansion, short-cut wartime training, and . . . massive infusion of non-professionals." But perhaps most important was the "unification of the Armed Forces—levelling, standardizing, bureaucratic, relentless, hostile to Service pride and traditions—[which] had as an unvoiced but deadly real tenet the mongrelization of the Services, the humbling of elite units and the elite spirit." Marine traditions did suffer during this era, and much of its historical education was dropped from its classrooms.[77] From this perspective one might argue that it is remarkable that Marine Corps culture has remained intact and strengthened *despite* its experiences in the two great wars rather than *because of* them.

The general notion of Marine elitism, however, did not seem to suffer in the aftermath of World War II and was about to receive a significant boost in Korea. The 1950 "Frozen Chosin" Reservoir episode supplies the closest thing to a scientifically controlled experiment that warfare ever likely allows—and one in which the Marines clearly outperformed the Army. Allan Millett, who typically restrains his prose to an academic tone when writing on the Marines (despite the fact that he is a former Marine himself), could not resist a panegyric for those Marines who held the line in subzero temperatures in Korea: "Ravaged by the cold . . . the Marines fought with unmatched ferocity and determination. Some of the individual and small-unit heroics matched Greek and Nordic legends—except that they really happened." Of the Marines' necessary retreat, a "retrograde movement," he writes:

> General Smith correctly called the operation "an attack in another direction" in tactical terms, but for the UNC [United Nations Command], with the Eighth Army reeling back in eastern North Korea,

the campaign was part of a major strategic defeat. For the Marines, the campaign was a victory, for the march out from the Chosin saved X Corps and virtually destroyed seven PLA [People's Liberation Army] divisions. The 1st Division did so against heavy odds and at center stage for world military and press observers.[78]

In his history of the Marine Corps, *Semper Fidelis*, Millett writes, "At a cost of almost seven thousand casualties (about half from critical frostbite), the 1st Marine Division had polished the Corps's reputation for valor and skill at a time when Army divisions of the Eighth Army appeared infected with defeatism."[79]

It didn't hurt the Marine ego any that the Army's own Gen. Douglas MacArthur reported, "I have just returned from visiting the Marines at the front, and there is not a finer fighting organization in the world."[80] Marine experiences in conventional war only reinforced for the Marines, and for the American public, the swagger included in the third verse of "The Marines' Hymn":

> Here's health to you and to our Corps
> Which we are proud to serve;
> In many a strife we've fought for life
> And never lost our nerve.
> If the Army and the Navy
> Ever look on Heaven's scenes,
> They will find the streets are guarded
> By United States Marines.[81]

Even after the malaise imposed by the Vietnam War, Victor Krulak would claim, "Woven through [the Marine] sense of belonging, like a steel thread, is an elitist spirit. Marines are convinced that, being few in number, they are selective, better, and above all, different."[82] Aaron O'Connell, writing on Marine Corps culture, sees this concept as foundational: "At the root of the Marines' ideas about themselves were narratives of exceptionalism—an ideology that made them feel separate from and superior to everyone else, both soldiers and civilians. This exceptionalism, with its attendant sentiments of insularity and mistrust of outsiders, was the first principle of Marine Corps culture."[83]

And at what are they exceptional? Above all, fighting. In his 1944 attempt to analyze what makes the Marine Corps so special, what force binds its brotherhood and inspires its esprit de corps, Col. Charles A. Wynn writes:

> It is something deep down inside the soul of the Corps which I have often tried to analyze. It isn't because the Marines have served in every corner of the world; the Navy has done that. So has the

Army. It isn't because the Marines have won many of the greatest battles; some of the greatest battles fought by our forces have not used a single Marine. But ask a man why he enlisted in the Corps and his answer is always the same: "It's the best fighting force in the world."[84]

Gunnery Sergeant Lofland offers prose equally lyrical: "Some may refer to it as moral superiority. I call it esprit de corps. I know in my own mind that I am among the best fighting men in the world. I harbor firmly the belief that there are none better. I don't believe I'll ever lose, because I don't know of anyone good enough to beat me. For the past two hundred yards I've done it, and I'll continue to do it, because I think I can."[85]

Marines were unabashed in early twentieth-century advertising about their sheer enjoyment of fighting, and Marines continue that theme in a fashion congruent with modern sensibilities today. A rather unusual (for the Marines) ad campaign surfaced in the 1970s, claiming that "nobody likes to fight . . . but somebody has got to know how." Nathaniel Fick contends, unsurprisingly, that "it was dropped because Marines *did* like to fight and aspiring Marine officers wanted to fight."[86] Marines see themselves as the premier offensive force—not an occupation force (despite a long occupation duty history)—driven by "an unyielding conviction that they exist to fight."[87] Craig Cameron, with his aptly titled book *American Samurai*, summarized the Marine fighting ethic of the World War II years. Focusing on the dialectic between institutional identity and the increasing awe of its domestic American public, Cameron characterizes the result: "Marines regarded themselves as warrior representatives of their country, a kind of American samurai class."[88] Marines are made to "locate, close with, and kill the enemy."[89]

It provokes a wry smile to note that in Victor Krulak's seminal text, *First to Fight*, he begins his description of Marines with a chapter titled "The Thinkers" and then proceeds to fill those pages with warrior tales of superb fighting skills. Fighting valor is a focus all through the book, although the specific label "The Fighters" is reserved for the final section.[90] Even in an era of population-centric and civic-action heavy counterinsurgency campaigns, Carlton W. Kent, the sergeant major of the Marine Corps in 2008, struck an honest note in an interview to *Leatherneck* magazine. He flatly stated that all Marines need to get into combat. Marines "get bored" when not in combat. When deployed they expect to "engage the enemy."[91] They are warriors. Warriors fight. Although versatile and committed to "doing windows," when the mission requires significant downtime and involves limited combat or an excess of civic action projects, Marines are in danger of restless behavior.[92]

The Marine Corps is built around the infantry. Only the Marines Corps among US defense institutions has bestowed its name on the enlisted ranks.

The Army's personnel are officers and soldiers, the Navy has officers and sailors, and the Air Force is populated by officers and airmen, but the Marines are officers and Marines. The Marine orientation is "on the embattled man on the front lines."[93] The list of Marine Corps heroes—the "legends" of the Corps—is one of noncommissioned officers and subordinates. Some of these men went on to become commissioned officers, but most often their legends were made in enlisted ranks.[94] The two preferred nicknames—leatherneck and Devil Dog—are celebrations of the man at the tip of the spear: the infantryman, the grunt.

Commandant Charles Krulak echoes commandants of the past in calling the infantry "our most precious asset."[95] This valuation is internalized and assumed by grunts themselves. Those outside the infantry brotherhood suffer the derisive label POGs—people other than grunts—and receive no quarter at the sharp end of Marine humor.[96] Even Marine aviators find themselves in nebulous territory. A 1920 *Gazette* article highlighted the concern that some within the Corps had the feeling that aviators were "not real Marines."[97] The not so subtle hierarchy of grunt supremacy is reflected in the fact that the vast majority of commandant appointments have favored infantry over all other specialties. Gen. James F. Amos, commandant from 2010 to 2014, was the first naval aviator to hold the Marines' premier post. Despite his tenure, the attitude persists: "For many [in the Corps] there is infantry, and then everything else."[98] Even officers are told that they are "only support." A Marine mess hall ritual emphasizes leadership support as well as the essential nature of the lowest ranks: privates eat first; officers eat last.[99]

Further homage to grunt-level Marines may be experienced walking the chambers of the Marine Corps museum. It is very clearly a celebration of frontline men—not equipment or institutions or armor, but Marines—in the messy, grueling tasks of fighting war. In a bow to those men (and a few women), every Marine depicted in mannequin form in the museum has been individually crafted to resemble a real person—an actual serving or former Marine. Their faces stare back at onlookers who come to see what the Corps is about. It is about Marines.

## ROLE CONCEPTION

Role conception might be considered the preeminent "norm" or, alternatively, the flagpole for identity. The Marine Corps case makes clear that role conception is a key aspect of identity but is not the only, or perhaps even primary, feature. *Who we are* can remain a somewhat distinctive space from *what we do*. The Marine Corps's story is one of a rather consistent identity—elitist and fight oriented—stretched across episodes of significant role shift.

The first commandant to set a mark for Marine Corps role identity in the pages of the *Gazette* was the highly popular and articulate John A. Lejeune. Writing in 1922, he urged: "But let us not forget the object of our existence, which is to make and keep the Marine Corps a great fighting machine—the greatest on earth, bar none."[100] It was he who cast the Marines as a legion of hardened combat veterans "grown grey in war with very few intervals of peace" and immortalized this image by weaving it into Order 47, read every year on the Marine Corps's birthday.[101] Clear in Lejeune's mind, however, was that his Marine fighters were doing so as "part and parcel of the naval service." The heroic land duty performed in World War I was a necessary exception—the Marines' key roles remained within the traditional naval sphere. In addition to protecting Navy yards, Lejeune's 1920s-era leather-necks acted as guards for American legations in foreign countries, as landing forces to "protect American lives, rights and interests," as forces of occupation to "restore order and to maintain peace and tranquility in disturbed countries," as administrators in garrisons, as detachments for "service on board the vessels of the Fleet" and in aviation, and as "Expeditionary forces for service with the Fleet in war."[102]

In 1930 Commandant Ben Fuller assumed command of a Corps emerging from nearly two decades of small-wars conflict.[103] His tenure was largely captured by a tug-of-war between those in the Corps advocating further development of small-wars competency and those championing a more amphibious role: landing operations and the securing of advanced bases. Felt strongly among Marines was the need to differentiate themselves from the Army and to carve out distinctive space.[104] Fuller's speeches reflect, but do not reconcile, the doctrinal tension between these two distinctive roles. He opens his primary contribution to the *Gazette* with an impassioned attachment to expertise on the seas—"Cut the ancestral knot that binds us to the waters of the oceans, seas, bays, gulfs, rivers, lakes and other wet spots and with the same motion you cut the throat of the Corps"—and to the Navy—"Do not let the Naval-Mind of the Corps be changed to any other type of mind, that will leave only a memory, a history, of our grand and glorious Corps of the Ocean." At the same time, he heralds the essential role played in small wars: "Major wars, beginning with the Revolution and ending with the World War, have proved the splendid usefulness of the Corps to the Nation. But the magnificent record of constructive achievements, and successes in minor wars, during a period of over one and a half centuries has conclusively proved that the Corps is a necessary part of the United States Government." The bridge between these two banks is a claim to "versatility": "We know what our job was yesterday and we are struggling faithfully to do our work today, but who knows what it will be tomorrow? Probably something new and unique. It may be anything. Our job is intricate—diffused. It requires versatility."[105]

It was Fuller's successor, John H. Russell, who tipped the scales in favor of landing operations and amphibious doctrine. A longtime "fervent" amphibious war advocate,[106] Russell became commandant in 1934, a decisive moment in the Corps's history, and threw his support behind the nascent Fleet Marine Force.[107] Russell's advocacy for the amphibious camp might be regarded as somewhat surprising in light of his own small-wars service, which involved time spent in the Dominican Republic and over a decade in Haiti, including as high commissioner for eight years.[108] Not a surprise, however, is his dedication to forging doctrine for the Corps. Russell had, as a major eighteen years earlier, made a formal "Plea for a Mission and Doctrine," now considered one of the seminal pieces of Marine Corps doctrinal history. [109] A year before he became commandant, Russell laid a rhetorical foundation for the doctrine to come. Through the device of a fictional conversation between General X of the Marine Corps and Admiral Y of the Navy, Russell performed a bit of stage setting: General X points out that the Marines' "main job" is to "maintain expeditionary forces to seize advanced Bases and perform other land operations for the Fleet." Admiral Y concurs but points out that "you have not sold the idea one hundred per cent to the Navy or to your own Corps."[110] The remainder of Russell's piece is dedicated to doing just that. As commandant (for a short two and half years given the Corps's mandatory retirement age), Russell swung his weight behind the Fleet Marine Force but not without a bow to those advocating improved training in small-wars expertise.[111] During his tenure, doctrine was codified in both camps: the *Tentative Landing Operations Manual* and *Tentative Manual for Defense of Advanced Bases* on the amphibious side and *The Manual of Small Wars* for fighting in the bush.[112] Only one doctrinal emphasis, however, survived more than a handful of years in Marine Corps classrooms.[113]

Painful as it must have been for the Corps's small warriors, next-in-line commandant Thomas Holcomb's wholesale emphasis on amphibious landings in the run-up to World War II can only be viewed in hindsight as prescient. Both internal and external winds of change were blowing the amphibious direction for the Corps, not least of which was a looming threat from Japan.[114] Holcomb biographer David Ulbrich claims that Holcomb was selected as commandant in 1936 over several more senior, more obvious choices because "he fit a particular political profile inside the Corps that placed him in the ascendant clique. Holcomb favored the new dual mission of amphibious assault and base defense over the outmoded mission of constabulary security in small wars."[115] Holcomb's speeches throughout his tenure construct a narrative around this theme. According to Holcomb, not only are Marines amphibious by birth—they have worked since their infancy to refine a distinctive amphibious expertise. As "first out," their mission is to pave the way for the Army. Writing later, in the thick of World War II, he declares:

> In the course of this war, on a scale which the world has never before seen, it is possible to lose sight of what your particular job

is—of what the Marine Corps' job really is. The Marine Corps' primary function is to prepare the way for other troops. Ours is an amphibious operation. . . . For that purpose we have trained for over a hundred and sixty-seven years. We are today, I believe, the most proficient amphibious military body in the world, and I say this with due modesty.[116]

Holcomb's Corps certainly valued excellence in amphibious operations for its wartime utility but, perhaps more important, because amphibious expertise offered the Corps *distinction*. Craig Cameron, writing of that era, describes this mission set as the "great gift" to the Marine Corps, fulfilling its ultimate craving for "a single, great mission" and a distinctive role— one essential to national security—that would set it apart from the Army and Navy: "Amphibious assault made a sort of elite of the entire Marine Corps."[117] Holcomb was forthright about this status. Speaking in 1943, he pointed out that the Marine Corps's dedication to "the most exhaustive research of landing operations . . . throughout the world's written military history" provided Marines with an education that

does not make us better Army officers than the best Army officers or better Naval officers than the best Navy officers. They can run the Army far better than we can. They can run the Navy far better than we can. But by the same token, because of our specialized training, we can run amphibious and landing operations better than they can. With our tradition, experience, and our training, they could run amphibious operations as effectively as we can, but they do not spend their lives in this specialization. We do.[118]

Holcomb encouraged Marines to take exceptional pride in their expertise since "landing operations are, of course, the most difficult of all military maneuvers." The successful prosecution of these operations, in his view, laid the foundation for the Marine brand of esprit de corps.[119] A newly pinned Marine subjected to Holcomb's version of leatherneck history would see it as an unbroken path of preparation for amphibious assault:

The U.S. Marine Corps always has had a predilection for this kind of amphibious fighting. . . . For nearly one hundred and seventy years, Marines have been specializing in amphibious warfare, and I believe the Corps has fought more continuously than any other service. We conducted landing operations during the Civil War, and again during the Spanish-American War. The Marines landed at Guantanamo Bay in Cuba. They landed in Haiti, and Nicaragua, and at other places in Latin America and the Caribbean. They landed in China at the time of the Boxer Rebellion. Always, when trouble required the presence of United States forces, the Marines were first on the scene.[120]

It is interesting that in this rendition of history it is the *landing* at the beaches of Hispaniola that is the important bit rather than the nineteen-plus years spent there. Small wars, as a role and as a key aspect of Marine Corps identity, were, by the time of Holcomb's tenure, effectively washed from the scene.

Unabashed amphibious pride continued under Alexander Vandegrift, appointed commandant in 1944: "From our do-or-die beginning we have developed a great amphibious machine, the power of which has amazed the warring world." Enemies would do well to take note: "There can remain no doubt anywhere, least of all in Germany and Japan, as to who now calls the amphibious tune and wields the weapons of decisive might."[121] Given the unabashed confidence of these lines, it is somewhat of a shock that the Corps's next battlefront was domestic. Even before the war had ended, the US Army General Staff was ardently pursuing objectives that threatened the survival of the Corps, including usurping its signature expertise, amphibious operations.[122]

The fight for the Corps's life surfaced to public view under Vandegrift. His 1944–47 tenure registered a win with the enactment of the 1947 National Security Act, which forged a statutory role and mission for the Corps: "The Marine Corps shall be organized, trained and equipped to provide fleet marine forces of combined arms, together with supporting air components, for service with the fleet in the seizure or defense of advanced naval bases and for the conduct of such land operations as may be essential to the prosecution of a naval campaign."[123] Pleased as the Marines were with their new statutory protection, the law did not assure that the Corps would be provided the budgetary and organizational strength to do its job. Given the general unhappiness of the Army with the National Security Act, the Corps recognized it as essential to shore up organizational assurances via a second piece of legislation. It is therefore no surprise that Commandant Clifton Cates (1948–51) dedicated pages of the *Gazette* to detailing the fight for the organization's life. His summary plea to Congress was the warrior's call: "The Marine Corps asks nothing for itself except the right to fight again in the wars of the United States."[124]

It was Cates's successor, Lemuel Shepherd, who saw legislative victory for the Corps in the form of Public Law 416, signed by President Harry Truman in June 1952. It provided the Corps with a minimum of three combat divisions and three aircraft wings and mandated a place for the commandant at the Joint Chiefs' table when issues of direct concern to the Marine Corps were being discussed.[125] Shepherd's contribution to the *Gazette*, penned one year before his tenure, recognizes a lesson from the

Marines' painful political battle. Albeit central in their own eyes, the leathernecks' unprecedented contribution to amphibious assault seemed to have
found little anchor in the public imagination:

> In the eyes of the American people whom they serve, the history of
> the United States Marines is reflected essentially as a procession of
> noteworthy deeds by individuals and small groups. While this is not
> inaccurate as a characterization of Marines, insofar as their part in
> history is concerned, there is another—albeit less colorful—aspect
> of their accomplishments which would appear in the long analy-
> sis to deserve an even more prominent place in American historic
> annals. This is the effort of the Marine Corps, conducted over the
> past four decades, to rationalize the amphibious operation in terms
> of modern arms and modern operational concepts.[126]

The Corps continued to hold to amphibious assault as mission central but
began to dress up their role in other themes as well, resurrecting Fuller's
"versatility" and the long-standing virtue of "readiness." In describing to the
House Armed Services Committee of 1961 where the Marine Corps stood
and where it was headed, Commandant David M. Shoup (1960–63) reasserted focus on the fighting man and his willingness to depart to any clime
and place: "The purpose of the Corps is to provide combat forces of willing
and able Marines, prepared to fight whenever and wherever required." He
did not, however, abandon expertise in the amphibious role: "I believe that
the Navy–Marine Corps sea-air-ground team of today has perfected the art
of amphibious assault to a degree unknown before."[127]

Wallace M. Greene presided as commandant from 1964 to 1967 and
oversaw the Marines' landing as combat forces in South Vietnam in 1965.
A year later he described that event, as well as an additional landing in
the Dominican Republic, to the Joint Committee on Armed Services and
Appropriations in the Senate as examples of the Marines performing their
"classic role" of "an amphibious landing on a foreign shore in support
of National policy, as directed by the President." Greene pointed out that
near simultaneous landings on dual shores revalidated and emphasized
"the requirement to continue to maintain the most modern amphibious
capability in both the Atlantic and the Pacific." Amphibious capability
is first in the limelight, but Greene also boosted the Corps's versatility
credentials when describing its then current task set: patrolling and civic
action in the hamlets of Vietnam. Institutional willingness to be versatile
was apparent in his public statements on behalf of the Corps. His budget,
however, demonstrated that the priorities of the Corps remained amphibious. Despite the fact that Marines were currently waging a ground war
in Indochina, Greene acknowledged that his research-and-development

dollars remained "limited largely to those matters which fall within our statutory responsibility—that is, the development of the doctrine, tactics, techniques and equipment employed by a landing force in amphibious operations." His testimony to the committee concluded with an emphasis on combat readiness—the ability to "mount out on short notice and fight." The Marine degree of "readiness," Greene argued, represented "a priceless commodity, without parallel by any other nation."[128]

Leonard Chapman (1968–71), who oversaw the Marine Corps during the thick of the Vietnam War and its near conclusion, continued to emphasize the same two roles. Despite the role Marines were playing—years-long counterinsurgency forces fighting alongside the Army—Chapman held fast to "readiness" and to "amphibious" as Marine hallmarks. In a seminal "State of the Corps" piece penned in 1969, Chapman reminded his Marines of their true calling:

> Despite the heavy impact of our Vietnam commitment on the rest of the Marine Corps, we have managed with certain personnel and logistic restrictions to maintain our readiness to meet other commitments which could arise. As part of the Navy / Marine Corps team, we never lose sight of the responsibilities inherent in our role as this nation's force in readiness for the projection of seapower ashore or such other duties as our country may require.
>
> Congressional legislation established our primary mission: to prepare for and execute landing force operations as part of an amphibious task force.[129]

The Marine Corps continued to gain experience in complex, land-based counterinsurgency operations while defining itself in terms of immediate, short-burst combat readiness via advanced landing operations. Small wars are thick in Marine heritage but had been experienced as nearly ad hoc episodes with each round, never codified into doctrine until after the Banana Wars and shelved to oblivion nearly immediately afterward. In a particularly ironic twist, history records that Marine officers going to Vietnam were schooled not by their own *Small Wars Manual* or their own antiguerrilla history, but by the US Army doctrine of counterinsurgency in vogue in the run-up to Vietnam. The Marine Corps was so far divorced from its own small-wars heritage that the *Small Wars Manual* was left under dust in favor of the 1962 Fleet Marine Force Manual 8-2, *Operations against Guerrilla Forces*, a collection of borrowings from Army doctrine. Combined Action Platoon program Marine and scholar Michael Peterson points out that this historical irony is all the more painful because the Army's doctrine was a less useful fit for Vietnam than the Marines' doctrine would have been. The Army doctrine focused on experiences fighting partisan irregulars attached to external forces rather than homegrown insurgents of the sort the authors of the *Small Wars Manual* had faced. The Marines' doctrine would have been better suited to dealing with the Viet Cong.[130]

Robert E. Cushman, the commandant who shouldered the task of putting the Corps back together after the Vietnam War (1972–75), spoke before the Senate Armed Services Committee with new enthusiasm for the versatility role alongside the two roles emphasized by his predecessor. In short sum, he cast the Corps as "the Nation's versatile amphibious force-in-readiness." Versatility for Cushman meant a Marine Corps "organized, equipped, trained, and readied to cover the widest possible spectrum of crisis situations."[131] Decades later, Commandant James T. Conway (2006–10) defended the notion that Marines can act as both a sea-based force and "in sustained operations ashore," in much the same way. Using "adaptability" rather than versatility as the rhetorical calling card, his *Marine Corps Vision and Strategy 2025* pledges, "We can adapt quickly with unparalleled speed across an extraordinary range of military operations."[132] Marines have come to openly claim the versatility role. They are the nation's jacks-of-all-trades, capable of the full range of military force tasks outside traditional warfighting.[133] Marines are *willing* to "do windows" but are not always particularly enthusiastic about it. They readily claim the concept of versatility and embrace it as an identity marker, but they enjoy doing some windows far more than others.

The Marines' traditional centerpiece—amphibious assault—has morphed a bit and has added a companion in its transition to the present. Very often termed "expeditionary" rather than "amphibious" in the rhetoric of the current force, the operational core of today's Marines remains deeply anchored to their identity as "soldiers of the sea." As an "expeditionary naval force," the Corps is "organized, trained, and equipped to conduct naval campaigns and operate on and from naval platforms, or to fight in protracted campaigns ashore."[134] Marines "assure littoral access" through both soft- and hard-power projection.[135] The Marines' formal literature acknowledges that references to amphibious "assault" need to give way to the far more inclusive term "amphibious operations." In addition, the past counterinsurgency-rife decade has forced the Marines to add (again!) a place for counterinsurgency competency alongside its adventures on the sea. Its *Marine Corps Operating Concepts* states:

> Often thought of exclusively as an amphibious *assault* force, the period 1942–1945 was the only time in our history that the Marine Corps was organized, trained, and equipped for that one mission and did only one mission: amphibious *assault*. During the subsequent Cold War the Marine Corps was optimized for sea-based crisis response. Amphibious *operations*—of all types—remain a Marine Corps forte but not exclusively so. For the last 65 years, Marines have operated from the sea as part of a naval team and

conducted other sustained operations—principally referred to as "small wars."[136]

"Force-in-readiness" has changed the least for the Corps across the decades. The *Marine Corps Vision and Strategy 2025* document maintains a core obligation to "respond swiftly, with little or no warning, to emerging crises," to "maximize speed and freedom of action through seabasing," and to maintain "high standards of readiness across the force."[137] The Marines' third edition of *Operating Concepts* sings much the same tune. It lists "responsiveness" alongside "naval character" and "military professionalism" as one of the three key characteristics of the twenty-first-century Marine Corps and defines "responsiveness" as a state of being "ever-ready" to rapidly engage a well-prepared force.[138] General Amos, who as assistant commandant drafted Conway's *Vision and Strategy 2025*, became steward of the Marine Corps himself in October 2010 and branded the Corps the nation's "expeditionary crisis response force."[139]

The determined pledge of Marine Corps leadership to achieve this tripartite package—versatility/adaptability, amphibious/expeditionary, and edge-of-the-seat combat readiness—must engage the hard reality that, for any force, neither budgets nor personnel numbers allow for highly trained specialties across the full spectrum of conflict types. Marines aspire to be jacks-of-all-conflict-trades, but even they must choose over which types to be "master." Writing within a few years of the 2011 withdrawal of US forces from Iraq, Lt. Col. Frank Hoffman congregated the most pronounced doctrinal factions within the Corps into four camps. The first, which he labels the "Small Wars School," is reminiscent of the same in the Marine Corps of the 1930s. The modern camp argues that Iraq and Afghanistan are a far more compelling blueprint of things to come than are visions of a large-scale conflict of traditional arms. For this camp, it is failing states, transnational threats, and jihadism that should play front and center in the threat-planning mind. An essential assumption of this doctrinal posture is that irregular warfare is "not only different and of greater priority," but also that "it cannot be successfully conducted by general purpose forces that only marginally prepare for it."[140] Adherents demand of their brothers that they move on from Iwo Jima envy and the notion that the Corps's mission continues to be built principally on the Pacific experience.

The second camp, "Traditionalists," is so named because its members represent the doctrinal position most intermeshed with Corps culture. Traditionalists remain focused on fighting and winning large-scale interstate war and insist that "the Corps' raison d'être is founded in its amphibious capability and that its force structure, equipment, and training must be focused on projecting power 'from the sea.'" Traditionalists are not unaware that the majority of Marine effort in the last fifty years has been spent in small-wars fashion; they simply believe "that such scenarios are not amenable to military intervention and that these contingencies should not be the focus for American strategy or its military." The future conflicts worth fighting, they argue, will be conventional in nature.[141]

The third school, "Full Spectrum Operations," is the doctrinal form of the day among a critical mass of American ground force commanders (Army included).[142] This school is willing to accept that no one specialty may be optimized in an effort to train and supply for the full range of conflict contingencies but argues that an effort toward multicapable flexibility is as good as it gets. Commandant Conway's "medium weight" force concept—"being heavy enough to sustain expeditionary warfare and light enough to facilitate rapid deployment"[143]—falls along these lines. This school takes Marine Corps versatility at its word and hedges risk by investing in the quality, education, and mental agility of forces.

Finally, Hoffman sees a "Division of Labor" camp, which advocates that some forces train, are equipped, and are organized into force designs specifically for irregular warfare, while the larger part of the force maintains focus on conventional training and armament. In this, the Division of Labor adherents reject the sort of hubris demonstrated by some members of Corps leadership in the pre-9/11 era who dismissed anything short of conventional combat as a general category of "other" and assumed that the Marine Corps "generally know[s] how to do [evacuations of noncombatants], nation-building, counterinsurgency, and several other peripheral operations associated with [operations other than war]."[144] Division of Labor advocates agree with the Small Wars School that "regular and conventional warfare are markedly different modes of warfare" than irregular enterprises and therefore must be trained toward in genuinely distinctive ways. In addition to placing priority on preventative mechanisms that include stability operations, Division of Labor advocates would mandate highly specialized training for irregular scenarios in order to avoid being the jacks-of-all-trades who are masters of none.[145]

If historical pattern and organizational culture are sound indicators, the Corps will tumble about in this irregular-versus-regular discussion but will inexorably move toward a role distinction emphasizing conventional competence launched from the sea. In the meantime, the Marines are maintaining that theirs is a domain void of domain. The Corps is a general-purpose force that lives in the "seams"—a role posture defined within the *Marine Corps Operating Concepts*:

> The Army, Navy, and Air Force enjoy the clarity of focusing on the domains of land, maritime, and air. Their ties to these domains have naturally led to their individual and distinctive cultures, philosophies, and doctrines. . . .

Where domain-optimized forces have experienced friction is at the seams between the domains and in responding to sudden changes from the expected character of conflict. Unlike the other Services, the Marine Corps has not relied on a single geographic domain to ensure our place in national defense and service to the Nation. This distinction has at times been an institutional vulnerability that has led to attempts to reduce or eliminate the Corps based on perceived redundancy. It has, however, also been a source of great strength that has fueled competitive innovation, strategic and operational foresight, and the ability to view the battlespace "where four map sheets intersect" with a perspective not tied to a single cultural or domain bias. The Marine Corps has repeatedly demonstrated its institutional and operational adaptability by effectively bridging the nation's most critical seams between domains.[146]

General Amos, who was commandant during the last two years of Marine service in Iraq, provided a slightly more defined approach in public speeches: "We Marines don't really have a domain—we have a *lane*, and that lane is crisis response. I told my fellow Service chiefs, I'm not interested in poaching on your domain at all. But ours is a lane that cuts across all of these domains. If there is some duplication, I think it's not only affordable, it's necessary."[147] Grounding the Corps's sense of self through its rather turbulent search for a "lane" in the "seams" has been a set of commonly founded and consciously cultivated norms and ritualized values. Marines know who they are—how Marines look, how they behave, and what they believe—even if the role they perform remains a consistently open question.

## NOTES

1. The *Marine Corps Gazette* was begun in March 1916 as a publication for the officer corps. *Leatherneck*, begun in November 1921, is aimed at the enlisted ranks.
2. "The Epic of Dixmude," *Marine Corps Gazette* (March 1917): 85.
3. Cooling and Turner, "Understanding the Few Good Men."
4. Ricks, *Making the Corps*, 185.
5. Builder, *Masks of War*.
6. Ibid., 9. See Frank Hoffman's defense of the Corps's strategic voice: "Marine Mask of War."
7. Ricks, *Making the Corps*, 188–89. The Army War College does not have a record of this event or a transcript of Builder's speech (which is not totally unusual per its operating procedures). Rick's accounting of the lecture appears to be the only published record of it.

8. Ibid., 19.

9. Estes, *Handbook for Marine NCOs*, 72.

10. United States Marine Corps (hereafter USMC), *Sustaining the Transformation*, unpaginated introduction.

11. Woulfe, *Into the Crucible*, 11–12.

12. Dye, *Backbone*, x.

13. Oral history file AFC 2001/001/46366 MS01, Veterans History Project, American Folklife Center, Library of Congress.

14. Smith, *The Few and the Proud*, 174–75.

15. The Gallup question reads: *Just off the top of your head, which of the five branches of the armed forces in this country would you say is the most prestigious and has the most status in our society today—the Air Force, the Army, the Marines, the Navy, or the Coast Guard?* Polling taken in 2001 indicated that 36 percent of Americans rated the Marines the most prestigious branch, with the Air Force coming in second at 32 percent. By 2004 the Marines had widened this gap considerably, coming in at 39 percent, with the Air Force falling to 28 percent. This trend has continued over America's counterinsurgency years until 2011, when the Army displaced the Air Force for second place, with the Marine Corps climbing still higher: Air Force 15 percent, Army 22 percent, Marine Corps 46 percent (Navy 8 percent, Coast Guard 2 percent). Data retrieved November 23, 2012, at http://www.gallup.com/poll/148127 /americans-army-marines-important-defense.aspx.

16. O'Connell, *Underdogs*, 1.

17. USMC, *Sustaining the Transformation*, 19.

18. Oral history files AFC 2001/001/43420 MS02, AFC 2001/001/72369 MS01, AFC 2001/001/71698 MS02, AFC 2001/001/50169 MS02, and AFC 2001/001/53039 MS01, respectively, Veterans History Project.

19. This is a reference to the 1984 television commercial in which raw steel is forged into the blade of a Marine officer's sword, offered as metaphor for the transformation a young man would undergo through Corps tutelage.

20. Krulak, *First to Fight*. This book appears on the most highly recommended tier of the Commandant's Professional Reading List.

21. A reference to the US emergency phone number, 911—not a reference to the terrorist event of 9/11.

22. Hoffman, "Marine Mask of War," 2–3.

23. Capt. Owen O. West, "Who Will Be the First to Fight?" *Marine Corps Gazette* (May 2003): 54–56.

24. Col. John A. Lejeune, later commandant of the Marine Corps (1920–29), wrote with definitive clarity: "Let us not forget that we are, first of all, infantrymen, and have inherited the glorious traditions of that arm of the service." Lejeune, "The Mobile Defense of Advance Bases by the Marine Corps," *Marine Corps Gazette* (March 1916): 18. This theme is represented across multiple *Gazette* articles of this era.

25. Millett, *Semper Fidelis*, 29.

26. Unless the issue is "toughness," in which case it is the Air Force that is the object of ridicule.

27. Classic among these pieces is Maj. John H. Russell, "A Plea for a Mission and Doctrine," *Marine Corps Gazette* (June 1916), which sparked a discussion in the Corps that lasted in the journal's pages for the better part of a year.

28. Michael E. O'Hanlon, "Be All the Army Can't—or Won't—Be," *Marine Corps Gazette* (November 2010): 10. The paranoia surrounding this issue was only amplified by a speech given by Secretary of Defense Robert M. Gates to Marines in August 2010 in which he stated explicitly that "the Marines do not want to be, nor does America need, another land army." See http://archive .defense.gov/speeches/speech.aspx?speechid=1498. The same theme is evident in the 2010 edition of the *Marine Corps Operating Concepts* (June 2010), in which general officers felt compelled to put in print, "Often mischaracterized as land forces, the Marine Corps is actually part of the Naval Service—*soldiers from the sea.* . . . As such, Marine Corps forces are primarily designed to be employed, supported, and sustained at and from the sea." USMC, *Marine Corps Operating Concepts* (emphasis in original).

29. Robert M. Gates, George P. Shultz Lecture, San Francisco, August 12, 2010, http://archive.defense.gov/speeches/speech.aspx?speechid=1498; Ricks, *Making the Corps*, 38, 62; Spooner, *Marine Anthology*, 340

30. "Excerpts from the Statement of the Major General Commandant, U.S. Marine Corps, before the Committee on Naval Affairs of the House of Representatives on the Estimates for the Marine Corps on January 23, 1918," *Marine Corps Gazette* (March 1918): 67–68.

31. S.Sgt. Rudy R. Frame Jr., "The Battle of Belleau Wood," *Marine Corps Gazette* (November 2012): 20.

32. Millett, *Semper Fidelis*, 301–2.

33. Fehrenbach, *U.S. Marines in Action*, 63.

34. Millett, *Semper Fidelis*, 304.

35. Cameron, *American Samurai*, 24.

36. USMC, *United States Marine Guidebook*, 2-1 ("teufel hunden" bold in original).

37. Simmons, *United States Marines*, 100.

38. USMC, *United States Marine Guidebook*, 2-6.

39. This particular variation accessed on October 29, 2012, at http://www.military -quotes.com/forum/marine-corps-knowledge-t1721.html.

40. Each of whom believes "he's the toughest guy in the room." Fick, *One Bullet Away*, 144.

41. Ricks, *Making the Corps*, 44.

42. Fick, *One Bullet Away*, 4.

43. Smith, *The Few and the Proud*, 103, 86, 26.

44. Ibid., 112.

45. Ibid., 91.

46. Millett, *Semper Fidelis*, xvii.

47. Cameron, *American Samurai*, 36.

48. Sgt. Clarence B. Procter offers self-congratulatory prose typical of *Gazette* articles in the 1913–18 era when he "modestly" defends the then-contemporary recruiting slogans used by the Corps: "Recruiting: Past, Present and Future," *Marine Corps Gazette* (March 1918): 33.

49. USMC, *Sustaining the Transformation*, unpaginated introduction.

50. Krulak, *First to Fight*, xv.

51. Ricks, *Making the Corps*, 37.

52. O'Connell, *Underdogs*, 35–36.

53. USMC, *Warfighting*, 59.

54. Ricks, *Making the Corps*, 29.

55. Fick, *One Bullet Away*, 12.

56. Ricks, *Making the Corps*, 40, 43, 88; Price, *Devil Dog Diary*; Smith, *The Few and The Proud*; Woulfe, *Into the Crucible*; *The Marines*, PBS documentary (2007).

57. Sledge, *With the Old Breed*, 8.

58. This Marine Corps slogan ran consistently through advertising of the 1970s and early 1990s.

59. Gy.Sgt. John H. Lofland III, "I Am a Marine!," *Marine Corps Gazette* (November 1976): 23. See also Price, *Devil Dog Diary*, 188–94; Dye, *Backbone*, x.

60. Burk, "Military Culture," 457.

61. Fehrenbach, *U.S. Marines in Action*, 1.

62. Terriff, "Warriors and Innovators," 217.

63. Fick, *One Bullet Away*, 72. O'Connell provides an interesting discussion of the similarities between Marine Corps culture and religious orders, noting, among other features, that members of the Corps draw regularly on the language of religion, practice extreme discipline, engage in rituals, and cultivate a profound connection to the spiritual where Marine "ancestors" reside. O'Connell, *Underdogs*, 5–8.

64. Krulak, foreword of Woulfe, *Into the Crucible*, ix.

65. The US Marine Corps has a staff within the Historical Division devoted entirely to researching and relaying unit histories. Marines entering a unit learn its heritage, heroes, battle glories, and sea stories early on. Marines sealed to their unit via this heritage speak in condescending tones about Army equivalents who know nothing of the heritage of the unit to which they belong. Connable, "Culture Warriors," 4.

66. Lofland, "I Am a Marine!," 23.

67. Ricks, *Making the Corps*, 88.

68. Col. Charles A. Wynn, "A Marine Is Different," *Marine Corps Gazette* (May 1944): 14–15.

69. Ricks, *Making the Corps*, 64.

70. Fick, *One Bullet Away*, 72.

71. Maj. Frank E. Evans, "The Marines Have Landed," *Marine Corps Gazette* (September 1917): 213.

72. Thomason, "Marine Brigade," 33.

73. Ricks, *Making the Corps*, 37.

74. Smith, *The Few and the Proud*, xx.

75. Bradley, *Flags of Our Fathers*, 3.

76. Smith, *The Few and the Proud*, 271.

77. Col. R. D. Heinl Jr., "The Marine and His Traditions," *Marine Corps Gazette* (November 1964): 23–25.

78. Millett, *Semper Fidelis*, 493. For additional accounts, see Simmons, *United States Marines*, 195–210; Fehrenbach, *U.S. Marines in Action*, 155–65; and Cameron, who writes, "Like Guadalcanal, enough has been written on the legend of 'frozen Chosin' that fact and fantasy have tended to merge." *American Samurai*, 228–30.

79. Millett, *Semper Fidelis*, 495.

80. A Marine "favorite," this citation appears nearly anywhere collections of Marine quotes are assembled, including doctrinal texts. See Estes, *Handbook for Marine NCOs*, 8.

81. Third verse of "The Marines' Hymn." Known as the oldest of the US military anthems (it was in familiar usage by the mid-1800s), its precise origination date and author are unknown. It was formalized as the Marine anthem in 1929. Sturkey, *Warrior Culture of the U.S. Marines*, 61–62. A complete set of lyrics may be found in Sturkey's work and on the official Marine Corps public site at http://www.marineband.marines.mil/About/Library-and-Archives/The -Marines-Hymn/.

82. Krulak, *First to Fight*, 155.

83. O'Connell, *Underdogs*, 4.

84. Wynn, "A Marine Is Different," 13.

85. Lofland, "I Am a Marine!," 23.

86. Fick, *One Bullet Away*, 33.

87. Dye, *Backbone*, xi.

88. Cameron, *American Samurai*, 30.

89. Smith, *The Few and the Proud*, xix.

90. Krulak, *First to Fight*.

91. R. R. Keene and Sara Wirtala Bock, "An Exclusive Interview with the 16th Sergeant Major of the Marine Corps," *Leatherneck* (November 2008): 27.

92. When asked what Marines do with their downtime, one Recon Marine, a member of an elite branch and one who loves his Corps, responded with humor in warning: "Marines are, like, dumb. Like, really, really dumb. I mean, like, they're intelligent, but they're also, like, dumb, like if you leave them in a room they'll figure a way how to blow the room up with nothing in the room except for them and the room." Oral history file AFC 2001/001/78228 MS02, Veterans History Project.

93. Ricks, *Making the Corps*, 19, 192.

94. For a sampling, see Estes, *Handbook for Marine NCOs*, 3–4. Chesty Puller is a notable exception. Although he enlisted, it was while serving as an officer that he earned his five Navy Crosses and his Distinguished Service Cross.

95. USMC, *Sustaining the Transformation*, unpaginated introduction.

96. A significant percentage of the widely popular Marine-based comic strip *Terminal Lance* (found at http://terminallance.com/) is dedicated to taking punches at POGs. For typical YouTube fare, search "POGs vs. Grunts."

97. Maj. Alfred A. Cunningham, "Value of Aviation to the Marine Corps," *Marine Corps Gazette* (May 2013): 99.

98. Salmoni and Holmes-Eber, *Operational Culture*, 280.

99. Fick, *One Bullet Away*, 23, 180.

100. Maj. Gen. John A. Lejeune, "Preparation," *Marine Corps Gazette* (March 1922): 55.

101. Maj. Gen. John A. Lejeune, "A Brief History of the U.S. Marine Corps," *Marine Corps Gazette* (March 1923): 19.

102. Maj. Gen. John A. Lejeune, "The United States Marine Corps," *Marine Corps Gazette* (December 1923): 249–54.

103. Wendall C. Neville succeeded Lejeune as commandant but died sixteen months later without leaving his mark on the pages of the *Marine Corps Gazette*.

104. For a detailed history of this internal conflict, see Bickel, *Mars Learning*.

105. Maj. Gen. Ben H. Fuller, "The Mission of the Marine Corps," *Marine Corps Gazette* (November 1930): 7.

106. Ulbrich, *Preparing for Victory*, 40.

107. Bickel, *Mars Learning*, 205–27.

108. "Major General John H. Russell, U.S.M.C.," *Marine Corps Gazette* (November 1936); Schmidt, *United States Occupation of Haiti*, 95–221.

109. Russell, "Plea for a Mission and Doctrine."

110. Brig. Gen. John H. Russell, "A New Naval Policy," *Marine Corps Gazette* (August 1933): 13.

111. Ulbrich, *Preparing for Victory*, 38.

112. The manuals' titles are represented here as Russell wrote them in his capstone contribution to the *Gazette* upon retirement. Brig. Gen. John H. Russell, "Final Report of Major General Commandant," *Marine Corps Gazette* (November 1936).

113. Bickel, *Mars Learning*, 220–24.

114. Holcomb's education at the Naval War College focused on Japan as the most plausible primary US enemy. Ulbrich, *Preparing for Victory*, 32.

115. Ibid., 40.

116. Lt. Gen. Thomas Holcomb, "First to Fight," *Marine Corps Gazette* (November 1943): 16.

117. Cameron, *American Samurai*, 36–38.

118. Holcomb, "First to Fight," 16.

119. Lt. Gen. Thomas Holcomb, "Marines in War and Peace," *Marine Corps Gazette* (December 1943): 4.

120. Ibid.
121. Lt. Gen. Alexander A. Vandegrift, "Amphibious Miracle of Our Time," *Marine Corps Gazette* (October 1944): 3.
122. In Krulak's accounting, this was born from an Army determination to "eliminate forever its deficiencies in amphibious matters and its dependency on Marines for amphibious expertise." Krulak, *First to Fight*, 18.
123. Ibid., 51. See also James D. Hittle, "The Marine Corps and the National Security Act," *Marine Corps Gazette* (October 1947).
124. "Summary of the Marine Corps Position," *Marine Corps Gazette* (December 1949): 17.
125. Krulak, *First to Fight*, 58. For detailed accounts of the political machinations that led to this moment, see ibid., 17–58, and O'Connell, *Underdogs*, 98–147.
126. Lt. Gen. Lemuel C. Shepherd Jr., "Passing in Review," *Marine Corps Gazette* (April 1951): 62.
127. "Corps Standing Tall: Ready, Willing, Able," *Marine Corps Gazette* (April 1961): 1.
128. Gen. Wallace M. Greene Jr., "Commandant's Report," *Marine Corps Gazette* (May 1966): 21, 22, 25, 27.
129. Gen. Leonard F. Chapman Jr., "State of the Corps," *Marine Corps Gazette* (May 1969): 30.
130. Peterson, *Combined Action Platoons*, 18.
131. Gen. Robert E. Cushman Jr., "Walking Tall," *Marine Corps Gazette* (April 1975): 19.
132. USMC, *Marine Corps Vision and Strategy 2025*, 8.
133. The "do windows" reference is well understood and used with frequency within Marine Corps circles. Capt. Chris Seiple does a particularly nice job of capturing the many "other than war" tasks that doing windows comprises: "Window into an Age of Windows: The U.S. Military and the NGOs," *Marine Corps Gazette* (April 1999): 63.
134. USMC, *Marine Corps Vision and Strategy 2025*, 8.
135. USMC, *Marine Corps Operating Concepts*, 1.
136. Ibid., 2 (italics in original).
137. USMC, *Marine Corps Vision and Strategy 2025*, 5, 8.
138. USMC, *Marine Corps Operating Concepts*, 8. See also Estes, *Handbook for Marine NCOs*, 9.
139. Eliason, "Interview with James F. Amos," 12–17.
140. Lt. Col. (Ret.) Frank G. Hoffman, "Posturing the Corps for the 21st Century," *Marine Corps Gazette* (December 2012): 28.
141. Ibid., 29. It is not military chiefs, however, but civilian masters who determine which battles the nation fights—a point that seems to be missing from the Traditionalists' analysis.
142. Hoffman cites the tone and substance of the Army's Field Manual 3-0, *Operations*, as evidence and notes that many of the tenets of the Full Spectrum School may also be found in USMC, *Marine Corps Vision and Strategy 2025*.

143. USMC, *Marine Corps Vision and Strategy 2025*, 5; seconded by Commandant Amos in Eliason, "Interview with James F. Amos," 15.
144. Col. Gary W. Anderson, "Campaign Planning for Operations Other Than War," *Marine Corps Gazette* (February 1996): 45.
145. Hoffman, "Posturing the Corps," 30.
146. USMC, *Marine Corps Operating Concepts*, 3.
147. Eliason, "Interview with James F. Amos," 15.

# CHAPTER 4

---

# BROTHERS IN ARMS
## Marine Norms and Values

In his groundbreaking work on service culture, Carl Builder labeled a service's key value its "altar for worship"—that which a service reveres or cherishes as an ideal. For the Navy, it is tradition and independence at sea; for the Air Force, technology; and for the Army, service to the nation.[1] Had he deigned to write on the Marine Corps, Builder might have perceived what becomes apparent across the bulk of Marine recorded histories. The key value for the Corps is the Corps itself.[2] Everything Marines do revolves around protecting and burnishing the essence, heritage, public persona, and future place of the Corps. Marines unapologetically reference "our beloved Corps." *Beloved*. Marines make mention of fighting for country, but Marines fight for Marines. They fight for brothers and the Corps. Although likely unconscious, the DI's creed makes the hierarchy of Corps over country somewhat overt: "These recruits are entrusted to my care. I will train them to the best of my ability. I will develop them into smartly disciplined, physically fit, basically trained Marines, *thoroughly indoctrinated in love of the Corps and country*. I will demand of them, and demonstrate by my own personal example, the highest standards of personal conduct, morality and professional skill."[3] The following sentiment, expressed by Sgt. Maj. Clint Kreuser, echoes the feelings of fellow Marines who sat on the "bench" outside combat in Iraq and Afghanistan: "Every Marine wants to go over there; that's where the fight is; that's where our Marines are."[4] Even if the "cause" behind an engagement is nebulous and efforts seem to be dysfunctional or failing, Marines go—or go *again*—to the fight because other Marines are there. This sentiment crosses generations. A Vietnam-era vet stated for the record: "In combat I fought for the Marine Corps. I didn't fight for this country or our flag. That wasn't due to any lack of patriotism, but because country and flag were too remote

10,000 miles away. A fighting man, when successful, needs something closer. Marines have it. Our Corps is our country."[5]

A seeming switch in perspective occurs when Marines are speaking to "civvies" (civilians) about their service. In these conversations, Marines tend to reference service to country in explaining their commitments and sacrifices. The pattern of discourse, however, continues to tie back to fellow Marines. Marines are making a demand of the American public to respect the sacrifice brothers have made in their name. This perspective tends to spill over into what Marines perceive as naive or offensively ignorant public notions about the role of war in preserving freedom. Marines often see themselves as the quiet guarantors of the "good life" swirling around them. Sgt. Jeremy D. Lima captures the sometimes irritated stance of a returned-home Devil Dog:

> I don't think war is fun or glorious or anything like that but, I am willing to do it again, in fact I want to do it again. I think the military services are absolutely necessary especially with the world is today [sic]. It seems that everyone (kids, parents, etc.) think that the military is the last resort and these kids are too good for the military, but in reality, if someone thinks that way, they must think they are too good for freedom. Everyone likes to do their own thing whether that is playing sports, playing music, read books or spend [sic] time with family and friends, but no one is willing to defend that, they just take it for granted.[6]

A number of bumper-sticker-borne narratives capture the Marines' attitude toward what they perceive to be uninformed antiwar protesting:

> Except for ending slavery, Fascism, Nazism, and Communism, WAR has never solved anything.

> PATRIOT DISSENT is a Luxury of Those Protected By Better Men Than They.

> If You Can't Stand Behind the Troops . . . Stand in Front of Them . . . PLEASE!

Marines fight for Marines, but they do expect the nation to honor the sacrifice made in its name.

Commandants' speeches, training manuals, official histories, and doctrinal texts are all rich repositories of additional values, norms, and beliefs officially pursued by Marine Corps leadership. To determine which of these are genuinely internalized by members of the organization—which are believed, cherished, and acted on with the sort of regularity that constitutes "culture"—official texts must be matched against grassroots narratives, the heritage tales celebrated and voluntarily passed from one cultural generation to the next. Grassroots narratives may come in various forms, including oral histories, poetry, humor, slogans, and legend. Oral histories and legends provide a particularly rich source of data, since each typically offers the additional benefit of providing context and insight into the "why" behind genuinely admired cultural values or ritualized practices.

For all its ubiquity, Marine Corps legend is surprisingly difficult to pin down. One might expect to find it in the pages of the *Marine Corps Gazette* or *Leatherneck*, but a search reveals limited offerings. The stories "everyone knows" are often not in print. Marine leadership is not naive to the essential importance of legend to the fighting spirit of the Corps; in fact, the absence of legend in the pages of the *Gazette* is likely evidence of that. Putting legend in print may put it in jeopardy. A service journal would require of itself a responsible level of research to validate the historic authenticity of any particular legend. This research may result in significant downgrades of some rather cherished institutional "memories." Stewards of these tales are far wiser to keep them as motivational oral history, passed down in classrooms, from mentor to boot, and within units by word of mouth.

Those who act as oral history repositories within a societal band are labeled "key informants" in ethnographic terms. Most ethnographers do not rely on wide-sweep survey techniques but pick out common threads in an interwoven culture through conversations with key interlocutors. These are members of the culture who know a lot about the particular aspects of a culture, are highly articulate, and are willing to share their knowledge.[7] Born in 1925, retired major Rick Spooner represents a classic key informant where Marine legend is concerned. A veteran of World War II, Korea, and Vietnam, Spooner dedicated his life to the Corps and has done the same with his retirement. His restaurant near Marine Corps Base Quantico, the Globe and Laurel, is considered a cultural icon for the Corps. Military memorabilia cover its walls and ceilings. Most important, Spooner himself remains a repository of oral history. He is often solicited as a speaker and is revered as the man in possession of the full repertoire of leatherneck yarns. A testament to his cultural credentials is the fact that any on base at Quantico who want to introduce a newcomer to their culture immediately suggest lunch at the Globe and Laurel.[8]

In 2010 Spooner relented to significant peer pressure and put his "mostly fiction" version of Marine Corps legends into a book. His work weaves stories stretching from the Banana Wars years through the last days of the Pacific campaign. The themes are not all glory days. If anything, Spooner's primary theme is a love for the Corps *despite* the absurdities and ironies and sometimes blood-soaked life it offers.[9] For the outsider, probably the most surprising aspect of Spooner's collection is its emphasis on the upsidedownness of Marine Corps life. The wrong people get promoted, slick do-nothings or screw-ups get medals, and men of genuine talent and warrior skill often end up on the wrong side of merit boards. The redeeming theme, however, is that "brothers" know what is going on, even if the Marine "machine" does not, and that is what matters.

## NORMS AND VALUES

The critical massing of norms, values, and beliefs about self and others across these legends is remarkably consistent when a similar exercise is applied to contemporary oral histories. The themes that emerged across both official and grassroots sources are highlighted in the sections that follow.

### Band of Brothers

The Marines' "mystical brotherhood" is woven through by an enviable esprit de corps lived, treasured, and valued by leathernecks who guard it with a zealous loyalty.[10] Several of the *Gazette*'s earliest recorded commandant speeches highlight esprit de corps as a priority. Maj. Gen. John Lejeune framed esprit de corps as both obligation and treasure: New recruits "received from [the Corps] the benefit of the practical knowledge and experience of the old-time Marine, and the marvelous *esprit de corps* which has been handed down from generation to generation."[11] Later: "Every officer and every man should have it. Each one of us should use all his strength to add to it. It is a sacred thing. It is our priceless heritage from the past. It has come to us from the heroic dead."[12] The conscious cultivation of Marine esprit, however, had not yet been institutionalized as a priority. In a September 1921 submission to the *Gazette*, 1st Lt. Sidney J. Handsley lamented the lack of formal mechanisms for learning the traditions, symbols, and history of the Corps. His argument for remedying this deficit was the establishment of a more robust esprit de corps—one that would remove "that utter sense of loneliness" by binding fellow Marines together within the heritage of "meaning" ensconced in their hymn, symbols, and rituals, "the meaning [of] which," Handsley worried, "too often, he only learns by chance."[13]

Over time, the Corps refined—well beyond its sister services—the art form of consciously cultivating esprit de corps and mooring it to a common sense of history, heritage, and symbols. This effort is fueled by a recognition that a strong esprit de corps is a fighting asset.[14] In the thick of World War II, Commandant Thomas Holcomb reminded his force: "As every Marine knows, the preparation for service is not limited to the development of technical skills. There is also the development of an esprit de corps to assure that our men's native and acquired fighting skills will be vitalized by an indomitable determination to win, against any odds."[15] Vietnam-era commandant Wallace Greene acknowledged much the same: "It is this spirit that has enabled us to bear adversity without complaint and to win victories over seemingly impossible odds."[16]

Maj. Jason Spitaletta, a student of psychology within the Corps, points out that Marines today are biased to receive esprit de corps because of the brotherhood reputation the Marine Corps projects. Recruits go in looking for it, presume that it will happen, and it does.[17] Marine recruiting posters boast that "orphans" arrive at Parris Island and a family emerges.[18] This brotherhood feature of the Corps was made yet more famous by Medal of Honor recipient Dakota Meyers who, in a nationally televised interview, explained his medal-winning defiance of orders in his attempted rescue of team members: "We are taught obedience to orders, but I can tell you what we are taught more, importantly, is the brotherhood."[19] Meyers is not alone in his heroics in the name of brotherhood. Jorje Cruz, a staff sergeant and Recon Marine, won the Navy Cross for retrieving his brothers: "I couldn't see myself, even if it meant dying, leaving those guys behind. . . . Those are the guys that were . . . , like, my big brothers because they taught me everything." About returning to civilian life: "You never find that comradery [sic] again."[20]

Although new recruits are certainly biased to receive the gift of brotherhood, and the Corps's propaganda usefully reinforces it, the near universal consistency of strong, very often verbalized emotive attachment to the Corps brotherhood—from all Devil Dog ranks and stations and across grassroots narrative forms—indicates that the "brotherhood" within this insular military society is the genuine article. Major Spitaletta sums up: "We value the relationships with one another more so than anything else."[21] When asked what he enjoyed most about the Marine Corps, L.Cpl. Kaleb Bench said simply, "The other Marines."[22]

The Marines' strong brotherhood exists *in spite of*, rather than because of an amelioration of sexist slights and ethnic slurs within the Corps. Women and ethnic minorities have struggled across time to be afforded equal status and positions of influence within Marine ranks.[23] Marine discourse includes both high praise for its female members in articles written for its service journals, as well as exceptionally crass and degrading banter in less public settings. The 2017 Marines United scandal in which a number of male Marines contributed to a social media site that boasted the display of nude photos of female service members without their permission prompted a strong response from women in the Corps. Their "open letter" to fellow Marines directly targeted a culture in which "women are devalued, demeaned, and their contribution diminished." To their brothers, it read: "This is about the time you said, 'We don't need any more females in this section,' as if there were a quota. It's about the time you made the joke about the female Marine and her face, her hair, her voice, her private life, or her sexual orientation. This is about pretending you don't hear women when they speak. And about looking only at men when you speak. Or treating sexual assault as a burden."[24]

Female Marines continue to navigate this uneven ground with surprisingly high morale. Although it is not unusual for infantry Marines to voice the attitude that the Corps "is no place for females," many female Marines make strong claims of equanimity for themselves.[25] "They call Marines . . . 'The Few and the Proud.' They call us females the 'Fewer, and the Prouder.' . . . I love the Marine Corps!"[26] Fewer indeed: The Marine Corps has both the fewest absolute number of women and lowest percentage within its force across the US armed services.[27] The incorporation of women into combat roles remains hotly debated, and female Marines themselves have argued both sides—although a clear majority publishing within the *Gazette* favor greater inclusion across military occupational specialties, including infantry.[28]

Marines acknowledge that they crack racist jokes and make ethnicity an open target for energetically hurled insults. They rebuke accusations of racism, however, and claim their verbal sparring is proof that "being a Marine transcends any other form of identity, to include those associated with gender or race."[29] Randy Shepard, director of strategy over the Marine Corps advertising account for the last two decades, would qualify that point. He believes the Marine Corps has long experienced a recruiting problem when it comes to diversity because "the culture of the Marine Corps, and in particular the infantry, is white, Southern, and Protestant."[30] Research conducted by his organization, J. Walter Thompson, indicates that while America is becoming increasingly diverse, the Corps has shifted little in the last twenty years from its 71 percent white composition, making it increasingly "whiter" than the overall population.[31] Although Marines have convinced themselves that there is little harm done with racist jibes within ranks, past bouts of racism made enemies out of civilian populations in the Caribbean during the Marine occupation there and would certainly provoke the same reaction from any future population subject to its derogations.

No matter their color or gender, in near complete accord contemporary Marines who have left the service declare that what they miss most is "other Marines." Marines tend to see themselves as a breed that can be little understood by outsiders, both in terms of behavior and bond. Their norms are perceived as out of sync with civilian society: "We had fight clubs . . . and you see Marines out there just knocking it out and fighting each other. And then when they were done they were, like, beer it is and they would drink down, like, a 30-rack of beer and laugh about it. I mean, a different breed of animal, a Marine is."[32] The bonds forged can only be framed in familial terms, or something stronger: "They're like brothers and sisters. . . . You go through so much together that you couldn't go through . . . with your own blood, so they almost become your own blood just through experience so it's hard not to talk to them. . . . There are a few that you'll never forget that will almost be part of you forever."[33] "We became a band of brothers as they call it, it truly is."[34] Admiration for peers and superiors bears a striking contrast to what might be found in corporate civilian society: "[My fellow officers and

Marines] were extraordinary. Of course you don't get along with everyone, but . . . it's being around people that appreciate the core values that you hold dear. You know the core values in [the] Marine Corps are honor, courage, and commitment . . . and the individuals that participate in that are, I mean, they are heroes."[35] The "other Marines" valued are not only contemporary buddies, but also connections in spirit and practice to Marines who have come before. Homage to the Corps's heritage and heroes is ritualized in the Marine Corps birthday celebration every year on the tenth day of November. On this day, the commandant sends out a birthday message that reminds troops of Marines long gone (but not forgotten!) to whom they owe a future of honor.[36] Typical of birthday prose is Commandant Randolph Pate's in 1956: "We must strive constantly to add luster to the glorious record of those Marines who have gone before us. Only by so doing can we prove ourselves worthy of our heritage. Only thus can we proudly bear the title of United States Marines."[37] Commandant John A. Lejeune originated the tradition of the birthday ball (which Marines *must* "voluntarily" attend), as well as Marine Corps Order 47, which lauds the history of the Corps and is read annually. Commandant Lemuel C. Shepherd formalized the cake-cutting ritual.[38] The first piece of cake, cut with a Mameluke sword to celebrate warrior heritage, goes to a guest of honor, the second to the oldest Marine present, and the third (or a remainder of the second piece) to the youngest Marine present—signifying the bond between the two generations, the passing down of heritage. Marines take their Corps's birthday seriously and will cobble together a cake no matter their situation, including in combat zones. It is a ritual performed on the same day all around the world, a reminder of heritage and brotherhood from which they derive strength.

Rituals such as the birthday ball and cake-cutting ceremony reinforce a primary theme running throughout Spooner's legend collection: The Marine Corps is a family. Retired Marine and scholar Aaron O'Connell describes the Corps in the same terms. The Marine Corps provides "a connection to a larger family that reaches across time and space. This is one of the principal benefits of membership in the Marine Corps: a broad and deep sense of kinship that encompassed all Marines, past and present, living and dead."[39] Its members protect each other internally and out. Even the worst of Marines are defended from outsiders. This may mean defending physical life or personal reputation. To save a lieutenant whom they detest, Spooner's fictional platoon risks life and limb: "In either case, he was down and for all their disgust, the men of the Third Platoon had to save him. He may be the lieutenant they most wanted to see marooned on a desert island, but he was a Marine."[40] The reputations of individual Marines are protected in order to protect the reputation of the Corps as a whole. Protection of brothers, and of the Corps, is laudable, and without question this demonstration of fierce internal loyalty contributes to the strong bonds of brotherhood that remain the most attractive, and reliable, feature of the Corps. In counterinsurgency scenarios, however, especially those of extended duration involving state-building efforts, brotherhood ties of this intensity threaten to undermine evenhanded jurisprudence on behalf of locals when Marines are in charge and their brothers violate local norms, legal practices, or are abusive in their treatment of the native population.

The Corps as an institution and the brotherhood it affords are the most sainted values on the USMC altar of worship, but the Corps has no shortage of additional "values." The Marine Corps values *values*. Marines are overt about it. They advertise values, drill values, preach values. The three that reign supreme are courage, honor, and commitment.[41] Recruits repeat these three times daily in boot camp: "Honor. Courage. Commitment. Kill, kill. Marine Corps!"[42] Marines are indoctrinated to see themselves as the bastions of a long-forgotten conservative America, the still-standing sentries of a noble value triumvirate. The list of values officers must memorize, drill, and recite is much longer: bearing, courage, decisiveness, dependability, endurance, enthusiasm, initiative, integrity, judgment, justice, knowledge, loyalty, tact, and unselfishness (not to be left out, officers retain the "Kill!" chorus, which is belted out by candidates at full volume as a response to such banal commands as to take one's seat).[43] Courage, honor, and commitment have pride of place as mantra, but in directives from leadership to the Corps these are not the values that commandants spend most of their time discussing in detail. "Professionalism" and "discipline" absorb far more speech and directive time than do courage, honor, and commitment.

## Professionalism and Discipline

Marines see themselves as the "consummate professional[s]."[44] The Corps's seminal doctrinal text, *Warfighting* (known among Marines as MCDP-1), defines professionalism as being "*true experts in the conduct of war*," achieved by "intelligent leaders with a penchant for boldness and initiative down to the lowest levels."[45] No other attribute is more highly regarded or more repeated as praise in Spooner's legends. "Savage is one of the best-damned Marines I've ever known. With a handful of men like him, you could storm the gates of hell and overrun the Devil's brigade. He's a professional, through and through."[46] Spooner's use of the term captures the same spirit as the official definition, as does Fick's experience as a Force Reconnaissance Marine. Among Recon Marines, an elite branch within the Corps, being called "hard" is "the greatest compliment one could pay to another." Fick explains: "Hardness wasn't toughness, nor was it courage, although both were part of it. Hardness was the ability to face an overwhelming situation with aplomb, smile calmly at it, and then triumph through sheer professional pride."[47] The same combat-valor orientation to "professionalism" appears in this admiring account of the early twentieth-century Corps that included Marine legend Smedley Butler:

But there was this Marine Corps. A small, go-to-hell outfit of 2,900 troops, its 77 officers were mostly Civil War veterans, tall, straight, bearded professionals who dressed their pride in gaudy blue uniforms, carried Mameluke hilt swords, fed their thirst with chewing tobacco, their fatigue with drinking whiskey, cursed with the metric vigor of Kipling, drilled their troops night and day, knew everything there was to know about their three weapons, the Lee straight-pull 6mm rifle, the Gatling gun and the Hotchkiss revolving canon. Weird, unorthodox, demanding men, they fought like hell and they won. To be accepted by them, to be admitted to this small band of brothers. . . . Well, here was something intensely personal, something proud and glorious and exciting that no amount of fatigue and pain and death could diminish, here was a place where you could sometimes find the moment of truth, and this was what Capt. Butler chose to do with his life.[48]

These images strike a sharp contrast with expanded notions of "professionalism" practiced in the modern-era Corps. This century's Devil Dog warriors continue to see coolness under fire as central—"Our Marines performed under pressure. That's what Marines do."[49]—but while on military base are expected to exhibit "professionalism" through a set of what might seem anachronistic civilities.[50] Strict protocols regarding saluting, verbal salutations, body language, and tidiness of uniform are among a set of interesting social rigidities actively practiced within the Corps's ranked brotherhood. In this, leathernecks present one of many paradoxes. When on base they are more courteous, conscious of protocol, and obsessive about uniformed appearance than their sister services, but when deployed downrange they take pride in acquiring more dirt, smell, and muck than most humans could stand—and banter in language that makes civilized ears burn. One of Spooner's legendary teams called themselves the "Raggedy Assed Marines," with more than a touch of pride in their "salty," worn-and-torn combat appearance.[51] This image resides alongside a contradictory, near fanatic ethos to keep their persons and uniforms clean. E. B. Sledge, in his memoir of the World War II years, notes that being physically filthy

> bothered almost everyone I knew. Even the hardiest Marine typically kept his rifle and his person clean. His language and his mind might need a good bit of cleaning up but not his weapon, his uniform, or his person. We had this philosophy drilled into us in boot camp, and many times at Camp Elliot I had to pass personal inspection, to the point of clean fingernails, before being passed as fit to go on liberty. To be anything less than neat and sharp was considered a negative reflection on the Marine Corps and was not tolerated.[52]

A favorite quote of the Corps that neatly captures this dueling set of values is purported to have been said by Eleanor Roosevelt during a visit to Quantico in 1945: "The Marines I have seen around the world have the cleanest bodies, the filthiest minds, the highest morale, and the lowest morals of any group of animals I have ever seen. Thank God for the United States Marine Corps!"[53]

The aspect of "professional" most important to Marines in any particular moment seems to be driven by both physical and historical context.[54] Almost no mention is made of professionalism in commandants' speeches until the 1970s, when resuscitating certain aspects of professionalism after Vietnam became paramount to the Corps's image. Commandant Leonard F. Chapman Jr. took up the baton of "professionalism" during his tenure (1968–71) and used it to beat a steady drum into his final year, emphasizing not only military proficiency and physical fitness but "cleanliness and squared-away appearance" as well.[55] Chapman was the first commandant to give priority attention to military appearance in the *Gazette* but was certainly not first to note it as a hallmark of Marines. Pride in military appearance stretches back to the Marines' earliest days.[56] The subject was addressed in the *Gazette*'s very first editions. Capt. Frank E. Evans began his treatise on the signature Mameluke sword with the following:

> The Marine Corps has been notably free from slavish imitation or hasty adoption of the customs and traditions of the sister services. In no department has it more tenaciously held to its own distinctive attributes than in its uniform and equipment. . . . This independence of spirit has had much to do with the sturdy *esprit de corps* and its steady growth, and the fostering of a purpose that the customs and traditions of the Corps are not to be lightly discarded.[57]

Marines are enamored of their dress blue uniform and are fairly certain that all others feel likewise. The Corps uses the advantage of handsomest-of-the-services regalia to full effect in television advertising. Several generations of recruiting commercials ended with the image of a "squared-away" Marine in striking dress blues. Superficial as the draw was, it worked. Sgt. Jose Robert Reyes is not the only young recruit to go starry-eyed over Marine fancy dress: "One day I was in the cafeteria and . . . I saw this . . . staff sergeant and . . . he just walked in there with his uniform and he even had a sword and he just looked bad ass and I was like wow I wanna look like that."[58] Spooner confesses the same. As a shoeshine boy, he "fell in love with the Corps the first time he ever saw a Marine." Marine appearance was the key draw to service: "Always in dress blues, marching down the street, looking tall and squared away, and never letting me shine their shoes . . . always referring me to the sailors. . . . The Marines were too proud to let a kid shine their shoes. And I thought, 'Wow, they're special, they're different, they're wonderful!'"[59]

Effective as Marine dress is in courting the vanity cravings of America's youth, the purpose of sharp appearance runs a level deeper. Of the voices extolling Marine Corps spit and polish, Commandant Chapman is most overt about function: "All of this dressing up has a purpose: to enhance our professional image within ourselves. Professional service to the people of the United States is our goal in everything we do; from the way we think to the way we act; and from the way we know our profession to the way we look."[60]

A squared-away appearance has become, for Marines, synonymous with professionalism and discipline. Great care is taken with keeping all aspects of the uniform sharp: chevrons are touched up with black marker when they begin to show wear, trousers are bloused over boots in a regulated fashion, "covers" (hats) have sharper angles than those of other forces, and "high and tight" haircuts are signature Marine. The basic thinking is "sloppiness begets sloppiness," and small infractions will lead to larger ones.[61] Marine leadership is venerated, in part, because their uniforms are crisper than recruits can seem to achieve. One contemporary Marine recalls the larger-than-life image of his DIs—listing their appearance credentials first: "So the drill instructors are really like the hallmark of what it means to be . . . a Marine. . . . Their uniform is perfect, [they're] motivated, loud, in physical shape, smart . . . everything that a Marine should want to be."[62]

Impressive as it may be, the Marine version of being squared-away—looking sharp—can come at the expense of practicality: Hands are not allowed in pockets, even in cold weather, nor are wallets. Not all regard this "tradition" as endearing and esprit-building. Maximilian Uriarte, author of the widely popular and decidedly irreverent Marine comic strip *Terminal Lance*, has dedicated more than one of his humorous offerings to the pockets topic with the following tactical observation:

> I've said it before and I'll say it again: quite possibly the most absurd nuance of the Marine Corps is not being able to put your hands in your pockets—even when it's bitter cold outside. I've heard the old tales and adages of Chesty Puller saying something along the lines of, "A Marine with cold hands and empty pockets is a fool." . . . In any case, this really just comes down to one simple belief of mine: pockets exist on the uniform for a reason. If it's cold outside, *warm your hands.* . . . The Marine Corps should encourage such an action, since cold hands could very well adversely affect the way a Marine performs his job.[63]

Absurd though it may be, hands-out-of-pockets is Marine tradition, and infractions have consequences. One retired Marine wrote to the *Gazette* about the deleterious impact that casual regard for this rule by leadership had on his troops twenty years earlier. In anticipation of a visit from the commandant, his troops "field-dayed" their barracks to a "fanatical" degree of perfection. The commandant's visit and speech were short. Back at the barracks, the sergeant noticed that his troops were depressed. Upon inquiry, one of his young privates "sneeringly" retorted, "He had his hands in his pockets the whole time he spoke to us." The author notes that this may be a small thing, but "Marines do not put their hands in their pockets, ever." His message to leadership is that Marine Corps's standards and traditions matter, and matter most for those who command and inspire.[64]

Strictly constructed as they are, it is inevitable that Marine values of form and appearance will clash with values of pragmatism or utility when downrange. Traditions may matter, but carrying the squared-away mentality into all forums may create unintended negative consequences and perhaps even undermine more strategically significant values. A Marine blogger featured on the *Foreign Policy* website complained that appearance, correct processes, and form were often privileged in the Corps over genuine results in the field. The value hierarchy, as he perceived it, seemed to be "it's okay to fail to provide any added value, so long as the PowerPoint slides are free of typos, no serialized gear is lost, and everyone attends the Sexual Harassment Prevention training."[65] The opportunity cost imposed by one value set can often have serious consequences for another.

A close companion to the Marine version of professionalism is "discipline," a value and practice given consistent attention across commandants' speeches ("The men who are the best disciplined, of whatever country they are, will always fight the best."[66]) and referenced by DIs as the primary objective of boot camp.[67] Boot camp's ritualized practices: drill, inspections, and rigid requirements of form and appearance are "essential for effecting the transition from civilian to Marine. They [teach] recruits to submit to authority, to venerate tradition, and to sacrifice comfort, safety, and even life, all in the name of Marine Corps discipline."[68] Recruits chant verses about discipline and are instructed to become embodiments of its essence— clean-cut, self-possessed men standing apart from "nasty" civilian society.[69] Marines are quickly socialized to regard "undisciplined" as a deeply humiliating insult.[70] The result: In their oral histories, Marine veterans are more likely to cite "discipline" as the way the Marine Corps changed his or her life than any other characteristic.

The textbook definition of discipline for modern Marines is holding oneself responsible for one's "own actions and others responsible for their actions," as well as a commitment to "maintaining physical, moral, and mental health, to fitness and exercise, and to lifelong learning."[71] In practice, however, the aspects of "discipline" referenced by most Marines who comment on this value (usually in the form of an insult levied at another service) are appearance and fitness. Marines chastise other services (primarily the

Army and National Guard) for sloppiness in uniform or fatness.[72] Being overweight is often treated as synonymous with being undisciplined—a significant failing. "Being soft or overweight is not merely against regulations; it demonstrates a departure from the warrior culture."[73]

When in the field, however, it is combat discipline that becomes paramount. This comprises both coolness under fire and possession of the grit and raw dedication required to accomplish the mission. Pain, misery, and insurmountable odds are to be muscled through. "To Marines, failure is never an option."[74] When faced with an overwhelming condition, "You suck it up, you deal with it, you deal with the situation."[75] The Marine conception of discipline has also come to include the restraint required when conducting offensive operations against an elusive enemy hiding within sometimes hostile civilian communities. Responding to an excess of force used by Marines in Haditha, Iraq, in 2006, Lt. Gen. Jim Mattis reinforced the expected discipline standard: "No matter how provoked, a marine has to suck it up, stay friendly one minute longer and not turn into a racist. The goal is to diminish the enemy, not to recruit for him."[76]

Marines claim that their professionalism and discipline account for a higher degree of success than other services in training foreign forces in the field. They argue that indigenous trainees respond better to a mentor they can respect, who brings stature, bearing, and professionalism to the equation. Marines actively cultivate a distinctive body language—"bearing." They train to hold themselves differently, look people directly in the eye, inspire confidence, exude competence, and radiate the sort of leadership that others will yearn to emulate.[77] When proper bearing is achieved, Marines believe the natural result is admiration and a desire for emulation. It is important to note that Marine focus here is on *who they are* and *how they present themselves*, rather than the other side of the equation: treatment of and effective training for indigenous trainees.

Characteristics and behaviors not included in the requirements of Marine-defined professionalism and discipline deserve attention as possible blind spots. Discipline, in the Marine mind, is not incongruent with extraordinarily rough habits, including heavy alcohol and tobacco use, womanizing, and caustic language. Underage binge drinking and the rampant availability of pornography and tobacco are all part and parcel of enlisted life. (Terminal Lance makes a point of this by crafting a "food pyramid" for corporals, which places tobacco as the mainstay, supplemented with alcohol and energy drinks, reinforced by porn to reduce the "pain" of Marine life absurdities.[78]) The Corps has made an attempt to ameliorate substance abuse, with limited effect.[79] Issues of sexual assault have only recently received serious attention. Admiring as he is of the Corps, Thomas Ricks notes that the Marine Corps does worst of the services in Department of Defense (DOD) assessments of sexual harassment.[80] Up until January 2012, a search of "sexual assault" or "sexual offenses" over the entire *Gazette* and *Leatherneck* histories (each nearly one hundred years) yielded fewer than twenty articles. Commandant James F. Amos's "war on sexual assault" prompted by the DOD's searing internal report examining the problem in 2012 has demanded far more attention be paid to the issue.[81] Writing with passion in 2014, Lt. Col. David Bardorf acknowledged that the Pentagon's findings regarding the scope of the problem within the Marine Corps "gashed the soul of a Service that prides itself on its core values of honor, courage, and commitment." Further acknowledged is that "prevention will require cultural change and engaged leadership" and will likely be achieved only over an extended time horizon.[82] Rallying as a response to the Marines United scandal, female Marines publicly rededicated themselves to speaking up, to providing more attentive mentorship to female recruits, and to not allowing fear of ostracism or retaliation to keep them quiet. They know they are playing the long game: "We have no illusions. Changing a culture is even harder than changing policy."[83]

The discursive habits among Marines are a likely contributor to the cultural environment now under scrutiny as too permissive of sexual offenses.[84] While tightly scripted in what is said to officers and how one addresses civilians on base, Marines' repartee with one another—often projected into public view (in forms such as memoirs, blogs, comics, and YouTube videos)—is rife with base, sexually charged references interwoven with gratuitous profanity. Marines would not disagree with this charge. They take a certain pride in it. Flexing creative and witty muscle by inventing a new form of even further degraded insult is part and parcel of the alpha male brotherhood. In this, Marines have become genuinely "desensitized" to the impact of exceptionally coarse language and sexually explicit references. They tend to scorn the offended and discount the prospect that some of their bumpier relations with foreign nationals may stem from this practice. The ban on cursing that exists for DIs (and recruits) at Marine Corps boot camp indicates that, at some level, the Corps recognizes that profoundly offensive language is *offensive* and a signal of indiscipline. Nonetheless, queries regarding the possibility that Marines might apply the same clean-cut standards to vocabulary that they do to haircuts are most often met with quick rebuke: "It will never happen."

## Teamwork and "The Individual Marine"

The unique brotherhood of the Marines presents another set of paradoxical values that make up an essential component of their Corps: the tension between valuing teamwork and valuing the individual Marine. Marines do indeed value the team, a concept drummed into them both psychologically and physically in boot camp. Spooner's legends continue this theme into the field. Despite the availability of larger-than-life Marine heroes, his collection of tales, for the most part, focuses on the ordinary Marine and his unit.[85]

Cameo appearances of famous Marines are peppered throughout but do not dominate the story line. Teamwork—moving as a unit, training, patrolling, and even socializing in brotherhoods—is the consistent image throughout.

An emphasis on teamwork is not surprising coming from the Marine Corps. Far more surprising, especially for those who have been socialized to regard being called "individual" as insult, is the emphasis in commandants' speeches on "the individual Marine." Commandants do speak of brotherhood but more often of *the individual Marine*. From Thomas Holcomb in 1943: "The emphasis *still* is on the *individual*. As always, each man is trained just as if the outcome of the entire war depends on *his personal success*—as indeed it does to a higher degree than he is likely to realize."[86] David M. Shoup in the run-up to Vietnam: "The Marine Corps continues to emphasize the importance of the small unit leader and the individual Marine. Success in battle ultimately depends on them."[87] And Leonard F. Chapman Jr. in the thick of it: "[Chapman's] summation of this first trip to Vietnam as CMC [commandant of the Marine Corps] ('But not my last') is an even firmer conviction that the key to successful Corps operations in Vietnam rests solely with the individual Marine."[88]

The paradox is made sensible when context and repetition reveal that the commandants' concern is nothing like the American cultural notion of "individual"—a focus on personal needs and rights—but rather a concern for the excellent craftsmanship, fine-tuning, and careful maintenance of an *individual weapon*. The Marine is a *weapon*. In this, the paradox is undone, and the prose becomes a natural fit with leatherneck culture. The "transformation" glamorized by Marine Corps advertising is a promise that the Corps will take untried, somewhat ordinary human material and transform it into a state-of-the-art lethal weapon. Recruits expect this of the Corps. At the end of their training, they want to stand with fellow Devil Dogs Col. Norman L. Cooling and Lt. Col. Roger B. Turner and say, "The principle [*sic*] weapon system aboard an amphibious ship is not the main battery or the aviation squadron—it is the Marine."[89]

## Combat Prowess

Weaponizing Marines comes with its own set of norms cultivated across the institutional history of the Marine Corps. The concept that dominates Marine identity, that theirs is "the finest fighting institution in the world,"[90] manned with "fighters who are ready, willing, and able to win,"[91] is married to a set of practices aimed at making that claim a reality. Unpacking the norms and values that attend the Marine brand of fighting and what they perceive as the fighting characteristics that "win" is essential to understanding their combat practices and how these might suit in a counterinsurgency environment. The Marine-as-fighter persona is reinforced in even the most mundane organizational norms. Marines do not dig foxholes. They dig "fighting holes." Foxholes are for hiding in. Fighting holes are a "weapon to kill the enemy."[92] Ricks tracks the implications of the "fighting" value on leadership advancement within the Corps. In the platoon he is following, Recruit Lee is made the "guide" for his group because he performed best in "combat hitting skills."[93]

Though not specifically trained toward, bravery bordering on insanity—an extreme form of audaciousness (a value that *is* consciously cultivated)—is "oorahed" in the Corps and is a signature of many legendary heroes. What might be diagnosed as clinical psychosis in civilian society is loved and revered if it is geared toward the good of the Corps. Describing his boot camp DIs, one Marine reminisced:

> Instructors were hardcore, Gunnery Sgt. Lamar among them. He was a former sniper, a man of high morals, very honorable, and could bring on the pain. Gunnery Sgt. Leonard was a regular guy and the easiest, not a good platoon sergeant. Sgt. Wyatt was sadistic but the best of all because he was hard, a sniper and was crazy. He would destroy us to no end until you liked it. Then he would increase the temperature in order to make you hate it. He was constantly trying to break morale. [He'd] talk crap to belittle you and laugh at you, but he was the most respected drill instructor in the whole platoon. He tried the hardest to teach us stuff, spent extra night[s] when he didn't need to, and [went] . . . out of his way to make the platoon learn.[94]

The resultant Marine fighting ethos has mixed results. Craig M. Cameron claims that attempts to achieve the impossibly high standard of bravery under fire worked well for World War II–era Devil Dogs and other times "conflicted with more rational, commonly accepted military practices, and at these times the marines paid a price in blood incommensurate with their accomplishments."[95] On the flip side, Marines relish the upshots of a reputation that precedes them. State Department political officer Kael Weston had this to say about the Marines' reception in his area of Afghanistan: "The Afghans love the Marines. They fear the Marines the most, but in a warrior culture they respected them the most. They know that when the Marines are in town, the sheriff is here. The Army guys are not bad, [but] they are not as aggressive. The Afghans respond to the aggressiveness."[96] This sentiment was echoed, but in more negative form, by a Marine veteran from Afghanistan who noted that civilians near the base would stop what they were doing and emit vibes of fear, awe, or apprehension when the Marines walked by. If soldiers passed by, they would just keep sweeping.[97]

The excellent craftsmanship and fine-tuning required in making Marines the lethal weapons they aim to be comprises many of the martial arts but none more important than marksmanship. "Every Marine a rifleman" is not just a motto. It is institutional practice. Cooling and Turner note:

> Because Marines do not recognize artificial battlespace divisions such as those associated with the deep, close, and rear fights, the Marine Corps seeks to train every Marine as a rifleman. In other words, regardless of a Marine's military occupational specialty (MOS), he or she is expected to be able to proficiently fight hand-to-hand and with infantry weapons systems up to and including heavy machine guns. . . . Consistent with its warrior culture, Marines do not think of themselves as pilots, logisticians, or infantrymen. They are Marines, and they can all fight.[98]

The rifle is central to the collective Marine persona and identity, so it is unsurprising that in Spooner's legends the combat expertise valued most is marksmanship—mentioned significantly more times than any other skill. In his stories, success is consistently attributed to "carefully aimed rifle fire," compelling other forces to note the "fighting skills and remarkable marksmanship of the American Leathernecks."[99] It is worth noting that it was not until the early Banana Wars era that marksmanship became signature fare for Marines.[100] It is a norm, however, that Marines have developed and come to own. Commandants' speeches supply no end of emphasis on competence with the rifle. Leading the Corps in the years just before combat forces hitting beaches in Vietnam, Commandant Shoup, famous for his "Shoupisms," quipped that although not all Marines had the new M14 rifle, not "a single enemy will remain unshot for this reason."[101] Presiding on the other side of the Vietnam years, Commandant Cushman reminds his commanders that "even with the advanced weaponry available to the Corps today, the individual Marine and his rifle is still the key to combat success. . . . 'One round–one hit' will be as valuable to the Marine leader of the next war as they have been to the leaders of all wars which comprise our proud history."[102]

Marines overtly celebrate their enjoyment of a firing weapon. Of the twenty-six "Fighter Identity and Ethos" slogans cataloged during research for this book, nearly half were "firing-oriented," including such gems as "Happiness is . . . a belt-fed weapon," "When in Doubt . . . Empty the Magazine," and "MARINE SNIPER: You Can Run but You Die Tired." General Mattis caused no small dustup with the American public (but only further endeared himself to Marines) when, during a public panel discussion, he cheerfully declared of his modern adversaries: "Actually it's quite fun to fight them, you know. It's a hell of a hoot. It's fun to shoot some people. I'll be right up there with you. I like brawling. You go into Afghanistan, you got guys who slap women around for five years because they didn't wear a veil. You know, guys like that ain't got no manhood left anyway. So it's a hell of a lot of fun to shoot them."[103]

Enthusiasm aside, the "they can all fight" bit of Marine mentality may be dangerous if applied with slogan-borne hubris. Infantry Marines see themselves (understandably) as preeminent in this regard, a class apart from POG "riflemen." Training is required of all, but training may not guarantee combat-ready proficiency. An overconfidence in the "every Marine a rifleman" mantra may have serious consequences when stretched too far. Marines in Vietnam's Combined Action Platoon (CAP) program existed by their wits and infantry training at the squad level and had little patience for replacements from the "rear" if these draftees hadn't invested sufficiently in their marksmanship.[104]

Genuine skill with the rifle may not be spread evenly throughout the Corps, but the egalitarian spirit of "all as fighters" permeates this service to a degree significantly deeper than its sisters and forges a general valuing of fighting skill over any other sort of military competence. When without firing metal, Marines are expected to remain a weapon personified and must use whatever is at hand. From Spooner's lore: "The company gunnery sergeant made a good argument for carefully aimed rifle fire as he passed the word to all hands that if they were to run out of ammo because of the loss of the dump, they would fight with bayonets, K-Bar knives or their bare hands."[105]

## Man versus Machine

The Corps, more than Army, Navy, or Air Force, emphasizes man over machine in its doctrine.[106] The Marine Corps's text *Warfighting* makes explicit the Corps's emphasis: "No degree of technological development or scientific calculation will diminish the human dimension in war."[107] General Mattis, in the 2006 introduction to the Corps's *Small-Unit Leader's Guide to Counterinsurgency*, reinforces this point when applied to insurgents: "There is no magic bullet, nor technological breakthrough that will win this fight for us. The human factor, more than ever, will determine the victor in this test of wills."[108] While technology is appreciated and employed, it is the frontline Marine—the grunt—that is the Corps's main investment. Lt. Col. Frank G. Hoffman cites as evidence that "the Corps invests a larger portion of its budget in personnel than any of the Services, and invests more on a per capita basis on selection, initial training, and development."[109]

*Warfighting* overtly downplays any romance with high technology: "Equipment should be easy to operate and maintain, reliable, and interoperable with other equipment. It should require minimal specialized operator training."[110] Later: "There are two dangers with respect to equipment: the overreliance on technology and the failure to make the most of technological capabilities. . . . Technology cannot and should not attempt to eliminate humanity from the process of waging war." The manual further warns that one must not become so reliant on technology as to be rendered dysfunctional without it.[111] Cooling and Turner argue that the Corps has achieved this in practice: "The Marine Corps notably avoids relying on technology to the extent of the other Services" but is not unwilling to benefit from the industrial might of its motherland. It maintains a cautious relationship with technology—benefiting from but not becoming overly dependent on it for success.[112] In this, the Marines take pride in representing a significant contrast to their sister services. They do not "man" the equipment. They equip the man.

As much as this mentality is celebrated within Marine circles, it may come as a bit of surprise to those who regard them from afar. Compared to the US Army and US Air Force, the Marine Corps may be man-centric, but in the world of international militaries they still present a formidable technological presence. Ben Anderson, a British journalist observing the changing of the guard from the British Army to US Marine forces in Helmand Province in 2009, registered a level of awe when the Marine machine landed: "The British Army had shown incredible bravery and suffered horrendous losses, yet it was impossible not to see the US Marines, with their billions of dollars' worth of new equipment, unlimited support, aggressive ambition and unapologetic bluster, as the big boys coming to take charge."[113]

Marines reside in a technologically advanced and technologically driven national military. Theirs will be a constant battle to keep eyes fastened on manpower while awash in the siren calls of technological fixes to warfare's problems. This tension is represented in the *Gazette*, which celebrates the investment in frontline Marines but spends a significant number of its pages on technological advancements or prompts for innovations, including calls for competency across the cyber spectrum. Some Marine authors have openly derided the infantry focus necessary for maneuver warfare and claim it as anachronistic in the cyber age.[114] An award-winning essay in the *Gazette* complained of cultural elements that stifle adequate development of expertise in advanced computer-based systems, capturing this mentality through the words of an infantry lieutenant colonel who quipped: "The more I learn about these computers the smaller my biceps get."[115]

Tension notwithstanding, Marines remain the consciously cultivated technological underdog of the US military services. In this, they do maintain an advantage for US forces in counterinsurgent warfare. Devil Dogs' caution in their relationship with technology and continuing institutional emphasis on self-reliance and on-the-fly fixes place Marines in a better-prepared position than their American military counterparts to serve in austere environments and navigate fighting terrain where advanced weapon technology may not follow. As much as it is valued, the Corps will have to continue a conscious and well-defended fight to keep its focus on investment in personnel rather than technologically advanced military property as it pushes through the twenty-first century.

## Penny Pinching

Not all Marine distance from technology is due to martial philosophy; some of it is due to fiscal austerity. Marines have made forced frugality a Devil Dog virtue by embracing "a willingness to make do with less."[116] Lt. Gen. Victor H. Krulak titles part IV of *First to Fight* "The Penny Pinchers" and credits Commandant Archibald Henderson (1820–59) with establishing institutional frugality as something beyond necessity: a Marine principle.[117] Even Builder, despite his scholarship emphasis on the Army, Navy, and Air Force, pauses to take note of Marine Corps thrift, commenting on the "hand-me-down equipment" wielded by men and women who take "more pride in who they are than in what they own."[118]

Again, this mentality must be viewed through the optic of a first-world nation that spends in excess of $400 billion on its military.[119] Despite their membership in the globe's most technologically advanced and lavishly funded military force, Marines may argue that they are being sent to perform a hegemon's tasks with only a fraction of its resources. Marine authors of all sorts love to prove the point by quoting Corps budget numbers to the public. Typical of commandants before him, Commandant Amos took to the budget-boasting stage in 2011 with numbers to prove that "the Marine Corps has always given our Nation the 'best bang for its buck.'" During the fiscal year he cited, 2010, "the United States Marine Corps consumed only 8.5% of the DOD budget, while it provided our Nation 31% of its ground operating forces, 12% of its fighter/attack aircraft and 19% of the Nation's attack helicopters." Marines have learned to make a virtue, and public hay, out of getting the short end of the stick: "At the end of the day, Congress and the American people know that the Marine Corps is a value and that we only ask for what we truly need."[120]

To make up for their limited means, the Corps cheerfully consumes hand-me-downs,[121] hoards goods like Depression-era grandmothers, and has made a virtue of the "honorable art of institutional theft."[122] One Marine recounts a joyful swag grab in Kuwait: "We were doing . . . camp take down. . . . A bunch of Brits had left already and we were taking down all their tents. And my guys were just going crazy over the gear they left. . . . It was like Christmas for them. . . . It's something in the Marine Corps so when we get hand-me-downs and find stuff [like] that it's just like a holiday."[123] Both practical and paranoid, "Marines have been known to hoard goods such as folders, toilet paper, MREs [meals ready to eat], magazines, etc., as the rainy day—or existential threat to the unit or Corps—might be around the corner." Accepted behaviors in the "theft" category include "appropriating" Army-issued goods whenever the opportunity arises. "Appropriating" also means stripping kits of needed gear within Marine Corps circles. "As the Marine aphorism goes, 'there's only one thief in the Marine Corps. Everyone else is just getting their stuff back.'"[124] In good DOD fashion, Marines have made an acronym of their pickpocket practice: STEAL (Strategically Taking Equipment to Another Location).[125] One Vietnam-era CAP Marine fondly recalls a "hero" from his unit:

> Lt. Silvia, our Delta Company Commander, was kind of a legend for two reasons. First, he was a great thief, he stole one of those big generators from the Air Force Base just so he and the guys could keep their beer and pop cold. Second, [h]e was coming back down . . . [Road One] and took small arms fire . . . so he called in artillery . . . waited for a reactionary squad and checked out the enemy KIA's [killed in action] with just a pistol. . . . Got to love that.[126]

Thieving and fighting credentials both. A solid Marine.

By necessity, the frugality norm mandates an attendant valuing of ingenuity to make up for material shortcomings. In this the Marines seem to defy Colin Gray's characterization of US armed forces: "Strategic necessity is the mother of military invention, and since the 1860s, at least, Americans have had little need to invent clever work-arounds for material lack."[127] Marines would beg to differ. Marine lore is full of work-around stories, the necessity of which seem to defy explanation given the largesse of Big Tent Army.[128] The explanation is not just the American military's material contempt for the Marine Corps—it is also a natural repercussion of being out in front of supply lines. Again, the Corps has made a virtue out of material shortages and publicizes it as a natural fit with life in the "seams." Commandant Amos points out that the Corps is ideally suited for expeditionary crisis response, in part, because "we're trained and willing to live pretty austerely."[129] Austerity, in this case, might be best captured by Fick, who lived it. Marines are frugal not only in substance, but in other dimensions as well: "The Marine Corps has an institutional culture of doing more with less, and that includes not only less money and less equipment but also less time, less certainty, less guidance, and less supervision."[130]

## Suffering

Doing more with less comes with a dose of externally imposed misery. Marines deem this insufficient and impose more. In Spooner's tales, "sweating, tired Marines wearing gas masks and marching along a dusty road under a blistering tropical sun" are made to do air raid drills over and over again. Disgusted, "Fearless Frank" asks, "Why do we always have to practice to be miserable?" Ross shoots back with, "'Cause when we really are miserable we'll be so accustomed to it that it won't seem so bad."[131] Ross may be right.

Relishing the rough life seems to fit Marines for their selected "lane." Marines are far more comfortable and happy with expeditionary duty than soldiers. They know how to "pack their trash" and make the worst circumstances seem like a party. In Ricks's words, they "tend to display a kind of funky joie de vivre, especially in the field," where he watched them make a Mogadishu party out of random chunks of meat, several tiny bottles of Tabasco sauce (stolen from the Navy galley), and Little Richard's greatest hits pumping from a Walkman hooked to miniature speakers. "They knew how to live—a sharp contrast to the infantry squad from the Army's 10th Mountain Division that I saw in Haiti sitting bored in a tent, reading dirty magazines, and grousing about its cold rations."[132] Marines are conscious of their distinctiveness in this category. When asked what separated Marine from Army units in Iraq, Cory Carlisle—a Marine lance corporal who was medically retired in 2006—reflected on his service in Fallujah by saying, "Tactically—and this is huge—we are happy in misery. . . . In fact, it's funny because [now that I am out] I am almost nostalgic to be miserable."[133]

Ricks argues that misery and suffering have become intrinsic values for Marines.[134] O'Connell agrees and argues that this is one way in which Marine Corps culture parallels a religious order:

While members of the Army, Navy, and Air Force . . . speak approvingly of tradition, morale, and the bonds of fraternity, their training literature, memoirs, and service journals make no mention of "spiritual unity" or ghosts, and they do not refer to their service as a "religion," as the literature of the Marine Corps did. Nor did the other services have quite the same deep veneration of suffering, which offered prestige in exchange for a demonstrated capacity to endure hardship.[135]

O'Connell argues that recruits learn to measure their worth according to their capacity to suffer. "Recruits learned, in ways they would not forget, that what made Marines exceptional was their ability to endure more pain than members of their sister services."[136] One Marine veteran conveys the status Marines derive from living the rough life:

The first [tour in Iraq] we pretty much didn't have any supplies. We got like three pairs of socks that we'd have to try to wash with a rock and a bar of soap to try to clean off because they were rock hard. We didn't take showers for a few months; clothes were quite dirty and grimy after a few months of not being washed. We really didn't get a whole lot of food. Sometimes we would have to ration off the water because they didn't bring enough to us. That's part of what sucks about being ahead of everybody, but at the same time it makes you feel like more of a badass than them and you run off with a certain factor of pride.[137]

O'Connell points out that the Marine veneration of suffering has tactical repercussions. His research indicates that the Marine approach in the Pacific during World War II resulted in quicker successes but a higher casualty rate than the Army's. Perhaps counterintuitive for a civilian, "the presence of a rival service performing similar missions but with fewer casualties did not degrade the Marines' esprit de corps; it increased it." For Marines their higher casualty numbers proved they were taking the blunt end of the fight and were more deserving of admiration, even when both services achieved the same objectives.[138]

Cory Carlisle sees the Marine valuing of misery as offering positive tactical advantages in a counterinsurgency fight. From his perspective, embracing misery and suffering means that Marines are not afraid to go out and get their hands dirty in the messy frontline tasks of population-centric operations. He perceives the Army as having a threshold it wants to stay within. The Marine Corps has a much wider berth of things its grunts are willing to do because they are capable of being miserable. In Carlisle's experience, "boot camp is about making you be as miserable as they possibly can." After suffering the consistent tortures the Corps inflicts, "combat is a breeze."[139] While certainly said with a smile and no small dose of hyperbole, Carlisle means to make a point. Marines do relish misery, and they believe it affords them a tactical edge.

## NOTES

1. Builder, *Masks of War*, 18–20.
2. Lt. Col. Frank Hoffman, USMC (Ret.), who also stepped in to fill this gap, agrees for the most part with this assessment. Hoffman also adds teamwork and subordination of the individual to the common good, combat readiness, and expeditionary ethos as altars of worship for Marines. Hoffman, "Marine Mask of War."
3. Smith, *The Few and the Proud*, 253 (italics added).
4. Ibid., 270.
5. Gy.Sgt. John H. Lofland, "I Am a Marine!," *Marine Corps Gazette* (November 1976): 23.
6. Oral history file AFC 2001/001/53039 MS01, Veterans History Project, American Folklife Center, Library of Congress.
7. Bernard, *Research Methods in Anthropology*, 187.
8. A further testament is the cameo on Spooner that O'Connell provides as opening material in the first chapter of *Underdogs*, his recently published book on

the Corps. O'Connell describes the Globe and Laurel as "part restaurant, part museum, and part Marine Corps shrine." O'Connell, *Underdogs*, 24–26.

9. Spooner, *Marine Anthology*, ix.

10. Krulak, *First to Fight*, 156.

11. Maj. Gen. John A. Lejeune, "It's in Their Blood," *Marine Corps Gazette* (December 1921): 415.

12. Maj. Gen. John A. Lejeune, "Preparation," *Marine Corps Gazette* (March 1922): 55.

13. 1st Lt. Sidney J. Handsley, "Esprit de Corps," *Marine Corps Gazette* (September 1921): 311, 310.

14. O'Connell asserts: "Few military organizations think of their culture as a form of power; the Marines do so explicitly, protect it zealously, and deploy it offensively." O'Connell, *Underdogs*, 19.

15. Maj. Gen. Thomas Holcomb, "Our 168th Anniversary: A Message from the Commandant," *Marine Corps Gazette* (November 1943): 5.

16. Gen. Wallace M. Greene Jr., "Special Message from New CMC," *Marine Corps Gazette* (January 1964): 1.

17. Maj. Jason Spitaletta, USMC, correspondence with the author, October 25, 2011.

18. These findings coincide with Ricks's tracking of recruits from boot camp through the inevitable disappointments of post–boot camp life. Despite letdowns in other areas, Ricks finds the "brotherhood" good still intact. Ricks, *Making the Corps*, 249.

19. Dakota Meyers, interview, *Daily Show with Jon Stewart*, October 24, 2012, http://www.cc.com/video-clips/4chwwp/the-daily-show-with-jon-stewart -dakota-meyer.

20. Oral history file AFC 2001/ 001/78228 MS02, Veterans History Project.

21. Maj. Jason Spitaletta, USMC, correspondence with the author, October 25, 2011.

22. L.Cpl. Kaleb Bench, correspondence with the author, August 18, 2008.

23. Salmoni and Holmes-Eber, *Operational Culture*, 280–81.

24. Letter provided via Dan Lamothe, "Frustrated with Misogyny, Hundreds of Female Marines Have Joined a Group Pressuring Male Colleagues to Change," *Washington Post*, April 11, 2017, https://www.washingtonpost.com/news /checkpoint/wp/2017/04/11/frustrated-with-misogyny-hundreds-of-female -marines-have-joined-a-group-pressuring-male-colleagues-to-change/?utm _term=.c41898d5c891. Commandant Gen. Robert Neller acknowledged that the root of the sexual harassment problem was cultural and renewed the Corps's commitment to addressing it. Jeff Schogol, "Top Marine: Nude Photo-Sharing Scandal Shows 'We've Got to Change,'" *Marine Times*, March 14, 2017.

25. See chapters 18 through 22 on female Marine stories in Smith, *The Few and the Proud*.

26. Oral history file AFC 2001/001/49712 MS02 [1], Veterans History Project. See also AFC 2001/001/73183 MS01 and AFC 2001/001/37518 MS01.

27. Capt. Karen M. Walker, "Women Leading Men," *Marine Corps Gazette* (May 2009): 41–44.

28. For arguments in favor, see Capt. Jessica M. Hawkins, "Female Assignment Policy," *Marine Corps Gazette* (September 2012): 73–76; Maj. Amy "Krusty" McGrath, "Women in Combat," *Marine Corps Gazette* (November 2012): 47–49; Capt. Lia B. Heeter, "Women in Combat," *Marine Corps Gazette* (July 2013): 29–32; and Capt. Marissa Loya, "Combat Exclusion Policy: Outdated and Impractical," *Marine Corps Gazette* (September 2013): 78–80. An argument against is found in Capt. Katie Petronio, "Get Over It!: We Are Not All Created Equal," *Marine Corps Gazette* (July 2012): 29–32.

29. Cooling and Turner, "Understanding the Few Good Men," 8.

30. Randy Shepard, correspondence with the author, November 2, 2011.

31. Randy Shepard, "How the U.S. Marines Brought Rambo and Bono Together through Research (and Why)," demographics research and commercial campaign assessment paper prepared for J. Walter Thompson Co. and selected as a Jay Chiat Awards Winner, (2012). Pdf available at http://stratfest.aaaa.org/2012-winners/.

32. Oral history file AFC 2001/001/78228 MS02, Veterans History Project.

33. Oral history file AFC 2001/001/72364 MS01, Veterans History Project.

34. Oral history file AFC 2001/001/52380 MS02, Veterans History Project.

35. Oral history file AFC 2001/001/74501 MS01, Veterans History Project.

36. Spooner captures the Marine ethic of keeping their dead alive through one squad leader's consistent refrain: "No one is really dead until he is forgotten." His reminder is twofold: It is the obligation of every Marine to inspire vibrant remembrance of those that have fallen, and consequently, no Devil Dog need fear death in the Corps. Spooner, *Marine Anthology*, 241.

37. Commandant Gen. Randolph M. Pate, "Commandant's Birthday Message," *Marine Corps Gazette* (November 1956): 98.

38. Sturkey, *Warrior Culture of the U.S. Marines*, 21.

39. O'Connell, *Underdogs*, 40.

40. Spooner, *Marine Anthology*, 266.

41. United States Marine Corps (hereafter USMC), *Marine Corps Values and Leadership*.

42. Ricks, *Making the Corps*, 62.

43. Fick, *One Bullet Away*, 18.

44. USMC, *Marine Corps Values and Leadership*, 4-1.

45. USMC, *Warfighting*, 56, 57 (italics in original).

46. Spooner, *Marine Anthology*, 64.

47. Fick, *One Bullet Away*, 145.

48. Robert B. Asprey, "The Court-Martial of Smedley Butler," *Marine Corps Gazette* (December 1959): 30.

49. Oral history file AFC 2001/001/53039 MS01, Veterans History Project.

50. Ricks, *Making the Corps*, 92–93.

51. Spooner, *Marine Anthology*, 302–3.

52. Sledge, *With the Old Breed*, 92.

53. See an iteration on *Leatherneck*'s website: http://www.leatherneck.com/forums /showthread.php?1647-Eleanor-Roosevelt-s-quote.

54. The ability of Marines to acquire muck or allow one's blouse to come untucked will rest largely on the disposition of the closest sergeant major. The "classic" portrayal of an overzealous sergeant major enforcing dress standards in a combat-heavy arena (Iraq) is found in *Generation Kill*, an HBO series based on the book of the same title by Evan Wright (and validated by a second accounting of the same events in Nathanial Fick's *One Bullet Away*). This pseudo-documentary series is widely regarded among members of the Corps as the most true-to-life film of them ever made.

55. Gen. Leonard F. Chapman Jr., "A Letter from the CMC," *Marine Corps Gazette* (June 1970): 16.

56. Millett notes as early as 1863 a reputation for "military efficiency, discipline, and appearance." Millett, *Semper Fidelis*, 97.

57. Capt. Frank K. Evans, "The Sword of the Corps," *Marine Corps Gazette* (September 1916): 268.

58. Oral history file AFC 2001/001/68026 MS01, Veterans History Project.

59. O'Connell, *Underdogs*, 25; Spooner, *Marine Anthology*, 196–97.

60. Gen. Leonard F. Chapman Jr., "Purpose, Readiness, Quality, Progress," *Marine Corps Gazette* (April 1971): 16.

61. Fick, *One Bullet Away*, 22.

62. Oral history file AFC 2001/001/67587 MS01, Veterans History Project.

63. Maximilian Uriate, *Terminal Lance*, http://terminallance.com/2011/01/21 /terminal-lance-98-unexpected-guest/. See also http://terminallance.com/2010 /01/12/terminal-lance-3-looking-professional/.

64. "HB #4: Losing Our Traditions," *Marine Corps Gazette* (May 1999): 16.

65. Thomas Ricks, "We're Getting out of the Marines Because We Wanted to Be Part of an Elite Force," *Foreign Policy* (January 4, 2013), http://foreignpolicy .com/2013/01/04/were-getting-out-of-the-marines-because-we-wanted-to-be -part-of-an-elite-force-2/.

66. Maj. John H. Russell Jr., employing a quote borrowed from British rear admiral Richard Kempenfelt (1718–82) in a precommandant write-up, "A Plea for a Mission and Doctrine," *Marine Corps Gazette* (June 1916): 114.

67. Smith, *The Few and the Proud*.

68. O'Connell, *Underdogs*, 37.

69. Ricks, *Making the Corps*, 71.

70. "Have I trained a bunch of nasty undisciplined privates?!" Woulfe captures "typical" DI discourse with recruits entering the Crucible phase of training. Woulfe, *Into the Crucible*, 10.

71. USMC, *Marine Corps Values and Leadership*, 2–3.

72. Marine humor often reflects this theme. See http://twitpic.com/8gpdp5.

73. Cooling and Turner, "Understanding the Few Good Men."

74. Ibid.

75. Sgt. Dax Carpenter, commenting on his approach to severe posttraumatic stress disorder while still in combat. Oral history file AFC 2001/001/57035 MS01, Veterans History Project.

76. Quoted in West, *Strongest Tribe*, 155.

77. Dye, *Backbone*, 19–29.

78. Uriate, *Terminal Lance*, http://terminallance.com/2010/04/16/terminal-lance -30-the-lance-corporal-food-pyramid/.

79. Jason Raper, "Marine Corps Substance Abuse Program: It's Time to Implement Change," *Marine Corps Gazette* (July 2012); Tom Bartlett, "Alcohol Abuse," *Leatherneck* (September 1982); H. J. Sage, "Marines and Alcohol," *Marine Corps Gazette* (December 1976). For a particularly candid assessment of this problem as assessed by a Marine, see Thomas James Brennan, "In the Military, the Drinking Can Start on Day 1," *New York Times*, October 1, 2012, http:// atwar.blogs.nytimes.com/2012/10/01/in-the-military-the-drinking-can-start -on-day-1/.

80. Ricks, *Making the Corps*, 204.

81. The search terms "sexual assault" and "sexual offenses" yielded eighteen articles up until January 2012. A little over four years later (September 2016), the number had jumped to 101.

82. Lt. Col. David Bardorf, "Stamping Out Sexual Assault," *Marine Corps Gazette* (July 2014): 25.

83. Letter provided via Lamothe, "Frustrated with Misogyny."

84. Michael DeSa, "The Fray in Our Institutional Fabric," *Marine Corps Gazette* (December 2014): 14–18.

85. Chesty Puller, Dan Daly, "Manila John" Basilone, and Smedley Butler typically top the list.

86. Holcomb, "Our 168th Anniversary," 5 (italics in original).

87. Anonymous, "Corps Standing Tall; Ready, Willing, Able," *Marine Corps Gazette* (April 1961): 1.

88. "Individual Marine Is Key, Says CMC," *Marine Corps Gazette* (February 1968): 1.

89. Cooling and Turner, "Understanding the Few Good Men."

90. Capt. August Immel, "My Tribe Is the Marine Corps," *Marine Corps Gazette* (July 2010): 59.

91. Maj. John E. Coonradt, "Corps Values," *Marine Corps Gazette* (September 1998): 27.

92. Fick, *One Bullet Away*, 28.

93. Ricks, *Making the Corps*, 76.

94. Oral history file AFC 2001/001/17844 MS01, Veterans History Project.

95. Cameron, *American Samurai*, 36.

96. Kael Weston, correspondence with the author, February 1, 2012.

97. Oral history file AFC 2001/001/48860 MS01, Veterans History Project.

98. Cooling and Turner, "Understanding the Few Good Men."
99. Spooner, *Marine Anthology*, 48, 74, 76, 82, 249.
100. Ulbrich, *Preparing for Victory*, 16
101. "Grim Determination, but No Hate," *Marine Corps Gazette* (December 1961): 1.
102. "CMC Issues Challenge," *Marine Corps Gazette* (June 1975): 4.
103. "General: It's 'Fun to Shoot Some People,'" CNN.com, February 4, 2005, http://www.cnn.com/2005/US/02/03/general.shoot/.
104. Oral history file 2599, USMC Vietnam War Oral History Collection, Marine Corps Archives and Special Collections, Gray Research Center, Quantico, VA. See also Klyman, "Combined Action Program," and oral history file 2367, USMC Vietnam War Oral History Collection. Transcription by Lacey Lee, February 21, 2012.
105. Spooner, *Marine Anthology*, 249.
106. A distinction must be made for the US Army Special Forces, part of the larger US Army but a subculture apart in their focus on cleverness and ingenuity in order to complete mission sets. Hoffman, "Marine Mask of War," 2.
107. USMC, *Warfighting*, 14.
108. Mattis, foreword, *Small-Unit Leader's Guide*.
109. Hoffman, "Marine Mask of War," 2.
110. USMC, *Warfighting*, 65.
111. Ibid., 67.
112. Cooling and Turner, "Understanding the Few Good Men."
113. Anderson, *No Worse Enemy*, 60.
114. Maj. Michael S. Chmielewski, "Maybe It's Time to Reconsider Maneuver Warfare," *Marine Corps Gazette* (August 2002).
115. Maj. Robert M. Flowers, "It Is Broken," *Marine Corps Gazette* (May 2004): 45.
116. USMC, *Marine Corps Operating Concepts*, 8.
117. Krulak, *First to Fight*, 141.
118. Builder, *Masks of War*, 208.
119. US Department of Defense, "DoD Releases Fiscal 2015 Budget Proposal and 2014 QDR," news release NR-111-14, March 4, 2014, http://archive.defense.gov/releases/release.aspx?releaseid=16567.
120. Speech given before the Marines Memorial Association, San Francisco, and printed in the *San Diego Union Tribune*: "Military: Gen. James Amos Outlines Vision of Marine Corps," *San Diego Tribune*, February 8, 2011, http://www.sandiegouniontribune.com/sdut-military-gen-james-amos-outlines-vision-of-marine-2011feb08-story.html.
121. Ricks, *Making the Corps*, 199.
122. Krulak, *First to Fight*, 150–51.
123. Oral history file AFC 2001/001/65466 MS01, Veterans History Project.
124. Salmoni and Holmes-Eber, *Operational Culture*, 278.
125. Dye, *Backbone*, 9.

126. Response from Steve Markley, CAP veteran, to a CAPMarines@yahoogroups query regarding CAP legends, October 31, 2012.

127. Gray, "Irregular Enemies," 39.

128. For one that features a Humvee repair via boot band (an article mandatory to "squared-away" appearance) and bootlace, see Dye, *Backbone*, 10–18. For another that details the out-of-pocket expenses involved in jerry-rigging Humvees with civilian-fare CB antennas, see Fick, *One Bullet Away*, 166.

129. Eliason, "Interview with James F. Amos," 15.

130. Fick, *One Bullet Away*, 320.

131. Spooner, *Marine Anthology*, 319–20.

132. Ricks, *Making the Corps*, 21.

133. L.Cpl. Cory Carlisle, correspondence with the author, January 15, 2015.

134. Ricks, *Making the Corps*, 150.

135. O'Connell, *Underdogs*, 42.

136. Ibid., 36.

137. Oral history file AFC 2001/001/67094 MS01, Veterans History Project.

138. O'Connell, *Underdogs*, 54.

139. L.Cpl. Cory Carlisle, correspondence with the author, January 15, 2015.

# CHAPTER 5

# "WE DO WINDOWS"

## Marine Norms and Perceptual Lens

The norms Marines cultivate and the perceptual lens that gives them meaning are shaped by the lane in the "seams" that they have claimed: ready versatility. The Corps's commitment to "doing windows"—whatever task its nation asks of it—is buttressed by a set of norms and values that include speedy action, consciously cultivated flexibility, an emphasis on innovation at the point of friction, a somewhat loose regard for doctrine, and insistence that executive decision making be pushed to junior levels for maximum flexibility and effectiveness. Marines shore up their claim as the nation's most ready and versatile force by immersing recruits in a culture that prioritizes above all else a commitment to mission. As an organization, the Marine Corps maintains a steady state of paranoia concerning its institutional viability. Given the Corps's history on the nation's organizational chopping block and its narrow escapes over time, Corps leadership continues to remind new initiates that their institutional survival depends on a nation enamored of its Marine Corps. The overriding perceptual lens is that full-spectrum mission accomplishment, at whatever cost, is the key to keeping the Marine Corps in business.

## NORMS

The norms, or preferred modes of behavior, that Marines expect of themselves define the force in important ways. Norms capture not only what is acceptable and routine but also the infractions that separate "in" from "out" group members. The norms that are most celebrated often feed into aspects of identity and offer behavioral evidence that a highly prized reputation is well earned. The repercussion can be that favored norms are pursued for purposes beyond their immediate utility within any particular context.


## Bias for Action

Omnipresent throughout Marine tales, doctrine, self-descriptions, and training is lived evidence of the Marine maxim, bias for action. Enshrined in Marine Corps doctrine, repeated as a catechism by officers, and attributed to George S. Patton Jr. is the ardently held belief that "a good plan violently executed *now* is better than a perfect plan executed next week."[1] For Marines, "intense" and "motivated" constitute verbal praise. "Boots" are rewarded for "aggressiveness" and "audacity." Kael Weston, a State Department officer who served with Marines for several consecutive years in both Iraq and Afghanistan, described the result: The "Marine instinct is to sprint, they are twitch muscle guys."[2]

The way this plays out in the field is described by Marine veteran Joseph Mariani:

> [My story starts with] a sign in Afghanistan hanging in the office of the NATO political advisor from Britain. It was the "Keep Calm and Carry On" poster from the blitz, and I was struck by how out of place it was, almost to the point of being offensive. The more I thought about it, the more I realized that this was because the sign stood for exactly the opposite of both side[s] of the Marine Corps culture. While one certainly wants to be cool under fire, there are necessarily things in war that demand determination, resolve, and emotion. Every General or senior Colonel I worked with were bundles of kinetic energy. LtGen Mills, who I worked under in both Iraq and Afghanistan, is 61 years old going on 90, but he ran 6 miles every night after work, and at a pace faster than most men half his age. Keeping sedately calm is simply not an option for Marines. And while this certainly gives rise to the YouTube chauvinism of Marines that is so annoying, it also provides the motivation and determination to accomplish the mission regardless of difficulty or cost.
>
> But that resolve alone cannot accomplish anything. Simply holding your nerve and battering away with a conventional strategy is exactly what had failed the Army in Anbar up to 2006. The other half of Marine Corps organizational culture is the rejection of the "Carry On" of the poster. With Marine forces replacing NATO troops across Helmand in 2010, the distinction was clear. Many NATO commands, even some elite Royal Marine Commando units, were content simply to hold their FOBs [forward operating bases], patrol intermittently, and, as a result, come under regular attack

when they ventured out. Marine commanders refused to simply accept the status quo for the 7 months of their deployments and across the Helmand river valley, they increased the rate of patrols and the scope of engagement with the population. It was the drive to find innovative solutions, not accept the status quo, that shaped Marine strategies in Iraq and Afghanistan.[3]

Marines are required to demonstrate initiative and employ the "70% Solution"—acting now on imperfect information rather than waiting to amass enough for a perfect judgment call.[4] Subordinates are expected to tell their superiors what they can do, not what they cannot.[5] The 1997 Marine Corps publication *Warfighting* defines boldness as "the characteristic of unhesitatingly exploiting the natural uncertainty of war to pursue major results rather than marginal ones"—a mode of action that will inevitably result in mistakes. The Marine Corps accepts that. On the other hand, *Warfighting* doctrine advises dealing "severely" with "errors of inaction or timidity."[6]

The Marine Corps bias for action is tied to at least two key features of Marine role: readiness and the ability to thrive in the chaos of a war environment. The most constant "mission" of the Corps across its varied role history has been *readiness*. Pursuant to this norm and mission set, immediate response is daily drilled into recruits during boot camp.[7] One of the few books of fictional literature listed on the commandant's reading list—*Starship Troopers*—is a sci-fi allegory of the Marines themselves. In it, author Robert Heinlein captures the essence of quick response as "on the bounce." It may be the most oft-repeated phrase in the book.[8] The immediate response impulse, married to an expeditionary nature, fosters in the Corps an "in and out mentality" where combat operations are concerned.[9] Marine expeditionary units (MEUs) execute these sorts of operations with regularity. In the last few years, in-and-out operations have included coming ashore to assist flood victims in Pakistan, rescuing a ship and crew from Somali pirates, rescuing a downed pilot (in less than ninety minutes!) in Libya, and assisting with earthquake relief and nuclear containment in Japan.[10]

When major operations are on the horizon, "paving the way" for other troops—those better suited for garrison duty—is the role Marines would prefer to fill. Their determined stubbornness to stick to the first-in/first-out role contrasts with their own early history, which was heavy with years-long occupation duty, and their twentieth- and twenty-first-century experience, in which it has been the rare exception (most famously in the Pacific campaign of World War II) for the Marine Corps to "pave the way" for other troops rather than staying alongside them for the length of the ground war and the stability operations that followed.

A second potentially problematic mentality for success in population-dense counterinsurgency operations is the Marine attachment to the notion of war as chaos. This is not, on the whole, an illegitimate assumption. War, and any battle, large or small, *is* chaos. *Warfighting*, as doctrine, is meant to prepare Marines for this environment. It is a treatise on being able to thrive in chaos—in the thick of friction, uncertainty, fluidity, disorder, and complexity. "It is precisely this natural disorder which creates the conditions ripe for exploitation by an opportunistic will."[11] If sufficient disorder to destabilize the enemy, and thus gain the advantage, does not exist, it is recommended that Marines create it: "We must not only be able to fight effectively in the face of disorder, we should seek to generate disorder and use it as a weapon against our opponents."[12] So what of a mission to stabilize rather than create chaos? To engage in civic action and patiently cultivate intelligence rather than pursue the enemy? The "small-twitch" muscles that perform so admirably in high adrenaline, constant-motion environments may threaten to short-circuit in stabilizing operations, which require restraint and a calming influence.

Marines study the tempo of war as a dimension in which victory is won by those with superior initiative and speed. *Warfighting* doctrine instructs: "In general, whoever can make and implement decisions consistently faster gains a tremendous, often decisive advantage."[13] A well-trained Fick echoes this mentality in his memoir: "Winning a firefight requires quick action by leaders. The key is to make decisions about your enemy and act on them faster than he is acting on decisions made about you."[14] Speed as a weapon, and as a stand-alone value, is so ingrained in Marine ethos that it often comes at the cost of lives. Comparing Army and Marine strategies in the Pacific, O'Connell notes that the Army was willing to conserve manpower by using methods that were effective but slow. The Marines, however, "trained for quick, decisive engagements." For them, "speed of conquest was critical; the carnage it produced was the unfortunate but necessary price for victory." The Army regarded the Marine approach as "reckless and unimaginative." The Marines, by turn, believed that the Army fell short in the key virtues of audacity and tenacity. Across their combined operations, "the Marines had higher casualty ratios but took more ground," and "the Army worked more slowly but conserved lives in ways Marine tactics did not."[15]

An insurgent force may also see the temporal sphere as a weapon but in perhaps very different terms than the Marine Corps: one of protraction and exhaustion.[16] An insurgent who knows Marines well may attempt to bait them into rash action, causing them to trample political aims in pursuit of the enemy. Maj. Jason Spitaletta characterizes the dominant personality type in the Corps as "higher strung" and notes that this is not conducive to "tactical patience." Therefore, "if in stability operations the best action is no action, it is counterintuitive" to enlisted Marines. Because of their bias for action, they may "force things unnecessarily." He notes that in a foreign theater Marines "tend to want to assume the lead and dictate how things are run," even when the more effective long-term strategy might be "enabling"—supplying support from behind.[17]

## Adapt and Overcome

The ability to adapt, innovate, and improvise is not just recommended behavior—it is core to Marine identity. Two of the five sections of Victor H. Krulak's *First to Fight* are dedicated to this topic: "The Innovators" and "The Improvisers."[18] These titles capture the action not as a transitive verb, but as an identity noun—a trait woven into the nature of the members of the Corps. In assessing the character of a Marine, USMC veteran Charles Wynn writes, "The Marine goes everywhere, does everything. It is taken for granted that nothing is impossible. He is simply ordered to do a given job. He goes and does it. Nobody tells him how. He works it out on the spot. He invariably succeeds. It never occurs to him that he may fail."[19]

"Adapt and overcome" is verse, doctrine, and expected practice. The third edition of the *Marine Corps Operating Concepts* manual (2010) opens with this injunction: "Military excellence is defined by the excellence of our Marines; their thinking, ability to innovate, adapt, and to overcome the challenges presented by complex environments, threats, and conditions."[20] Krulak claims that "improvisation has been a way of life for the Marines" and highlights the technological advancements initiated by the Corps throughout its history. He expands on this theme by pointing out that the Corps has had to remake itself as an institution—moving from "expeditionary duty in the colonial infantry role" (Haiti, China, Dominican Republic, Nicaragua) to masters of the amphibious assault and, one might further add, to today's expeditionary crisis-response force.[21]

Scholars and historians are more tempered concerning the Corps's innovative accolades. A read of Allan Millett's account of early leatherneck history makes it clear that in many instances Marine role "innovations" were largely forced on them. A rather constant theme of Marine early history is the Corps's failure to innovate even when the need is obvious and possible avenues are available. For instance, Millett records that it was pressure from the Navy, not the Corps itself, to "reorganize the Marine Corps into permanent expeditionary battalions that could develop and defend temporary advanced naval bases for the battle fleet." Marine commandant Maj. Gen. Charles Heywood (1891–1903), for his part, remained tied to the Corps's nearly obsolete duties of seagoing military service—ship guards, naval gunnery and landing party service, and a security force for Navy yards and stations. Millett characterizes the forced changes to Marine Corps roles as exogenous pressures: the forward development of the Navy and the expansionist thrust of American diplomacy.[22] It is worth noting that Millett's history, to the point referenced, predates the Marines' self-imposed image of "innovative." It is important to consider what effects embracing, inculcating, and marrying identity to such a trait have had on innovation within the modern service.

Terry Terriff examines this question via two contemporary examples: the shift from frontal assault to maneuver warfare and the less successful attempt by Commandant Charles Krulak to institutionalize "a culture of constant innovation."[23] In the first instance, Commandant Alfred M. Gray accomplished an "innovation" in the Marine way of war by turning the organization toward maneuver warfare. Terriff points out that this was no small feat, resisted by a number of factions within the Corps and successful only because of the enormous effort applied and the credibility of Gray himself. Gray personified significant investment in the "old way" of war and was therefore able to use his position as commandant and his warfighter reputation to wield the leadership necessary for the change. New identity goods in a familiar frame, "smart warrior"—alongside revised education, field training, and proven success in the field—were additional requisites for altering the annihilation warfare mind-set of a rather change-adverse body of Marines.[24]

In the second instance, Charles Krulak's attempt to institutionalize (via training and fighting methods) an identity trait already claimed by the Marine Corps—innovators—largely failed. Krulak's initiation of the Marine Corps Warfighting Laboratory (MCWL) was meant to "experiment with forward leaning concepts and technologies" and "test them to failure" in order to assess which held promise for future engagements and which did not. At the conclusion of his efforts, his officer corps was polled and the majority returned a painfully ironic assessment. The officers "viewed their service as being very open to innovation, [but] . . . also thought that the Marine Corps had no present need to innovate." Rather than seizing on the opportunity to explore innovations, the critical mass of the Corps stumbled at the open-endedness of Krulak's concept and gradually turned the MCWL into a typical deliverables-based unit for current operating forces.[25] These two episodes provide instructive lessons, and somewhat cautionary tales, for those who would hold up the Marine Corps as an innovative standard.[26]

Terriff's summary claim is that the Corps's past record of innovation "makes clear that it is willing to innovate, but this does not mean that its self-perception of being a body of 'innovators' means it accepts innovation easily."[27] Terriff's finding—that the image the Marine Corps cultivates as an innovative institution may be a far higher standard than is lived—is not entirely surprising. At the strategic and institutional levels, the Corps, like other services, faces obstacles to change as a result of its own strong identity, projected image, and carefully cultivated norms. Marine Corps efforts to continue to pursue an identity that celebrates innovation—drumming it into new recruits and reinforcing it through internal writings among officers— are not for naught, however. Demanding flexibility and creative solutions from officers and grunts on the ground may mean that Marines, while not living the ideal of institutional innovation to the levels they tout, are still better than other services at immediate-term improvisations and mission-relevant inventiveness in situations of uncertainty. Maj. Gen. Larry Nicholson claims that this is the aspect of Marine culture particularly well suited for counterinsurgency. "We prize above all else, innovation at the point of friction." He points out that this is what the Corps selects for in its officer candidates and rewards in its noncommissioned officers (NCOs). The Corps looks for individuals who can "think on their feet" and then trains them to become even better at it.[28]

Deborah Avant reinforces this concept in her work on military doctrine. Her scholarship leans heavily on Charles Krulak's testimonial of Marine innovation, contending along with him that flexibility has become "a part of the professional ethos of the marines."[29] She takes Krulak at his word—that the Marines have historically been rewarded for innovation and not usually punished if innovations fell flat. Ricks observed as much during his stint with Marines and claims that the Corps, consequently, is most adept among the American services at addressing its own faults.[30] He cites a culture of open and candid criticism, even from the bottom up. It is due to this ethos, in part, that USMC intelligence officer Ben Connable claims that the Marine Corps of the 1930s makes the grade in John Nagl's "learning organization" test: "it promoted suggestions from the field, encouraged subordinates to question policies, institutionally questioned its basic assumptions, generated local SOPs [standard operating procedures], and had a senior officer corps in close touch with men in the field."[31]

Connable builds on this claim to assert that the modern Corps is more skilled than sister services at "operating in culturally complex environments."[32] Marine doctrine assumes contextual complexity, and training follows in the same spirit by imposing swift switches of both task and location on recruits, a regimen designed to force would-be Marines to deal with situations of flux and rapid change.[33] Writing of the mind-set that shaped Marine training standards in the 1990s, James Woulfe explains, "One day they could find themselves reacting to confusing changes of environment in a short period of time. They might feed the hungry one minute and be engaging a deadly enemy with rifle fire the next." Tomorrow's Marines must be trained against getting comfortable because "their lives depend on their ability to adapt quickly to the changing situation."[34] Individual lives depend on it and, according to Victor Krulak in *First to Fight*, so does the outcome of the battle: "Try as hard as you can to be ready . . . but be willing to adapt and improvise when it turns out to be a different battle than the one you expected, because adaptability is where victory will be found."[35]

Marines are primed to contend with fast-paced, chaotic environments. Connable's claim of deftness in "culturally complex" environments is a bit of a different matter. In this the Marine Corps presents a strange dichotomy. It has been the most forward-leaning of the services in emphasizing cultural competence and investments in research and training.[36] As the men at the tip of the spear, many Marines grasp that culture impacts the way humans behave and may play a significant role in battlefront terrain. Connable's claim that Marines also possess "an innate ability to adapt to foreign cultures," however, may be a bit of a stretch.[37] Ethnocentrism drawn from their own American culture, an in-and-out mission mentality, and brotherhood insularity all inhibit substantial investment in understanding an alien culture on the part of individual Marines. Few of today's Marines would disagree that cultural competence in one's area of operations is useful. Even Spooner makes place for a cultural expert among his historical heroes: First Lieutenant Savage is a hero not for combat valor but because he exercises sound judgment and effectively trains the Haitian gendarmes by speaking their patois, understanding their culture, and respecting them as soldiers. It is notable, however that Savage is also portrayed as exceptional—a bit of a "one of a kind."[38]

Nathaniel Fick captures the typical relationship in the latter decades of the twentieth century between Marines and foreign cultures: "I realized that although [Marines] traveled a lot, they rarely saw the places they visited. Marines aren't travelers in the traditional sense. They view foreign countries either from behind a gun sight or through the haze of a night on liberty. Perspective skews to one dimension, as if the Marines are the players and everything else is a prop."[39] Fick confesses: "During planning in Kuwait, and during the first few days of the [2003 invasion], we repeatedly made the same mistake: assuming that the Iraqi military would do what we would have done in their situation."[40] Although cultural competence is emphasized to near exhaustion in the *Small Wars Manual*, Marines had not, up until the twenty-first century, systematically translated this into operational practice.

## Regard for Doctrine

The strong emphasis on adaptability and improvisation has had the effect of a somewhat rebellious-son attitude among Marines toward standard operating procedures and doctrine.[41] Capt. Joseph Mariani acknowledges the tension that characterizes the Marine relationship with doctrine. Although MCDP-1 *Warfighting* is considered "the bible" by most Marines, and one of Mariani's peers "was almost thrown out of a moving MRAP in Iraq for arguing against doctrine to his boss," the doctrine itself "is vague enough to admit almost infinite interpretations." The net result is that Marines

> also take pride in not following doctrine. There is an often repeated story at TBS [the Basic School] that Marine Advisors arrive for partnered training with another country. As they begin exercises the Marines notice the host country officers becoming increasingly agitated until a shouting match breaks out. Finally, the Marines walk over and ask what the problem is. One of the host country officers explains, "we worked for weeks reading and studying your doctrine so that we would be ready to work well when you arrived. But once you began the mission we discovered that you don't even

follow your own doctrine." The best I can say is that like religion, the Marine Corps has a few guiding principles which constantly have to be redefined to fit the context of the time and place. And it is that process, more than any particular outcome of it, that makes the Marine Corps the Marine Corps.[42]

Marine reverence for its doctrine is genuine, even if not scrupulously applied. They take pride in *Warfighting*, which is at the same time slim in verse and wide in application. In comparing doctrine generated by the Corps to that produced by its sister services, Williamson Murray writes, "The one oasis in the desert that is military doctrine remains the Marine Corps. Its doctrinal manuals connect with the real world and to the fact that the American military is supposed to be preparing and thinking seriously about war." He praises the common sense manifest in *Warfighting*, which aims to give Marines "a realistic and intelligent understanding of war's uncertainties, ambiguities, and horror."[43] Marines enjoy bragging that the Army envies the Corps's concise, intelligently flexible, and user-friendly doctrine and that soldiers are often found with a copy of *Warfighting* in hand at joint exercises. Marines may have affection for their doctrine in part because they see it as playing a less prescriptive role than the doctrine of their service counterparts. Cooling and Turner note, "Marine commanders know their doctrine and frequently apply it, but true to their naval heritage, they retain the prerogative to deviate from it. Marine authored doctrine also tends to be broader and less prescriptive than that authored by the Army."[44] Blagovest Tashev, a cultural contractor who has worked for several years alongside Marines at Quantico's Center for Advanced Operational Culture Learning, argues that for Marines

doctrine is a departing point. Marines believe that doctrine is a guideline, a warfighting philosophy, rather than a directive because only mission analysis can determine how exactly a mission is to be done. Policy cannot be a cookie cutter because according to Marines' outlook (and their doctrine, *Warfighting*) the world is replete with uncertainty, chaos, and friction. That is why policy is a point of departure. Thus, what other services see as Marines' unwillingness to be team players and just follow the rules, are simply the consequences of their doctrine; and yes, it is cultural.[45]

## Leadership

When asked what he had done in the Corps that most epitomized being a Marine, Dale Nicholas said, "The leadership." Nicholas is a corporal. As a *corporal* in the Marine Corps, leadership defined him. Leadership was "having six guys who look up to you, you are the role model. What you do, good or bad, they pick up on. You have to do what they are going to look up to." [46] Joe Mariani explains a junior officer's perspective on Marine Corps leadership:

> The command and responsibilities entrusted to junior officers (and junior NCOs for that matter) in the Marine Corps is not . . . matched in the other services. The Army promotes officers so quickly that anyone below the rank of captain is merely a warm body to fill a chair. In deployments to Iraq I would have trouble getting my counterparts from Army commands on the phone because they thought that a [lieutenant] could not possibly be the senior analyst for a regional command. Where else but in the Marine Corps would a 25 year old 1stLt be entrusted with $14 million dollars in equipment, and the only guidance I got from my commander was "as long as you don't get anyone killed, do whatever you have to do to improve ground sensor collection in Afghanistan." [47]

These two vignettes capture the twofold essence of leadership in the Corps. One aspect focuses on leadership traits (the sort of character and behavior one expects from a leader), and the second focuses on leadership dispersal—the Marine Corps commitment to push authority to the lowest levels.

In his 1916 "Plea for a Mission and Doctrine," future commandant John H. Russell Jr. foreshadows both aspects in an effort to advocate a more serious approach to leadership training within the Corps. He believed that leaders need not be born but could be made and that the Corps was falling short in training "intelligent initiative." [48] The modern Corps works to do exactly that. In fact, Julia Dye, a hoplology scholar with both academic and personal attachments to the Marine Corps, argues that "the Marine Corps treasures leadership above virtually all other qualities in the ranks; even above and beyond such obvious military virtues as bravery and tenacity in the face of danger or hardship." [49]

Spooner's legends highlight a number of the character and professional traits expected of leaders. Leaders living the Marine standard are professional, cool under fire, and competent, but most important, they take care of their men. Leadership on the front lines meant an ability to maintain discipline and, when necessary, innovate. The aspect of leadership most valued throughout the stories, however, was a willingness to get down at the level of the enlisted man, tutor him, and share his hardship. Spooner describes then major "Tony" Waller (an authentic and often publicly controversial figure) as one who "made it a point to spend time with each of his subordinate units as they moved through the fields and villages. He encouraged his Marines and reminded them of their responsibility to uphold the proud traditions of the Corps. The Marines loved and respected Waller and they did their utmost not to let him down." [50]

Waller was not portrayed as exceptional, but rather as fulfilling the Marine ideal alongside others of caliber. The same traits that endeared leaders to their men in Spooner's tales are the traits that contemporary Marines note as distinguishing of great leadership:

> Probably the finest officer I knew was not my last main officer but the commanding officer before him, Lt. Col. Mike Dana. I mean he was a man's man. He was not scared to come to work and work all day with us on a 5 ton or on a generator replacing a head gasket. And then the next day he's over at motor-t or HT and all he does is move gear all day. Then the next day he's over at fuel. All he does is fuel vehicles all day. He was not afraid to do what he asked every marine in his command to do. . . . He knew everybody by name, he knew everybody's wife's name, and for the most part he knew what was going on with your family. I remember—and this is what stands out for me most with him—I had a bad time because my dad went in for heart surgery and I'd never talked to the man but I had talked to some people in my platoon and after I got the news Col. Dana came to my room in the barracks after hours and asked if I was OK and if I needed some leave. And to me, that's what makes an officer right there.[51]

Drill instructors training new recruits are schooled to demonstrate this paternal mode of leadership from the boots' first day: "There is no way that I will eat until every single one of my recruits has eaten. There is no way that I will go to sleep until my recruits are in bed. Those are things that just don't happen. . . . That's just the Marine Corps leadership."[52]

A Marine leader should not only demonstrate paternal regard for each Marine under his or her command—he or she must also become expert in the arts of war: its history and philosophies. A Marine leader will also exemplify intelligence, exceptional boldness, and a willingness to dish out and receive candid assessment.[53] When the Corps's leadership ideal is achieved, it results in a veneration without peer in the other services. One Marine major acknowledged that "the Marine Corps exhibits hero worship to the extent the Roman legions did."[54] This sort of sheer loyalty and determined admiration of key leaders is perhaps best captured in the words Captain Mariani used after returning from a 2010 deployment: "If General [John F.] Kelly showed up at my door tonight, I would follow him barefoot to Afghanistan."[55]

Marines are socialized to hold their senior leaders in high esteem and to treat them with a sort of reverence. Maj. Ben Connable points out that the commandant of the Marine Corps can use his position of superior trust and legitimacy to good effect for the Corps. The commandant's popular status and the Corps's smaller service numbers means "the Commandant can sometimes effect paradigm shifts against strong currents of internal and external protest. This authority has proven critical to the ability of the contemporary Marine Corps to adapt to asymmetric threats. Commandants have often served as the ultimate champion of maverick or revolutionary ideas."[56]

Marine leadership recognizes that the trust it demands and socializes into new Marines is a precious commodity. Doctrine emphasizes the path Major Waller exhibited in attaining trust: "Only by their physical presence—by demonstrating the willingness to share danger and privation—can commanders fully gain the trust and confidence of subordinates."[57] Trust in leadership is the requisite good for inspiring combat effectiveness in fighting men. "Leaders should develop unit cohesion and esprit and the self-confidence of individuals within the unit. In this environment, a Marine's unwillingness to violate the respect and trust of peers can overcome personal fear."[58]

Not all leaders measure up. Examples of outrageously poor leadership (of the sort typically kept from public view) and its repercussions for Marines are portrayed with painful accuracy in the popular war memoir turned television series *Generation Kill*.[59] A Marine blogger hosted by Tom Ricks on the *Foreign Policy* website expressed his own frustration at belonging to an "elite" organization that refused to clean house:

> I'm talking about the Field Grade Intelligence Officer in Afghanistan who didn't know who Mullah Omar was. I'm talking about a senior Staff NCO in the intelligence community who could not produce a legible paragraph. I'm talking about a Battalion Commander who took pride in the fact that he had done zero research on Afghanistan, because it allowed him to approach his deployment with "an open mind." . . . The problem is not so much that these individuals pop up every now and then, as every organization has its bad eggs, but rather that we see them passed on through the system, promoted and rewarded. *If we are truly the elite organization we claim to be, how do we justify the fact that we allow these individuals to retain positions of immense influence, much less promote through the ranks?* How do we justify this endemic tolerance for mediocrity or outright incompetence?[60]

Uneven talent in the leadership pool poses a risk for the second tenet of Marine Corps leadership: an ethos of distributing leadership to junior levels. Even in the wake of the discipline problems endemic to the Vietnam War, Commandant Robert E. Cushman Jr. argued, "Train them; back them up; *Let* them lead; and *Make* them lead."[61] Cushman's admonition is the essence of Mission Command as captured in today's *Marine Operating Concepts*:

> Rooted in service culture and fundamental to our warrior spirit, Mission Command is a cultivated leadership ethos that empowers decentralized leaders with decision authority and guides the

character development of Marines in garrison and combat. Mission Command promotes an entrepreneurial mindset and enables the strong relationship of trust and mutual understanding necessary for decentralized decision making and the tempo of operations required to seize the initiative, degrade enemy cohesion and strengthen our own cohesive relationships in the crucible of combat.[62]

Mission Command is an outgrowth of Commander's Intent, a founding principle within *Warfighting*, which encourages initiative within the bounds of the commander's primary objectives: "The purpose of providing intent is to allow subordinates to exercise judgment and initiative—to depart from the original plan when the unforeseen occurs—in a way that is consistent with higher commanders' aims."[63] Subordinates should understand the intent of commanders at least two levels up. Senior leaders set the tone, convey intent, and let subordinates figure out the details.[64]

The Marine Corps works harder than its sister services at training juniors for leadership and ought to be credited with such. Ricks, alongside other authors, notes this as a distinguishing factor: "Much more than the other branches, [the Marines] . . . place pride and responsibility at the lowest levels of the organization."[65] The genuine effort to empower Marines at the lowest levels might be contrasted with the Army, which gives mission command of this sort lip service but remains fairly rigidly hierarchical in practice.[66] Marines typically have more discretion than their rank equivalents in the other services and have developed a consequent comfort with operating autonomously in small groups.

Applying decentralized decision making to the field, however, is rife with risk. It is difficult for senior commanders to resist using technological advancements in communications to micromanage those beneath them. In fact, a new irony in the Corps is that "the push to enable the strategic corporal through technology [has] unintentionally resulted in the tactically focused colonel."[67] Despite the Corps's clear and unambiguous doctrinal focus on pushing decision making to the lowest possible levels, the risk factor acts as impediment. Maj. Jeffrey Davis notes that Marines "talk a lot about a culture [that allows] . . . failure but it does not sit comfortably. . . . Letting guys loose and trusting them to do the right thing—[it is hard] . . . for the culture to adopt and accept that."[68] Hard especially when the eye of the public media is trained on young Marines who inevitably arrive on the scene with "a linguistic gap, maturity gap, and a number of issues that contribute to friction" and whose failings are less likely to be forgiven in limited rather than existential wars.[69]

Art Corbett, the author of the Mission Command section of the *Marine Corps Operating Concepts*, assesses that his Corps would live the Mission Command ideal in fuller form if engaged in "real" war. He argues that "elective, peripheral wars that do not pose an existential challenge or attack core national interests" can cause leaders to become distracted by "equally peripheral issues and political correctness" and are therefore "breeding grounds for risk aversion."[70] Corbett's point is painful irony, since it is in irregular operations that competent, decentralized leadership is of critical value. This irony is only one of many variables that sustain the unequivocal Marine preference for "real war."

## PERCEPTUAL LENS

Victor Krulak combines three relevant cultural frames (norms, values, and perceptual lens) in summing up the Marine mentality: "[The Marines'] complex personality was—and is—dominated by a conviction that battle is the Marines' only reason for existence and that they must be ready to respond promptly and effectively whenever given the opportunity to fight."[71] "Battle" in this context is not just a convenient term—it is a sincere description of Marine focus. As recently as 2004, the Corps reinforced its perception of the "two critical services" it performs for the nation: "We make Marines and we win battles."[72] Marines win battles. It has traditionally been up to the Army to win wars. The Marines' perspective that they are "first to fight" and "perform missions at the lower end of the range of military operations" means a more tactically focused eye.[73] Successful missions are the key to winning battles; thus, for the individual Marine an "ethos of 'mission, mission, mission'" reigns supreme.[74] From Krulak's perspective, it is why America keeps its Marine Corps.

### Mission, Mission, Mission

The theme of "accomplishing the mission"—no matter how senseless it may seem (e.g., chasing a seagull at boot camp)—is a constant thread running through training histories and conversations with Marines. "Mission" in this sense is nearly wholly tactical. It involves accomplishing the task immediately at hand. It is not antistrategic, as long as someone higher up is thinking strategically, but it may mean that leadership training at the lower levels (squad, platoon, perhaps company) emphasizes leadership *within* the tactical mission rather than leadership to *adjust* the tactical mission if it is not accomplishing strategic objectives.

The civil-military division of labor in the United States means it is incumbent on politically elected leadership to determine grand strategy—the employment of military means to achieve political aims. Perhaps as a sort of mental defense shield, enlisted Marines consciously or unconsciously refrain from grappling with questions of a strategic nature. Marine staff sergeant

Christine Henning commented on her camaraderie with other females while stationed in Iraq: "We don't really see each other that much but, when we do, we don't talk about the war. We try to talk about other things when we are sitting in our hooch watching TV. So I don't know what they think. I don't really know what I think either but I am glad that I am part of the war trying to help the Iraqi people have a better life."[75] A second Marine voices similar sentiments and provides some insight into the utility of being strategically indifferent:

> I've been in many situations I thought were unjust. I still don't trust the government. After being in Iraq, I really started to distrust the government and what they were willing to give our lives for. But, I am a United States Marine. I'm not a politician, my job is to defend the United States against all enemies foreign and domestic. I do not get to choose who those enemies are. That is the job of the government. I'm just a pawn in the whole scheme of things. I just do my job, keep my Marines alive, and live to fight another day.[76]

Spooner's legendary leathernecks projected the same consigned disregard for the "why" behind the mission. They deployed "not because they wanted to, none did. Not because they were fearless, none were. It certainly was not for patriotism or because they were heroes. They would go simply because they were Marines following orders."[77] Roch Thornton, a Vietnam-era Marine, argues the near impossibility of understanding the strategic arc of the war for most grunts: "From an infantryman's point of view there's no real beginning, middle and ending . . . there's only the middle. You're dropped into a dirty, dangerous situation. You try to do your job and not get killed. Then it's over. Little of it makes any sense so you spend the rest of your days trying to figure it out."[78]

The mental focus on the mission in front of them allows Marines to do what other humans would shrink to do—whether it is crawl in filth, vertically patrol enemy-infested caves, or walk over hundreds of their own dead to continue the assault on the enemy. Marines believe in themselves and in "mission accomplishment"—no matter how dirty, hard, bloody, or fatal. Tyler Boudreau served as a captain in the early years of the Iraq War and found that when he returned home and was discussing his experiences with civilians, they complained that he was "always going on about mission" when he talked about Iraq:

> This is what civilians don't get about the military. The mission statement is our life blood. It is the impetus for all action. It's that important. . . . The mission statement isn't merely some abstract idea ginned up by a few bureaucrats stuffed in a Pentagon cubicle.

It is the soldier's reason for being. It is his purpose. It is why he's
been sent to war.

. . . A commander can drop dead in the midst of a fight, but his
unit will persist. They will press on without him because they don't
fight for him. They fight for the mission, for the end-state. In the
absence of his direction, they will recall what he said before he died.
They'll remember the "commander's intent" and they will continue
to operate on that basis. That's mission-type orders. And that is why
the mission statement is so critical to know and understand. That's
why it's not just a matter of semantics. The mission statement is
why our troops fight.[79]

Marine heroes do not possess a common set of personality traits or
leadership characteristics. They range from disciplined to maverick, cool
and taciturn to outrageous and undiplomatic; their human strengths and
failings cover the full range. What they do have in common is a commitment to mission accomplishment against all odds and with uncommon
bravery and audacity. These men are not heroes because they save Marine
lives. They are heroes because they accomplished the objective. In fact, if
the objective required a high number of lives, this only increases Marine
prestige in accomplishing the mission. Focusing on the Marines of the
Pacific campaign, O'Connell observes that continuous assault was a "cultural" course of action that "was preferred to safer but less Marine-like
tactics":

In short, the Marines continued forward because their ideas about
proper Marine behavior gave them no alternative. Death was not
unimaginable; it could be incorporated into the Marine's stories
about his own identity. Failing one's comrades or appearing to prefer the Army, however, could not. As one Marine noted in his last
letter to his wife before being killed in the assault on Tarawa: "The
Marines have a way of making you afraid—not of dying but of not
doing your job."[80]

High casualty rates could be incorporated into the Marines' cultural
themes of prestige earned via suffering and dying. O'Connell claims that
"the Corps' steadily increasing casualties in World War II—which were
twelve times greater in the last year of fighting than they were in the first—
further convinced Marines that their service was superior to the others
around them." The bloody price of their victories compounded the insularity
of the Corps and only deepened its members' attachment: "The narratives
of Marine exceptionalism continued to function, even when the service's
principal marker of difference was greater suffering and dying."[81] Spooner's
legends carry much the same theme. A lot of Marines die. They do not "get

away," nor is it the heroic or best among them who survive. Sacrifices at this level can be made because the Marine, and the decision to put him in harm's way, are part of accomplishing the mission, and accomplishing the mission is what keeps the Corps alive.

## Clinical Paranoia

Terry Terriff identifies organizational paranoia as the key driver of Marine Corps culture.[82] He is in good company. Ricks, during his time in Devil Dog quarters, came to the same conclusion: "This abiding sense of vulnerability, and the consequent requirement to excel to ensure that survival of the institution, is *the* central fact of Marine culture."[83] As did O'Connell: "Perhaps the most recurrent theme in the Marine Corps of the early Cold War was a notion of being under siege from without, both by enemies in combat and by other forces in the executive branch of the U.S. government."[84] The Corps's fight to survive is the primary plot line of Krulak's *First to Fight* narrative. He details the Corps's tenuous existence and its last-minute pullback from the brink of extinction—not once, but multiple times over the course of its history.[85] Marine paranoia is not unfounded, but Terriff usefully distinguishes why their paranoid perspective merits the label "cultural": "What distinguishes the organizational paranoia of the Marine Corps as a cultural trait, rather than simply a reasonable response to environmental conditions, is its pervasiveness and persistence, even when there is no one out to get the Corps, and the propensity it creates to perceive any and all challenges, real or imagined, significant or insignificant, as putative threats to the very survival of the Corps as a service and to react accordingly in a forceful manner."[86]

Norman and Cooling believe that this trait has served the Corps well. Paranoia has been a healthy force "driving the Marines to constantly evaluate their competence and direction against the challenges and opportunities associated with emerging and future operational environments."[87] The Marines' own anthropologists credit paranoia as the impetus for its institutional drive to excel and perform at a higher level than the other services.[88] Hoffman points out that the Marines' lack of settled domain means they have reason to be concerned with their legitimacy as an organization—"a Marine Corps is a luxury for most countries"—and agrees that this institutional paranoia usefully promotes innovation.[89] Terriff argues that paranoia prompts the Corps to be forward-looking and on its guard so as to not be rendered obsolete by changes in the strategic-military environment. Further, it is keen to make sure that its forward-leaning adjustments to the strategic environment do not overlap so much on the functions of other services that it is seen as redundant. Those sensitivities are most pricked when comparisons are made to the US Army.[90]

## Amphibious Roots

The Marine Corps must be not only better, but different. Thus, Maj. Gen. Larry Nicholson has two words to explain the Corps's current return to amphibious roots: "service relevance." The Corps must show that it can bring something that the US Army can't bring. "The Army can do COIN [counterinsurgency] and can do it very well. The Army can't do amphibious operations."[91] It is interesting to note that today's "return to amphibious roots" refrain is a near replay of Commandant Robert E. Cushman Jr.'s call in the aftermath of Vietnam: "We are pulling our heads out of the jungle and getting back into the amphibious business."[92]

2nd Lt. Valerie J. Cranmer challenges the notion of a Marine identity based in amphibious assault and argues that it is small wars that make Marines unique. Cranmer first notes the ridiculousness of basing one's "roots" on the historic but inconsequential amphibious landing at New Providence in 1776, then goes further: "Amphibious warfare is an integral and important facet of Marine Corps history, strategy and ethos. However, to say we are a Service based in offensive amphibious warfare is the myth. The Navy by nature is amphibious and without it we could not perform an amphibious assault. Also, the Army conducted arguably the most well-known amphibious assault on Normandy in World War II. It is our roots in small wars that alone separates us, not amphibious assault."[93] Cranmer might also have noted that the "Marines' Hymn" celebrates involvement in a small war with its reference in its very first line to Tripoli. While this skirmish in the Barbary Wars may not have been any more strategically significant than the New Providence amphibious landing, it did demonstrate far more élan and ingenuity in execution.

Cranmer's essay explores cultural rather than security-oriented reasons for Marine rejection of the small-wars heritage: "There remains a . . . feeling of impending doom if the Marine Corps develops an alternative specialization in tactics dealing with counterinsurgency (COIN) or small wars."[94] Marines believe that they have a knack for counterinsurgency—that they are much better than the Army at this type of service—but they don't relish this perceived fact.[95] Cranmer goes on to argue, convincingly, that Marine resistance to small wars may be linked to the lack of glory from such engagements and, more important, popular approval.[96] In the context of Marine organizational survival, this makes a good deal of sense. The Corps has survived, more than once, on sheer popularity with the public and with Congress. O'Connell recounts the immediate post–World War II political battle waged against it. The sharpness of the fight, and its outcome, made clear to Marines that "their only trustworthy allies lay outside the executive branch: Congress, the public, and their own veterans."[97] Reflecting on this history, Victor Krulak's sobering reminder rings in the ears of all living Marines: "In terms of cold mechanical logic, the United States does not *need* a Marine

Corps. However, for good reasons which completely transcend cold logic, the United States *wants* a Marine Corps."[98]

The Marine Corps leadership guide acknowledges in its very first pages that Devil Dogs have a special relationship with their national public: "Feared by enemies, respected by allies, and loved by the American people, Marines are a 'special breed.'"[99] Avant notes that Marines keep a weather eye on the civilian institutions that keep them alive and prepare to adapt themselves accordingly.[100] Keeping this relationship healthy requires that every Marine be a publicist.[101] Marines are expected to be personally modest but enjoy full boasting rights on their Corps. One gray-haired Marine in Spooner's legends is reflecting back on his decades spent in the nation's service and the men he fought alongside: "He knew warrior-monks who were professionals, some were bonafide [sic] heroes but most denied it. Real Marines brag about their Corps but not about themselves."[102] Over the course of the last seven decades, Marines have taken the publicity task to heart and have become accomplished enough to inspire the ire of their political opponents. An exasperated President Harry S. Truman, in a moment of poor judgment, wrote into correspondence: "For your information, the Marine Corps is the Navy's police force and as long as I am President that is what it will remain. They have a propaganda machine that is almost equal to Stalin's." Truman was made to publicly apologize for the "Stalin" bit of his comment, but modern Marines repeat the legend with a bit of wry pride.[103]

Leathernecks perceive popular adulation to be in jeopardy, however, if the Corps becomes the force that takes up and executes small wars, a type of war Cranmer characterizes as "slaughter of a civilian populace, torture, and the prolonged struggle that sucks every resource from the country like a leech." Cranmer cites the Good Neighbor Policy of 1933 as an attempt to distance the American government from the "unpopular interventions in South America." Roosevelt, in so doing, "left the Marine Corps hanging out to dry" as the public face of such interventions. In Cranmer's estimation, "there has never been a small war that has been good or popular." Amphibious assault, on the other hand, belongs in the camp with "good wars" and is therefore far more likely to meet with popular approval and support.[104]

Marine attitudes that stability operations in irregular settings are "unglamorous and, perhaps, un-Marine,"[105] founded in painful instances of public censure during earlier counterinsurgency eras, stand in contrast to national opinion today. Both the Army and Marine Corps have received a significant boost in popularity and esteem in the eyes of the American public during this century's counterinsurgency campaigns. The Marine Corps's prestige numbers have moved up ten percentage points since 2001, raising their already number-one position among the services significantly higher than it had been on the eve of 9/11.[106]

Marines survive as an American institution because of the championing of Congress and the love of the American people. They survive as a *physically capable* force only with sufficient budget. A second piece of rationale offered by Marines concerning the current "return to amphibious roots" trajectory is based on fiscal considerations. The Marines are conscious of the fact that conventional war preparation demands a healthier-sized budget. Bigger budgets result in sounder footing as an institution: The more deeply invested the nation becomes financially in a particular service, the more likely they are to hang on to it. Owing to organizational paranoia, the Marines are well aware of their own slim fit where budgets are concerned and, despite their native frugality, would like a weightier budget anchor attached to their organizational ship.[107]

## CONCLUSION

The aspects of identity, norms, values, and perceptual lens captured across the previous three chapters represent cultural factors that have evolved over the long stretch of Marine Corps history. Both historical context and the specific counterinsurgency issues faced by Marines have determined which of these cultural factors have taken center stage in any particular moment in time. The next three chapters, in part II of this book, examine Marine Corps culture in its dialectic with counterinsurgency operations within two eras: the Banana Wars and the Combined Action Platoon program ensconced in the larger Vietnam War. These are examined closely, with an eye toward identifying which lessons survived the gauntlets of national and organizational cultures and were pulled forward into the Corps's first foray into twenty-first-century counterinsurgency: Iraq, the subject of the fourth chapter in part II.

When analyzing service culture, Builder advised looking at a service's history and behavior rather than "the words they may use to mask or explain themselves."[108] In the following chapters, however, it is not only Marine behavior that is of interest, but the words and perceptions they employed to rationalize their activities. When officers and Marines of each era were forced to prioritize norms and values and articulate a defense of their actions, they provided a window into the operational cultural narratives shaping their perceptions and resultant activity. The dialectic between the cultures they brought with them and the trial-and-error learning curve within consecutive counterinsurgency theaters produced a set of innovations—lessons learned—as well as a set of lessons recognized as important but not implemented—lessons lost. The nature of these, as well as the nature of the cultural blind spots that remained, is the summary subject to which we now turn.

## NOTES

1. United States Marine Corps (hereafter USMC), *Warfighting*, 87.
2. Kael Weston, correspondence with the author, February 1, 2012.

3. Capt. Joseph Mariani, correspondence with the author, November 3, 2011.
4. Dye, *Backbone*, 2–18, 100.
5. Fick, *One Bullet Away*, 87.
6. USMC, *Warfighting*, 44, 58.
7. Ricks, *Making the Corps*, 27.
8. Heinlein, *Starship Troopers*.
9. Kim Hodges, formerly a Marine, now an Army lieutenant colonel, in correspondence with the author, August 1, 2011.
10. Eliason, "Interview with James F. Amos," 13.
11. USMC, *Warfighting*, 11.
12. Ibid., 12.
13. Ibid., 85.
14. Fick, *One Bullet Away*, 181.
15. O'Connell, *Underdogs*, 49.
16. Kilcullen, *Accidental Guerrilla*, 30–35.
17. Maj. Jason Spitaletta, correspondence with the author, October 25, 2011.
18. Krulak, *First to Fight*.
19. Col. Charles A.Wynn, "A Marine Is Different," *Marine Corps Gazette* (May 1944): 15.
20. Flynn, foreword, USMC, *Marine Corps Operating Concepts*.
21. Krulak, *First to Fight*, 109, 73.
22. Millett, *Semper Fidelis*, 137–38.
23. Son of the previously referenced Victor Krulak.
24. Terriff, "Warriors and Innovators," 222–34.
25. Ibid., 233.
26. See, for instance, Siegl, "Military Culture and Transformation," 103–6.
27. Terriff, "Warriors and Innovators," 235. A historic issue that highlights both the service's gender issues and its reluctance to innovate might be the arduous process undertaken by a few female pioneers in overturning the regulation requiring automatic discharge for female Marines who became mothers. See chapters "Mary Sue League" and "Jeanne Botwright" in Smith, *The Few and the Proud*, 229–41.
28. Maj. Gen. Larry Nicholson, conversation with the author, January 11, 2012.
29. Avant, "Institutional Sources," 421.
30. Ricks, *Making the Corps*, 20.
31. Nagl, *Learning to Eat Soup*; Connable, "Culture Warriors," 4.
32. Connable, "Culture Warriors," 2.
33. USMC, *Warfighting*, 9.
34. Woulfe, *Into the Crucible*, 20.
35. Krulak, *First to Fight*, 179.
36. See Holmes-Eber, *Culture in Conflict*, for additional insight on Marine efforts.
37. Connable, "Culture Warriors," 2.
38. Spooner, *Marine Anthology*, 70–91
39. Fick, *One Bullet Away*, 109. A far crasser view comes in the form of a Marine Corps bumper sticker: "Travel to Exotic Places, Meet New People, KILL THEM."

40. Fick, *One Bullet Away*, 201.

41. Avant, "Institutional Sources," 421.

42. Joseph Mariani, correspondence with the author, November 3, 2011.

43. Murray, "Does Military Culture Matter?," 149–50.

44. It must be noted that the Marine Corps continues to borrow a good deal of its doctrine—that which it deems outside its core competencies—from the Army. Cooling and Turner, "Understanding the Few Good Men."

45. Blagovest Tashev, correspondence with the author, February 14, 2012.

46. Dale Nicholas, correspondence with the author, September 20, 2011.

47. Joseph Mariani, correspondence with the author, November 3, 2011.

48. Maj. John H. Russell, "A Plea for Mission and Doctrine," *Marine Corps Gazette* (June 1916):113, 120.

49. Dye, *Backbone*, xvii.

50. Spooner, *Marine Anthology*, 41. For other examples of ideal leadership, see pages 30, 47, 199–200, and 242.

51. Oral history file AFC 2001/001/65466 MS01, Veterans History Project, American Folklife Center, Library of Congress. It is important to note that this same Marine had equally powerful stories of the negative sort of about officers whom he held in the lowest possible esteem.

52. Smith, *The Few and the Proud*, 262.

53. See USMC, *Warfighting*, 56–58.

54. Maj. Jason Spitaletta, correspondence with the author, October 25, 2011.

55. Joseph Mariani, correspondence with the author, November 3, 2011.

56. Connable, "Culture Warriors," 7.

57. USMC, *Warfighting*, 80.

58. Ibid., 15.

59. An HBO series based on the book of the same title by Evan Wright (and validated by a second accounting of the same events in Nathanial Fick's *One Bullet Away*).

60. Accessed at http://ricks.foreignpolicy.com/posts/2013/01/04/we_re_getting _out_of_the_marines_because_we_wanted_to_be_part_of_an_elite_force (italics in original).

61. Gen. Robert E. Cushman Jr., "The Challenge of Leadership," *Marine Corps Gazette* (August 1972): 15.

62. USMC, *Marine Operating Concepts*, 16–17. Quotation originally in italics.

63. USMC, *Warfighting*, 89.

64. Ibid., 91, 60.

65. Ricks, *Making the Corps*, 19. See also Cooling and Turner, "Understanding the Few Good Men," and Dye, *Backbone*.

66. Alywin-Foster, "Changing the Army," 32.

67. Maj. Jason Spitaletta, correspondence with the author, October 25, 2011.

68. Maj. Jeffrey Davis, correspondence with the author, October 26, 2011.

69. Spitaletta, correspondence with the author, October 25, 2011.

70. Art Corbett, correspondence with the author, January 20, 2012.

71. Krulak, *First to Fight*, 3.

72. USMC, *Sustaining the Transformation*, 17.

73. Cooling and Turner, "Understanding the Few Good Men."

74. Salmoni and Holmes-Eber, *Operational Culture*, 281.

75. Smith, *The Few and the Proud*, 248.

76. Oral history file AFC 2001/001/46366 MS01, Veterans History Project.

77. Spooner, *Marine Anthology*, 270.

78. Roch Thornton, correspondence with the author, October 8, 2016.

79. Boudreau, *Packing Inferno*, 30–31.

80. O'Connell, *Underdogs*, 58.

81. Ibid., 28–29.

82. Terriff, "Innovate or Die," 477.

83. Ricks, *Making the Corps*, 197.

84. O'Connell, *Underdogs*, 10–11.

85. Krulak, *First to Fight*.

86. Terriff, "Innovate or Die," 484.

87. Cooling and Turner, "Understanding the Few Good Men."

88. Salmoni and Holmes-Eber, *Operational Culture*, 277.

89. Hoffman, "Marine Mask of War," 3.

90. Terriff, "Innovate or Die," 484.

91. Maj. Gen. Larry Nicholson, conversation with the author, January 11, 2012.

92. Terriff, "Innovate or Die," 486. Cushman's original quote can be found in Gen. Robert E. Cushman, "A Weapon System Defined," *Leatherneck* (June 1972).

93. 2nd Lt. Valerie J. Cranmer, "The Myth of Our Amphibious Roots: How Our Small Wars History Has Been Usurped," *Marine Corps Gazette* (October 2011): 18.

94. Ibid., 12.

95. Michael E. O'Hanlon, "Be All the Army Can't—or Won't—Be," *Marine Corps Gazette* (November 2010): 12.

96. Cranmer, "Myth of Our Amphibious Roots," 14.

97. O'Connell, *Underdogs*, 13.

98. Krulak, *First to Fight*, xv (italics in original).

99. Blackman, foreword, *Marine Corps Values and Leadership*.

100. Avant, "Institutional Sources," 421.

101. Ricks, *Making the Corps*, 198.

102. Spooner, *Marine Anthology*, 344.

103. O'Connell, *Underdogs*, 142.

104. Cranmer, "Myth of Our Amphibious Roots," 14–16.

105. Ibid., 14.

106. Scott Schonauer, "Poll: War Boosts Image of Army, Marines," *Stars and Stripes*, June 20, 2004, http://www.stripes.com/news/poll-war-boosts-image-of-army

-marines-1.21183; Gallup Poll results retrieved November 23, 2012, http://
www.gallup.com/poll/148127/americans-army-marines-important-defense
.aspx.

107. Terriff, "Innovate or Die," 483.
108. Builder, *Masks of War*, 4.

# PART II

# MARINES ACROSS A CENTURY OF COUNTERINSURGENCY PRACTICE

# CHAPTER 6

# SETTING THE STAGE

*Small Wars and the American Mind*

Many of the lessons lost, lessons embraced, and persistent blind spots that make up the fabric of the Marine counterinsurgency experience are not a product of Marine Corps culture alone but are the natural outgrowth of the national culture from which Marines are drawn. Both because of troops' sensibilities as Americans and the additional pressure of an American public requiring a behavioral standard, American culture plays a major role. When American cultural proclivities are reinforced by the cultural preferences of the American military as a whole and Marines in particular, these cultural predispositions—whether strategically sound or not—acquire particularly robust form.

The Banana Wars episodes and later the Combined Action Platoon (CAP) program in Vietnam reveal a pattern of consistently competing cultural mores—some of these drawn from national heritage, some inspired by membership in the larger strategic culture of the nation's military service, and some endemic to the Marine Corps itself. Which of these emerged as most influential on behavior may not have been easy to predict at the outset and offer some insight into the complicated picture of learning from war.

Before proceeding further, a brief snapshot of each small-wars intervention is in order. The pages of this chapter cannot afford a detailed examination of the political machinations that drove each of these conflicts and the personalities who waged them. Happily, this is treated in good form elsewhere.[1] What is necessary here is an overview sufficient for the purpose of painting a broad portrait of basic aims, length of stay, contours of the effort, and general outcomes.

# THE BANANA WARS

The small wars in question—Haiti from 1915 to 1934, intervention in the Dominican Republic from 1916 to 1924, and the suppression of rebels in Nicaragua from 1927 to 1933—are each counterinsurgency episodes that comprised both an enemy-centric effort and a comprehensive civic-action program aimed at nation-building. Small wars, as Marines came to understand them during this era, were a full-spectrum affair, significantly more complicated than major war. The *Small Wars Manual* acknowledges the simplicity of mission and objectives in major war—"the defeat and destruction of the hostile forces"—and juxtaposes this basic objective with the far more complex missions of wars in the bush: establishing and maintaining law and order, aiding or replacing the government, ensuring the safety and security of American nationals, and destroying any organized hostile force while employing methods that ensure a "minimum loss of life and property" and "leave no aftermath of bitterness or render the return to peace unnecessarily difficult." This is complicated further by an absence of clear directives from Washington. When in doubt, a leatherneck officer without specific mission orders should "deduce his mission from the general intent of higher authority, or even from the foreign policy of the United States."[2]

During their Caribbean engagements, Marines chased after (and killed) a good many "bandits" (as their foes were called), always in favorable ratios, and in the end successfully quelled, if not defeated, insurgent activity in Haiti and the Dominican Republic (although not in Nicaragua, where Augusto César Sandino remained at large even as the Marines departed). Marines recruited, trained, and partnered with a national constabulary in all three nations. Meant as an apolitical, national force to replace divided partisan armies or the militias of regional power brokers, the constabulary forces were devised for the dual purposes of soldiering and policing. In each of the three cases, Marines continued to officer these forces until their politically determined exit required that they make hasty authority transfers to newly minted local officers.

Marine efforts to govern the two states over which they held nearly uncontested power—Haiti and the Dominican Republic—included a strong focus on "law and order" (with an emphasis on order), economic recovery to sometimes unprecedented levels, improved sanitation and health conditions, roads built and communication systems upgraded and extended, and enhanced educational opportunities. Although military exigency certainly inspired many of these infrastructural improvements, evidence abounds that Marines also pursued their full spectrum of tasks with sincere intent to improve the quality of life for locals.[3] Their efforts, they believed, provided an example of a "valuable and novel political idea, ideal, that a government can be one of popular service."[4] Nevertheless, in all three Caribbean cases, Haiti, the Dominican Republic, and Nicaragua, America's First to Fight troops were pressured to depart, their time in-country leaving a bitter taste in the mouths of the local populations and their own American public.

Although the Caribbean conflicts occurred in close temporal proximity (Haiti and the Dominican Republic simultaneously), there existed very little transfer of knowledge from one conflict to the other.[5] This, combined with the extraordinary paucity of direction from civilian masters, meant that Marines (and their sometimes Navy counterparts) were left to devise policy from scratch in each round.[6] Vague instruction from Washington concerning strategic objectives is not typically appreciated by any security or foreign policy institution, but for a mission-centric institution such as the Marine Corps it proves particularly maddening. Complaining as artfully as he could manage it, Col. George C. Thorpe, a veteran of the Dominican engagement, wrote in 1919:

> It would seem that it would be a fine thing if troops in the trop-
> ics, and especially in the Dominican Republic and Haiti, were told
> exactly what their mission is. In the first place, it would help if our
> government could announce its policy in reference to these coun-
> tries—if it could say definitively what its program was intended to
> be, so that its representatives out among the people of these coun-
> tries could tell them exactly what our government conceives its mis-
> sion to be there. Uncertainty is always unsatisfactory. Men can face
> a very black future if they but know what it is. But an uncertain
> future, even with bright possibilities is annoying and unsettling.[7]

Frustrating though it may have been to the Marines who lived it, the dearth of civilian oversight creates for the modern researcher a useful context for examining the prioritizing and execution of counterinsurgency and nation-building practices when left to Marine discretion.

## Haiti

The Corps that landed its Marines in 1915 was no stranger to Haitian shores. The United States had sent its leathernecks to Haiti over a dozen times between 1857 and 1915.[8] The particular event precipitating Marine involvement in 1915 was the killing of the President Vilbrun Guillaume Sam, whose dismembered body was paraded through the streets, an act pro-voked by his bloody breach of Haitian norms regarding treatment of the political opposition. Haitian political upheaval was more typical than rare.[9] This particularly nasty incident drew the interventionist attention of the United States, not out of pure concern for "protection of American citizens and property"—its usual chestnut—but also a more strategic fear that Euro-pean powers, specifically France and Germany, would take advantage of

Haitian political disarray and economic debt to intervene and take control of the Haitian side of the Windward Passage. Such proximity to the Panama Canal was too close for American comfort.[10] Thus, in preemptive displacement of possible European geostrategic ambitions, the United States sent in the Marines.

The Marines did not at first perceive their role in Haiti as much beyond the normal in-and-out quelling function.[11] As it became clear that their civilian masters had a more enduring mission set in mind, the Marines settled in.[12] Their primary foe in this endeavor was a motley bunch termed *cacos*, after a local bird of prey. These opportunistic "revolutionists" abided in the hills until their services were solicited by some would-be political figure who could pay the appropriate bill.[13] Once amassed, *cacos* represented a formidable force of somewhat practiced guerrillas who plundered their way to the capital, Port-au-Prince.[14] For the Haitian Chamber of Deputies, it was the norm to choose an executive, even under the most chaotic of circumstances, once the previous one was deposed. The choice was typically the candidate with the greatest show of *caco* strength.[15] Once "succession" had taken place, the *cacos* returned to the hills.

Sympathetic to the candidate who had amassed their support and had been foiled by Marine intervention in succeeding Sam, the *cacos* took up a steady policy of harassment of Marine forces.[16] Their efforts intensified as it became clear that the Marines not only intended to stay, but also intended to displace *caco* bands from the role of Haitian kingmaker (and perhaps eliminate them).[17] The Marines flattened the first string of rebellions in just over a year.[18] Marine efforts at domestic improvement—specifically road-building using the French-era practice of *corvée* (forced labor in lieu of taxes)—prompted a second, more brutal rebellion that stretched from 1918 to 1920.[19] Marines continued to patrol and suppress spasms of insurgent violence after this period, but the vast bulk of energy was channeled into state-building.

Over the course of nineteen years (1915–34), Marines usurped most of the effectual powers of government, engaging in blatant election-fixing, the dissolution of governing bodies, and the passage of a US-penned constitution.[20] Criticism by the Haitian press of these heavy-handed moves was not allowed.[21] One Marine defended the comprehensive gag order as sensible given the unprofessional disposition of the Haitian press: "Edited in the polemic tradition of France, Haitian journals had only secondary regard for dissemination of news and none at all for truth. Enjoying freedom and security unknown before the Marines arrived, they delighted in attacking the U.S. occupation with irresponsibility and scurrility licensed by Haitian courts that refused to convict an editor."[22]

Marines not only usurped the powers of government—they also established its military arm by recruiting, training, and officering a national constabulary force, the Gendarmerie, which both administered and enforced

comprehensive government policy. This included policing as well as participating in an impressive string of material improvements: lighthouses, new
communication systems, clean water, roads, much improved health and sanitation systems, and agricultural advancements.[23]

Impressed as they were with Marine state-building achievements,
American public opinion toward Marine practices in the Caribbean nation
began to sour as reports filtered out of gratuitous killings of natives—many
in somewhat dubiously documented "attempts to escape"—excesses that
culminated in a formal Senate inquiry in 1921.[24] The evidence of Marine
misconduct shamed the American public, which held a high opinion of
itself as "rescuer" and "friend to poor nations." Haitian student revolts in
1929 sparked a skirmish with Marines resulting in fifty Haitians dead or
wounded—a display of violence that shocked Washington and signaled the
beginning of the end of American occupation.[25] Preparation for an extended
withdrawal began, and the last Marine departed Haitian shores in 1934.

Within a very short period, the public works that had consumed so
much time, energy, and treasure fell into decay: telephone lines broke down,
roads eroded and became overgrown, and many of the strides forward in
health and sanitation collapsed. Local politics reverted to the spoils system with the Gendarmerie (renamed the Garde d'Haïti) passed as a tool
from one Haitian strongman to another.[26] Marine accounts of the Haitian
experience do not analyze its aftereffects. Rather, the remembered history
within the Corps credits its Marines with vast strides forward in progres-
sive state-building and effective training of a local constabulary. The tales
that live in Marine legend are those of fabled figures Smedley Butler and
Herman Hannekan: Butler for his audaciously aggressive patrols (including
a race up a drainpipe against live fire in order to take a *caco* stronghold at
Fort Rivière)[27] and Hanneken for his patient intrigue and gutsy infiltration
of insurgent leader Charlemagne Péralte's inner circle, resulting in Péralte's
death and the collapse of the second Haitian rebellion.[28]

## The Dominican Republic

The Marines' arrival in the Dominican Republic in 1916 was again founded
on the need to shore up a profoundly unstable government on an island
that was a potential launching pad to the Panama Canal. The move, like
the intervention in Haiti, was part and parcel of a larger strategic impulse
to exert US hegemony in the region.[29] The Dominican head of state—Juan
Isidro Jiménez—had been toppled by his own war minister. Aging and somewhat sickly, he refused to be part of a Marine march on the capital, Santo
Domingo, to take it back. Instead, he resigned on the spot. The Marines,
nudged on by the State Department, moved forward without Jiménez's
support and marched to the capital anyway to take on his usurper, Gen.

Desiderio Arias. Rather than face the Marines head-on, the Dominican general and those forces loyal to him fled Santo Domingo and holed up in the interior city of Santiago. Marines brought in reinforcements and in just under a month succeeded in occupying key coastal towns and ousting Arias from his stronghold.[30] Most Dominicans kept to the sidelines and out of the way of the Marines, assuming that the US presence was only temporary and would end with a new election, which Arias had promised to respect.[31]

One by one the candidates that the Dominican Congress put forward for the presidency were deemed unsuitable by US representatives. When it elected one of them anyway, the United States imposed severe financial sanctions and refused to recognize the president-elect.[32] Political overlording of this sort raised the ire of Dominicans and generated anti-American feeling. These sentiments only intensified in ensuing months as locals encountered abusive behavior from the occupying Marines.[33] When, seven months into the occupation, it became clear that the Dominican Congress was moving to support Arias in the next round of promised elections, the State Department directed the Navy to intervene and assume the full powers of government until a "suitable" candidate could be found.[34] The Dominican Army was disbanded and disarmed.[35] Marines declared martial law and implemented a comprehensive military government, which would endure for nearly eight years.

The Marines' military government was characterized by seemingly contradictory impulses. The first was an emphasis on order at the expense of democratic practices. The primary victim was often the press. The military government enforced strict censorship: Dominicans were fined, abused, or jailed for even light criticism of the military occupation.[36] The second impulse was a sincere dedication to do what was good for Dominicans. Marines engaged in comprehensive public works projects, including reforming education, building roads and other key infrastructure, improving health and sanitation, and establishing an apolitical constabulary. The combined elements of this paternalistic posture meant that the Marines left no doubt as to their superior station vis-à-vis the indigenous population but also that they were dedicated to protecting their Dominican charges from predatory US commercial interests and pleading the Dominican case for favorable financial arrangements.[37] Marine efforts in economy and finance resulted in an unprecedented but not long-lasting boost to the Dominican economy. Although Marine leaders were sincere, the goodwill they generated in improving the welfare of Dominican citizens at a state level was undermined by serious abuses of citizens by Marine personnel at the local level.

Five and a half of the Marines' eight years in the Dominican Republic—from early 1917 until the middle of 1922—were spent fighting a largely unsuccessful counterguerrilla campaign against a disparate bunch—some anti-Americans, some bandits, some unemployed peasants, and some displaced strongmen from the countryside. This insurgency was not a direct follow-on from the Arias rebellion but rather a reaction to Marine moves into the east, which threatened the station of local power brokers who had traditionally posed a counterweight to the central government.[38] The insurgency was hydra-headed in the extreme, led in sometimes competing factions by multiple strongmen, and grew in strength as Marine activities in the east inspired the ire of locals. Bruce Calder, author of the seminal text on the Marine occupation from the Dominican perspective, points to key deficits in the Marine perspective: "The marines long failed to comprehend the nature either of their opponents or of the war they were fighting," which condemned them to "make the same mistakes again and again" and kept them from controlling the eastern half of the republic.[39] The official Corps history, looking back, seems to mourn the inability to morph the fight into a conventional one: "Against Marine superiority in artillery, machine guns, small-unit maneuver, and individual training and marksmanship, no Dominican force could hold its ground. However, with too few men to cover too much terrain, inadequate mounted or motorized forces, and often poor communications, the Marines usually could not force the elusive enemy to stand for a decisive battle."[40]

By the time Marines, along with their trained Dominican constabulary and civilian recruits ("civil guard"), began to bring effective pressure to bear on the insurgents, popular sentiment in both the Dominican Republic and the United States to withdraw Marine forces had already achieved an indignant critical mass. The public announcement of a Marine withdrawal inspired insurgents to call a truce with the Marines closing in on them and accept amnesty at the negotiating table by laying down arms.[41] Marines were required in 1922 to transfer most functions of government to a provisional Dominican administration and focus strictly on completing grand public works projects and training Dominican leaders to take over the Guardia Nacional. Pushed out by popular will, the last Marine departed Dominican shores in 1924.

Within very few years, most endeavors in the Dominican sphere had reverted to the 1916 standard. Politics were equally corrupt and personality-driven, the economy was beholden to the same few interests, health and education improvements had proved unsustainable, and peasants rejected the agricultural practices offered by US advisers in favor of traditional methods. Two key changes remained, however. The national government, by virtue of the Marines' dismantlement of the strongman-based *caudillo* system, became a much stronger and uncontested force in the lives of most Dominicans. Improved roadways and communication lines aided the government's reach into previously insulated areas of the country. The Guardia Nacional, trained by the Marines, proved capable of maintaining order. As head of this service, Rafael Trujillo used it to spy internally, take over the reins of government, and wield a dictatorship for thirty-one years.[42]

## Nicaragua

Many Marines, and a number of those writing on the Corps, regard the 1927–33 Nicaraguan affair as "probably the most significant small war experience in Marine Corps history."[43] A few distinguishing variables offer themselves up by way of explanation. Augusto César Sandino, a lieutenant in the Liberal Army unwilling to lay down arms alongside his fellow partisans in the US-brokered peace agreement between Liberals and Conservatives, represented a far more formidable foe than Marines had faced in their previous Caribbean conflicts. He was, whether the Banana Wars–era Marines chose to admit it or not, a genuine political revolutionary rather than an opportunistic bandit.[44] To this end, he managed to supply his followers with machine guns, dynamite bombs, and hand grenades in addition to studied tactics in guerrilla warfare. Sandino's forces appeared to have had at least rudimentary marksmanship training and reduced the Marine advantage of superior firepower skills by attacking at night.[45] Sandino's success in eluding Marines for five consecutive years is partially attributed to the additional asset of outside help from Mexico and an external sanctuary in Honduras.[46] Neither insurgent group in the Marines' counterinsurgencies on Hispaniola had been able to exercise the advantages of geographically proximate allies. Thus, the fighting aspect of the Marines' engagement in Nicaragua went on for much longer than it had in either Haiti or the Dominican Republic, and its inconclusive finish prompted a far more significant level of Marine frustration and discussion.[47]

The inflated status of the Nicaraguan conflict within Marine small-wars circles remains intriguing, however, since the Corps's political power was most limited in this conflict in comparison with the other two. In Haiti and the Dominican Republic, the Marines not only directed military affairs— they also supervised or directly executed the entire government. Thus, the comprehensive power exercised by the Marines and range of possible lessons learned across the full counterinsurgency- and state-building spectrums would seem to render either Haiti or the Dominican Republic as the more interesting case study. That the Nicaraguan campaign wins this historical position seems to reinforce Marine interest in improving direct fighting skill—the skill set most robustly challenged and refined in Nicaragua— over improving the state-building skill sets often mandated in small-wars environments.

Although some of the small-wars lessons from Haiti and the Dominican Republic were available by way of a small selection of officer courses, informal mentorship, and articles submitted to the *Marine Corps Gazette* by the time Nicaragua rolled around, behavioral evidence in the Marines' first forays against Sandino reflects almost none of the lessons learned.[48] Small patrols had been discovered as the most effective approach in both Haiti and the Dominican Republic, but Marines initially pursued Sandino in default form: in large columns both "slow and blunt."[49] Small-unit combat patrolling became the "cornerstone of success" in Nicaragua but was rediscovered through much the same learning process as had been undergone on both sides of Hispaniola.[50]

The Marines were aided in their anti-insurgent task by an aggressive and innovative aviation arm; Marine aviation "came of age" in the Nicaraguan conflict.[51] Fire support by air was pioneered—including history's first dive-bomb attack—with sometimes surprising success.[52] Resupply by air and the evacuation of the wounded, both novel concepts at the time, enabled increasingly savvy (and smaller) patrols to remain in the field for weeks in pursuit of insurgent forces rather than be tethered to garrison post.[53] Most famous of these roving patrols was Chesty Puller's Company M, which became the "terror of the Sandinista contingent" in its area of operations.[54]

The Marines' primary accomplishment in Nicaragua was not the defeat of an insurgent force but rather oversight of two rounds of free and fair elections. Michel Gobat, who in the main tends to be profoundly critical of the Marines' intervention in Nicaragua, nevertheless cedes credit to them on this point: "The historical evidence thus suggests that Nicaragua's US-managed elections were not simple charades. However tentatively, they fostered political equality, participation, accountability, and contestation—outcomes that political scientists deem key to the creation of a democratic polity."[55] Marines accomplished this by keeping Sandino's forces sufficiently at bay and by a steady and conscious demolition of the *caudillismo* system of regional power brokers in the Nicaraguan countryside.[56] It was for this secondary purpose that the Guardia Nacional de Nicaragua was originally constituted.[57]

The Nicaraguan Guardia was based on the same organizational concept employed in Haiti and the Dominican Republic and experienced many of the same challenges: low-quality recruits who were characterized by tendencies toward abuse of the population, inattentiveness to discipline, and a steep learning curve in all martial arts. In short, it was "not an effective organization for the first year and a half of its existence."[58] In the end, however, the Guardia was deemed a success by its Marine officers as both the best-trained—it was fighting the Sandino insurgency almost entirely on its own by 1930—and most loyal (despite ten mutinies, seven of them lethal!) of the Caribbean constabularies.[59] Like its two predecessors, the Marine-trained national constabulary in Nicaragua engaged in both internal and external policing and became the republic's strongest state institution, armed with unprecedented reach into the countryside.[60]

After five years of fighting and oversight of two elections, the Marines were pulled from Nicaragua. Intense political and fiscal pressure from home—present from the beginning—was only exacerbated by the negative press skillfully cultivated by Sandino's cause célèbre, the disenchantment of a disgruntled elite in-country, and democratic processes that signaled an indisputable marker of Nicaraguan readiness to take the helm.[61] The Marines did not get Sandino.

Sandino, however, agreed to amnesty in the wake of the Marines' departure. His Sandinistas agreed to disarm and come in from the field. They were later assassinated by the Guardia forces of Jefe Director Anastasio Somoza, this to include Sandino himself after an evening dining with Somoza.[62] Somoza, in turn, took advantage of the upheaval to unseat the elected president and, Guardia in hand, establish a family dictatorship that would rule Nicaragua for forty-five years.[63]

The Marines, for their part, left the Caribbean with accrued small-wars competence but a decidedly bitter bent toward irregular conflicts, which required so high a price and were often treated as inconsequential at home. Writing in 1937, Capt. Evans Carlson voiced a common feeling:

> [Small-wars] deaths tended to emphasize to the people of the United States that the work of training a national constabulary was far from being a peaceful and safe occupation. The yeoman work of this nature which so often falls to the lot of the Marines is too frequently considered by the folks at home as a normal peacetime function which is free of the hazards which are ordinarily associated with a major war. But a man is just as dead if he is killed in a minor engagement of a minor expedition as he is if he succumbs in the greatest battle of a major war. It perhaps takes more courage to carry on in a minor war for often the individual lacks the moral support which is provided by the propinquity of large numbers in a major operation.[64]

## INTERVENING YEARS

The Caribbean episodes imposed stress on a range of Marine norms and values and inspired a discussion of best practices in counterinsurgency environments. As the discussion matured, its proponents resolved that the lessons identified must be incorporated into practice by the Marine Corps through changes in training. Toward this end they assembled a new doctrinal text: the *Small Wars Manual*. Had the Marines' next major engagement been faced in the bush, the lessons drawn from this manual might have been trained into action and cemented into Marine fighting form. Instead, Marine attention turned to the Pacific, and the *Small Wars Manual* was shelved.[65] The result: The bulk of previously established default norms within the Corps persisted, even those in sharp contrast with the most emphasized lessons learned in the laboriously assembled *Small Wars* text.

Not all was lost, however. The temporal proximity of Vietnam to the Banana Wars meant that some in senior positions during the 1960s carried with them the informal tutoring of mentors who had served in the Carib-bean.[66] Out of this mix an experimental Marine-driven program within Vietnam was born. Fewer than 1.5 percent of the Marines in Vietnam served in the CAP program.[67] Its impact on the annals of studied counterinsurgency history, however, has registered far above its numerical weight.

## VIETNAM: THE CAP PROGRAM

Several official histories of the CAP program cast it as a direct outgrowth of the Banana Wars experience. Victor Krulak, one of the program's strongest and most senior supporters, argued, "Senior Marine officers and those who had an interest in Marine Corps history knew that the Combined Action idea had been applied with success before—in Haiti . . . , in Nicaragua . . . and, probably most effectively, in Santo Domingo."[68] Other Marine voices are more circumspect about the CAP program's Banana Wars heri-tage. William Corson, one of the program's most famous and controversial directors, challenged the assumption that the CAP program represented a natural follow-on to the Banana Wars experience or that it duplicated its lessons. He argued, alongside others, that the CAP program, rather than being an accumulated set of "lessons learned" from previous irregular eras, was instead a program that fell much more along the lines of Marine inno-vation—an evolving project of many fathers that grew organically out of an effort to protect airfields and lines of communication running through hamlets.[69] The program sprang from a need to augment limited personnel numbers along defense lines. In response, some enterprising Marine offi-cers decided to team Marines with Vietnamese Popular Force (PF) soldiers already present in the respective areas.[70] The program ran in continually evolving fashion from 1965 to the end of 1970, at which time it was phased into a separate program that watered down many of the CAP's distinctive features.[71] The CAP program's mission was entirely dissolved after six years (in spring 1971).[72]

The CAP program was so innovative that many saw it as outside tradi-tional Marine boundaries. Bruce Allnutt, who in 1969 completed a compre-hensive nine-month review of the program, claimed that even at its height some "traditionalists" were decrying the CAP effort as being "outside the Marine Corps' historical mission."[73] Further evidence of that sentiment comes from the enlisted CAP Marines themselves. When asked what advice he would pass along to a new Marine joining his unit, a seasoned CAP Marine cautioned, "The major thing is . . . you must be open-minded because this line of work is different than anything else . . . in the Marine Corps."[74]

A review of the CAP program's beginnings and evolution does seem to indicate that as much as the Caribbean may have been in the minds of the Corps's most senior ranks, the corporals and privates who served in the program and shaped its practices were doing so with little conscious regard for lessons their progenitors may have learned there. They were instead—in their own minds—engaging in a rather novel experiment in counterinsurgency. A brief set of instructions, an in-country two-week course, and their own previous training and cultural inclinations guided their behavior.

The Marines' ad hoc program, circumstantial and informal as it may have been, provided a basic structure far more effective in counterinsurgency practice than Army general William C. Westmoreland's conventional approach in Vietnam. Some of the successes in the CAP program may be attributed to the mentorship of senior officials by Caribbean-era Marines, other successes came from predispositions within Marine culture, and still others were the result of somewhat accidental circumstances that turned out favorably for counterinsurgency practice.

The CAP program operated within a territorially bounded Marine zone within the larger Vietnam War and thus poses some striking differences to the operational objectives and tactical posture pursued in the Banana Wars. The CAP approach might be labeled "aggressive garrison duty." A squad of typically fourteen enlisted Marines—no officers—and one Navy corpsman were assigned to work with Vietnamese PF soldiers (whose numbers raised the force strength to platoon level, about thirty men) in a specific village (comprising a number of hamlets) and were instructed to "deny the enemy [the] recruits, food, and intelligence . . . needed to achieve victory."[75] They were also to kill the enemy. Aggressive local patrolling, ambushes, and patient intelligence collection were the primary tactics toward this end. But unlike their Caribbean predecessors, Marines did not actively pursue the enemy beyond the bounds of the village. Should their nightly efforts at ambush successfully produce a clash with the enemy, most CAP Marines (when communications equipment and weather cooperated) could call in their coordinates and receive immediate illumination and artillery support launched from the nearest base.

Marines in the CAP program trained local rather than national militia forces. Popular Force members (PFs) were, most often, village males who represented the least of the South Vietnamese military brethren.[76] The individual Vietnamese within these forces ranged the full spectrum of both military competence and cooperative sentiment toward US forces. Marines did not officer these forces; rather, the CAP unit was designed to operate with parallel American and Vietnamese chains of command. In practice, the operating command structure varied with personality and CAP-specific agreements reached between PF and Marine squad leaders.[77]

For the Corps, the oft-touted primary success of the program was that "no CAP hamlet ever returned to VC [Viet Cong guerrilla] control."[78] This did not mean that CAP units were not lethally overrun. Some were. But these were replaced by other CAP units within twenty-four hours. Although many PFs proved themselves worthy allies and indispensable guides of local terrain and culture, PFs on their own, without the support of Marine forces or artillery, were not able to fend off the surge of North Vietnamese Army forces that eventually took the countryside. Marine-trained PFs provided a sometimes excellent force multiplier but not a stand-alone military force.

CAP Marines were instructed to engage in civic-action projects in order to "win the hearts and minds" of villagers and "work themselves out of a job" by transferring skills to locals and ceding legitimacy to the South Vietnamese government. Their civic action, however, was provided at a far more humble level than the major public works projects of the Caribbean era. Though accidental and circumstantial in genesis, this Boy Scout level of civic action—a by-product of the Marines' frugal circumstances, their familiarity with village life, and action-oriented protective instincts—proved more successful in inspiring the sincere gratitude of locals and in achieving sustainability than most larger operations did.

In the end, although the US military force to which they belonged incurred the anger and often hatred of the South Vietnamese population, CAP Marines maintained generally positive relations with the villagers most affected by their presence, some remarkably so. Many Marines, in return, became deeply attached to the villagers they served. In commenting on the extraordinary rate of extended tours among Marines in the CAP program and his own voluntary extension in America's most controversial war, CAP squad leader Philip Leiker explained why he couldn't leave Vietnam: "I felt like I would be deserting my family."[79]

Whether in the tropics of the Caribbean or the jungles of Vietnam, many of the lessons learned, lessons lost, or lessons not recognized at all are best explained as a product of a widely shared American culture rather than anything the Marine Corps cultivated on its own. Dominating the scene is an American mind-set that defined US ambitions abroad and inspired notions concerning what its military forces might accomplish. Marines, in their initial endeavors, accepted and amplified American notions concerning both Yankee obligation and know-how in righting small nations and bringing them into the functioning fold, including fundamental changes to local infrastructure and culture. Resistance from Caribbean locals was explained through racist prisms that justified a continued expansion of administration and control. Racist perceptions widely shared across the American public, and particularly pronounced within the southern part of the country from which a healthy segment of leatherneck recruits were drawn, meant an easy slide into callous treatment of dark-skinned populations and a string of consequent abuses that made the Corps a political target at home.

Marine behavior within the CAP program was remarkably different from that of early Marine counterinsurgents or that of Marines operating within the wider war in Vietnam. As such, it demonstrates that within the right context a more strategically productive collection of norms and values—an alternative operational cultural narrative—may be pulled to the

fore. Practice with this alternative set of norms and values formed new habits for CAP Marines and altered, in productive ways, their perceptual lens.
Marine behavior was turned on its head, to good effect, within the CAP
program, not so much because of reduction of racism at home but because
of dedication to mission on the part of Marines and a survival strategy
that capitalized on the American instinct to protect the underdog and to
help small nations. Good treatment of villagers within a CAP unit's area of
operations was important for instrumental reasons: Marine squads placed
within those villages were vastly outnumbered and could survive only
through maintaining good relations with locals. What started out as instrumental practice became for many of the Marines of the CAP program an
intrinsic value as well, something enjoyed for its own feel-good benefits. Life
with Vietnamese villagers altered the lens employed by Marines. They came
to see the war through local eyes, enhancing both intelligence-collection
efforts and informing Marine assumptions about what villagers might reasonably be asked to do.

## THE AMERICAN MIND: "WHEN THERE'S A WILL, THERE'S A WAY" NAIVETÉ

An American perspective that exerted enormous influence across the years of
the Caribbean episodes and of Vietnam was the can-do and *should-do* attitude that American Marines brought with them to their nation- and state-
building ventures. Shared in common with the American public at large
was a Marine notion that the United States was embarking on a civilizing
enterprise: building order from chaos and doing so for peoples who could
not do so for themselves. The introduction of the *Small Wars Manual* makes
this clear: "The purpose should always be to restore normal government or
give the people a better government than they had before, and to establish
peace, order and security on as permanent a basis as practicable. Gradually
there must be instilled in the inhabitants' minds the leading ideas of civiliza-
tion, the security and sanctity of life and property, and individual liberty."[80]
    Initially, the Marines approached this comprehensive mission set as sim-
ply another task to be done. Only after significant years in-country do we
detect any recognition in the ranks that the task taken on is bigger than one
military force might pursue. However, these sentiments, while peeking out
of the window from time to time, are no match for the general argument
going in: Americans, and most certainly Marines, are able fixers of such
messy things as small nations that cannot seem to get their act together. A
small, backwater nation of indigents is no match for determined American
plans to bring it order, security, and prosperity.[81] Maj. E. H. Ellis, one of
the most influential of Marine small-wars voices, starts his seminal article
"Bush Brigades" with "Uncle Sam undoubtedly stands preeminent in every

'New Movement'; whether it be national or international, he is always to be found distinctly at the front. 'Clean Up' weeks are his specialty and he will 'clean up' anything or any place—a disease or a nation."[82] Marines saw this as an American tradition or capacity and were certainly not going to prove incapable of doing it.

Speaking as both a Marine and an officer in the two-year-old Gendarmerie d'Haïti, Capt. Frank L. Bride expresses exquisite naiveté on the task before him. In his mind, a functioning, prosperous government should be the work of a few years' time: "The *Gendarmerie* was, in fact, facing the problem of reconstruction for this government down to its most minute detail. It was hoped and believed that within a few years this land which is abundant in all things which nature plans for the welfare of humanity, would be running without hitch or friction; that all connected with the government would consider country first and personal gain as a secondary consideration."[83] Indigenous cultural change at a foundational level was part of the assumed package in all Caribbean episodes. Bothersome though it may be, Marines intended to oversee "the irksome months or years of reconstruction, when there must be effected a continual and vital change in native methods of life in all its respects."[84]

Those "few years' time" produced a body of seasoned Marines divided in their views regarding their ability to impact local culture. Some remained dedicated to a baldly ethnocentric and functional approach, convinced that natives introduced to a superior practice would most certainly see the error of their ways. One Marine colonel comments on the subject of eradicating cock-fighting in the Dominican Republic, perceived as "disgusting entertainment" by Americans:

> Our first inclination is promptly to illegalize cock-fighting. We favor prize-fighting. No doubt we are right and that cock-fighting should not be. The way to accomplish that is by the process of substitution instead of elimination. If *Guardia* officers can show the native something better than cock-fighting he will not be very slow to adopt the improvement. The officer will get his troops and other natives interested in baseball, tennis, and other athletic games, which are not only more entertaining than cock-fighting but more improving, and gradually the native will prefer these pastimes to the chicken affair.[85]

Lt. Col. Henry C. Davis, also a veteran of the Dominican years, reflects on his service in a totally different vein. In an otherwise profoundly ethnocentric article, he writes, "It is typically American to believe that we can exert a subtle alchemy by our presence among a people for a few years which will eradicate the teaching and training of hundreds of years, which will remold character according to our lines and which will educate races which have been kept in the grossest ignorance by the powers ruling over them. It is a hopeful theory, but it lacks common sense."[86] These men are not separate in era—they are writing within months of one another—but have come away with diametrically different perspectives on the prospect of enacting a lasting shift in norms within the local population. The result is a paradoxical *Small Wars Manual* that intends to remake society but, in referring to training local forces, supplies this caution: "Each race of people has its peculiar characteristics and customs. These may be modified somewhat under influence, but cannot be entirely destroyed or supplanted. These characteristics and customs should always be recognized and considered when dealing with persons of different races."[87] Although a selection of Marines may have recognized the profound difficulties in altering local cultures as a "lesson learned," their nation, and wider institution, did not. Thus, this continuing blind spot in the American polity propelled its forces into a similarly comprehensive attempt at a culture-altering nation-building effort in Vietnam. Suffering little damage by defeat there, this mentality accompanied Marines into their twenty-first-century conflicts in the Middle East and South Asia.

## PATERNALISTIC RACISM

Marine ambitions to remake the cultures of the Caribbean nations they oversaw were made more problematic by the ethnocentric attitudes they brought with them. Notions of national superiority combined with rather uninhibited racism. Racism, deeply embedded by the American experience with slavery and compounded by ignorance of local conditions and culture, drove perceptions of what was likely, what was possible, and what solutions would work with the indigenous population.[88] One Lt. Col. Henry C. Davis, a self-declared expert on Latin culture, described to fellow Marines a proper understanding of Latin American natives. Acknowledging that much of the lackadaisical work ethic that he witnessed was a product of years of insecurity and theft of crops by local bandits, his remedies are nonetheless filtered through an overwhelming superiority complex. Excerpts include:

> The Dominican is constitutionally opposed to work in the cane fields. He will cut wood, occasionally; he will till his land, spasmodically; he will drive a bull cart, indifferently; but he will not work in the cane. . . . The Dominican is himself indoctrinated with one thing—respect for FORCE. I do not mean to say that a brutal application of force is all that he understands or respects, but I do most emphatically say that to gain his respect one must have and exert the strong hand in dealing with him. . . . He does not want to be patted on the back and told he is an equal. He has had a master

his entire life; he recognizes the necessity of a master, and he wants a master. . . . Men who respect themselves are bound to make those under them respect them. This the Latin understands, and this he looks for in the man whom Fate has, for the time being, placed in charge of his destinies.[89]

Racist notions in Marine minds were validated and exacerbated by their initial contact with the physical conditions of Hispaniola.[90] Up close it was an entirely different scene than the alluring green hills that had beckoned from sea. In the words of one of the more colorful Marines who landed on the Haitian side, the oft-quoted Faustin Wirkus:

> It hurt, It stunk, Fairyland had turned into a pigsty. More than that, we were not welcome. We could feel it as distinctly as we could smell the rot along the gutters. . . . In the street were piles of evil-smelling offal. The stench hung over everything. Piles of mango seeds were heaped in the middle of the highway, sour-smelling. It was not merely that these, mingled with banana peels and other garbage, were rotting—the whole prospect was filthy. . . . Haitians of the working class have the ugliest feet in the world. In my bewilderment I somehow blamed them for the horrid things on which they stood. We were all annoyed.[91]

Racism did not abate significantly with contact. A year into the Haitian intervention, a fictional tale billed by the *Gazette* as "without question the best short story that has been written of Hayti [*sic*]" painted a land of exotic evil, massively degraded under black rule from its previous French-inspired enlightenment. In black hands it had become "a place of evil reputation," which had replaced monastery bells with "the midnight mutter of voodoo drums" and veneration of the Virgin with that of the serpent.[92]

Marine racism, perhaps unsurprisingly, tended to become more pronounced in direct proportion to skin hue. For instance, racial prejudice was stronger toward Haitians (usually darker skin) than it was toward Dominicans, but even within particular republics Marines tended to attribute intelligence (even if not likeability) to the same gene that carried lighter skin.[93] Describing his training efforts within the Dominican Guardia, a Lieutenant Fellowes writes:

> As a general rule, the degree of intelligence increased with the decrease of the ebony tinge. The blacker recruits were generally simple-minded giants who did what they were told simply from the habits of discipline, and lacked sense of responsibility and initiative. Those who were of clearer complexion usually were more intelligent, and could be trusted with responsible jobs.[94]

Nicaragua was often described by Marines as an attractive posting, but even there Marines brought the full spectrum of ethnocentrism to bear: racism, paternalism, and superiority. Despite the fact that Nicaraguan elites saw themselves as "white," their American guests "typically considered all native Nicaraguans to be nonwhite (usually of mixed race) and thus culturally inferior" and by virtue of their inferiority prone to civil disorder. These views were expressed in articles penned for North American journals—articles that were read by local elite. These tended to exaggerate exotic aspects of Nicaragua and cast the country in a primitive light.[95]

In its best form, racism came in the guise of paternalism. The "for your own good" mentality possessed by Marines provided cognitive justification of their strict and coercive measures, usurpation of decision-making authority, and ongoing presence in order to achieve what was "best" for the country. Mary Renda documents a consistent strain of paternalism in Marine attitudes toward the occupation of Haiti. She quotes the most famous of the Haitian expeditionary figures, Smedley Butler, in testimony to Congress during its 1921 and 1922 investigations: "We were all embued [sic] with the fact that we were the trustees of a huge estate that belonged to minors. That was the viewpoint I personally took, that the Haitians were our wards and that we were endeavoring to make for them a rich and productive property, to be turned over to them at such a time as our government saw fit."[96] Documented elsewhere, Butler's private remarks reflected the attitudes of most Marines when he dubbed his Gendarmerie subordinates "my little chocolate soldiers" and cast his ambitions as an effort to do his "level best to make a real and happy nation out of this blood crazy Garden of Eden."[97] Renda argues that this paternalism came in the form of "domination, a relation of power, masked as benevolent by its reference to paternal care and guidance, but structured equally by norms of paternal authority and discipline." Paternalism was not an alternative to violence "but rather as one among several cultural vehicles for it."[98] Although America's resolve to do "what was best" for the republics was not insincere, its marriage to racist paternalism ensured incurring the sharp resentment of the nations' populations. Marines alone cannot be saddled with the blame for bringing racism with them—they did this by virtue of their American heritage—but they must own the belligerent actions they vindicated through this perceptual lens, actions that fell enough outside the American norm—racist as it was—that it was rejected by the Marines' own domestic public and brought shame and indignation down on their service.

## Marines Behaving Badly: The Banana Wars Years

Marines of the Banana Wars era were racist, rough, somewhat divorced from domestic civilian life, trained toward violence as a problem-solving device, and dangerous when bored. To cite only one example, Marines acting as legation guard in Nicaragua well before the civil war of 1926 got themselves court-martialed and pulled out of the country for fighting with local thugs, sacking the offices of journalists who had insulted them, and engaging in a knock-down-drag-out brawl with police that became fatal.[99] It should have been a surprise to no one, therefore, that the Marines landing on the beaches of the Caribbean for long-term state-building duty posed a plausible liability for local civil-military relations.

Marine leadership was not unaware of the potential strategic impact of Marine treatment of locals and issued orders mandating that their relations be positive and friendly. In this sense, the need for positive relations with locals was not a blind spot in the Banana Wars era. Well before admonitions for good treatment were penned in the pages of the *Small Wars Manual*, Marine officers overseeing the deployment of their troops to the Caribbean stressed diplomatic and courteous behavior. Col. Joseph Pendleton, then the commanding officer of the Fourth Regiment of Marines landing in the Dominican Republic, admonished his troops:

> Members of this command will therefore realize that we are not in an enemy's country, though many of the inhabitants may be inim-ical to us, and they will be careful so to conduct themselves as to inspire confidence among the people in the honesty of our inten-tions and the sincerity of our purpose. Officers will act toward the people with courtesy, dignity and firmness, and will see that their men do nothing to arouse or foster the antagonism towards us that can be naturally expected toward an armed force that many inter-ested malcontents will endeavor to persuade the citizens to look upon as invaders.[100]

Orders of a similar sort were issued in Haiti.[101] While many Marines may have taken this advice to heart, a critical number did not.

The well-intended paternalistic benevolence of some members of the Corps cannot be denied.[102] Some members of the Marine Corps took a gen-uine interest in the welfare of the local population and went to great lengths, some of them exercising personal connections, to improve the lot of the pop-ulation they perceived as in their care. These efforts did not bear the fruits of gratitude that they might have, however, given the context created by other Marines exercising more abusive behavior and by the generally paternalistic and condescending manner in which even the most favorable actions were dispensed. Marines tended to sympathize with the most impoverished of the local citizens and cultivated a concomitant disdain for the local elite who seemed callous to, or culpable in, the suffering of their countrymen.[103] Although peasants often appreciated Marines rising to their defense in eco-nomic and political matters, the end result was a hostile relationship with the national elite—those with whom the Marines had to cooperate in order to achieve nation-building aims and those who possessed the most robust communication connections to the US Congress and domestic public.[104]

The American penchant to side with the underdog and to disdain an established aristocratic class meant that Marines exhibited little restraint in demonstrating their repugnance of the local elite and were happy to act as obstructionists to elite agendas. With typical leatherneck contempt for the entitled upper class, Captain Frank Bride writes:

> The better educated as a whole had a tendency to promenade the streets with a cane as an inseparable companion and discuss among themselves the best thing to be done and the easiest way for some-one else to do it. "Easy money" was the golden motto. . . . If a man can read and write he immediately aspires to join the class of "do-littles," probably becomes a government employe [sic] and perhaps, in the past, aspired to direct the secret affairs of some senator or deputy who could not read or write.[105]

Marine contempt for the elite encouraged officers and enlisted to find opportunity to diminish their upper-class stature, sometimes in the form of "humiliating arrests for petty offenses."[106] Anti-elite sentiment was sharpened by the fact that the elite were not white. Scholar Hans Schmidt writes, "Negroes were accepted, sometimes with fondness, so long as they 'stayed in their place,' while those who exhibited wealth, education, or ambition were subject to attack as 'uppity niggers.'"[107] Even those members of the elite with whom the US occupiers had reasonably good relations were subjected to inferior treatment. Butler, who did not exhibit the levels of vitriolic racism spewed by some, was still no respecter of nonwhite persons, even if they were head of state. When traveling with the mixed-race Haitian president Philippe Sudré Dartiguenave, Butler slept in the bed while the president slept on the floor.[108]

Physical abuse of the population tended to be more pronounced in areas of skirmish and conflict. Marines were frustrated by the elusiveness of their insurgent quarry and tended to take this out on civilians who resided in the same geographic area.[109] There are clear indications that Marines practiced "open season" from time to time—wreaking brutality on Haitians without discrimination between bandit and citizen, burning homes and destroying property. The atrocity that seems best documented (much is rumored) is the illegal killing of Haitian prisoners "trying to escape." Despite active efforts at the very highest levels of the Corps to keep this in-house and out of congressional sight, reports continued to leak out until the situation became a major national issue.[110]

While some Marines behaved abusively, others set high standards for productive counterinsurgency conduct. Capt. Merritt A. "Red Mike" Edson, who would become famous for his aggressive and successful patrols in

Nicaragua and his command of the Marine Raiders in World War II, gained the confidence of the Miskito Indians in a critical area of Sandino influence through his patient cultivation of personal relations, including providing security assurances to those who dropped their tenuous relationship with Sandino and aided his Marines. These methods contrasted markedly with fellow Marines who burned the houses of those suspected to be guerrilla sympathizers and shot enough prisoners "trying to escape" that Marine command felt compelled to issue orders of restraint.[111]

Despite Edson's strategic advances in cooperating successfully with the Miskito to track down and upend Sandino insurgents, his patient and indigenous-based methods were not adopted by the rest of the Corps. Worse still, his assurances of security were not respected by higher officers, and the Miskito were left to their fate after Edson was pulled out.[112] Edson's approach required careful cultivation of relationships rather than destruction of goods—an approach that ran contrary to Marines' hardwired bias for quick action. Edson's strategically sound methods, despite being field tested by a well-respected officer, remained extraordinary rather than becoming the norm.

In less kinetic areas, abuses were still widely felt, sometimes flaring to unconscionable levels but most often tending toward obnoxious rudeness, racist epithets, and disrespect rather than outright brutality.[113] Marines had to be barred from the local cantinas in Nicaragua where they were prone to get drunk during outings "terminating either in arguments, fistic encounters or a visit to the commanding officer and eventually the calaboose."[114] Attempting to warn fellow Marines off such behavior, 1st Lt. Robert Kilmartin cautioned that although assaulting a citizen of the Dominican Republic is a "small matter," it will get big publicity.[115] The culmination of "do-nots" emphasized in the Marines' *Small Wars Manual* provides a window into other unhelpful practices pursued at the time: "When passing or halting in the vicinity of dwellings occupied by peaceful natives, do not take fruit, eggs, or other things without fair payment; do not gamble or drink with natives; do not enter native houses without clearly understood invitation; do not assume a hostile attitude."[116]

The immediate failing for the Corps was not in the preexisting prejudice of Marines—this came as part and parcel of a racist nation offering up some of her most caustic members to leatherneck ranks. The failing was one of Marine Corps leadership as demonstrated by its lackluster effort to discipline, and therefore restrain or eliminate, abusive behavior. Marine leadership recognized the behavior of Marines as unfavorable but made few serious efforts to curb it. The Corps's initial limited effort entailed a mostly fruitless search for linguistically proficient and nonracist Marine personnel for officer posts in the various guardias, alongside a charade of limited and dramatically uneven redress of sometimes very serious grievances (destruction of property, rape, torture, murder) by a court structure run by Marines and unable to force itself to dispense jurisprudence in anything but closed-ranks fashion.[117] This was in complete contravention of the *Small Wars* wisdom that followed: "One of the most important duties of the inspector in small wars is to investigate matters which involve controversies between individuals of the force and local inhabitants. These investigations should be promptly, thoroughly, and fairly made, bearing in mind the interests of the individuals concerned and those of our Government. The finding of facts should be recorded and filed for future reference to meet those charges of impropriety which so often follow our withdrawal from the theater of operations."[118]

The only tactical solution to have any real effect was to keep Marines as segregated from the local population as possible.[119] On this point, Lt. Col. Harold H. Utley recommended supplying goods directly from the States that might otherwise be found in local markets, in order to avoid putting enlisted Marines "in direct contact with the natives—native people, native liquor, native women, native prices—all of which can be prevented by the exercise of a little foresight."[120] When conducting a patrol, Marines were ordered to stay outside of saloons and houses and to interact as little as possible with the natives.[121] Even within constabulary units, Marine officers often kept the peace through segregation.[122]

Not until the Senate inquiry of 1921 forced Marine abuses into the lime-light did the Corps take its own crackdown efforts seriously. Once they did, in the form of Brig. Gen. Harry Lee, who aggressively prosecuted offenses and actively pursued a change in the mentality of the troops stationed under his command in the Dominican Republic, it became clear that impact could have been made much earlier on.[123] Lee was able to put a stop to most of the serious abuses in his jurisdiction, but the weight of past practices and the persistent remnants of racism prevented the creation of productive relationships with locals on any scale.

Banana Wars–era behavior toward locals produced a number of negative strategic consequences. In all three Caribbean cases, Marines caused grievances sufficient for joining insurgent ranks. Marine abuses produced enemies sometimes faster than they could defeat them.[124] In the case of Haiti, Marines were directly responsible for forced-labor policies (the *corvée*) that inspired an entirely new round of insurgency.[125] To compound the matter, the Gendarmerie was underprepared to help Marines respond, owing in large part to Marines' racist perceptions, which kept them from "trusting" their Haitian enlisted men with guns and allowing them target practice.[126]

Unsurprisingly, the racist behavioral context also had an impact on the collection of intelligence. Although the *Small Wars Manual* speaks of cultivating positive relations with locals in order to elicit useful intelligence, there is no evidence that Marines were able to achieve this in any systematic way during the Banana Wars.[127] Individual innovations occurred; for instance, one Sergeant Darmond serving in Haiti—already ahead of his peers by being fluent in the local language—was celebrated for his intrepid and successful patrols and efforts to capture bandits alive. "A reformed bandit does us more good than a dead one. Dead men tell no tales, but live ones, treated right, tell tales and they tell the tales we want them to tell. They told that the white man wasn't such a bad lot and that the Haitian people could have confidence in them, but they must behave themselves."[128] Unfortunately, Sergeant Darmond's techniques did not catch on.

Marine intelligence efforts instead involved comprehensive mapping (none had yet been done of several areas), aviation reconnaissance, ground patrols, quizzing foreign nationals living in the region, and attempts to glean information from natives by either pecuniary rewards or force.[129] Drawing from an identity favoring offensive action and a national heritage that believes all things can be solved with money, the Marines initially saw intelligence as something to be bought with straight cash: "In the employment of natives, either regularly or for a given occasion, money is usually the keynote of the Intelligence system."[130] When short on cash, Marines used force: "It is safe to say that at least 50 per cent. of the so-called harsh measures used in bush warfare could be eliminated by providing the troops with adequate information money."[131] Marines assumed that the bandits benefited from intelligence freely offered up by the population. The *Small Wars Manual* accepts this as a steady state, lamenting that Marine "operations are based on information which is at best unreliable, while the natives enjoy continuous and accurate information."[132]

Racism tinged even this perspective. Rather than attributing the absence of useful voluntary intelligence from the population to their own abusive actions, Marines often blamed this failure on deficient local intellect. Marines paid cash for what they regarded as intelligence of very wobbly reliability, citing the limited morality of the natives in question: "Name the information you want and pay for it when verified. Natives invariably, when they talk, tell you what they think you want to hear. Their sense of right and wrong, time, distance, etc., is usually about zero per cent., but by sticking and striking averages fair results can eventually be obtained."[133] Utley, in one of his seminal small-wars pieces written for the *Gazette*, cites the logic of British small-wars expert Col. C. E. Callwell: "Callwell says that the ordinary native found in the theaters of war peopled by colored races lies simply for the love of lying." Even when attempting the truth, "his ideas of time, numbers and distances are of the vaguest. My own impression is that he will exaggerate numbers and minimize distances in nearly every case."[134]

The logical fallacy is striking. Locals, in the Marine perception, were capable of providing the enemy with perfectly accurate and detailed advice about where Marines resided and intended to patrol but were intellectually incapable of providing the same sort of information about the enemy back to Marines. The double-layer perceptual lens—one layer racism (low esteem for the mental acuity of the population) and one layer insular egocentrism (a refusal to see clearly the mistakes of one's own group as causal in the unhelpfulness of locals)—prevented Marines from addressing this problem in a way that may have reversed some of the strategic backlash and helped them cultivate a more fruitful intelligence relationship with residents in the know. Instead of engaging in critical introspective analysis, Marines blamed negative relations with indigenous populations on the "gullibility and ignorance" of the population, which was exploited by agitators, the local press,[135] or "so-called Americans who under one pretext or another will assist in originating and spreading tales of alleged 'atrocities' said to have been committed by our troops."[136] The Marines' refusal to acknowledge their own culpability may be due, in part, to their perception that their own abuses paled in comparison to the extensive abuses meted out by peer European powers on indigenous populations.[137] Although this may have been true, their comparatively restrained level of abuse was still sufficient to incur the ire and even hatred of members of the population.[138] The fact that this was modest in proportion to global standard was likely a benefit lost on those who suffered it.

Looking back on these experiences, the *Small Wars Manual* authors hoped to construct doctrine that would turn the situation around. Their verbiage indicates optimism in fostering a different sort of intelligence relationship with locals in the future, based on an improved "attitude adopted toward the loyal and neutral population" but without abandoning the prospect of coercion: "The natives must be made to realize the seriousness of withholding information, but at the same time they must be protected from terrorism."[139] Whatever intelligence wisdom was gained in the process of prosecuting the three Banana Wars and ruling Haiti and the Dominican Republic, it came too late in those theaters to have an effect. The fact that in all three cases Marines had to use means other than sound, volunteered intelligence to locate the enemy—using their own small patrols as bait to draw out the enemy, systematically canvassing large areas with constant patrolling, or surveying the landscape by air—indicates that their intelligence rapport with the population remained poor.[140]

Hostility between Marines and the indigenous populations ensured that they would eventually be driven from each country and that the national narrative concerning their experience there would be a negative one. More important for Marines, the negative narrative would play in their home country. The American population soured on the Marine interventions, not because Marines failed to "get bandits," but because of national shame regarding the treatment of locals. As early as 1922, the pages of the *Gazette* were acknowledging the repercussions. Lieutenant Kilmartin, the same who dubbed assaulting a citizen of the Dominican Republic a "small matter," used love and loyalty to the Corps and the strong dedication to not tarnish its image in an attempt to inspire good behavior toward indigenous citizens:

Every time a member of this brigade commits an act of abuse upon a citizen or resident of the Republic he brings forth the criticism of the Dominican people. And where does that criticism fall? Upon the man who committed the abuse? No, but upon the United States and its officials and officers, your president receives the blame; your whole government receives the blame; your Marine Corps and my Marine Corps receives the blame, and especially your commanding general and officers of this brigade.[141]

Despite this plea, the impulse for abuses continued in Haiti and the Dominican Republic and was carried through the years in Nicaragua. Institutionally, this damaged the Corps's place in the American national heart and affected, in at least the short term, its ability to accrue institutional strength via talented recruits and the sympathies of a budget-setting Congress. Hoping, perhaps, to influence the next generation of Marine small warriors, the authors of the Corps's *Small Wars* doctrine beat a steady drum throughout its text, admonishing changes in Marine behavior: "In major warfare, hatred of the enemy is developed among troops to arouse courage. In small wars, tolerance, sympathy, and kindness should be the keynote of our relationship with the mass of the population."[142] Although this lesson may have been recognized, the lesson that was internalized was of a different sort. Marines came to believe that the methods required to defeat adversaries in small wars would unavoidably lead to a blackening of public opinion. "We must never, in our zeal for the perfection of plans for a Small War, overlook the fact that behind and over us is that force known as 'Public Opinion in the United States.'" Therefore, "measures justifiable in a regular war, tactically sound, and probably the most efficient available, must frequently be eliminated from the plan of campaign as not being in accord with public policy in the existing situation."[143] This aspect of the Marine perceptual lens led them to codify into doctrine what they believed to be a bitter and unavoidable reality: "An ordinary characteristic of small wars is the antagonistic propaganda against the campaign or operations in the United States press or legislature."[144]

Marines in the CAP program did not study the *Small Wars Manual*, but they managed, nonetheless, to do a better job of living some of its precepts. In so doing, they garnered more favorable (albeit limited) press. Marines arriving to the CAP program were no less ethnocentric in their beliefs about America's ability to accomplish its purposes and possessed paternalistic notions about the Vietnamese largely reflective of the sort held by their Caribbean counterparts. What made a significant difference in the CAP Marines' behavior was a rudimentary selection process favoring less-prejudiced Marines, brief training in Vietnamese language and culture, a confined geographic location, and an altered mission optic featuring real incentives for careful treatment of locals. The CAP Marines' mission set and operational context drew a different set of values and norms to the fore, one that shaped behavior in marked contrast to that of the bulk of US military forces operating in Vietnam around them.

## Marines Reformed: CAP

The Marine Corps of the Vietnam era continued to reflect the prejudices shared across the American public. CAP historian Michael Peterson points out that the Marines were the last of the services to desegregate in the 1950s and their view of Asian nationals tended to be captured in epithets such as the widespread "Luke the Gook."[145] Vietnam-era boot camp training emphasized an every-Vietnamese-a-Viet-Cong approach and inculcated hostility toward them.[146] Marines drawn into the CAP program may not have been racist at the socially ingrained levels of Marines entering black Haiti and the Dominican Republic, but they often reacted strongly, and negatively, upon initial contact with Vietnamese villagers. A Marine who had grown up in the squalor of Harlem was still unprepared for the realities of impoverished Vietnamese village life and reacted with "awe and revulsion" upon entry to his CAP unit.[147] One CAP interviewee who was three months into a CAP tour after leaving a line unit confessed, "Well up north I was never used to having the Vietnamese around me because I hated them. . . . The number one thing that I hated in this world was the Vietnamese."[148] His sentiments about the Vietnamese were unusually harsh for a CAP Marine (he was one of the rare interviewees from the CAP program to ever refer to the Vietnamese as "gooks") but demonstrate that these sorts of attitudes were in the mix. On balance, one CAP Marine surmised, "You don't have to love them, just don't hate them. Lots of CAP Marines didn't like the Vietnamese."[149] Racist attitudes, although initially present, were tempered and sometimes entirely ameliorated during a tour in the CAP program by virtue of three programmatic realities: an attempt to screen participants, unforgiving peer pressure from fellow CAP members to treat locals well, and the intrinsic value of developing positive and rewarding relationships with villagers over time.[150]

For many assessors of the CAP program, including CAP Marines themselves, the overriding sentiment that emerged was that "not just any Marine" could fill a CAP billet. The precepts of the CAP program were clearly not perceived as an easy and natural fit for those warriors made within Marine culture. The *Gazette*'s introductory article on the CAP program billed CAP service as requiring "a special kind of breed, even among the New Breed."[151] "You needed a special kind of Marine to be in a CAP," agrees CAP vet Warren V. Smith. "I hate to say this, but you had to be a gook lover. That's what they used to call me. I wouldn't say I was a gook lover though, I just treated the Vietnamese the way I'd want to be treated."[152]

The senior Marine officers who encouraged the development and growth of the CAP program understood the need for careful selection of CAP Marines. The CAP screening process was designed with high standards in mind but was not applied with consistency in practice. In its ideal form, Marines who were selected for the program had volunteered for it and also came highly recommended by a commanding officer. These Marines had strong marks in conduct and proficiency, had been in-country for at least two months but had at least six months remaining, were interested in living and working with the Vietnamese people, were exceptionally mature, had not been wounded more than once, and were high school graduates.[153] In practice, the selection process was rather haphazard. In some eras and regions, Marines coming in were tightly and systematically screened.[154] In other cases, Marines were "volunteered" out of their units because they were not liked by their commanders and the commanders knew or cared little about the CAP program—a "cleaning out the trash" approach.[155] Some Marines volunteered out of line units not because they were interested in CAP service, but rather because they misperceived it as an opportunity to get out of the line of fire.[156]

When it became difficult to find infantry Marines with the proper mentality—too many had seen too much action and had been hardened against the Vietnamese—the CAP program started pulling Marines from rear-echelon duties or assigning them directly to CAP duty from training in the States.[157] The patchy selection process was listed as a key shortcoming by Francis T. McNamara, a Foreign Service officer serving as a political adviser to the US military, who systematically reviewed the program in 1970. Interestingly enough, his concerns focused on the resultant youth and lack of combat experience of squad leaders—an opinion seconded by CAP Marines—rather than issues of ethnocentrism or underdeveloped people skills.[158] He also recommended a return to voluntary service from among Marine ranks for the program rather than the direct-assignment approach, since the predominantly volunteer era seemed to exhibit higher degrees of enthusiasm for the CAP program's population-oriented principles.[159]

Regardless of military occupational specialty or eventual designation to the CAP, Marines were all trained in the same Marine boot-camp style. Once assigned to a CAP, these Marines would continue to lean heavily on their infantry training but needed some "retooling" in mind-set for the program. At its best, the CAP program offered its Marines additional in-country training on Vietnamese language and customs at a special CAP school for three to four weeks. Marines had diverse reactions to this effort. Some proved resistant,[160] while others noted the value of this brief training and advocated for significantly more.[161] The value of understanding local culture and receiving adequate linguistic training is probably the subject that receives the most lip service and least practice across historical Marine Corps lessons recognized.[162] The need for cultural competence is a lesson recognized across multiple texts (*Gazette* articles, orders, and doctrine) and is often spoken of in ardent prose but is consistently lost in competition with more kinetically oriented training. Given the extraordinarily limited culture and linguistic training provided to Marines before their entry into highly isolated and profoundly insecure CAP village life, it is no wonder that a summary assessment of the program provided the following strong recommendation: "The Vietnamese-language training is inadequate and has seriously hampered the ability of some teams to gather intelligence and to protect themselves."[163]

Language barriers inhibited the core missions of CAP Marines, which included training PFs to patrol proficiently, engaging productively with villagers, and gathering operational intelligence. Marines, imbued with strong incentives to make up for the training they lacked, spoke in a limited English-Vietnamese pidgin with their PF counterparts and used a range of hand gestures in order to be understood. Any misunderstandings with PFs were difficult to resolve owing to the language barrier: "On three or four occasions we had language problems with the PFs. The translation would be lost and somebody would get insulted, and before you knew it there'd be eight Marines on one side and twenty-five or thirty PFs on the other locked and loaded."[164] If it wasn't misunderstandings that caused danger, it was the inability to use the charade-like hand signals when PFs and Marines worked together during the dark hours of night patrols.[165] Some CAP squads were fortunate enough to be assigned a linguist, but most had to make do, often training interested children to speak English and translate for their parents. Those who possessed Vietnamese language ability reported friction precipitously reduced: "They'll give you information that's usually very vital and you'll have no problem at all with the Vietnamese."[166]

Whatever the level of training received, newly arrived CAP recruits were made to conform to a certain standard of conduct by their peers. This was informed at the highest level by a decidedly unique mission optic: "We were first and foremost to become deeply involved, on a personal basis, with the Vietnamese people; helping them throughout their daily lives in whatever small way we could. . . . Our second responsibility was to train new warriors in each village."[167] Although the mission set provided the grand rationale, an immediate and unforgiving instrumentality provided the genuine incentive: If Marines treated villagers badly, they put themselves and their entire squad at much greater risk. Therefore, Marines policed their own and each other's behavior. If a Marine caused problems with the villagers, he was ousted by the squad and shipped back to a line unit.[168] CAP squads could not afford to incur the ill will of the often VC-supporting villagers around them.

CAP Marines were initially motivated toward good treatment of locals for this key instrumental reason—it helped keep them alive. Over time, however, many internalized population-centric norms for emotional-preference reasons rather than raw instrumentality. As time passed and relations with the villagers warmed, Marines found both instrumental and intrinsic value in forging positive and personal ties and saw it as the secret to their success: "I think living in the villages, amongst the people, we showed them that we could face the same dangers they did. We didn't abuse them or their women, either physically or verbally. We honored their customs and traditions."[169] One Marine emphasized eating the food, even when it was difficult, in order to gain the people's trust.[170] The result of this combination of goodwill interactions, according to a lance corporal, was that "some of them shared their hootches [sic], their food, their laughter, and their tears with us."[171] A norm combining both strategically instrumental and intrinsically satisfying rewards is likely to take particularly robust form. CAP Marines evidenced their commitment to this new normative set by the rate of tour extensions: Sixty percent of CAP Marines voluntarily extended their tours for an additional six months when they had the option to return home.[172]

Marines came to see the strategic benefits from positive treatment, in part from experiencing the opposite effects that members of other services produced. Capt. R. E. Williamson, an organizer of CAP units in their earliest years (1966–67), spent a good deal of time detailing this logic in a *Gazette* article to fellow officers. He cited a number of incidents in which military expediency was privileged over local considerations and a strategic backlash resulted. These included interrogating citizens whom the elected village chief had already cleared, thereby undermining his credibility with his citizens as protector; barbed-wire incursions into valuable grazing land; and summary cancellations of local market days. "Sometime after the above incidents these same people were subjected to a somewhat more serious affront to their human dignity. An extended perimeter required the desecration of ancestral burial grounds. Bulldozing the burial grounds of an entire village marked its inhabitants as unworthy and virtually non-beings."[173]

CAP Marines, aware of their villagers' sensibilities, acted protectively toward them and felt enormous indignation toward Army and Marine units that did not.[174] Army units coming through paid little regard to the people, often damaging or stealing precious property.[175] In these sorts of instances, CAP Marines were tempted to come to blows with their own countrymen. One recounts:

US Army. Yeah. They come into my area, there was five of them, and they were wolf whistling and getting pretty close to the gals and the mama-sans ... were getting very upset and I'm off a distance and I see this little thing and I can hear them doing the nasty talk, and ... I thought I hated *them*. I really hated them. (laughs) And they're lucky I didn't kill them because I said, "What are you doing here?" And I was kind of rag-tagged, and I was walking with my rifle kind of loose handed and—I mean, I live here! ... And they gave me a bad time. Like, "You don't look like you're— Are you one of those guys that's just kind of hiding out in the village, you're not a Marine anymore?" So I pulled the rifle up and undid the safety and said, "No I'm serious, you do not hassle the ladies in my hamlet and you better leave now. I'm serious."[176]

Inevitable mishaps caused by troops moving through the area were often exacerbated, to near fatal degrees,[177] by a lack of communication between "friendly" units and the CAP force.[178] CAP Marines possessed a front seat to observe the effects: "So whatever the troops do over here because of ignorance comes right back on the American government and this isn't good, it doesn't make for good relations with the people, and you'll find that they're not responsive when something like this happens."[179] Relationships that were fostered in the village were often damaged by events beyond the Marines' control or by the accidents of war. In one case an American truck killed a village girl. In quick response, the CAP team secured solatium payment and put two tank treads in the road to slow down traffic.[180]

Internal friction within the CAPs stemmed from multiple sources. Constant thieving by PFs was a problem and caused strained relations in nearly every platoon.[181] Some platoons suspected that significant numbers of their villagers and PFs were VC and therefore made little effort to build relationships with them.[182] Relationships were also damaged if Marines were unable to provide basic security and protect the villagers from VC assassinations.

Despite the friction of war and the youth, inexperience, limited training, and almost nil linguistic skills of CAP Marines, results from a 1970 survey conducted by McNamara revealed that Vietnamese villagers were "generally quite happy with the CAP Marines." They appreciated the medical service provided by the Navy corpsmen as well as the Marines' attempts at civic action and praised their "general standard of conduct." Key in this assessment was the fact that the Marines stayed long-term in the village, so if any unfortunate incident did occur, the friction was more easily resolved. The villagers knew the Marines by name and could report them with accuracy through the PF chain of command. The result, according to McNamara's study, was that these incidents were therefore typically resolved "on the spot."[183]

Although the priority given to specific missions within the CAP program fluctuated over time, the basic set remained the same: protecting the village from VC intimidation, taxation, and harm; training PFs; engaging in civic action; and gaining intelligence from villagers. On the last point CAP Marines were ordered to organize local intelligence nets in a formal manner.[184] Marines rarely did this but managed to achieve superior intelligence in their own way.[185] They tended toward indirect methods that relied on close observation rather than the often brutal direct methods employed by PFs or other Vietnamese.[186] Some commanders deemed the Marines' steady flow of indirectly acquired intelligence the most valuable contribution of the CAP program.[187]

In sharp contrast to the Banana Wars enlisted men, Marines of the CAP program were admonished to make their community contacts "continuous and personal," and they did. They recognized that without constant interaction with villagers, one would miss or misinterpret subtle communications being sent contextually.[188] Marines who ingratiated themselves to villagers were allowed closer involvement in, and understanding of, village life. Marines visited local homes, attended village ceremonies, and ate on the local market. Marines came to know "their" villagers and the personal habits, customs, and physical signatures of normal life in their "ville." "We became familiar with most of the people . . . [so] we'd recognize any stranger immediately."[189] Marines also recognized village habits and so could refrain from fire when a familiar profile appeared outside after curfew.[190] This collective familiarity imbued young American Marines with a heightened "sixth sense" for shifts signaling danger:

> But living with those people, you got to know their habits, you got to know their movements, and you even got to know their reactions. So when they were out working—harvesting rice is an example—and you were on patrol, you could tell if they were anxious and nervous about you being there. You could pick up on, *Okay, something's not right here.* Call it a sixth sense or whatever, but the hair would stand up on your back because mama-san and papa-san wasn't in their natural state of mind.[191]

The CAP sixth sense proved to be, perhaps, its most essential intelligence and counterinsurgency tool. Villagers were not always forthcoming with information, and CAP Marines tended to be pragmatic in their analysis of why, often more so than their distant commanding officers.[192] The enlisted men on the ground were aware that many older Vietnamese had sons and daughters in the VC. These children could be held as hostages to ensure cooperation.[193] Those villagers less affiliated with the VC were often just worn out. "Some of the farmers provided us with intelligence, but most just wanted to get on with their lives. They couldn't care less about the war, although it touched them in some way nearly every day."[194] One CAP Marine summed up somewhat sympathetically: "The villagers were so tired of the war they really didn't care who controlled things. They just wanted to be left alone."[195]

In some CAPs, the successful relationships built up with villagers yielded reliable intelligence:

> After we had been in the village for a while and people came to trust me . . . they used to come up to me with different things. Like an old mama-san would be walking by me and would—without directly addressing me—she would say, "Don't go into (ph) Anh Hung

tonight," you know. That would tell me that something was going to be happening in the area tonight. So of course, being Marines, we went in there. But that's how we got our intelligence was mainly from the people. The intelligence we got from the Marine Corps, oh, God, it was just absolutely terrible. It was always way out in left field somewhere and it really never pertained to anything that happened to us. . . . And what intelligence they did have a lot of times just didn't come out to us, so most of the time we just relied on the Vietnamese.[196]

For others, the familiarity of living in the ville—the ability to detect small changes that meant that the VC were in the area—served as their most important intelligence asset.[197] When villagers were mum, intelligence could still be gleaned contextually: "Our main mission was to prevent the VC from stealing the farmers' rice and harassing them. One way of knowing if the VC were in the area was to keep an eye on the vats the farmers kept their rice in. If they were empty, Charlie had passed through. The farmers would never tell us anything, so we didn't know if we were helping them or hindering them. It was very frustrating."[198]

One CAP squad member summed up the rather obvious distinctive quality of CAP intelligence rather nicely:

Q:  Your CAP seems to be unusually successful in gaining intelli-
    gence from the people. To what would you attribute your suc-
    cess in this regard?
A:  Well, the first reason is, and one of the main functions in the
    program, is to work closely with the people. I think in the
    past guerrilla wars that have been carried on that the Allied
    forces or the American forces or French or whoever it may
    be separated themselves from the people and did not allow
    themselves to get the information the people have to offer.[199]

Unfortunately, much of the intelligence that the CAP squads had to offer was ignored at strategic levels. One of their serious frustrations was that their intelligence was often dismissed since it was passed forward by junior Marines rather than officers. This included warnings in advance of the Tet Offensive.[200] CAP leaders' observations and analysis were not translated up the chain of command because command did not put enough stock in enlisted opinions. "That was one of the problems with the CAPs—we didn't have any officers with us. They thought we exaggerated."[201] As a result, most CAP intelligence was gleaned and applied locally, which was helpful in that immediate area but a missed opportunity for larger strategic effect.

Looking back, a number in the Corps deem the CAP program largely successful. It undermined VC influence in the villages where it operated, won the help of locals to a much higher degree than that experienced by line units, and produced Marines far more satisfied with and committed to their Vietnam service. These advantages notwithstanding, the same Marines are not sure if the program could be replicated on a grand scale. They are not confident that the character requirements of the program could be met by a sufficient number of Marines. That opinion is held both by officers and enlisted. "I think the CAP program was the most successful thing we had going in Vietnam," said one officer, "but I also think too much emphasis was placed on not offending the people we were protecting. We expected tact and diplomacy from young American Marines who did not possess such qualifications, nor had they been trained for such a mission."[202] A former enlisted CAP member commented, "I don't think we could ever have found enough Marines with the intelligence and sensitivity to make it work on a large scale, nor could we have provided the language and cultural training."[203]

The benefits of hindsight, and perhaps a more comprehensive view of the program as whole, offer an alternate perspective on the viability of a large-scale Marine effort along CAP lines in future counterinsurgency theaters. The first point to note is that the program worked decently well *despite* hitches in its selection process. Bad apples that were allowed through the initial screening, or passed through because there was no screening at all, were removed by the far more efficacious vetting of peer review on the ground.

Second, duty of the type pursued in the CAP program posed no threat to the warrior image. CAP Marines saw plenty of action, and CAP duty acquired a reputation as a death trap, with high casualty rates.[204] The *perception* of those rates was even higher. One Marine recalled being buffeted by bloody tales on his way to CAP duty: "All the 'old salts' rotating back to the States stopped in and told us some real horror stories about the CAPs. They kept telling us how they were being overrun. These war stories began to get to us and we contemplated asking for a transfer, but we decided to stick it out and see what these CAPs were all about."[205] To the extent that Marines value suffering and audacious bravery in the line of fire, the isolated, counterinsurgency CAP life provided it.

Third, the idea that there were simply not enough sufficiently mature Marines in the force to expand CAP-like duty does a disservice to one of the Corps's key identity markers and normative functions: training, molding, and incentivizing junior leaders. If commanders across the Corps understood and supported a program based on the CAP principles as a signature Marine mission and selected their highest-caliber NCOs to lead CAP squads (rather than tossing in their unit misfits), the amplified status of belonging to the program might produce a surprising number of young men and women willing to exercise the maturity to fill it. As noted in the introductory chapter, today's Corps is drawing recruits from a generation of American youth who are attracted to the dual roles of warrior and humanitarian. The Corps's most recent recruiting ads capitalize on this impulse and provide images of both. Although warrior scenes of combat skill continue to dominate, heroic images of Marines forging warm bonds with foreign nationals have the potential to draw in recruits tailor-made for future programs modeled on the CAP concept. Whether these sorts of Rambo/Bono (to borrow the J. Walter Thompson term) Marines begin to fill the ranks of service will likely have less to do with the availability of capable recruits and more to do with the cultural induction process—"the transformation"—the Corps chooses to pursue.

## NOTES

1. For excellent work on the origins and details of the Banana Wars, see Bickel, *Mars Learning*; Langley, *Banana Wars*; Schmidt, *United States Occupation of Haiti*; Calder, *Impact of Intervention*; and Gobat, *Confronting the American Dream*.
2. United States Marine Corps (hereafter USMC), *Small Wars Manual*, ch. 2, "Organization," 2. Owing to the chapter-specific pagination style of the original *Small Wars Manual* (reproduced in the reprinting), all citations will include a chapter reference as well as relevant page number.
3. For an example of such sentiments, see Capt. Frank L. Bride, "The Gendarmerie d'Haiti," *Marine Corps Gazette* (December 1918): 298.
4. Brig. Gen. John H. Russell, "The Development of Haiti during the Last Fiscal Year," *Marine Corps Gazette* (June 1930): 106.
5. Bickel, *Mars Learning*, 94, 108, 112.
6. Schmidt, *United States Occupation of Haiti*, 108–9; Millett and Gaddy, "Administering the Protectorates," 105, 110; Calder, *Impact of Intervention*, 1.
7. Col. George C. Thorpe, "Dominican Service," *Marine Corps Gazette* (December 1919): 325.
8. Langley, *Banana Wars*, 115; Boot, *Savage Wars of Peace*, 159.
9. Langley, *Banana Wars*, 119; Boot, *Savage Wars of Peace*, 157.
10. Millett, *Semper Fidelis*, 181; Boot, *Savage Wars of Peace*, 159.
11. Millett, *Semper Fidelis*, 184.
12. Bickel, *Mars Learning*, 69; Schmidt, *United States Occupation of Haiti*, 71.
13. Millett, *Semper Fidelis*, 178.
14. Bickel, *Mars Learning*, 71; Boot, *Savage Wars of Peace*, 157.
15. Langley, *Banana Wars*, 123.
16. Ibid., 186.
17. Robert Debs Heinl and Nancy Gordon Heinl, "The American Occupation of Haiti: I. Pacification, 1915–1921," *Marine Corps Gazette* (November 1978): 32; Bickel, *Mars Learning*, 70; Boot, *Savage Wars of Peace*, 162.
18. Schmidt, *United States Occupation of Haiti*, 82–86.
19. Heinl and Heinl, "American Occupation of Haiti: Pacification," 35; Edward Bimberg Jr., "Black Bandits of Haiti," *Leatherneck* (August 1941): 9; Schmidt,

*United States Occupation of Haiti,* 100–3; Millett, *Semper Fidelis,* 196; Bickel, *Mars Learning,* 72.

20. Bimberg, "Black Bandits of Haiti," 6; Langley, *Banana Wars,* 123–25; Schmidt, *United States Occupation of Haiti,* 98–99; Boot, *Savage Wars of Peace,* 166–67.
21. Boot, *Savage Wars of Peace,* 161; Schmidt, *United States Occupation of Haiti,* 75.
22. Robert Debs Heinl and Nancy Gordon Heinl, "The American Occupation of Haiti: II. Problems and Programs, 1920–1928," *Marine Corps Gazette* (December 1978): 54.
23. Bickel, *Mars Learning,* 75–80; Heinl and Heinl, "American Occupation of Haiti: Problems and Programs," 53.
24. Millett, *Semper Fidelis,* 199, 202–3; Schmidt, *United States Occupation of Haiti,* 105–7.
25. Millett, *Semper Fidelis,* 210.
26. Schmidt, *United States Occupation of Haiti,* 233–35.
27. See Simmons, *United States Marines,* 89–92.
28. Fehrenbach, *U.S. Marines in Action,* 34–45.
29. Calder, *Impact of Intervention,* xxvi.
30. Boot, *Savage Wars of Peace,* 167–69; Langley, *Banana Wars,* 133–43.
31. Calder, *Impact of Intervention,* 10.
32. Ibid., 10–19; Langley, *Banana Wars,* 137.
33. Calder, *Impact of Intervention,* 15.
34. Millett, *Semper Fidelis,* 191.
35. Bickel, *Mars Learning,* 108.
36. Calder, *Impact of Intervention,* 21; Millett and Gaddy, "Administering the Protectorates," 108; Millett, *Semper Fidelis,* 193.
37. Calder, *Impact of Intervention,* 43–53, 69–85.
38. Bickel, *Mars Learning,* 108.
39. Calder, *Impact of Intervention,* xxviii.
40. Fuller and Cosmas, *Marines in the Dominican Republic,* 16.
41. Calder, *Impact of Intervention,* xxviii.
42. Ibid., 61, 238–52.
43. Lt. Col. Richard J. Macak Jr., "Lessons from Yesterday's Operations Short of War: Nicaragua and the Small Wars Manual," *Marine Corps Gazette* (November 1996): 56.
44. Millett, *Semper Fidelis,* 246.
45. Bickel, *Mars Learning,* 157–58.
46. Langley, *Banana Wars,* 194, 206.
47. Cable, *Conflict of Myths,* 96.
48. Bickel, *Mars Learning,* 144, 161, 167.
49. Millett, *Semper Fidelis,* 248.
50. Bickel, *Mars Learning,* 171; 1st Lt. J. G. Walraven, "Typical Combat Patrols in Nicaragua," *Marine Corps Gazette* (December 1929).
51. Millett, *Semper Fidelis,* 252.

52. Ibid., 247; Bickel, *Mars Learning*, 177; Langley, *Banana Wars*, 190.

53. Bickel, *Mars Learning*, 171–73, 176; Langley, *Banana Wars*, 208; Millett, *Semper Fidelis*, 251.

54. Cable, *Conflict of Myths*, 106.

55. Gobat, *Confronting the American Dream*, 215.

56. Millett, *Semper Fidelis*, 250.

57. Gobat, *Confronting the American Dream*, 205–6, 217.

58. Bickel, *Mars Learning*, 169. See also Millett, *Semper Fidelis*, 252–54, 257.

59. William L. Bales, "The Guardia Nacional de Nicaragua," *Marine Corps Gazette* (October 1932): 18–19; Millett, *Semper Fidelis*, 256–58; Langley, *Banana Wars*, 205; Macak, "Lessons from Yesterday's Operations Short of War," 59. See also Langley, *Banana Wars*, 205.

60. Gobat, *Confronting the American Dream*, 205–6, 216–19.

61. Bickel, *Mars Learning*, 163–64; Langley, *Banana Wars*, 183, 188, 193; Millett, *Semper Fidelis*, 248, 259; Gobat, *Confronting the American Dream*, 215, 232–66.

62. Bickel, *Mars Learning*, 178.

63. Millett, *Semper Fidelis*, 260–61.

64. Capt. Evans F. Carlson, "The Guardia Nacional de Nicaragua," *Marine Corps Gazette* (August 1937): 13.

65. Schaffer, "1940 Small Wars Manual," 49. As was the Caribbean experience generally. Bickel, *Mars Learning*, 142.

66. Peterson, *Combined Action Platoons*, 16; Cable, *Conflict of Myths*, 161.

67. Allnutt, *Marine Combined Action Capabilities*, 11.

68. Krulak, *First to Fight*, 190. See also Hemingway, *Our War Was Different*, 3, and *Fact Sheet on the Combined Action Force*, 1, declassified document provided on the US Marines Combined Action Platoons website, http://capmarine.com/cap/data.htm.

69. William Corson, oral history in Hemingway, *Our War Was Different*, 49; Allnutt, *Marine Combined Action Capabilities*, 9; Peterson, *Combined Action Platoons*, 23.

70. Allnutt, *Marine Combined Action Capabilities*, 9; Klyman, "Combined Action Program."

71. For examples of the CAP's evolving priorities and functions, see M.Sgt. George Wilson, Gy.Sgt. Jack Childs, S.Sgt. Norman MacKenzie, and Cpl. Michael Sweeney, "Combined Action," *Marine Corps Gazette* (October 1966); *Fact Sheet on the Combined Action Force*, 1–2; Allnutt, *Marine Combined Action Capabilities*, 21; and Peterson, *Combined Action Platoons*, 35, 39.

72. Hemingway, *Our War Was Different*, 4–15.

73. Allnutt, *Marine Combined Action Capabilities*, 3. For a contrary opinion, see Peterson, *Combined Action Platoons*, 22.

74. Oral history file 3679, USMC Vietnam War Oral History Collection, Marine Corps Archives and Special Collections, Gray Research Center, Quantico, VA. Transcription by Jacquelyn Thompson, February 22, 2012.

75. Hemingway, *Our War Was Different*, 17. See also *Fact Sheet on the Combined Action Force*, 3–4.

76. Some CAPs trained Regional Forces (RFs), which were somewhat higher on the Vietnamese military ladder.

77. Allnutt, *Marine Combined Action Capabilities*, 17. For an example of largely productive relationships with PF forces, see West, *The Village*. For an example of unproductive relationships, see the two-part *Gazette* series by Maj. Edward F. Palm, "Tiger Papa Three: A Memoir of the Combined Action Program," *Marine Corps Gazette* (January 1988), and "Tiger Papa Three: The Fire Next Time," *Marine Corps Gazette* (February 1988).

78. Hemingway, *Our War Was Different*, 11.

79. Philip Leiker, correspondence with the author, February 15, 2013.

80. USMC, *Small Wars Manual*, ch. 1, "Introduction," 32.

81. Langley, *Banana Wars*, 118.

82. Maj. E. H. Ellis, "Bush Brigades," *Marine Corps Gazette* (March 1921): 1.

83. Bride, "Gendarmerie d'Haiti," 296 (italics added).

84. Ellis, "Bush Brigades," 14.

85. Thorpe, "Dominican Service," 324 (italics added).

86. Lt. Col. Henry C. Davis, "Indoctrination of Latin-American Service," *Marine Corps Gazette* (June 1920): 156.

87. USMC, *Small Wars Manual*, ch. 12, "Armed Native Organizations," section III, "Operations and Training," 18.

88. Millett and Gaddy, "Administering the Protectorates," 111; Langley, *Banana Wars*, 127; Calder, "Caudillos and *Gavilleros*," 123.

89. Davis, "Indoctrination of Latin-American Service," 155–56.

90. Millett, *Semper Fidelis*, 186.

91. Quoted in Schmidt, *United States Occupation of Haiti*, 68.

92. Rex Beach, "Rope's End," *Marine Corps Gazette* (June 1917).

93. Millett and Gaddy, "Administering the Protectorates," 111.

94. Lt. Edward A. Fellowes, "Training Native Troops in Santo Domingo," *Marine Corps Gazette* (December 1923): 231.

95. Gobat, *Confronting the American Dream*, 257.

96. Quoted in Renda, *Taking Haiti*, 13.

97. Boot, *Savage Wars of Peace*, 166.

98. Renda, *Taking Haiti*, 15.

99. Millett, *Semper Fidelis*, 240.

100. Maj. Samuel M. Harrington, "The Strategy and Tactics of Small Wars," *Marine Corps Gazette* (December 1921): 479.

101. Schmidt, *United States Occupation of Haiti*, 78.

102. See the panegyric of Capt. William Knox in Thorpe, "Dominican Service," 318.

103. Millett, *Semper Fidelis*, 209; Schmidt, *Maverick Marine*, 80–85; Gobat, *Confronting the American Dream*, 218; Boot, *Savage Wars of Peace*, 166; Langley, *Banana Wars*, 133.

104. Millett, *Semper Fidelis*, 209.

105. Bride, "Gendarmerie D'Haiti," 296.
106. Gobat, *Confronting the American Dream*, 219.
107. Schmidt, *United States Occupation of Haiti*, 80.
108. Millett and Gaddy, "Administering the Protectorates," 105.
109. Of special note is Charles Merkel, the "Tiger of Seibo," who habitually arrested local people for the crime of reserving information. He became notorious for gruesome torture and the burning of two small villages. Langley, *Banana Wars*, 146–47. For other accounts of abuse, see Calder, "Caudillos and *Gavilleros*," 123–25.
110. Schmidt, *United States Occupation of Haiti*, 104–7.
111. Brooks, "U.S. Marines and Miskito Indians," 71–72.
112. Ibid.
113. Calder, *Impact of Intervention*, 15. Such abuses were often categorized as "public drunkenness or rowdyism." Millett, *Semper Fidelis*, 188. For typical attitudes toward locals, see Wes Ley, "A Recruit in Santo Domingo," *Marine Corps Gazette* (August 1927). Some of this was blamed on the morally deteriorating effects of tropical heat. Thorpe, "Dominican Service," 321–24.
114. "Nicaragua and the United States Marines," *Marine Corps Gazette* (March 1924): 8.
115. 1st Lt. Robert C. Kilmartin, "Indoctrination in Santo Domingo," *Marine Corps Gazette* (December 1922): 379.
116. USMC, *Small Wars Manual*, ch. 6, "Infantry Patrols," 32.
117. On efforts toward the selection process, see Thorpe, "Dominican Service"; Millett, *Semper Fidelis*, 188; and Schmidt, *United States Occupation of Haiti*, 88. On the issue of lopsided justice, see Millett and Gaddy, "Administering the Protectorates," 109, and Calder, "Caudillos and *Gavilleros*," 15, 126.
118. USMC, *Small Wars Manual*, ch. 2, "Organization," 36. These sentiments are reinforced in Ellis, "Bush Brigades," 14.
119. Heinl and Heinl, "American Occupation of Haiti: Problems and Programs," 54–55; Millett, *Semper Fidelis*, 211.
120. Lt. Col. Harold H. Utley, "The Tactics and Technique of Small Wars: Part III. Functions of the Personnel (First) Section of the Staff," *Marine Corps Gazette* (November 1933): 43.
121. Bickel, *Mars Learning*, 96.
122. Maj. Herman Hanneken, "A Discussion of the Voluntario Troops in Nicaragua," *Marine Corps Gazette* (November 1942): 250.
123. Millett, *Semper Fidelis*, 205–7.
124. Ibid., 200; Renda, *Taking Haiti*, 11; Calder, "Caudillos and *Gavilleros*," 124–25.
125. Schmidt, *United States Occupation of Haiti*, 100–2; Bimberg, "Black Bandits of Haiti," 9; Millett and Gaddy, "Administering the Protectorates," 105. For a description of the abuses of the *corvée*, see Heinl and Heinl, "American Occupation of Haiti: Pacification," 35; Millett, *Semper Fidelis*, 196.

126. Schmidt, *United States Occupation of Haiti*, 103; Millett and Gaddy, "Administering the Protectorates," 105; Millett, *Semper Fidelis*, 187, 197.

127. Ellis claims "scant attention" had been given to the subject of intelligence up to this point and suggests that the Corps take a population-centric approach and become more serious about it. Ellis, "Bush Brigades," 13. Bickel claims that the Marines did slightly better on the intelligence front in the Dominican Republic than in Haiti. Bickel, *Mars Learning*, 112–15, 122–23. See also Fuller and Cosmas, *Marines in the Dominican Republic*, 67–68; Langley, *Banana Wars*, 145.

128. Sergeant Daramond quoted in "One-Man Armies of Haiti," *Leatherneck* (September 1931): 13.

129. For an overview of intelligence methods excluding those involving force, see Lt. Col. Harold H. Utley, "Tactics and Techniques of Small Wars: Part II. Intelligence," *Marine Corps Gazette* (August 1933): 47. Though omitted from Utley's article, physical abuse to extract information was so common that new ideas were offered up in the *Gazette*. This particular approach involved slapping the jugular vein with a flat wooden tool. Maj. John A. Gray, "Cul de Sac," *Marine Corps Gazette* (February 1932): 42. It is unclear whether these practices fell within the sort renounced in the *Small Wars Manual* some years later: "Methods of extracting information which are not countenanced by the laws of war and the customs of humanity cannot be tolerated. Such actions tend to produce only false information and are degrading to the person inflicting them." Ch. 2, "Organization," 28.

130. Utley, "Tactics and Techniques of Small Wars," 47. The *Small Wars Manual* also advocates the "liberal use of intelligence funds" in order to obtain "information of hostile intentions." Ch. 2, "Organization," 5.

131. Ellis, "Bush Brigades," 9, 11.

132. USMC, *Small Wars Manual*, ch. 1, "Introduction," 15.

133. Capt. G. A. Johnson, "Junior Marines in Minor Irregular Warfare," *Marine Corps Gazette* (June 1921): 160.

134. Utley, "Tactics and Techniques of Small Wars," 46.

135. Russell, "Development of Haiti ," 83; Ellis, "Bush Brigades," 12–14.

136. Maj. Harold H. Utley, "An Introduction to the Tactics and Technique of Small Wars," *Marine Corps Gazette* (May 1931): 51.

137. See this argument made by Ellis, "Bush Brigades," 10, and supported by Utley, "Introduction to the Tactics," 51.

138. Johnson, "Airpower and Restraint in Small Wars: Marine Corps Aviation in the Second Nicaraguan Campaign, 1927–33," 62. For an example of kinetic restraint due to women and children being present, see "Events in Nicaragua since February 28, 1928," *Marine Corps Gazette* (June 1928): 144.

139. USMC, *Small Wars Manual*, ch. 1, "Introduction," 27.

140. Fuller and Cosmas, *Marines in the Dominican Republic*, 37; Millett, *Semper Fidelis*, 200.

141. Kilmartin, "Indoctrination in Santo Domingo," 379.

142. USMC, *Small Wars Manual*, ch. 1, "Organization," 32. See repeated admonitions of this sort within this chapter on pages 23, 24, 30, and 45, as well as in ch. 12, "Armed Native Organizations," section V, "Civil and Military Relationship," 24.

143. Second quote printed in all capital letters in original for extreme emphasis. Utley, "Introduction to the Tactics," 51, 52.

144. USMC, *Small Wars Manual*, ch. 1, "Introduction," 28.

145. Peterson, *Combined Action Platoons*, 45.

146. Tim Duffie, CAP veteran, lecture at Utah State University, February 16, 2012.

147. Hop Brown, oral history in Hemingway, *Our War Was Different*, 22.

148. Oral history file 2926, USMC Vietnam War Oral History Collection.

149. Duffie, Utah State lecture.

150. This often pertained to intra-Corps racism as well. One black CAP Marine claims that racism toward his color—so pronounced in some areas of the Corps that it drove him to aggressive behavior—disappeared during his service with the CAP: Brown, oral history in Hemingway, *Our War Was Different*, 24, 26. For a thorough examination of the distinctly less racist attitudes of CAP veterans vis-à-vis other Marines of the Vietnam era, see Southard, *Defend and Befriend*.

151. Wilson et al., "Combined Action," 31. William Corson, one of the most outspoken directors of the program, set a high standard: "If they entered the job with an ethnocentric attitude, they would not succeed." Corson, oral history in Hemingway, *Our War Was Different*, 50.

152. Warren V. Smith, oral history, in Hemingway, *Our War Was Different*, 141.

153. Klyman, "Combined Action Program." An even tighter screening program was designed on the basis of extensive research of Vietnamese culture and the right type of Marine for the job but was never implemented. See Peterson, *Combined Action Platoons*, 41–42.

154. Capt. Tom Moore, oral history in Hemingway, *Our War Was Different*, 151.

155. Tom Harvey, oral history, ibid., 72; Brown, oral history, ibid., 26; Klyman, "Combined Action Program."

156. Harvey Baker, oral history in Hemingway, *Our War Was Different*, 61.

157. Peterson, *Combined Action Platoons*, 73.

158. For CAP Marines' opinions on this topic, see oral history file 2367, USMC Vietnam War Oral History Collection, transcription by Lacey Lee, February 21, 2012, and oral history file 2599, ibid.

159. Francis T. McNamara, letter to Lt. Gen. Melvin Zais, attached as addendum to *Fact Sheet on the Combined Action Force*. For a detailed look at the shifting selection process over the life of the program, see Klyman, "Combined Action Program."

160. For complaints from a captain attempting to get Marines to take cultural training seriously, see oral history file 753, USMC Vietnam War Oral History Collection, transcription by Noah Johnson, February 23, 2012.

161. Peterson, *Combined Action Platoons*, 48; Klyman, "Combined Action Program"; Brown, oral history, in Hemingway, *Our War Was Different*, 23; oral history files 2202-2341 and 2202-2599, USMC Vietnam War Oral History Collection.

162. For enthusiastic admonishments to know the culture and speak the language in the *Small Wars Manual*, see ch. 1, "Introduction," 13, 18, 19, 22, 26, 28, 41; ch. 2, "Organization," 1, 17, 18, 28; ch. 6, "Infantry Patrols," 12; ch. 13, "Military Government," 10–13; and ch. 14, "Supervision of Elections," 12.

163. McNamara, letter to Zais. See also Allnutt, *Marine Combined Action Capabilities*, 26.

164. Rocky Jay, oral history in Hemingway, *Our War Was Different*, 115.

165. Klyman, "Combined Action Program."

166. Oral history file 2202-2341, USMC Vietnam War Oral History Collection.

167. Goodson, *CAP Mot*, viii–ix. Not all agreed that the priorities be laid out in this order; see Chuck Ratliff, oral history in Hemingway, *Our War Was Different*, 28.

168. Allnutt, *Marine Combined Action Capabilities*, 29. For a specific discussion of a Marine who had to be removed, see oral history file 753, USMC Vietnam War Oral History Collection, transcription by Noah Johnson, February 23, 2012. For a discussion of one who was not removed soon enough, see Dr. Wayne Christiansen, oral history in Hemingway, *Our War Was Different*, 133–34. Even the corpsman, valuable as he was, was not immune: CAP 1-3-9 shipped one back for poor conduct. Philip Leiker, lecture at Utah State University, April 5, 2013.

169. Brown, oral history in Hemingway, *Our War Was Different*, 27. Another Marine details the lengths his squad went to in order to protect the reputations of Vietnamese women in his ville: oral history file 2724, USMC Vietnam War Oral History Collection.

170. Tom Krusewski, oral history in Hemingway, *Our War Was Different*, 90.

171. Jay, oral history, ibid., 117.

172. Krulak, *First to Fight*, 190. See also Peterson, *Combined Action Platoons*, 26.

173. R. E. Williamson, "A Briefing for Combined Action," *Marine Corps Gazette* (March 1968): 42.

174. For instance, see Harvey, oral history in Hemingway, *Our War Was Different*, 82; Jay, oral history, ibid., 118; and oral history file 2599, USMC Vietnam War Oral History Collection.

175. Oral history file 2202-2341, USMC Vietnam War Oral History Collection.

176. Interview with CAP Marine Trust Israel, November 9, 2013, transcription in possession of the author.

177. Warren Carmon, oral history in Hemingway, *Our War Was Different*, 168–69.

178. Smith, oral history, ibid., 140–41.

179. Oral history file 2202-2341, USMC Vietnam War Oral History Collection.

180. Allnutt, *Marine Combined Action Capabilities*, 27.

181. Ibid., 27; Klyman, "Combined Action Program."

182. Interviews with CAP Marines Mark Brady (CAC Bravo 2-1, later CAP Charlie 3) Michael Smith (CAP 4-3-2 and CAP 2-2-1), and Roch Thornton (CAP 2-7-2), November 9, 2013, all transcribed and in possession of the author.

183. McNamara, letter to Zais.

184. For an example of an effort of this kind, see oral history file 2141, USMC Vietnam War Oral History Collection.

185. Allnutt, *Marine Combined Action Capabilities*, 40–42; Brown, oral history in Hemingway, *Our War Was Different*, 25; Jimmy Sparrow, oral history in Hemingway, *Our War Was Different*, 45. "We were invited to village Tet parties and sometimes we even received some good intelligence because of what we did for them." Skip Freeman, oral history, in Hemingway, *Our War Was Different*, 104; oral history file 2141, USMC Vietnam War Oral History Collection.

186. Oral history file 2367, USMC Vietnam War Oral History Collection, transcription by Lacey Lee, February 21, 2012. "Our Kit Carson scout showed no mercy when he was interrogating a suspect." L.Cpl. Paul Hernandez, oral history in Hemingway, *Our War Was Different*, 174.

187. Allnutt, *Marine Combined Action Capabilities*, 42. For an assessment from Lt. Col. Sherwood A. Brunnenmeyer, a director within the CAP, see oral history file 2898, USMC Vietnam War Oral History Collection, transcription by Kristen Amundsen, February 22, 2012. See also oral history file 2304-6, ibid., transcription by Victoria Cattanach, February 21, 2012.

188. Williamson, "Briefing for Combined Action," 42.

189. Hernandez, oral history in Hemingway, *Our War Was Different*, 174.

190. Oral history file 2599, USMC Vietnam War Oral History Collection.

191. Interview with CAP Marine Wayne Hickman, CAP 2-3-2 (November 9, 2013), transcription in possession of the author.

192. For an intelligence discussion from a frustrated officer, see Maj. H. G. Duncan, oral history, in Hemingway, *Our War Was Different*, 156.

193. For instance, see oral history file 2202-2341, USMC Vietnam War Oral History Collection.

194. A. W. Sundberg, oral history in *Our War Was Different*, 111. See also Art Falco, oral history, ibid., 162.

195. Jay, oral history, ibid., 117.

196. Interview with CAP Marine Mark Reshel CAP Papa 1 (November 9, 2013), transcription in possession of the author.

197. Christiansen, oral history in Hemingway, *Our War Was Different*, 133; Klyman, "Combined Action Program."

198. Hernandez, oral history in Hemingway, *Our War Was Different*, 171.

199. Oral history file 3679, USMC Vietnam War Oral History Collection, transcription by Jacquelyn Thompson, February 22, 2012.

200. Peterson, *Combined Action Platoons*, 56.

201. Krusewski, oral history in Hemingway, *Our War Was Different*, 60.

202. Duncan, oral history, ibid., 156.

203. Edward Palm, oral history, ibid., 39.
204. According to Peterson, mid-1967 statistics gave CAP Marines a 75 to 80 percent chance of being wounded once, a 25 percent chance of being wounded twice, and 16 to 18 percent chance of being killed. Peterson, *Combined Action Platoons*, 88. See also Duncan, oral history in Hemingway, *Our War Was Different*, 154.
205. Hernandez, oral history in Hemingway, *Our War Was Different*, 170.

# CHAPTER 7

# CONTRASTING NATION-BUILDING IN THE CARIBBEAN AND VIETNAM

*Efficiency and Order as Enemies of Democracy*

Held in high esteem within American culture and elevated to near sacred regard with the US military are values of efficiency and order and norms that privilege quantifiable results. Marine efforts at both civic and kinetic counterinsurgency tasks were, and continue to be, heavily influenced by this reinforced cultural formula. Their efforts in the Caribbean reflect the well-meaning pursuit of order and stability but with strategically undermining consequences. Order and efficiency were privileged over messy attempts to encourage indigenous self-governance, and pressures to achieve tangible and quantifiable improvements in state-building produced strong incentives to diminish local involvement in order to speed up results.

There is no substantial evidence that the Marines' pursuit of efficiency and order during Banana Wars nation-building stands in contrast to what other branches of the US military might have done. The prioritization of efficiency and order within Marine organizational culture, supported and rewarded by the larger framework of US military culture, was only encouraged by the valuing of the same in most of American society. In this sense, it is more appropriate to cast Marine actions as a natural outgrowth of American national culture and US military culture rather than leatherneck culture alone. Marines, raised in a democratic system that they viewed as exceptional and superior, attempted to duplicate this system by undermining nearly every principle on which it is founded. Marines built the states they oversaw, not according to the principle every American school child is taught as foundational—separation of powers—but according to a value that the US military prizes far more highly when nation-building abroad: efficiency. American citizens prize the ideal of separation of powers and pluralism but, in the practical aspects of legislating economic and social life, complain ceaselessly about its cumbersome processes and copious inefficiencies. Both in their social patterns and in economic endeavors, Americans reward productive and efficient behavior and punish those who do not seem to be able to accomplish much in a timely fashion. The prioritizing of efficiency, therefore, has identifiable national and military cultural roots. It is the Marines' military identity and organizational norms, however, that dominated in shaping the specific means they pursued to achieve it.

Marine efforts supplied unprecedented material and economic boosts in both Haiti and the Dominican Republic (where they controlled political and economic life to a higher degree than in Nicaragua), and at astonishing low cost, by establishing political regimes that modeled the efficiency of centralized authority. The reach of their authority was extended both by material improvements to infrastructure and by a Marine-trained security force whose loyalties were tethered to the newly constructed centralized governance structure rather than to national ideals or the indigenous population. Although unintended, Marine and American blind spots concerning this formula laid the groundwork for long-term dictatorships in the wake of American withdrawal.

The Combined Action Platoon (CAP) program's decentralized organizational structure focused on protecting locals from VC influence rather than building a centralized force to defend the nation. By virtue of the tactical considerations that inspired its inception, this program empowered popular-level resistance rather than contributing to centralized and autocratic governance. Although CAP Marines remained imbued with all of their forebears' material impulses, their thin scraps for budget made large-scale infrastructural improvements impossible and relegated them to neighborly acts of civic action, a hearts-and-minds approach that yielded surprisingly profitable results in force protection and intelligence.

## STATE-BUILDING IN THE CARIBBEAN

Executive Order No. 47, the Marine order founding the Guardia Nacional Dominicana, stresses "bringing it to and . . . keeping it in a high state of efficiency" as top priority.[1] To achieve this, Marine-trained constabularies increased their own strength by removing competing sources of power.[2] In all three Caribbean cases—Haiti, the Dominican Republic, and Nicaragua—resistance to the newly muscled centralized government reared in the form of informal and often corrupt regional power brokers acting as pseudo governing units. The American occupiers found their interference intolerable. Marines did not intend to be inhibited by local ne'er-do-wells in their own efforts to do good in the name of an adolescent, but growing, central government. Thus, when indigenous factions—of whatever sort—resisted the consolidation of power, the military response was to assert further control under the mantra "restoring internal order." Asserting control over one aspect of society often led to attempts to control those to which it was linked, until the Marine-manufactured constabularies became thoroughly intertwined in all levels of governing.[3]

So strong was the valuing of efficiency and the perception of centralized power as a necessary tool for delivering state benefits more widely and more rapidly that Marines were happy to extend this logic to the unseating of recalcitrant locally elected officials as well. The move was perceived by Marines in Haiti as a useful cleaning-up and expediting process:

> There was a gradual disappearance of local government, and commissioners appointed by the President took the place of the horde of office holders who in previous years had spent most of their time exacting under the guise of "taxes" a harsh tribute from the people.
>
> While this system of government may have been criticized by some in view of the control exercised over it by American officials, it certainly lent itself to the expeditious reformation of the country and the government.[4]

The Marines made the same moves in the Dominican Republic, usurping local power in order to "reduce the ability of provincial governors and local officials to disrupt the peace and frustrate national programs."[5] Col. Rufus Lane, who served as minister of foreign relations, justice, and public instruction within the Dominican military government, acknowledged that provincial governments had previously been "a very prominent factor in the administration" of the country but that these duties had since been taken over by the military government in order to execute policy more efficiently. The centralizing reach of the military government did not stop at the provincial level. Rufus goes on to explain:

> The municipal governments were, under the constitution of Santo Domingo, nominally independent. The officers were elected and they had certain legislative powers within the confines of their municipalities. In fact, however, all municipal governments were subject to the control of national government, and under the military occupation the tendency towards the ascendency of the national government was increased. These municipal governments were highly inefficient and wasteful and seemed to be incapable of carrying responsibility in reformatory measures. The Department

of the Interior and Military Police gradually assumed the functions of these governments, with the prospect that at no distant date even nominal independence will disappear.[6]

Although the Marine occupation of the government was less comprehensive in Nicaragua, even there Guardia officials took over police and judicial functions, replaced sheriffs, and ousted local mayors whom they deemed corrupt. In so doing the "Guardia emerged as the main link between the peasantry and the state" and evolved into the country's "most powerful and cohesive state institution."[7] Marines did not succeed in defeating insurgents in all three Caribbean episodes but did succeed in centralizing and extending the reach of the state. Traditional power brokers were demolished or scattered by the national constabularies, which served as the counterinsurgent army but also carried the mandate of internal police force and provider of social services. Marines created not only the most powerful martial instrument in the country, but the most powerful political instrument as well.[8] Newly constructed roads, telephone and telegraph services, and a wide variety of other infrastructure improvements allowed the US military to pursue "bandits" with more efficiency, allowed the state to govern with more oversight, and increased the government's reach into rural societies previously insulated from central administration.

Marines believed they were accomplishing their core objective: establishing stability and building the apparatus of state. The American assumption at the turn of the twentieth century, as now, was that most state-based problems could be solved through proper economics. The *Small Wars Manual* sums up as much: "Revolution is the term generally applied to sudden political changes, but the expression may be employed to denote any sudden transformation whether of beliefs, ideas, or doctrines. In most cases the basic causes are economic."[9] The perceptual lens through which Marines in the Caribbean determined their course of action was an economic and materials-centric one. For instance, rather than addressing the low quality of recruits to their newly established guardias as an identity issue—affiliation with foreign troops, especially imperious ones, was likely to threaten a reputational stain for well-regarded and talented locals—the *Small Wars Manual*'s authors continued to see low-quality recruiting as a problem to be solved through material inducements: "The rates of pay should be such as to attract the best type of natives to join the constabulary. By making the rates of pay attractive, natives of the highest type will be encouraged to make the constabulary a career."[10] Even loyalty could be bought:

The confidence and loyalty of the native troops is promoted by careful supervision of their material needs. More often than not, they will have been accustomed to meager salaries irregularly paid, scant food carelessly provided, as well as indifferent shelter, clothing, and equipment. When they are regularly paid in full on the date due, when fed adequately as provided by the allowance, and when good shelter, clothing, and equipment are provided, native troops will usually respond in the quality of service rendered.[11]

On the whole, the Marine approach in the Caribbean focused primarily on material offerings rather than positive person-to-person contact with locals. Although numerous directives at the time (and later in the *Small Wars Manual*) supplied a steady stream of admonitions to know the culture in nuanced fashion and treat locals well, it ran aground on a value set, both quintessentially American and reinforced by the Corps, that favored efficiently achieved material accomplishments.[12] Marines intended to get the country built up and "working again" and this as fast as possible. Bringing natives on board during the process would slow it down and create innumerable inefficiencies.[13]

John Russell, summing up Marine efforts in June 1930, noted that all of the impressive nation-building under his tutelage had been accomplished *despite* the Haitian people: "These achievements have been accomplished in the face of the handicaps of the mentality and tradition of the people, in the face of the frequent non-cooperation and at times actual hostility of the courts."[14] Lt. Col. Henry Davis, the previously noted self-styled expert on Latin culture, strikes much the same tone in advice he published for the benefit of fellow Marines:

> I spoke to them in their own language, not fluently, but with increasing facility as time went on. I tried to understand their viewpoint, and I believe I succeeded as far as any one else could in the time I was there. But they were also made to understand from the very first night I was in Macoris that the American commander was the boss and that his word in the absence of orders from higher authorities to the contrary was absolute law. It was a military government.[15]

Later, when discussing how to properly communicate government policy to the people, Davis continued:

> I found it of value to assemble the representative men at frequent intervals and try to make clear to them the wishes of our government as expressed through its representative, the senior officer present. This conference never took the phase of discussion of the merits of the case or the propriety of the action, but was merely an effort to have the representative men understand what we were trying to do at the time. To have allowed any discussion of the merit of the matter would at once have created the impression that an opinion was desired when nothing of the kind was the case.[16]

Nation-building has likely always been a misnomer but for Marines it was certainly so. Marines built the structure of the *state*, often, ironically, by overriding the voices of the *nation*. By confusing state and nation not just semantically but conceptually, Marines privileged material achievements (the infrastructure of state) over intangible achievements (fostering democratic and positive relations with the peoples of the nation) and therefore left behind a well-equipped state structure in the hands of a browbeaten and often resentful national community.

Perhaps the strangest feature of American cultural perception is the notion that the result of this combination—enormous material outlay orchestrated with disdainful and often abusive treatment of locals—should incur gratitude. The resistance of locals was not typically understood as a response to Marine indignities or heavy-handed methods but rather as a result of ignorance concerning the true intentions of the American occupation. The perception was that if only American *motives* and *intentions* were properly understood, locals would be eager to lend support. The *Small Wars Manual* recommends using "prominent native civilians" as proxy ambassadors. Taken on patrols, they could "do much to explain the mission of the intervening forces in the community, spread the gospel of peace, friendly relations, and cooperation, and counter the propaganda of the enemy." This effort was imperative since "the natives of the community are all potential enemies and many will become actively hostile if they are not convinced of the true objective of the occupation."[17]

Marines, even after members of their own Congress had shamed the Corps for its abuses and had consequently soured on state-building efforts abroad, continued to believe that their nation's "interventions or occupations are usually peaceful or altruistic."[18] Maj. E. H. Ellis argued that "in every case where the United States has taken charge of a small state it has been actuated by purely altruistic motives." The US is a "good angel" who attempts to interfere as little as possible in the lives of native peoples.[19] Privileging material outlay over personal behavior, American Marines referencing the occupation of the Dominican Republic defined and defended their nation's altruistic motives by pointing to dollars:

The object of the United States as explained in the beginning has never changed. It has been throughout the occupation to this time of returning the government to the Dominican people an unselfish object, looking only toward the betterment of the Dominican people and at great expense to the United States. It might be pointed out that the laws of nations give to one nation which occupies another's land, the right to support the occupation by taxation levied upon the country occupied. The United States has never even considered causing the Dominican people to defray the cost of the occupation in such a manner, but has itself borne the entire cost.[20]

A nation measuring its altruism by the material "gifts" it offers, and dispensing them through a service that means to act efficiently, presents a cultural formula that emphasizes physical accomplishments as primary objectives. Instincts toward material success were only compounded by the instrumental motivation of military necessity. Marine officers in the Caribbean could not afford the disease rates, inability to travel, and inability to communicate that the existing state of infrastructure often entailed. To achieve anything, these had to be remedied—and quickly. Instrumental needs combined comfortably with cultural inclinations. Marines preferred to focus their own action-oriented, efficient energies on tangible tasks, best accomplished without local interference, which could be chalked up in quantitative fashion for American domestic consumption.

Neither Marines nor their American civilian overseers saw the fallacy in this approach: that the preferred norms of action orientation and efficiency toward material successes were very likely to undermine the strategic ends that inspired American intervention in the first place, the need for a self-operating, stable, and democratic-leaning republic. The Marines pursuing these initiatives seemed blind to the inverse foundation they were laying: immense material and infrastructural improvements providing unprecedented reach into the countryside by a centralized, military-run government largely unaccountable to the people.[21] Nowhere in the *Small Wars Manual* are we provided an analysis of the contributions this formula may have made to a dictatorial aftermath in all three countries, despite clear acknowledgments that unprecedented government reach was being achieved. One Marine proudly notes: "These roads give military control of the whole Republic to the government and its military police force."[22]

Marine moves were congruent with, and accomplished, military values. Leatherneck efforts did create order and built state structures with admirable efficiency. Marines were very proud of both achievements. Reflecting on the state of Haiti in 1924, the Quartermaster Clerk John D. Brady remarked, "The period just passed has been the most peaceful and prosperous in the annals of the Republic; there was no semblance of an uprising and banditry has been non-existent. There has been a notable decrease in crime and offenses against the Haitian Laws."[23] General Russell notes that Marines managed to establish "law and order, uninterrupted, except for the banditism of 1919–1920 and the abortive disorders of November and December, 1929, for a period of fourteen years," a feat "remarkable when viewed against the background of previous conditions in the Republic."[24]

The legacy of this approach, however, was not likely the one Marines and their American sponsors had in mind. After the Marines departed, Haiti crumbled in short order, politically and economically, its future warlords somewhat aided by the national constabulary and improved infrastructure. In the Dominican Republic and Nicaragua, stability and order remained the legacy but under the iron fist of unprecedented lengths of dictatorship. Culpability for these legacies, in the minds of the populations who suffered them, belonged to the Marines. For the decades of the Somoza regime, Nicaraguans held to an anti-American narrative, blaming their current state on the leathernecks who had put it in motion. Many Nicaraguans viewed their country as having existed as a "quasi-US colony" until the Somozas were deposed in 1979. The three Somozas—Anastasio Somoza García and his two sons, Luis and Anastasio Somoza Debayle—were even dubbed "the last Yankee Marines."[25]

Before the Corps fully realized what a menace the president of the Dominican Republic, Rafael Trujillo—their onetime apprentice in the Guardia—was to become, they disseminated his praise of Marine mentors in the pages of the *Gazette*.[26] Even at this point, however, the reputation of the Ejército Nacional (the renamed Guardia) ought to have given them pause. A Marine general officer passing through the Dominican Republic in 1924—the first officer to visit there since the Marines had departed—paraphrased Trujillo's comments about the constabulary that the Marines had forged and he now wielded:

It seemed that in his opinion the military were not popular with the people nor with some of the leading politicians. This he explained was due to the fact that they wore the uniform of the Marines, and that their bugle calls and drums were a continual reminder to the people of the American occupation, which had not been popular with many of the people and the leaders. But Colonel Trujillo explained that he and his officers were proud that they were the offspring of the Marine Corps even though some of the leading politicians had used the expression—that the *Pòlicia* [*sic*], or *Ejercito*, was the *son of the American Marines*.[27]

Perhaps it is defensible that Marines of this era, in their pioneering moment of nation-building, did not see that their infrastructural improvements and enthusiastic amplification of a centralized government would become a precursor to dictatorship, but it is much less defensible today. Marine experiences and the lessons that could be gleaned with critical hindsight are largely lost on a forward-looking, ahistoric population. The dangers of the formula put in play during the Caribbean era remain largely undiscussed in Marine discourse and are absent from wider discussions concerning future counterinsurgency practice. Should they be considered, these would have something to say about the fallacy of measuring success through material achievements and would emphasize caution concerning the follow-on effects of constructing a centralized security structure unaccountable to the people and equipped with infrastructure that enables unprecedented reach into the countryside.

## LOCALS FIRST: THE CAP EXPERIENCE

CAP Marines pursued precisely the opposite course within their small area of operations within Vietnam—not through the conscious design of a dictatorship-wary strategy, but rather by circumstance of placement, starved budget, and a defensive mission set. As pointed out earlier, the CAP program began in defensive posture, protecting air fields and logistical lines important to the wider US military effort. As the program's successes in keeping the VC at bay became clear, its progenitors saw greater strategic ambitions for it—a sort of "ink blot" strategy that had the potential to squeeze VC influence from the countryside. Owing to institutional resistance from the US Army, the CAP program's ink-blot potential was never tested beyond five provinces within I Corps, a Marine area of responsibility, and peaked at in-country numbers of 42 officers, 2,050 enlisted, 2 naval officers, 126 corpsmen, and approximately 3,000 Popular Force or Regional Force members.[28] The vast majority of Marines in Vietnam performed service under Army command and in largely Army fashion.

One of the features of the CAP program that ran counter to the larger US military effort within South Vietnam was the empowerment of local hamlets rather than the increased centralization of the state. While recruits to the Caribbean constabularies were trained to break with local alliances and bind their identity to the centralized structure of the newly formed Gendarmerie or Guardia as a national institution, the loyalties of PFs remained local. PF identity was not forged anew in any meaningful way into the larger armed-force body within South Vietnam. Instead, PFs forged identity at the most local level as protectors of the population. PFs were trained for the express purpose of protecting their village and derived status from their ability to do so. Loyalty was to the villages and hamlets and could be extended to the Marines insofar as the Marines genuinely aided the cause of protecting PF friends and family. An identity of *localized protector* rather than enforcer of national government edicts on local populations represents a significant contrast with the form and function of Banana War constabularies. Given this substantial difference in priorities and posture, it is a touch ironic that it is the establishment and training of local forces that prompted the Marine's own "fact sheet" on the CAP program to draw parallels between the effort in Vietnam and the experience in the Caribbean.[29]

There is no evidence that the Marine Corps thought in any conscious way about empowering local forces as a balancer to national (and largely corrupt) institutions. Quite to the contrary, the general American military effort in Vietnam was aimed at providing exactly the sort of centralized, conventional armed force that had produced a tool for dictators in Haiti, the Dominican Republic, and Nicaragua. The local emphasis of the PFs was purely circumstantial and is representative of the historical happy accidents that Marines stumbled on by virtue of the operational realities of a roll-ing program. PFs were trained as a force multiplier. They were available to Marines as the "belittled and neglected . . . bottom rung in the Vietnamese military ladder."[30]

Marine-PF joint efforts were envisioned as the village-level tier of a multilayered military program to root out and kill the VC. From Victor Krulak, a key agitator and advocate from the program's beginnings: "The Combined Action Program's basic concept was to bring peace to the Viet-namese villages by uniting the local knowledge of the Popular Forces with the professional skill and superior equipment of the Marines. . . . The Viet-namese knew who the guerrillas were and where they hid; the Americans knew how to kill them."[31] Other assessors saw the Marine-PF relationship as key to fighting along population-centric lines: "By working with the PF and earning their respect and confidence, the Marines in the CAP are able to relate to the local people in a way that no conventional US military orga-nization could do. The PF therefore act as a link between the Marines and the local people. In a 'peoples war,' it goes without saying that this link is a vital asset."[32]

The record on PF performance was decidedly mixed. When comment-ing on their PFs, Marines often rated them individually rather than as a group—this one was trustworthy, that one useless, that one was almost defi-nitely VC, etc.[33] Others were primarily frustrated with them, sometimes to the point of treating them like the enemy.[34] Marines complained that PFs were easily insulted (exacerbated by the Marines' lack of cultural training), were lazy, often ran from a fight or refused to go out on patrols, and did not attend the training classes the Marines attempted to offer:[35]

> The CAP idea is a good idea as it is on paper but it doesn't always work out the way the big honchos figure it should. We have 30 PFs with us and approximately maybe three or four of these PFs are fighting men, the rest of them are just toy soldiers in green uniforms with rifles. They're professionals in one sense of the word, they're professional thieves, professional skaters. If they can get out of doing anything they'll do it. They expect everything and they don't give anything. They run when they're under fire, they sleep when they're on guard. They lie, they steal, everything you can think of.[36]

All Marines seemed aware of the mixed record, so in describing their own experience they would often offer a contrast: "The PFs we had . . . were very dependable. They wouldn't di-di [run away] like others did."[37] And some CAP Marines offered straight-up high praise for their PF counterparts, deeply grateful for local counterparts who were "really motivated" and "perform[ed] outstandingly."[38] When the CAP unit worked well, Marines tended to ascribe it to the PF's localized motivations:

The PF is one of the finest fighters that I have worked with in Vietnam though. I think it's due to the fact that he is out there protecting *his* family, *his* rice crop, and that he is there fighting as hard as he does. We have not had a problem with the PF of turning on us or running away from us during a firefight. In fact lately on our last four contacts, they have seemed real aggressive and we feel this comes through our training with them.[39]

The unintended result of Marines assuming "ownership" of Vietnamese villages—with or without the useful military help of the PFs—was that their loyalties became localized, sometimes pitting them against allied forces who were not equally concerned about protecting the persons and property of CAP villagers. A number of CAP veterans believe that they won their villagers' loyalty, and counterinsurgency help, in moments when they confronted rapacious or exploitive South Vietnamese troops—allied forces!—and chased them from their villages.[40] When villagers perceived that Marines were genuinely invested in their protection and in their interests, they began to offer their services in a more meaningful way. Rather than acting as a tool of the central government, Marines often acted as a local line of defense against it.

## Civic Action on a Shoestring

Marines in the CAP program found themselves somewhat insulated from the mistakes of American material overreach by virtue of circumstance. Disconnected from the larger war and budgetary victims of US forces commander William Westmoreland's disdain for the program, CAP Marines were left with few resources and dysfunctional Vietnamese political avenues for procuring them.[41] Still imbued with the spirit of their civic-action mandate, CAP Marines tended to fill their billet by scrounging resources from other services or digging into their own pockets. The results reveal both the benefits and limitations of state-building civic action as a strategic component of counterinsurgency.

Much of the grand-scale civic-action attempted by US military and civilian services in Vietnam yielded limited strategic benefit and was often unwanted or underresourced when placed in the material context of the population for whom it was built. Larry Cable explains that "confusion as to the nature of effective civic action assured that the superficially showy would prevail."[42] CAP Marines—much more attuned to village life than typical Army or Marine line infantrymen—tended to complain about the ethnocentric and unsustainable nature of the projects they saw go up around them: "They [Army, Navy, and line Marine units] make one mistake and that is they like to build something or do something that has immediate results and they oftentimes don't look into the future. For instance they will build a hospital and they will make no provision for providing the hospital with medical supplies, they will make no provision for feeding patients in the hospital or maintaining medical personnel there. They will make no provisions for a hospital maintenance."[43]

CAP Marines were not entirely immune to American enthusiasm for idealized, material-centric, impatiently executed civic-action practices. In his assessment of the program (focusing primarily on the years 1967 and 1968), Bruce Allnutt saw behavioral patterns very reminiscent of the Banana Wars years. Although the spirit of the program was different—in the CAP case, regulations specifically instructed Marines to make sure that a project was a village's choice, not their own—in practice things turned out rather the same. Marines found it frustrating to track down village officials or get them to commit to anything, so often, in defiance of the regulation, they decided on something themselves—many times a school-house (without having researched the availability of teachers). After waiting for weeks (or months) for their request for approval and supplies to be answered through the Government of Vietnam channels, Marines would run out of patience and scavenge from wherever possible the goods needed for the project. Once goods had been obtained, Marines were to encourage villagers to supply the labor for the project. When villagers' slow and nonchalant progress became too much for them, Marines—the epitome of American problem-solvers—scooped up the project and finished it themselves.[44] The project became American, start to finish. Unsurprisingly, these projects inspired little villager attachment or affection. If the project fell victim to VC destruction, villagers tended not to be overly upset. The prevailing attitude: "The Americans have many fine projects and programs, but none of them ever amount to much."[45]

Over time, CAP Marines began to recognize the senselessness of this approach and to resent it being foisted on them. They understood that even projects that had worked well in one area did not necessarily have transferability to another:

> Every time we had a civic action program we were sort [of] pushed into it at a wrong time. The attitude [from the people] was like, we don't particularly care for this sort of thing. . . . One time . . . we had word from higher up, that we were gonna dig wells for the people. They didn't need wells but we had to dig them anyway. . . . They got to thinking we are doing a lot of useless things.[46]

And CAP Marines agreed. They resented being the dispersal unit for hand-outs (usually soap and hygiene supplies) that villagers either didn't want or opted to sell on the market, and they resented the entitlement attitude among locals that they believed was being cultivated by American material outlays.[47] One captain with oversight over two CAPs delivered sage insight: "Generosity which cannot be returned breeds hostility, not affection."[48]

Those who were able to step aside from the American impulse for the grand-scale projects that played well back home and invest instead in the locally inspired spirit of the CAP program found that they met with much higher degrees of success.[49] Rather than building a school (an American favorite), one CAP unit constructed a grain-storage unit. Not only did this result in genuine gratitude from the population, it also accomplished significant disruption to the adversary's ability to obtain food. Marines tuned in with village life observed that this was the first time in a decade that villagers were able to keep all of their rice. They used the money to send their children to school and buy radios and bicycles. To show their gratitude, "marines of this position were receiving fifteen to twenty invitations a day to eat with . . . the Vietnamese in their village."[50] The villagers' attempt to return the favor, by sparing Marines from another meal of C-rations, became a useful measure of public attitudes and affection, an effective assessment tool duplicated decades later by savvy Marine officers in Al Qaim, Iraq.

Most CAP Marines were somewhat dubious about the strategic benefits that could be extracted from civic action. Their connection with villagers meant that they were more likely to see the conflict through local eyes. Villagers were often apathetic. And exhausted. "And being in this place so long, and in the heart of the fighting daily and nightly they're getting to be very tired and all they're living is just day by day until they wait to die."[51] Rather than attempting civic action to "win them over" and secure loyalty vis-à-vis the VC, Marines took a more pragmatic approach to minor acts of civic action and did it out of a rather instinctive impulse to be decent persons and make village life more enjoyable.[52]

Inhibited by limited supplies but armed with native make-do Marine ingenuity, many found ways to pursue modest civic action services despite their frugal circumstances. Two separate CAP Marines made use of the Army dump as a repository for supplies. In an effort to rebuild damaged homes, the first Marine transported villagers to the dump so they could scrounge any wood materials of value. Upon return, villagers sold these supplies to fellow villagers. With the pooled profits, the enterprising group could buy the more expensive materials needed, such as cement, off the local economy.[53] The second Marine talks about efforts to build a school, this time locally inspired:

> We built a schoolhouse, the people worked with us. The biggest thing was they couldn't get the materials, like the tin and nails and stuff. And we could go down to a place where they burned ammo boxes, and I took a crew down there myself and we pulled nails out of wood and straightened them ourselves to build a school house. And that was a combined deal with the civilians and military

working together there. And the people were really on our side. They didn't care for the way the VC treated them and I'd say that once you get the people on your side, where they don't want the communists in the area you got the war half won right there.[54]

Armed with this perspective, CAP Marines began fudging their reports to satisfy large-scale expectations,[55] and they curbed their practice to more "neighborly" activity such as sharing their one meal a day (if they got that meal) with PFs and villagers,[56] teaching kids to swim, or pooling platoon money to send village children to school or hire a teacher.[57] Marines found ways to secure farm implements and often used their native skills to help with farm work.[58] When in pursuit of an idea, Marines made up for shortages by "appropriating" goods from the Army or by issuing personal requests to folks back home.[59] Because medical attention was always the most appreciated of the civic-action forms, some CAP units sought out dentists for their village. Of their small-scale efforts, Allnutt noted, "They help satisfy the common American desire to 'do good' or help in some way, and they not uncommonly yield real benefit to the people."[60]

Marines engaging in low-level civic action of this sort found it more satisfying in a number of ways. Their perception was that villagers regarded their efforts as genuine. CAP Marines typically existed in a steady state of ragged disrepair. Their uniforms were filthy from night patrols, and by 1969 compounds had been discontinued. CAP Marines were now "mobile"—living and sleeping in the bush. Little of the American basket of plenty—save the enormous firepower they could draw on—characterized CAP Marine life. To the extent that a foreign fighter can invoke a sympathetic picture, some CAP Marines did. Their efforts to "help out," therefore, were met with a higher degree of village gratitude.

What strategic benefits did this yield? It is perhaps easier to talk about the strategic backlash that was *not* produced. Villagers tended *not* to develop entitlement mentalities to the same degree as was detected in other areas. CAP Marines did *not* destabilize their area with an inrush of goods or funds, nor did they build as many structures that villagers were unable to maintain. From the perspective of US national treasure, both are a plus. Far more important, however, Marines often softened what might have been purposeful plotting for their demise. Some Marines saved their own skins. One fairly dramatic example comes from a former CAP Marine who returned to his "ville" decades after the war was over. Friends in the village confessed to him that they had all been VC. Shocked, he asked why they had allowed his squad to live—especially when so many of their sister CAP units had been overrun. The villagers' formula was fairly simple: "You didn't hurt anybody intentionally. You were pretty good kids. You ran around the village and worked on kids with your first aid kits who had sores." Further, villagers reasoned that if they killed the CAP Marines, it would be a company of grunts on a search-and-destroy mission who would replace them. CAP Marines were protecting the village—not from the VC or the NVA, but from the American military machine.[61]

Among the short-term advantages of civic action, the primary benefits were an intermeshing with village life—often knowing the terrain far better than the enemy—and consequent contextual dividends in intelligence. Superior intelligence cannot be attributed wholly, or even primarily, to village gratitude stemming from American material gifts. Rather, it was a combination of relentless patrolling to establish security, a consequent well-developed sixth sense for the village, and neighborly civic action that encouraged consistent and warm interaction with villagers.

Sincerely offered civic action achieved some level of force protection but did not enhance the legitimacy of the South Vietnamese government, despite this being part of purported purpose. From a macro view, the American perception that drove these operations—that US-resourced civic action in the name of a host government can provide a lasting boost to the host government's legitimacy—is likely nothing short of strategic fantasy, one that does not seem to suffer much from consistent disproval. If local governing officials were cooperative (which many were), Marines were happy to attempt to pass the feel-good benefits of a civic-action accomplishment to them. In the main, however, Marine civic action did not incur legitimacy for local governments or Saigon; it incurred legitimacy for CAP Marines. In this sense it produced force-protection benefits, superior intelligence, and varying levels of counterinsurgent help. The goodwill and gratitude generated from these sincere acts could not be "gifted" to the South Vietnamese government. It went home with Marines.

## NOTES

1. Maj. Charles F. Williams, "La Guardia Nacional Dominicana," *Marine Corps Gazette* (September 1918): 196. Efficiency as well as "peace and order," according to 1st Lt. Robert C. Kilmartin, "Indoctrination in Santo Domingo," *Marine Corps Gazette* (December 1922): 383.
2. Gobat, *Confronting the American Dream*, 207, 216; Calder, *Impact of Intervention*.
3. Millett and Gaddy, "Administering the Protectorates," 111.
4. J. C. Fegan, "After Nineteen Years We Leave Haiti," *Marine Corps Gazette* (August 1934): 23.
5. Millett, *Semper Fidelis*, 193.
6. Col. Rufus Lane, "Civil Government in Santo Domingo in the Early Days of the Military Occupation," *Marine Corps Gazette* (June 1922): 135–36.
7. Gobat, *Confronting the American Dream*, 217–20.
8. Ibid., 4; Calder, *Impact of Intervention*, xii.

9. United States Marine Corps (hereafter USMC), *Small Wars Manual*, ch. 1, "Introduction," 20.

10. Ibid., ch. 12, "Armed Native Organizations," section II, "Organization of a Constabulary," 13.

11. Ibid., 9.

12. For reports celebrating Marine material and structural accomplishments, see Brig. Gen. John H. Russell, "The Development of Haiti during the Last Fiscal Year," *Marine Corps Gazette* (June 1930): 76–115; 2nd Lt. Leslie H. Wellman, "Mapping Activities and Compilation of Hand-books by the Second Brigade, U.S.M.C., in the Dominican Republic," *Marine Corps Gazette* (September 1923): 169; Lane, "Civil Government in Santo Domingo," 127–46; and "Conditions in Nicaragua," *Marine Corps Gazette* (November 1932): 88–89.

13. Bickel, *Mars Learning*, 83.

14. Russell, "Development of Haiti," 88.

15. Lt. Col. Henry C. Davis, "Indoctrination of Latin-American Service," *Marine Corps Gazette* (June 1920): 156.

16. Ibid., 157.

17. USMC, *Small Wars Manual*, ch. 6, "Infantry Patrols," 12.

18. Ibid., ch. 1, "Organization," 13.

19. Maj. E. H. Ellis, "Bush Brigades," *Marine Corps Gazette* (March 1921): 1, 11.

20. Kilmartin, "Indoctrination in Santo Domingo," 378–79.

21. For intensive treatment of these effects see Calder, *Impact of Intervention*; Schmidt, *United States Occupation of Haiti*; and Gobat, *Confronting the American Dream*.

22. Kilmartin, "Indoctrination in Santo Domingo," 382.

23. Quartermaster Clerk John D. Brady, "Haiti," *Marine Corps Gazette* (June 1924): 150.

24. Russell, "Development of Haiti," 87.

25. Gobat, *Confronting the American Dream*, 267.

26. Maj. Edwin North McClellan, "Down in the Dominican Republic," *Marine Corps Gazette* (May 1932).

27. "Santo Domingo after the Marines," *Marine Corps Gazette* (November 1930): 11 (italics in original).

28. Hemingway, *Our War Was Different*, 5; Klyman, "Combined Action Program"; *Fact Sheet on the Combined Action Force*, 1.

29. *Fact Sheet on the Combined Action Force*, 1.

30. Hemingway, *Our War Was Different*, 4.

31. Victor Krulak, foreword, ibid., x.

32. *Fact Sheet on the Combined Action Force*, 1.

33. Tim Duffie, CAP veteran, lecture at Utah State University, February 16, 2012.

34. Tony Vieira calls PFs "useless." Oral history in Hemingway, *Our War Was Different*, 41. Harvey Baker says he "didn't trust most of 'em." Oral history, ibid., 62. Rocky Jay called them "a bunch of draft dodgers" who were worse than useless and "always busting ambushes." He and a fellow Marine would "take

them out to the sand dunes and leave them out there all night just to get away from them." Oral history, ibid., 116. Maj. H. G. Duncan claims that in the era in which he oversaw CAPs in 1970, "there was hostility between Marines and PFs in almost all the CAPs." Oral history, ibid., 155.

35. Klyman, "Combined Action Program."

36. Oral history file 2614, USMC Vietnam War Oral History Collection, Marine Corps Archives and Special Collections, Gray Research Center, Quantico, VA, transcription by Megan Hansen, February 22, 2012.

37. Skip Freeman, oral history in Hemingway, *Our War Was Different*, 101. See also Wayne Christiansen, oral history, ibid., 131, and oral history file 2141, USMC Vietnam War Oral History Collection.

38. Oral history file 3679, USMC Vietnam War Oral History Collection, transcription by Jacquelyn Thompson, February 22, 2012; Art Falco, oral history in Hemingway, *Our War Was Different*, 159. See also Jimmy Sparrow, oral history, ibid., 45; Tom Harvey, oral history, ibid., 76; Tom Krusewski, oral history, ibid., 90; Warren V. Smith, oral history, ibid., 137.

39. Oral history file 2202-2341, USMC Vietnam War Oral History Collection, transcription by Megan Hurst, February 21, 2012.

40. Philip Leiker, lecture at Utah State University, April 5, 2013; Tim Duffie, "I Keep It in My Heart and Wait for You," posting on capmarine.com.

41. Corson, *Betrayal*, 178.

42. Cable, *Conflict of Myths*, 154.

43. Oral history file 2304-6, USMC Vietnam War Oral History Collection, transcription by Victoria Cattanach, February 2012. For the empty fate of schoolhouses, see John A. Daube, oral history in Hemingway, *Our War Was Different*, 122.

44. Anthropologist Leonard Mason notes the same pattern in American civilian life when engaging with Native Americans. Mason, "Characterization of American Culture," 1273–74.

45. Allnutt, *Marine Combined Action Capabilities*, 45–47. See also Klyman, "Combined Action Program."

46. Oral history file 2599, USMC Vietnam War Oral History Collection, transcription by Tawni Chambers, February 20, 2012.

47. Allnutt, *Marine Combined Action Capabilities*, 28, 44.

48. Capt. R. E. Williamson, "A Briefing for Combined Action," *Marine Corps Gazette* (March 1968): 43.

49. William Corson set and practiced the CAP standard for village-inspired civic action and describes it here: Corson, *Betrayal*, 154–73. See also Peterson, *Combined Action Platoons*, 40.

50. Oral history file 2251, USMC Vietnam War Oral History Collection, transcription by Noah Johnson, February 21, 2012. For an equally successful report on a village brick-making business, see oral history file 2304-6, ibid., transcription by Victoria Cattanach, February 21, 2012.

51. Oral history file 2614, USMC Vietnam War Oral History Collection, transcription by Megan Hansen, February 22, 2012.

52. West, *Village*, 176.
53. Oral history file 2304-6, USMC Vietnam War Oral History Collection, transcription by Victoria Cattanach, February 2012.
54. Oral history file 2571, USMC Vietnam War Oral History Collection, transcription by Tawni Chambers, February 21, 2012.
55. Allnutt, *Marine Combined Action Capabilities*, 48.
56. Jack Broz, oral history in Hemingway, *Our War Was Different*, 127.
57. Oral history files 2341, 2571, 2670, USMC Vietnam War Oral History Collection. Or teach English: Oral history file 2304-6, ibid., transcription by Victoria Cattanach, February 21, 2012.
58. Skip Freeman, oral history in Hemingway, *Our War Was Different*, 104; A. W. Sundberg, oral history, ibid., 110.
59. Tony Vieira, oral history in *Our War Was Different*, 42. For one that involved a swing set, see Tom Krusewski, oral history, ibid., 90.
60. Allnutt, *Marine Combined Action Capabilities*, 47.
61. Will Gilmore, correspondence with the author, January 31, 2012. For another example, see B. Keith Cossey, oral history in Hemingway, *Our War Was Different*, 88.

# CHAPTER 8

# COUNTERINSURGENCY READINESS FROM HAITI TO VIETNAM

*The Consequences of Craving Conventional War*

The overwhelming preference toward conventional warfare within the US military has served both to impede the development of counterinsurgency doctrine and to squelch some of the innovations Marines produced. The slow dawning of recognition in the Marine Corps that small-wars doctrine was needed and then the shockingly quick disregard of that which was laboriously forged are both products of this preference. Tactical innovations fared a little better. Marines tended, in each Caribbean case, to start with default conventional approaches against irregular enemies. Failure along the same repeated learning curve, rather than predeployment training, served as the educational device in each round. Gradually, Marines came to the same tactical conclusions in each theater and evolved toward small, aggressive patrols and decentralized leadership—tactics adopted early in the Combined Action Platoon (CAP) program and carried forward as Marine instinct into the campaign in Iraq. Other innovations slipped into lessons lost.

## DOCTRINE SLOW TO DAWN, QUICK TO FADE

The total absence of discussion of the insurgency problem in Haiti and the Dominican Republic within the pages of the *Marine Corps Gazette* during the early years of the occupations there implies an air of already achieved competence being carried out in business-as-usual fashion. The first article of any length on the subject in the *Gazette* (beyond quick references on such topics as the building of latrines or commemorations to fallen Marines) is in December 1916, a year and a half after the Marines landed on Haitian shores (in fairness, the *Gazette* had only been running since March 1916) and after the first *caco* rebellion was already defeated. Rather than revisiting the lessons learned in this conflict or formalizing some level of doctrine from the experience, the first article on Haiti is written in a form very like a travel brochure.[1] The writer dispatches advice to his fellow officers about the conditions that their families would encounter should the families choose to join the Marine adventure in Haiti. He addresses such vital topics as market fare, climate, and the appropriate gut to choose for one's tennis racquet. No mention is made of military exploits of any kind.

The next submission on Haiti is equally lightweight. It is purportedly on reconnaissance but reads more like a chatty diary entry, describing colorful scenes along a patrol, interactions with villagers on a path, the food eaten, the behavior of the burro, and a wide assortment of other entertaining details one might write in a letter home. It is written in the spirit of a lark, with no serious intent to convey advice or say anything much about a manner of reconnaissance patrolling.[2] In short, early writings demonstrate little tactical or operational curiosity about how the job is getting done and if it is being done well. The Marine perception seems to be that the situation is well in hand; it is small fare, and a serious discussion of such is unwarranted.

By 1928, after having spent thirteen years in Hispaniola fighting consecutive insurgencies, the Corps found itself still without a common body of lessons learned. The Marine's own Division of Operations and Training observed: "This type of combat, which might well be called 'bush warfare' is the one which has been most frequently encountered by marine personnel in the past, and yet is still unknown to many officers, either through a failure to be a participant with some expeditionary force, or through a lack of any available reports which might be studied."[3]

The naive perceptual lens regarding the ease of subduing "bandits" and building economically sound and politically democratic nations was eventually tempered by the Marines' lived experience. These lessons, however, remained locally learned and not shared across the service for many years owing to the Marine valuing of field experience over formalized education. The action orientation of the Marines was well entrenched in the early twentieth century. In 1916 Col. Ben Fuller (later to become commandant) described the Marine approach to education thus: "His education as a marine has always been obtained mostly by practical methods; what the older and experienced ones have learned in service is passed on to the new ones by actual demonstration; in unaccustomed circumstances and unfamiliar conditions he experiments for himself because of the lack of a doctrine and of thoroughly trained knowledge of the best practice."[4] Fuller believed this mode of instruction to be insufficient but also recognized that instruction within the war colleges run by the Army and Navy would not provide remedy. Designed to prepare generals to command an Army division or to provide the strategic lessons necessary to become a fleet commander, their courses did little to prepare Marine officers to command "an advance base or expeditionary force which may have to administer the affairs of a Caribbean republic."[5]

Attempts at training and education in theater were pursued in both Haiti and the Dominican Republic but with limited attendance and with little to no educational reach beyond the immediate theater.[6] Smedley Butler, like many leathernecks, took a certain pride in the lack of formal education possessed by bush Marines and derided too much education as having a detrimental effect on warrior spirit.[7] Butler characterized his superior in Haiti, Eli Cole, as being a "fine officer" but "over-educated." This, Butler believed, led him to overthink action to the point of risk-averse paralysis.[8]

Without comprehensive doctrine and only informal mentorship and trial-and-error learning curves to guide them, "Marine officers wound up 'reinventing the wheel' in each of the three insurgencies they encountered."[9] The negative consequences of this deficit were eventually recognized by small-wars practitioners. Several began an earnest discussion within the pages of the *Gazette*. Their aim was to prepare future counterinsurgency war planners with more than "a hazy knowledge of what has occurred in the past."[10] All three of the most significant voices of this period—Maj. E. H. Ellis, Maj. Samuel M. Harrington, and Lt. Col. Harold H. Utley—recognized that operations and tactics of small wars differed significantly from those of a conventional battlefield and thus required a separate sort of training.[11] An influential cadre within Marine leadership supported this idea, and after much discussion and analysis, the small-wars camp inside the Corps assembled its insights into the *Small Wars Manual*.

Marine preference for action over education slowed the formation of small-wars doctrine within the Corps. What sealed its fate, however, was circumstance, which pitted expertise in irregular warfare against preparation for future conventional conflicts. The shift to amphibious doctrine and the resultant squeezing of small-wars training out of the Corps's classrooms has been detailed in chapter 3. A second identity shift is examined here. Marines who served in the Corps before the great event of World War I may not have craved tropical counterinsurgency duty, but they certainly did not resent it as being outside their sphere. When this mission set came at the expense of participation in the world's largest conventional war, however, Marines soured on their Caribbean fare and began to regard it as beneath their military station.

## The Strategic Effects of Second-Rate Status

Although it took Marines a good while to take their Caribbean fights seriously by way of doctrine, one does not detect any aversion toward counterinsurgency duty within their writings during the initial years on Hispaniola. For those who had signed up for Marine life as profession, performing "warlike operations when a state of war does not exist" was assumed to be "fundamentally a function of the Marine Corps."[12] Skirmishes in tropical scenes were all well and good until they inhibited participation in "real" war. A good many Marines who ended up in service during the Banana Wars years had rushed to Marine offices in 1917 in order to sign up for the war of the century, not thinking much of Marine service beyond the great event in front of them.[13] These were recruits not pleased to be diverted to Hispaniola. Cut off from the Great War, they experienced intense frustration mirroring that of longtime salt Smedley Butler, then commandant of the Haitian Gendarmerie, who complained that Haiti was "becoming more and more detestable every day and the knowledge that I am not to be allowed to fight for my country, makes it even more unbearable."[14]

As a highly regarded Marine, Butler suffered the additional humiliation of being stuck in the tropics with second-stringers. It was well understood that the Corps was pulling its best off the island and sending them to the European front. Those left behind felt the sting of second class.[15] Lester Langley, whose scholarship examines US intervention across the Caribbean, believes this to have contributed to maltreatment of the population: "Those who stayed behind grew increasingly resentful of occupation duty; their frustration and bitterness over policing 'spigs,' as they often called Dominicans, made them less sympathetic toward their subjects or their plight."[16] Keith Bickel applies the same logic to those who returned from the front and "resented serving in the isolated tropics after having done their part in the war."[17] Hans Schmidt characterizes Haiti's irregular war as one that became perceived as a "frustrating and degrading experience" for superior forces who allowed the difficulty of the terrain, their own embedded prejudice, and the irregular nature of their foe to justify lapses in the "rules of civilized warfare" and consequent commission of atrocities.[18]

Part of the "degrading" condition was bound up in fighting a foe that Marines, especially with the war in Europe as backdrop, could not consider worthy. In their disdain, Marines tended to oversimplify their adversaries, casting them as bandits rather than proper military foes (even during the Sandino era in Nicaragua), and had difficulty imagining that any serious consideration need be given to the tactics of their defeat.[19] Throughout the Banana Wars years, Marines tended to underestimate their enemies' popular appeal, ascribing only criminal and predatory intent to the insurgents. This inhibited a strategically useful understanding of the adversary's narrative and kept US forces from clearheaded analysis of the contextual motives of new insurgent recruits. Maj. E. H. Ellis, one of the most influential writers on Marine small-wars doctrine, demonstrates this blind spot in his own seminal piece on "bush brigades." He describes the adversary as typically "outlaw bandits (bandits, ladrones, cacos) who rob and murder members of the forces of occupation and their own people indiscriminately."[20] Then he notes two sentences later that "the enemy will have moral support from most of his own people, material support from many, and will operate in their midst."[21] Ellis does not seem bothered with the apparent contradiction this logic seems to present or prodded with the need to unravel the nature of popular support in such a situation.

The bandit mentality persisted within the Corps, even after facing off with a genuine revolutionary in Nicaragua, and became enshrined in doctrine in the *Small Wars Manual*: "The mission of our forces usually involves the training of native officers and men in the art of war, assisting in offensive operations against organized banditry and in such defensive measure against threatened raids of large organized bandit groups as are essential to the protection of lives and property."[22] One line in the manual offers some glimmer of insight that adversaries of the future may be of a more sophisticated nature: "If marines have become accustomed to easy victories over irregulars in the past, they must now prepare themselves for the increased effort which will be necessary to insure victory in the future."[23] The bulk of assessments in the *Small Wars Manual* concerning the character of small-wars adversaries, however—born out of the leathernecks' tropical experience and validated in the Marine mind by overwhelmingly lopsided casualty rates in their favor[24]—did little to prepare Marines for the dedicated insurgents they would face in Vietnam.[25]

## LEARNED THE HARD WAY: SMALL PATROLS AND DECENTRALIZED DECISION MAKING

Despite the opportunity to do otherwise, Marines started each of their irregular Caribbean fights in highly regular fashion. Although Marines had no counterinsurgency doctrine of their own, they did have access to the Army's *Landing Force Manual*, which offered advice on small-patrol tactics and night patrols.[26] Rather than resort to them, however, Marines leaned on more familiar operational norms and started their counterinsurgency duties in Haiti, the Dominican Republic, and Nicaragua by garrisoning the major population centers first and situating themselves on the operationally defensive. Their initial offensive forays were in the conventional form of large columns marching in regular fashion.[27] Not all of these were disasters, but neither did they solve the "bandit" problem. Over time, Marine moves to protect towns became increasingly more aggressive and pushed farther into the countryside.[28] Given that the primary challenge for Marines was *finding* insurgents rather than killing them once discovered, Marines began using their own small patrols as "bait"—attempting to lure their adversary into attacking and then defeating them through expert marksmanship.[29]

In all three episodes, small, aggressive patrols emerged as one of the Marines' most successful tactics in the counterguerrilla field during the Banana Wars.[30] Many other approaches, such as concentrating the population into designated zones in order to isolate insurgents, were not.[31] By the time Marines came to the small-patrols tactical discovery (once again) in Nicaragua, the Corps became serious about documenting it.[32] An article titled "Events in Nicaragua since February 28, 1928" is a composite of patrol reports; a similar set of articles became serialized in the *Gazette*.[33] Relentless patrols did not always result in the discovery of insurgent leaders, or even the discovery of a respectable number of insurgent footmen to kill, but could typically claim success in keeping the adversary off balance. Marines were "constantly on the go, so that . . . [insurgents] in this area never knew when or where a patrol would drop in on them."[34] Marines hoped that by keeping their adversary on the run, they could cause erosion and perhaps fatal damage to organizational features of the insurgency, including information flow: "Above all, an active and aggressive campaign against the hostile forces in the field is the most effective method of destroying their intelligence service. A guerrilla band which is constantly harassed and driven from place to place soon loses contact with its own sources of information; it becomes confused and its intelligence system breaks down. As the occupation continues, superiority in this respect will gradually be obtained by the intervening forces."[35]

As late as 1933, small-wars doctrinal advocate Colonel Utley was still hedging on the now-proven tactic of small patrols. Rather than recommend it outright, he advised small patrol use "when the military situation permits," in order to diminish "the comparative superiority of the irregular" in tracking Marines' whereabouts.[36] The combined wisdom of the *Small Wars Manual* is more forthright: "It is desirable to keep the patrol as small as is consistent with the accomplishment of its mission. The larger the patrol the more difficult its control in combat, the more complicated its supply problems, and the more it sacrifices in the way of concealment and secrecy of movement."[37] It advises patrols both small and relentless: "By energetic patrolling of the area and vigorous pursuit of the hostile forces once contact is gained, the irregulars should be forced to disband completely or to move to more remote and less fertile areas. The pursuit of these small bands must be continuous."[38] Marines should expect to be outnumbered but not outfought. Their victory will come through "increased fire power through the proper employment of better armament, superior training and morale, and development of the spirit of the offensive." Mobility is key: "Infantry patrols of the intervening force must develop mobility equal to that of the opposing forces. The guerrilla groups must be continually harassed by patrols working throughout the theater of operation."[39] Looking forward, one would think CAP Marines were carrying this *Small Wars* chapter around in their pockets.

## Beating Guerrillas at Their Own Game: The Signature of CAP Patrols

CAP units were small by design and were mandated to make daily and nightly patrols right from the beginning of the program. Bruce Allnutt, speaking in 1968, notes that by far "the largest proportion of the time and energy of the CAP Marine is consumed in the planning, conduct, and reporting of strictly military operations—the patrols and ambushes." No matter the "pacification" level, Marines were required to engage in "continual, aggressive patrolling."[40] The geographically bounded nature of their patrolling, however, represents an important distinction from patrolling of the Banana Wars sort. The objective of CAP patrols was not to seek out the enemy and pursue him to extinction; rather, they were designed to clear and hold a specific village—to protect it from VC incursions and discourage any relationship with the VC at all. CAP Marines concerned themselves with the enemy who entered the ville, not the enemy without.[41] While limited in geographic reach, the mobile CAP units fit Marine psychology in being offensively oriented. "We learned to move together as if we were one, and we never made a sound. We were among the best at what we did."[42] Given the units' small size, their members had to create tactical depth by cross-training on all weapons and achieving universal familiarization with communications equipment.[43] Living in and patrolling a fixed geographic location lent CAP Marines immense advantages in knowledge of terrain. One recalled, "I guess the reason the Combined Action Program worked so well, at least in our CAG [Combined Action Group], was the fact we knew our AO [Area of Operations] so well. The regular grunt units left and returned six weeks later, but we knew every bush, stick, and bend in the river where an ambush could be set for us."[44] CAP Marines knew they were fighting in unconventional fashion, much closer to the ground, much more like the enemy, and not at all like conventional Army units. "This CAP compound [has] its advantages over the Victor Charlie due to the fact that we use guerrilla tactics against guerrilla tactics instead of the major conventional warfare as which are usually used in infantry tactics."[45]

The aggressive and geographically constrained patrolling style of the CAP Marines yielded a number of benefits. Villagers responded first and foremost to a clearly demonstrated ability to provide security. When Marines succeeded in protecting them, villagers tended to open up.[46] When they did not, the opposite occurred. One vet cites the example of Papa-3, which was "never effective" because a steady stream of battles showed villagers that Marines could "get their butts kicked." The security context played a central role in the effectiveness of any particular CAP unit.[47]

The first generation of CAP units set up day compounds in their villages where they slept, cleaned equipment, and offered the medical services of the corpsman—"medcaps"—for villagers. During the CAP program's early years, a number of compounds were lethally overrun, and it became increasingly clear that their static structure represented a juicy target for often overwhelming forces of the VC or infantry from the National Vietnamese Army. In response, Marine Corps leadership made a bold break to "mobile" CAP squads.[48] Such Marines didn't "live" anywhere—they remained constantly on the move throughout their village, taking up randomly selected day sites with village families (often the family would abandon its hooch for the day and turn it over to the Marines). Not all Marines were enthusiastic about the switch. Arguing for the compound approach, CAP scholar and former CAP Marine Michael Peterson notes:

> As a center of pacification, the compound . . . was a focal point for civic action. The peasants knew where to come for medical help (although they also knew where a mobile CAP could be found—the "bamboo grapevine" was very efficient). The CAP compound could be a much-needed haven of safety for hamlet officials and elders. And they were a warehouse for supplies earmarked for impending civic action projects. This is much more important than it appeared at first glance.[49]

Some Marines agreed. One argued strongly against the mobiles, saying that they were terrifying, didn't allow the men to build up supplies, or even acquire sufficient food. In addition, "civic action duty just fell by the wayside."[50] The mobile life certainly lacked in creature comforts. In one Marine's description: "We stayed on the move constantly. At night, when we could, we slept in the cemeteries. The Vietnamese believed that to enter a cemetery of their loved ones was bad. We also slept near dung piles out in the middle of rice paddies. The Vietnamese stayed away from there for obvious reasons. Our CAP always slept in full combat gear, rifles across our laps, propped up against gravestones, trees, rocks, whatever."[51]

Robert Klyman, whose thesis on the CAP program has merited both archiving in historical files at Quantico and a place on the CAP Marine website, says most Marines were enthusiastic about the switch to mobile CAP units since it required less "overhead" in time and materials invested in the compound and it made their unit harder to find and kill.[52] Compound-era Marines seemed to spend an inordinate amount of time fixing up the compound, getting it "squared away," and adding what comforts and defensive measure they could rather than spending that time in the village.[53] Klyman also emphasizes some of the advantages of mobile CAP units as observed by the directors of the program. Mobile CAP units forced Marines to live a lifestyle similar to the Popular Force soldiers (PFs). Marines were not seen to have any special privileges or accommodations, and this helped seal a closer bond with both villagers and the Marines' PF trainees. It also meant that Marines were out and about in the village (they had nowhere else to be!) instead of hanging out at the compound all day.[54]

In the end, Peterson concedes that the mobile CAP units "suffered fewer casualties and killed more of the enemy . . . which to the Marine commanders was the cardinal principle of war."[55] A 1970 fact sheet surveying CAP units across Vietnam put together by Marine Command notes that by being stealthy and unpredictable (a different ambush site every night), the mobile CAP units capitalized on the advantage of surprise, enabling them to take on much larger groups, and their small numbers were protected by elusiveness rather than "sheer bulk of forces and firepower alone." The enemy found it difficult to find and fix the CAP target in order to bring a superior force against it. Rather than defending a fixed position—the compound—the Marines' strategic optic became more comprehensively oriented on protecting the hamlet. The evidence the fact sheet supplies about the utility of this approach is fairly straightforward: "The enemy has succeeded in destroying some of our compound CAPs. He has never destroyed a mobile CAP." The reverse logic is undeniably compelling: "In pondering the relative merit of the compound CAP versus the mobile CAP, it might be well to reflect on how short this war would have been if the VC and NVA operated out of fixed compounds."[56]

## MISSION COMMAND: PLUSES AND PITFALLS

Banana Wars veterans, like their CAP successors, decentralized their leadership—more out of necessity than doctrine—and in the end came to see its value in strategic theory. The doctrine of the *Small Wars Manual* makes clear that "a force assigned a small wars mission should be tactically and administratively a self-sustaining unit. It must be highly mobile, and tactical units, such as the battalion, must be prepared to act independently as administrative organizations."[57] Further, "considerable authority must be granted all leaders to act independently and on their own initiative. In the absence of orders, action on the part of the patrol's subdivision is preferable to inaction."[58]

The lack of leadership training before and during the Banana Wars era, however, meant that interpretations of appropriate action varied significantly among those junior officers in decision-making positions and sometimes with serious consequences.[59] Even the Corps's official history concedes that "life in insolated outposts, where they often exercised wide authority under minimal supervision from superiors, offered temptations to corruption and the misuse of power to which a few Marines fell victim."[60] On a number of occasions, one rather infamously, Marine officers became so emboldened in their private tropical districts that they refused to follow orders. One of the most strategically damning episodes came in Haiti at the hands of Maj. Clark H. Wells, who continued the *corvée*—the old French law that mandated physical labor from locals in lieu of taxes—and in particularly brutal fashion, despite an order issued by Col. John Russell to desist.[61] The Corps paid the price in the form of a renewed *caco* uprising originating in Wells's area.[62]

CAP units, on the whole, fared significantly better in their exercise of junior leadership. This might be expected given the instrumental and intrinsic incentives to behave well when living an outnumbered life in a Vietnam ville but remains remarkable in light of the fact that CAP squads were composed entirely of enlisted Marines. One director of the program pointed out the enormous administrative responsibility that had been handed to these young men:

> It's interesting to note that you have a Sergeant running a Combined Action Platoon [the CAP Marines plus PFs] who maybe has at most three years in the Marine Corps. He has maybe had a high school education and maybe not and he is a United States ambassador to this particular village where he operates. It is also interesting to note that he is a Commander in the field, he has got to be his own Operations Officer, he's got to be his own Supply Officer and he has to be his own Administrator almost. The major supply sources of course came from the group but he was the guy that had to order and I think that it's amazing that we got as much out of those young fellows as we did.[63]

A second officer focused on the sensitive nature of commanding in the context of a civilian Vietnamese village:

> I think that what the Combined Action Program is—how it turns out, how successful it is—depends entirely upon the key man, the Combined Action Platoon leader. In this Combined Action Group our platoons are led by corporals and sergeants, mostly by corporals. This was perhaps the first thing that impressed me when I entered the program. The magnitude of the job that we've called upon this corporal to do; I compared it to the job I called upon my new lieutenants to do when I had the 1st Battalion 27th Marines prior to coming up here. I think there is a great deal more to the task of leading a Combined Action Platoon. It requires an understanding of the Vietnamese people, appreciation of their attitudes

and culture; it requires a finesse that the normal platoon leader doesn't often run into. Of course, the man we asked to do this job has had little of the background or little of the training that we normally give our platoon leaders. In effect I would say that in the Combined Action Program [we have an] almost . . . built-in leadership gap or leadership problem, yet it is the most remarkable aspect of the program, is how well these young corporals and sergeants rise to the task.[64]

CAP squad leaders exercised their autonomy by determining their mission priorities and by "innovations" in combat dress and patrol procedures. The fluctuating mission set of the CAP allowed squad leaders to determine locally driven priorities. Allnutt notes this as one of the program's foremost advantages—squad leaders were allowed the flexibility to accommodate their different situations and respond to "tactical environments and local conditions" in ways that made sense.[65] CAP Marines, far from the eyes of officers in the rear, tended to jettison all trappings of proper Marine kit and squared-away appearance that were not useful for preserving life in the bush. Marines discarded flak jackets, helmets, and any other gear that made noise.[66] PFs were drilled on patrol discipline—how to walk point, keep quiet, and maintain presence of mind under fire but unlike the Caribbean constabularies were not drilled in parade form and military appearance. In the oft present conflict between squared-away dress appearance and combat utility, CAP squads went all out for the latter.

Killer teams (KTs) were another innovation devised within the CAP units. These were small groups of typically two or three Marines and sometimes PFs who went out at night with no pack, flak jacket, helmet, or radio and often wearing VC-signature black "pajamas." They would haunt the hoochs of VC relatives or suspected sympathizers, and if "Victor Charlies" were discovered, they would track and kill them.[67] When the rear heard about this "innovation," it was ordered stopped immediately. CAP Marines themselves thought the idea very useful and continued to press for its inclusion.[68] Alternative orders did not force CAP squads to stop the KTs but to rename them: security teams.[69]

Mission command, CAP style, rested entirely on the Corps's ability to produce and select good leaders. Allnutt captures this concept with the appropriate emotive force:

The major variable affecting the performance of military operations is the leadership ability of the Marine squad leader. This man is the key to the entire operation, and on his ability all else hinges. He must lead in a vacuum, with no higher officers behind him to reinforce his authority, nowhere to pass the buck, and nowhere to hide (such as an NCO club) if things go wrong. He must have the strength of character to enforce his decisions against argument or complaint, and the endurance to live with his mistakes. And above all, in his isolated position, he must be an excellent tactician. Rarely is such responsibility placed in the hands of a 22 year-old (that is the average—some are 19) sergeant in other units. If he is strong, smart, and earns the respect of his men, the CAP is a superb fighting machine; but if he weakens (because "after all, I have to live with these guys"), loses control, or makes mistakes that destroy his men's respect for him, the CAP goes slack and becomes not only ineffectual or a liability, but also quite vulnerable to the enemy.[70]

Although the cumulative effect of the CAPs was largely a positive one, the lack of supervision and the extraordinary autonomy placed in young, largely untrained hands, meant that some individual CAPs succumbed to the worst of human caprice.[71] Mission command is not a risk-averse strategy. To hedge against those risks, the Corps will need to amplify both its significant investment in leadership training and its emphasis on ethics and discipline. This, combined with its newly enhanced recruiting image aimed at drawing civic-minded as well as warrior-bound young men to the Corps, has the potential to prepare a wider swath of NCOs for such weighty responsibility.[72] Although this may seem a tall order, it is not impossible. As he led the 2003 march to Baghdad, Maj. Gen. Jim Mattis propelled the First Marine Division's motto into Corps-wide mantra: "No Better Friend, No Worse Enemy."[73] To the Devil Dogs about to come face to face with Iraqis, he added, "First, do no harm." This signature commitment, if fully embraced by the Corps, provides precisely the identity platform for the best of CAP-style recruitment and training.

## NOTES

1. Capt. Randolph Coyle, "Service in Haiti," *Marine Corps Gazette* (December 1916).
2. Capt. Walter N. Hill, "A Haitian Reconnoissance [*sic*]," *Marine Corps Gazette* (March 1917).
3. To its credit, the Division of Operations and Training combined its observation on the dearth of available reports with a call that they be submitted so that the *Gazette* might disseminate them. This first article offers an initial few patrol reports by way of example. Sgt. Glendell L. Fitzgerald et al., "Combat Reports of Operations in Nicaragua," *Marine Corps Gazette* (December 1928): 241.
4. Col. Ben H. Fuller, "Should the Marine Corps Have Its Own War College?" *Marine Corps Gazette* (December 1916): 359. This sentiment is repeated fifteen years later by Maj. Harold H. Utley. See Utley, "An Introduction to the Tactics and Technique of Small Wars," *Marine Corps Gazette* (May 1931): 50.

5. Fuller, "Its Own War College?," 359.

6. Bickel, *Mars Learning*, 137–39.

7. Schmidt, *Maverick Marine*, 75, 111.

8. Boot, *Savage Wars of Peace*, 163.

9. Bickel, *Mars Learning*, 6.

10. Utley, "Introduction to the Tactics," 50.

11. Ibid., 50; Maj. Samuel M. Harrington, "The Strategy and Tactics of Small Wars," *Marine Corps Gazette* (December 1921): 480; Maj. E. H. Ellis, "Bush Brigades," *Marine Corps Gazette* (March 1921): 1–15. A disagreeing voice is Capt. G. A. Johnson, "Junior Marines in Minor Irregular Warfare," *Marine Corps Gazette* (June 1921): 152–63.

12. Utley, "Introduction to the Tactics," 50.

13. Simmons, *United States Marines*, 95.

14. Schmidt, *United States Occupation of Haiti*, 93.

15. Boot, *Savage Wars of Peace*, 170–71. See also Millett, *Semper Fidelis*, 199.

16. Langley, *Banana Wars*, 147.

17. Bickel, *Mars Learning*, 138.

18. Schmidt offers this enormously imbalanced kill ratio as partial evidence: 3,250 Haitians to 14–16 Marines. Schmidt, *United States Occupation of Haiti*, 104.

19. Boot, *Savage Wars of Peace*, 17; Cable, *Conflict of Myths*, 99. The United States Marine Corps (hereafter USMC) official history of the Dominican experience, written in 1974, does not characterize it as counterinsurgency but rather the "suppression of banditry." See Fuller and Cosmas, *Marines in the Dominican Republic*, 33. For typical prose regarding "bandits"—persisting even a near century later—see Lt. Col. Richard J. Macak Jr., "Lessons from Yesterday's Operations Short of War," *Marine Corps Gazette* (November 1996): 59.

20. Ellis, "Bush Brigades," 3. See also Capt. G. A. Johnson, who defines irregular warfare during the same period as "campaigns against nature, surprise, treachery, inferior weapons, tactics, and people. The enemy, if he has any tactics at all, usually descends to mere bushwhacking." In a particularly ironic twist, this author makes the point, some pages later, that one should "rather over-rate than under-rate the enemy in making your plans." "Junior Marines in Minor Irregular Warfare," 152, 161.

21. Ellis, "Bush Brigades," 3.

22. USMC, *Small Wars Manual*, ch. 1, "Introduction," 43.

23. Ibid., 8.

24. For instance, one article points out that in the accounting of the time more Marines in the Nicaraguan campaign had died of accidents and disease (sixty-five) than of wounds sustained in action (forty-eight). "The Marines Return from Nicaragua," *Marine Corps Gazette* (February 1933): 25.

25. CAP Marines learned quickly to hold their VC and NVA foes in high esteem. See Hop Brown, oral history in Hemingway, *Our War Was Different*, 25; Edward Palm, oral history, ibid., 39; Tony Vieira, ibid., 43; and oral history file 2367, USMC Vietnam War Oral History Collection, Marine Corps Archives

and Special Collections, Gray Research Center, Quantico, VA, transcription by Lacey Lee, February 21, 2012.

26. Bickel, *Mars Learning*, 91.

27. Ibid., 74–75, 120–21.

28. Bickel, *Mars Learning*, 85. The most dramatic of these were led by Smedley Butler in Haiti (Millett, *Semper Fidelis*, 187; Langley, *Banana Wars*, 131–33) and by Lewis Burwell "Chesty" Puller in Nicaragua (Macak, "Lessons from Yesterday's Operations," 59).

29. Bickel, *Mars Learning*, 87, 120; Fuller and Cosmas, *Marines in the Dominican Republic*, 37.

30. Bickel, *Mars Learning*, 87–88, 124.

31. On reconcentration, and "cordon operations," see Bickel, *Mars Learning*, 124–26; Millett, *Semper Fidelis*, 201–2; and Fuller and Cosmas, *Marines in the Dominican Republic*, 43.

32. 1st Lt. J. G. Walraven, "Typical Combat Patrols in Nicaragua," *Marine Corps Gazette* (December 1929): 245.

33. "Events in Nicaragua since February 28, 1928," *Marine Corps Gazette* (June 1928): 143.

34. Maj. John A. Gray, "Cul de Sac," *Marine Corps Gazette* (February 1932): 41.

35. USMC, *Small Wars Manual*, ch. 2, "Organization," 5.

36. Lt. Col. Harold H. Utley, "The Tactics and Technique of Small Wars: Part II.—Intelligence," *Marine Corps Gazette* (August 1933): 47.

37. USMC, *Small Wars Manual*, ch. 6, "Infantry Patrols," 8.

38. Ibid., ch. 2, "Organization," 6.

39. Ibid., ch. 6, "Infantry Patrols," 2.

40. Allnutt, *Marine Combined Action Capabilities*, 31–32.

41. *Fact Sheet on the Combined Action Force*, enclosure 7.

42. Chuck Ratliff, oral history in Hemingway, *Our War Was Different*, 29.

43. Paul Hernandez, oral history, ibid., 171.

44. Rocky Jay, oral history, ibid., 116.

45. Oral history file 2614, USMC Vietnam War Oral History Collection, transcription by Megan Hansen, February 22, 2012.

46. Allnutt, *Marine Combined Action Capabilities*, 26, 30.

47. Tim Duffie, CAP veteran, lecture at Utah State University, February 16, 2012.

48. Hemingway, *Our War Was Different*, 9.

49. Peterson, *Combined Action Platoons*, 62.

50. Interview of Gene Ferguson by Jack Shulimson, October 13, 1984, ibid., 61. Peterson owns the tape.

51. John A. Daube, oral history in Hemingway, *Our War Was Different*, 119.

52. Klyman, "Combined Action Program."

53. See oral history files 2141 and 2670, USMC Vietnam War Oral History Collection.

54. Klyman, "Combined Action Program."

55. Peterson, *Combined Action Platoons*, 61.

56. *Fact Sheet on the Combined Action Force*, 2.

57. USMC, *Small Wars Manual*, ch. 2, "Organization," 43–44.

58. Ibid., ch. 6, "Infantry Patrols," 48–49.

59. Schmidt, *United States Occupation of Haiti*, 70.

60. Fuller and Cosmas, *Marines in the Dominican Republic*, 32.

61. Millett and Gaddy, "Administering the Protectorates," 105.

62. Schmidt, *United States Occupation of Haiti*, 101.

63. Director Lt. Col. Sherwood A. Brunnenmeyer, oral history file 2898, USMC Vietnam War Oral History Collection, transcription by Kristen Amundsen, February 22, 2012.

64. Oral history file 3480, USMC Vietnam War Oral History Collection, transcription by Claire Ahlstrom, February 23, 2012.

65. Allnutt, *Marine Combined Action Capabilities*, 17–20.

66. Ibid., appendix E, E-5. See also Jimmy Sparrow, oral history in Hemingway, *Our War Was Different*, 44, and the wide range of motley photos on the CAP website, http://capmarine.com/.

67. Warren Carmon, oral history in Hemingway, *Our War Was Different*, 167; oral history file 3480, USMC Vietnam War Oral History Collection, transcription by Claire Ahlstrom, February 23, 2012.

68. Art Falco, oral history in Hemingway, *Our War Was Different*, 161.

69. Warren Carmon, oral history, ibid., 167.

70. Allnutt, *Marine Combined Action Capabilities*, 35. See also Klyman, "Combined Action Program," and H. G. Duncan, oral history in Hemingway, *Our War Was Different*, 155.

71. For examples, see Peterson, *Combined Action Platoons*, 89–92.

72. For a look at the thinking behind the Marine Corps's latest ad campaign, see Randy Shepard, "How the U.S. Marines Brought Rambo and Bono Together through Research (and Why)," demographics research and commercial campaign assessment paper prepared for J. Walter Thompson Co. and selected as a Jay Chiat Awards Submission Winner (2012). Pdf available at http://stratfest.aaaa.org/2012-winners/.

73. The motto was codified further in the Marine Corps's *Small-Unit Leaders' Guide to Counterinsurgency*, MCIP 3-33.01 (2006), 37.

# CHAPTER 9

# COUNTERINSURGENCY IN IRAQ

*Experiencing the Learning Curve*

Iraq would prove to be a critical test bed for Marine counterinsurgency instincts. The war the Marines had prepared for was over in three weeks. The First Marine Division demonstrated unmatched speed and logistical excellence in its push to Baghdad in 2003. Alongside their US and Coalition partners, Marines rapidly accomplished the immediate mission of defeating Iraq's military forces and toppling the country's leadership. Marines celebrate this early phase as an operation apart, a battlefield success in its own right. The larger strategic objective pursued by the US political administration, transforming the Iraqi polity into a functioning and stable democracy, remained ahead.

Baghdad's descent into looting and chaos and then into full-blown insurgency was not a contingency that received serious attention from US civilian or military planners in advance of the invasion. The rapid actualization of this problem set forced Marines on the ground to improvise their response. This process—dependent as it was on adaption by individual commanders on the ground and absent clear doctrine or universally agreed-upon strategy—resulted in significant variations in operation. Identifying a distinct Marine pattern during this early era in Iraq is further complicated by the initial sharing of operational space with US Army and other Coalition partner units. The approach employed by one unit was often scrapped by the next that rotated in.[1] Attempts to remedy this discontinuity came in ensuing years when areas of operation (AOs) were more clearly delineated and every effort was made to rotate units back in to areas where they had served on previous deployments.[2]

Approaches to the enemy differed not only because of the beliefs and inclinations of individual commanders, but also because of the sometimes dramatically different Iraqi subpopulations with whom the Marines worked.

The Marines' first area after the invasion was largely inhabited by Shi'ites, who were relatively happy to be liberated. The generally successful and largely peaceful leatherneck experience there did not reflect what they would face when they were redeployed to the hotbed of Sunni insurgency in Anbar Province in 2004.

Identifying and analyzing the operational effects of the counterinsurgency lessons Marines chose to implement in Iraq is further complicated by the involvement of civilian US actors overseeing the same space. Iraq represents a profoundly different case than that of the Banana Wars, where Marine service instinct could be readily identified and evaluated since it overwhelmingly dominated in both the political and security arenas, and that of the Vietnam War's Combined Action Platoon (CAP) program, where Gen. William Westmoreland left Marines to their own devices in the CAP AO. In Iraq, US civilian political leadership made decisions that sometimes upended Marine plans or significantly shifted the operating context. Disbanding the Iraqi military, dismantling the Ba'ath Party bureaucratic structure, and ordering both the start and then the premature end of the First Battle of Fallujah were all political decisions either made outside consultations with the military services or, in the case of Fallujah, made in direct contravention of Marine leadership advice. An evaluation of Marine success in stabilizing the areas under their jurisdiction is therefore not a story that can be told as a consequence of Marine methods alone or even, in cases such as those mentioned previously, as a consequence of Marine inclination at all. It is therefore with great care and an eye toward those spaces of time and place where Marines did exercise primary control over shaping the counterinsurgency environment that the lessons they chose to employ or innovations they pursued might be recognized and extracted for evaluation. The Iraq War serves as an important reminder to all services that some of the decisions and "best practices" most critical to strategic success may not rest entirely within military operational control. It is the civilian leadership they serve that determines the length of time allotted to engage the enemy, train indigenous security forces, and fulfill promises made to the population.

This chapter will first examine the small-wars "lessons learned" that the Marine Corps as an institution made available to its recruits during the post–Vietnam War years and was prepared to implement in the early years of the Iraq War. Key concepts emphasized during the 1990s provided guideposts to Marines who found themselves improvising in the highly chaotic environment of unraveling of civic order in 2003. They also paved the way for the stability operations Marines practiced in Shi'a territory for the remainder of their first deployment.

The chapter will next evaluate the extent to which these lessons were reinforced and built on in the interim period before Marines returned for a second deployment in 2004. Once it became apparent that the war in Iraq had become a counterinsurgency, what approach did Marines take in their planning? To what extent did planning draw on lessons from past counterinsurgency practice? Arriving back in Iraq in 2004 with "lessons recognized" in hand, Marines saw their well-considered plans for a population-centric approach sidelined by the First Battle of Fallujah. Under attack by insurgents and swimming in the sea of a hostile population, Marine instinct toward combat aggressiveness translated into what they perceived to be the option remaining: large sweep operations and raids. This approach yielded little lasting security but was perceived as useful in keeping the enemy "off balance." Marines themselves assessed little progress during the 2004–6 period, characterizing their actions as "treading water."[3] Looking back, however, many of them point to the eventual payoff of the Marines' persistent presence and their higher standards of conduct vis-à-vis the enemy. Owing to these two factors, outrages committed by al-Qaeda opened a window of opportunity that US soldiers and Marines were able to exploit. As early as 2005, key leaders within Army and Marine units forged ties with Sunni tribes that solidified into successful local alliances against the al-Qaeda insurgency and drove it toward extinction.

The practices that produced counterinsurgency success in Iraq were reflective of lessons recognized, if not always effectively practiced, by the Corps in earlier counterinsurgency fights. While many "innovations" in Iraq were standard practices during the Caribbean era or within the CAP, Marines in Iraq may be credited with refining and developing these in important ways. In that regard, Iraq represents a critical case study for understanding the lessons-learned process. Both US national culture and Marine service culture served to inhibit an early application of previously learned counterinsurgency lessons. However, when these practices were later employed with success and touted as Marine "innovations"—a key Marine value—Marines were able to quickly adapt to the "new" tactics and developed them to a far more sophisticated degree than their Marine forebears.

## LESSONS ON OFFER: KEY COUNTERINSURGENCY CONCEPTS IN THE POST-VIETNAM ERA

Combat aggressiveness has been and is the hallmark of the US Marine Corps. Instilled in Devil Dogs is a strong preference toward bare-knuckled fights when they are deployed abroad, even when this might not be the most productive course of action. Leatherneck history, however, has the potential to provide Marines institutional and historical advantages over other US services when faced with a small-wars fight. Many of the most noteworthy heroes of Marine legend gained renown in fights with irregulars, including Chesty Puller, Smedley Butler, and "Red Mike" Edson. In the 1990s, Marine leadership built on this heritage and leaned further forward than the other services in thinking through irregular bents on future warfare, including urban combat and the multiple challenges of delivering humanitarian aid, protecting civilians, and killing adversaries within three city blocks. Though this emphasis was touted in official rhetoric more than it was practiced in training, it nonetheless gave Marines valuable points of reference when they encountered such scenarios in Iraq.

The Marine Corps seems to have learned, more so than its US Army counterpart, the imprudence of abandoning entirely its assemblage of counterinsurgency lessons learned during decades of interim. Perhaps owing to stubborn pride in the successes of the CAP program and perhaps also thanks to its more consistent call to duty involving operations other than war, the Marine Corps kept a junior place for concepts of irregular war in its curriculum after the close of the Vietnam War. Marine officers were introduced to the contours of the CAP program, most read Bing West's novelization of life in a CAP unit, *The Village*, and West himself was an active contributor to discussions regarding irregular war concepts during the 1990s.[4] The post–Cold War decade for the Corps was certainly dominated by training focused on conventional operations, but it was also marked by key conceptual innovations from the top. Charles Krulak, son of Victor "Brute" Krulak—the primary force behind the CAP program during the Vietnam years—assumed the role of commandant in the mid-1990s and made it his mandate "to encourage—to demand—creativity and innovation to ensure that we retain an adaptive and flexible naval force able to anticipate events and win across the spectrum of conflict." Krulak acted on his self-imposed mandate by creating the Marine Corps Warfighting Laboratory (MCWL), which he tasked with pursuing a steady flow of creative innovation in order to meet future challenges. Krulak's vision emphasized the Marines' active pursuit of versatility across the full spectrum of potential fights, including "military operations other than war."[5] Though Krulak's efforts at innovation through the MCWL did not move many ideas beyond conceptual stages, two key concepts emphasized during his term of office—the three-block war and the strategic corporal—supplied future touchstones for Marine officers reaching for guidance during the initial stability operations phase of the Iraq War.[6] Adopted and cited with frequency and familiarity by officers serving tours in both Iraq and Afghanistan, Krulak's description of the three-block-war concept captured some of the key challenges of a counterinsurgent fight:

> Our enemies will not allow us to fight the "Son of Desert Storm," but will try to draw us into a fight on their own terms, more resembling the "Stepchild of Chechnya." In one moment in time, our Marines will be feeding and clothing displaced refugees and providing humanitarian assistance. In the next moment, they will be holding two warring tribes apart, conducting peacekeeping operations, and, finally, they will be fighting a highly lethal mid-intensity battle, all on the same day, all within three city blocks. We call this

the "three-block war." It is an environment born of change and adaptability. It will also be an age born of advanced technology and weapons that are readily available to friend and foe alike.[7]

The strategic corporal concept was also formed in anticipation of future irregular war. Krulak foresaw that the outcome of future operations, "whether humanitarian assistance, peacekeeping, or traditional warfighting," would be significantly impacted by the decisions of small-unit leaders operating far from the flagpole. These Marines would be required to deal with "a bewildering array of challenges and threats," which would require maturity and good judgment, often under extreme duress. Their decisions, subjected to "the harsh scrutiny of both the media and the court of public opinion" had the potential to impact not only the immediate tactical situation, but operational and strategic outcomes as well.[8]

As Krulak's predictions of three-block warfare came to pass in Iraq, Marines seized on the concept as prophetic and referenced it in order to ground their efforts in Marine identity and practice. Although the three-block-war concept had not translated into significant shifts in predeployment training and doctrine, it did allow Marine officers a service-specific optic for making sense of the complex task set in front of them and, perhaps more important, acted as a predesignated signal from the top that the current blend of humanitarian and kinetic tasks endemic to counterinsurgency were, in fact, authentic Marine Corps business. In this spirit, officers reporting back from the field during the first months in Iraq praised the switching of roles adopted by their troops as in line with the commandant's prescient vision. Describing the successful transition made by his Marines from the heavy aggression of mechanized war to pacification and stabilization efforts in Iraq's towns and villages during their first deployment in 2003, Brig. Gen. John F. Kelly reported back with pride that "this was Gen Charles C. Krulak's 'three block war,' and the Marines understood it and performed as if they were born to it."[9] Writing in 2004, a 1st Lieutenant Tsirlis affirmed, "Operations in Iraq are small unit fights for which our Marines are uniquely prepared. Former Commandant of the Marine Corps, Gen Charles C. Krulak's 'three block war' concept has unfolded before our eyes. The 'strategic corporal' is in effect." In the same breath that he cited these concepts, he acknowledged that any attendant skill set "received only a cursory level of instruction during The Basic School." Nevertheless, crediting a heritage drawn from the CAP program, as well as support and wisdom from the then-current division leadership of Gen. Jim Mattis, he summed up his confidence in the capacity of the Marine Corps to triumph in asymmetrical conflict: "The Marine Corps is uniquely suited for this type of warfare. Our illustrious history shows this to be true."[10]

General Mattis is often credited with pushing innovative counter-insurgency doctrine within the Corps. He is widely considered to be an

independent thinker who, as an unusually motivated autodidact, has cultivated a particularly high level of counterinsurgency (reduced to the acronym
"COIN" by the modern US military) expertise outside his military training.[11]
Mattis himself, however, insists that he is a representative product of Marine
institutions and culture. He explains that in addition to receiving training
on the CAP program, he, like other officers, had been issued a reprint of the
*Small Wars Manual*. This basic set of counterinsurgency lessons "prepared
me pretty well for COIN." He references the comprehensive reading list
mandated to officer ranks, the concepts of the three-block war and strategic
corporal, and the extended boot-camp and urban counterguerrilla training
put in place by visionary seniors to argue that "lessons recognized were easily examined in the literature and turned into lessons learned by the 90s" by
any who were willing to pursue them.[12]

## Guideposts to Stability Operations, 2003

Marines embarked on their Iraq campaign with General Mattis's eve-of-
invasion missive to all hands ringing in their ears:

> While we will move swiftly and aggressively against those who
> resist, we will treat all others with decency, demonstrating chivalry
> and soldierly compassion for people who have endured a lifetime
> under Saddam [Hussein]'s oppression. . . .
>     You are part of the world's most feared and trusted force.
> Engage your brain before you engage your weapon. . . . For the mis-
> sion's sake, our country's sake, and the sake of the men who carried
> the Division's colors in past battles—*who fought for life and never
> lost their nerve*—carry out your mission and *keep your honor clean.*
> Demonstrate to the world there is "No Better Friend, No Worse
> Enemy" than a US Marine.[13]

Mattis's order to engage in careful treatment of the civilian population was
reminiscent of that issued nearly one hundred years earlier by Col. Joseph
Pendleton when landing Marines on Hispaniola. Marines in Iraq, however,
were drawn from a nation that had experienced the Civil Rights Movement,
embraced far more tolerant social norms than Americans of the early twentieth century, and cultivated an identity as champions of human rights. In
addition, the searing experience of Vietnam meant that both the American
population and its service members were determined to avoid the bruising
and potentially strategically fatal consequences of undue harm to civilians
who inhabited the battle zone. The result was an American population and
a Marine Corps that demanded a higher standard of conduct from its troops
than their counterinsurgency predecessors.

The willingness of leathernecks in Iraq to make shifts toward effective counterinsurgency practices emerged from their commitment to mission rather than from enthusiasm to become counterinsurgency professionals. Population-centric counterinsurgency—for all its support from top Marine leadership—remains, for most Marines, in the ancillary category of "doing windows." In the early days of the Iraq campaign, Col. James A. "Al" Pace captured what he perceived to be a typical viewpoint among service members: "Whatever names you wished to give them—peacemaking, peacekeeping, peace enforcement, nation building, stability and support operations (SASO), or civil-military operations (CMO), they were all missions widely thought to be someone else's job and not missions 'appropriate' for America's combat forces." Devil Dogs believe their appropriate role is to move in, fight, and once hostile actions are over, be withdrawn.[14]

Decisions in the immediate aftermath of the invasion reflected this instinct. Col. Nicholas Reynolds recounts the way in which Gen. James T. Conway, commander of the I Marine Expeditionary Force (I MEF), reluctantly stepped to occupation duty after the capture of Baghdad was complete: "It was not a mission that General Conway relished. He wanted his MEF to fight the war and then to 'recock,' to get ready for the next war." Reynolds claims this as the natural pattern for Marines: "The idea was to assault the beaches, seize the objective, and then move on to prepare for the next assault, leaving the occupation duties to others." Recognizing in the chaotic aftermath of toppling the Saddam regime that that the Marines would have no choice but to involve themselves in postwar occupation of Iraq, I MEF announced that it would take up a "postwar stance" in southern Iraq, an announcement that "contained the Marines' trademark tinge of remorse about even having to conduct Phase IV [stability] operations."[15] Shouldering the mission in can-do Marine style, however, Brig. Gen. John Kelly quipped, "We'll do windows. It doesn't change our pay rate.'"[16]

In the weeks immediately following the fall of Baghdad, Marine officers demonstrated an instinctive understanding of a number of modern COIN principles.[17] They also showed impressive restraint in their relations with the Iraqi public.[18] In one particularly poignant example, Lt. Col. John Mayer found himself surrounded by an angry mob in the city of Al Hillah. As tensions continued to rise, someone threw a rock that hit him in the forehead. Mayer's response was to remove his helmet so that the mob could see the blood trickling down his face. Then, according to observer Bing West, he shouted through an interpreter: "Why do you throw rocks at me? Is this how you treat a guest?" The crowd continued grumbling but dispersed.[19]

On a more macro level, General Kelly records that the Marines resisted pressure from outside I MEF to amp up its artillery response once postinvasion hostilities began:

We once again resisted the suggestion to reply to these attacks with heavy firepower, a response that we felt would likely wound or kill innocent Iraqis. Even if innocents were not hit—and more importantly from a hearts and minds perspective—we felt it would severely erode our message that innocent Iraqi lives were as precious to us as our own. We calculated that the use of bombs and artillery against a fleeing enemy long gone before the first ordnance struck made no tactical sense, was in fact counterproductive, and would send the message that we held the lives of Iraqis in low regard. Some argued it would show Iraqis who was boss, or our resolve and power. We elected to rely on a high degree of field craft and the tactical expertise and confidence of our company grade infantry leaders.[20]

Kelly goes on to say that his unit continued to engage in civil affairs—particularly ordnance disposal—in order to win trust and "penetrate the civilian communities, many of which lived in terror of antiCoalition forces." The efforts of his Marines yielded "real intelligence" supplied by the populace and "developed a fragile relationship of trust."[21] Within the seven southern provinces it was assigned, the First Marine Division improvised effectively to organize governance and established security. Despite the on-the-fly nature of their stability operations and the lack of "blueprint," the division's chief of staff, Col. Joe Dunford, summarized that its assortment of approaches "worked out pretty well."[22] During the First Marine Division's brief occupational duty, Marines suffered only one combat death and left the area with a fair degree of optimism about the future.[23]

## IT'S AN INSURGENCY: LESSONS RESURRECTED FOR REENTRY, 2004

Fully aware by 2004 that they would be stepping into a burgeoning irregular fight, Marine leadership set about preparing their troops for redeployment. Charged with preparing the First Marine Division for reentry into Iraq, General Mattis made the *Small Wars Manual* required reading, hosted a security and stability operations conference that emphasized both population-centric counterinsurgency practice and Iraqi culture, and then buttressed this new training with briefings by Arab experts and veterans of the CAP program.[24] Over four thousand Marines were put through short Arabic-language courses and provided with a day-long session on Arabic cultural practices.[25] In his memoir, *Joker One*, platoon commander Donovan Campbell details the significant retooling of mind-set that took place during this period. Speaking of Mattis's directives, Campbell explains, "The general knew bone deep that in any counterinsurgency the people are the prize, and he took every step necessary to instill this strange population-centric mind-set into a force oriented toward high-intensity combat against a well-defined enemy." Campbell claims his unit took the general's intent on board and flipped its Marine default switch from "be fierce" to "be nice." His platoon entered Ramadi in 2004 expecting to "do far more school building than street fighting" and looked forward to "establishing rapport with the locals, . . . learning Iraqi culture and working together to improve their lives and their country."[26]

Training the Marine infantry toward a population-centric mentality and mission set, however, remained a perennial challenge. Noting that most grunts had entered the Corps in order to get into a fight, PFC Rich Mattingly reported in 2004 that officers conducting "three-block war" training spent most of their time and energy encouraging Marines to slow down and to rein in their "third block" mentality—a race to the firefight.[27] Marines arriving on the outskirts of Fallujah in the spring of 2004, therefore, were infantry grunts with combat default settings somewhat constrained by training in security and stability operations. Mission-centric, they stood ready to extend a "no better friend" hand to Iraqi locals.

Reports from the division's advance reconnaissance team informed them that the situation had moved beyond stability operations to real insurgency.[28] Recognizing the damage done by the blunt treatment dished out by the Eighty-Second Airborne Division preceding them—including civilian deaths resulting from firing at protestors in a Fallujah crowd—Marines were prepared to take a different tack.[29] Mattis planned a two-pronged counterinsurgency approach that included partnering his Marines with local Sunni police and security forces in the hunt for insurgents while engaging the population through economic projects to reduce the frustrations of unemployment and previous maltreatment.[30] These plans were sharply interrupted.

## Fallujah 2004

The two battles of Fallujah have, by Marines' own estimation, "given birth to new legends in leatherneck lore" and have claimed a hallowed place in the Marine gallery of signature battles.[31] Raw, lethal, house-to-house fighting of the sort that is venerated in Marine concepts of combat valor made Fallujah the "gem of the Iraq War" and the action within their decade-long effort that will be most often relived and recorded in institutional memory.[32] Despite the institutional commitment to a population-centric approach, many young Marines who served in Iraq during 2004 "routinely grumbled about restrictive rules of engagement [ROE] . . . and pined for more straightforward ass-kicking." Some, therefore, responded enthusiastically to the liberal ROE of the Second Battle of Fallujah. Embedded journalist Bill Ardolino sympathized, "It wasn't so easy for the Americans to get shot at or blown up every day without wanting to 'get some' in return." Most days,

Marines had to engage in severe restraint. The Second Battle of Fallujah offered them "a stand-up fight."[33] Important for Marine lessons learned, the First Battle of Fallujah also offered, as observed by Bing West, "a cautionary tale about mixing the combustible ingredients of battle and politics."[34]

On March 31, 2004, within a week of Marines replacing the Eighty-Second Airborne in Fallujah, four security contractors drove through the city, unescorted and without flagging their route to the Marines overseeing the area. Insurgents ambushed their two SUVs, riddled the occupants with bullets, mangled their burned corpses, and hung two of the desecrated bodies from a bridge. Scenes of the grisly affair outraged Americans and resurrected the trauma of Mogadishu, Somalia, a decade earlier. Washington demanded immediate retaliation. I MEF commander General Conway and First Division commander General Mattis pushed back against political pressure to react immediately. They stressed that the Marines had developed a patient and effective strategy to hunt down the killers and that reacting in anger with a full-scale attack against a city of civilians was strategically unwise. Marine leadership was prepared to channel its bias for action into carefully planned, targeted operations in order to achieve the strategic mission of political stability. In the daily report to superiors, the division's assistant commander, Brig. Gen. John F. Kelly admonished:

> As we review the actions in Fallujah yesterday, the murder of four private security personnel in the most brutal way, we are convinced that this act was spontaneous mob action. Under the wrong circumstances this could have taken place in any city in Iraq. We must avoid the temptation to strike out in retribution. In the only 10 days we have been here we have engaged the "good" and the bad in Fallujah everyday, and have casualties to show for our efforts. We must remember that the citizens and officials of Fallujah were already gathering up and delivering what was left of three victims before asked to do so, and continue in their efforts to collect up what they can of the dismembered remnants of the fourth. We have a well thought out campaign plan that considers the Fallujah problem across its very complicated spectrum. This plan most certainly includes kinetic action, but going overly kinetic at this juncture plays into the hands of the opposition in exactly the way they assume we will. This is why they shoot and throw hand grenades out of crowds, to bait us into overreaction. The insurgents did not plan this crime, it dropped into their lap. We should not fall victim to their hopes for a vengeful response. To react to this provocation, as heinous as it is, will likely negate the efforts the 82nd ABD paid for in blood, and complicate our campaign plan which we have not yet been given the opportunity to implement.[35]

Washington believed a show of force was necessary, so refused this advice and demanded the Marines go in. Marines saluted, gave residents two days to evacuate, and attacked.[36]

Marines acquitted themselves with legendary leatherneck fighting skill in the bloody streets of Fallujah. Watching the Marines rush into the fight, embedded reporter Robert Kaplan recorded their raw courage and tactical proficiency with awe:

> [Captain] Smith did not have to order his Marines straight into the direction of the fire; it was a collective impulse—a phenomenon I would see again and again over the coming days. The idea that Marines are trained to break down doors, to seize beachheads and other territory, was an abstraction until I was there to experience it. Running into fire rather than seeking cover from it goes counter to every human survival instinct—trust me. I was sweating as much from fear as from the layers of clothing I still had on from the night before, to the degree that it felt as if pure salt were running into my eyes from my forehead. As the weeks had rolled on, and I had gotten to know the 1/5 Marines as the individuals they were, I had started deluding myself that they weren't much different from me. They had soft spots, they got sick, they complained. But in one flash, as we charged amid whistling incoming shots, I realized that they were not like me; they were Marines.[37]

Marines will draw a number of lessons from the First Battle of Fallujah. A hindsight focus for the Corps has been the extent to which this engagement validated "nearly 10 years of urban experimentation and combat development," including "fighting among civilians, the three block war, and the use of asymmetrical tactics."[38] Their control over the outcome in Fallujah, however, was interrupted by the reaction of civilian leadership to the enemy's use of information operations, a lesson the Marines would learn the hard way in the first round in Fallujah and prepare carefully for in the second.

Days into the conflict, scenes of gore and dead children were sent to the airwaves by news outlets sympathetic to the insurgents' cause.[39] Whether the dead were a result of Marine military action or victims of the insurgents' own fire, both were skillfully played to a global audience as victims of Marine brutality. Reeling from the heart-rending images, key US allies and the Iraqi Governing Council demanded an end to the Fallujah assault. General Mattis assessed that Marine forces were days away from taking the city. The Iraqi leadership in Baghdad, with the support of key Coalition allies, continued their pressure on the White House, threatening to pull support if the Marine assault did not end immediately. In response, Washington concluded that the Fallujah operation was not worth the breakup of the

Coalition and ordered a halt.[40] While the halt may have been politically expedient, the message it sent to the insurgents was strategically damning. They perceived that they had sent the venerated US Marine Corps packing. Marines themselves were not sure what to make of the halt but consigned themselves to their orders: "Our job was not to be emotional. Our job was to put lipstick on that pig as best we could."[41] The Marines' History Division made a summary lessons-learned assessment: "The Coalition was quickly outmaneuvered by insurgent propaganda."[42] Put more colorfully, General Conway quipped, "Al Jazeera kicked our ass."[43]

The Marines would not, however, make the same mistake again. From early on in the war, they had consciously engaged in and improved on lessons learned regarding relations with their own domestic public via the media. Instructions in the *Marine Corps Gazette* as early as 2002 are very specific on this score:

> A reporter covering, but ignorant of, the Marine Corps can be an annoyance requiring valuable time that must be expended explaining very basic concepts. It's far better, however, to view this journalist as a piece of moldable putty upon whom the Marine Corps will make a lifelong impression. That a reporter is ignorant of what you do, or the rules under which you operate, makes him or her no less interested. And in any event, that reporter is going to convey something to the public. No matter what it takes, it is incumbent on every Marine to provide the access, candor, and insights necessary to produce an honest portrayal.[44]

The Marines' open approach to members of the media from the early days of the Iraq War reveals two important aspects of Marine culture. One is a consistent obsession with protecting the Corps's "special place in the American heart" in order to preserve its status as an institution.[45] The other is a level of confidence that observation of Marine activity—of recording the "naked event"—will yield public admiration.[46] Marines entering Iraq were encouraged to regard members of the media as an "entirely winnable constituency" and were told to switch away from words such as "handle," "escort," or "manage" in reference to media partners in favor of warmer terms that welcomed members of the press as "buddies" who were "adopted" into the division team.[47]

Heading this effort in the run-up to Iraq, General Mattis inspired confidence in his troops, reminding them that "left unsung, the noblest deeds will die" and exhorting them to provide the media with complete access, including interviews that would "show their courage to the world."[48] To authors and reporters, he issued a standing invitation: "Go anywhere, talk to anyone, and draw [your] own conclusions."[49] One reporter, skeptical that he would be allowed near the action, got a dose of Marine swagger from the division public affairs officer as a response: "I can put you in the back of an LVTP-7 amphibious assault vehicle with 18 angry grunts, drive you within 300 meters of the objective, and send you in the assault as the Marines storm the enemy's trench lines and drive bayonets into their hearts."[50]

Marines are nothing if not entertaining and, true to their word, provided "embeds" with front-row seats to the action and to Marines' signature banter all the way to Baghdad. Reporters came away impressed. Comparing their treatment in Marine units to that dished out by the Army, many were unreserved in their praise:

> In the three weeks I spent with the 1st Marine Division in Hillah, I was given unfettered access to everything the Marines did and said, even in the top-secret combat operations center. The commander, Maj. Gen. James Mattis, implicitly trusted his Marines to speak for him. He was not afraid of what would come out of their mouths. Consequently my experience was overwhelmingly positive—information rich, detailed and nuanced—and my articles reflected that.
>
> Contrast this with the Army's 3rd Infantry Division in and around Baghdad. News organizations talked to grumpy, hot soldiers who had less than glowing things to say about Pentagon leadership. The Army cut off reporters' access to them for more than three weeks, until Lt. Gen. Ricardo Sanchez reversed the policy.
>
> A soldier from the 1st Armored Division I met in the lobby of the Palestine Hotel deftly avoided a question about his view of the military situation. Moments later he admitted he had been instructed by his chain of command not to discuss such things with reporters, although he was allowed to chat about sports, his hometown and similarly benign subjects. Is it any wonder we are skeptical of official Army pronouncements?[51]

Marine public affairs specialists lamented the loss of embedded reporters once major operations against Iraq had concluded. They believed that press coverage of Iraq would have continued a steady stream of positive reports on Marine actions had the number of embeds across US military forces not been reduced from more than 770 to a mere 40.[52]

Leaning on that principle, Marines prepared to reenter Fallujah in the fall of 2004 by engaging their "every Marine a publicist" heritage and seeking out press personnel to observe and record their careful and disciplined preparations and to document their efforts to evacuate civilians from the city. Lt. Gen. John F. Sattler, who assumed command of I MEF in the lead-up to the Second Battle of Fallujah, reflected on the lessons of the first battle in order to shape the information environment for the second. Frustrated by media conceptions that Marines were "bombing indiscriminately" in the first go-round, he pursued a transparency strategy in advance of the second battle, inviting media personnel known for credibility and unbiased reporting to embed with the command operations center and become familiar with the Marines' painstaking targeting process.[53] In addition, Marines invited over ninety embedded reporters representing sixty different news outlets into their ranks.[54] Unlike the first action in the city of Fallujah, which Marines regarded as a spontaneous act of "retaliation," the second battle was a deliberately planned affair. Information operations were recognized as "high priority" and were delivered in a "massive effort" that included both printed messages and radio broadcasts.[55]

Marines minimized domestic backlash within Iraq by explaining to Fallujah residents exactly what was coming. Those charged with information operations made it very clear that Prime Minister Ayad Allawi believed all opportunities for a peaceful solution in Fallujah had been exhausted and that Marines would have his backing throughout the full operation there. The city was going to be attacked, and operations would not stop until it was cleared.[56] Marines and most observers agree that information operations were successful in convincing about 80 percent of the civilian population to depart.[57] Those citizens choosing not to leave were given specific instructions to stay in their homes.[58] Through messages communicated to both the resident population of Fallujah and to outside observers, Marines worked to ensure that they "owned" the information operations narrative this time around,[59] including successful psychological operations that misled insurgents about the direction of attack.[60] By the time the Marines launched their assault, their scores of embeds let the world see the Fallujah fight through Marine eyes, hour by hour.

According to General Sattler, "it worked."[61] Marines met with military success in clearing insurgents and, despite inflicting massive destruction on the city in the grim process of fighting an entrenched enemy, avoided political defeat.[62]

## "TREADING WATER": DEFAULTING TO LARGE SWEEP OPERATIONS, 2004-6

Neither productive engagement with the population in ousting the insurgents nor real progress toward stabilizing Iraq was achieved in the two years following Fallujah. Battlefield success against the insurgents in the city of Fallujah was necessary, but the heavy destruction that resulted did not garner goodwill with citizens there or in the surrounding region.[63] Iraqis who eventually came to partner with US forces characterize the years of US engagement up through 2006 as one mistake after another. They stressed that US forces did not understand Iraqi culture and consequently resorted to heavy-handed tactics and large sweep operations that arrested and interrogated many of the wrong people, moves that increased hostility and swelled the ranks of the insurgents.[64] An Iraqi governor sympathetic to the Coalition lamented, "We did not expect that [behavior] from a modern country such as the United States, where we are used to hearing about dialogue, human rights, freedom, and democracy. So the behavior of the Coalition forces and the mistakes that they committed accumulated. It fell right into the hands of the insurgents, and they took advantage of it."[65] Embedded journalist Bill Ardolino observes that the result was an Iraqi narrative comprising "tragedies, abuses, mistakes, and public relations disasters" that "consumed the local consciousness." Fair or not, these stories were told and retold, "while Americans' acts of kindness and attempts to establish security were little acknowledged, poorly understood, or overlooked." The negative story, in the 2004–6 period, dominated the scene.[66]

Early after the invasion, strict ROE were put in place in order to protect civilians. Despite these efforts, violence and abuses that harmed civilians remained in the mix. These practices occurred unevenly across time, AOs, and units and stemmed from a variety of factors. Some commanders remained aloof from population-centric thinking and made it clear to their subordinates that their mission was war with the enemy, not communion with the population. General indifference and sometimes anger toward what was perceived as a hostile population led to callous attitudes and abusive treatment.[67] A review of the content submitted to Marine journals during the first years of the Iraq War indicates an initial difference between the First Marine Division and the Second Marine Division in their dedication to a population-centric posture. Indicative of a more enemy-centric approach, the latter's words and actions exhibited less care in its engagement with the Iraqi population. For instance, in dispensing advice to fellow Marines deploying to Iraq, a unit within the Second Marine Division suggested keeping pepper spray on hand since it "works great" on prisoners of war, dogs, "and kids,"[68] a stark contrast in attitude and approach than that exhibited by the First Marine Division's General Kelly, who insisted that Iraqi lives and persons be regarded as "as precious to us as our own."[69] Despite its sometimes pronounced and counterproductive enemy-centric inclination, it would be the Second Marine Division that produced one of the most forward-leaning and successful counterinsurgency leaders, Col. Dale Alford, who pioneered the first in a number of successful campaigns to join forces with Iraqi tribes in pushing al-Qaeda from the region.

In other cases, harm to civilians occurred not because of differences in leadership but as the negative repercussion of an inability to communicate Marine intent to the population.[70] During their first years in Iraq, Marines operated with a chronic shortage of translators.[71] Some rough and even fatal treatment was simply the unhappy by-product of force-protection training that included orders to keep vehicles moving on crowded or pedestrian-heavy roadways and shooting drivers who failed to stop at checkpoints.[72]

The Marines' own account of the two years immediately following the battles of Fallujah characterize Marine operations as "semi-conventional"—a series of large sweeps, cordon and searches, raids, and patrols informed by limited intelligence from the population.[73] Marines engaged in spoiling attacks to keep the enemy on the defensive but did not have enough cooperation from indigenous forces to hold an area once cleared. The approach left them condemned to clear, clear, and clear again the same territory, a process some likened to "whack a mole."[74] Iraqis who consented to work with Americans were often targeted by insurgents when US forces moved on.[75] CAP veteran Bing West spent time on the ground in Iraq during this period and observed that "counterinsurgency existed as a slogan, but without changing the operational style of American battalions. In 2005, the battalions continued to do what they knew best: sweeps, mounted patrols, and targeted raids at night."[76] Having served as a participant observer in Marine operations in Anbar Province from 2004 to 2007, State Department political officer Kael Weston recounts that infantry units exchanged constant and bloody blows with insurgents—a "no-shit war"—but one that cycled without yielding strategic progress.[77]

Those officers participating in this phase were not unaware of the core problem: Marines could not progress in their attempts to win the population because their operations were fueling anger and were not providing security. Iraqis working with Americans were being assassinated weekly.[78] Without the ability to protect local allies, little headway could be made even given daily engagement with the tribes and consistent civic action.[79] The limited claims to effectiveness during this era are reminiscent of those from Nicaraguan patrols: keeping the enemy "off balance" and, in the Iraq case, the somewhat frequent discovery of weapons caches that could then be denied to the adversary.[80] Marines counted success by tallying dead insurgents and number of weapons found.[81] Those overseeing the civic action side of the war were left to wonder whether in the larger strategic picture the raids were doing more harm than good.[82]

Amid the violence on the ground in the fall of 2005, the fortunes of Marines were made worse by a particularly brutal incident. A squad in Haditha was struck by an IED (improvised explosive device), which tore apart a particularly beloved Marine. His fellow Marines responded with immediate force, killing five young Iraqis running away. After reporting sniper fire, they assaulted and cleared the rooms of nearby houses, killing nineteen civilians, including women and children.[83]

Reported in the American press as "horrific," the incident in Haditha became synonymous with Marine excess and brutality and threatened to undermine public support for leatherneck efforts at an already grim time in Iraq.[84] Although the Corps was roundly censured and investigated, Marines made their way back into the good graces of the American public in reasonably short order, likely because of their own sharp condemnation of the incident once the press had unearthed it. Marines felt the sting of the Haditha disgrace on their Corps and, despite instincts to close ranks with brothers, condemned the incident in their own journals. While Marines may have voiced sympathetic opinions elsewhere, authors to the *Gazette* made no excuses for the Haditha Marines and decried their action in the strongest possible terms, labeling it an "atrocity," a "massacre," and a "war crime," alongside such incidents as My Lai in Vietnam and Abu Ghraib earlier in Iraq. The prevailing recommendation was enhancement of ethical training in order to prevent like incidents from happening in the future.[85]

These Marines strike a very different tone regarding the role of the media than one finds in response to press highlights of abuses in the Banana Wars years. In *Gazette* articles referencing Haditha, the press is not vilified for reporting the incident—rather, Marines take responsibility for it and accept public censure as appropriate. Twenty-first-century Marines regard it as an operational reality that their mistakes will be sensationalized by a news-hungry media. Writing in 2006, 1st Lt. Matthew H. Peterson puts the onus on Marines to avoid giving media outlets negative material to work with:

> It has become a perennial truth that the media routinely exchanges truth for sensationalism, but I reject this argument as an explana-tion for the declining support for the Iraq war for two reasons. First, sensationalism is what the media does and always has done. To be outraged or even surprised by the media's behavior is tanta-mount to being mad at a snake for biting someone, but that is what snakes do. Second, while the media may misrepresent an event or fail to objectively present both sides of a story, rarely can the men and women of the press be credited with total fabrication. In other words, they may fan the flames, but they don't start the fire.[86]

## PREPARING FOR A TURNAROUND:
## LESSONS APPLIED, 2005–6

While Marines continued to slug it out downrange in the bleakest years of the Iraq War, Marine leadership at home was working with US Army counterparts to forge doctrine suitable for a modern counterinsurgency the-ater. When comparing this effort to the after-the-fact doctrine of the Banana Wars and the doctrine-free CAP program, it is clear that this century's Marine and Army forces were far quicker to appreciate counterinsurgency as a distinctive type of war and one deserving of doctrinal attention. In that sense, the lesson forged by Marine Corps predecessors in the *Small Wars Manual*—that counterinsurgencies are "wars of an altogether different kind, undertaken in very different theaters of operations and requiring entirely different methods from those of the World War"[87]—was recognized and applied earlier than in previous irregular conflicts. With support from fellow officers, General Mattis joined forward-leaning thinkers within the US Army to compile *Counterinsurgency Field Manual: FM 3-24*. Its emphasis on adaptive leadership and decentralized command meant a joint US military move toward long-standing Marine principles.[88]

Surveys in 2007 evaluating the manual's effect on attitudes and practice within the force recorded greater impact among Army officers than those within the Marine Corps. Forty-five percent of Army officers rated it as "extremely influential" and pointed to the manual's encouragement of adaption as its most influential feature. Marines rated the influence of the manual far lower, only 23 percent putting it in a "very influential" or higher category, since most considered its principles, especially those encouraging small-unit adaption, to be familiar territory. Ninety-four percent of Marine respondents agreed that their service encouraged innovation and improvisation, a significantly higher number than the 75 percent of Army respondents.[89]

Mattis recognized the need for his junior officers to have a pocket-sized companion reference to *FM 3-24*, so he mandated the creation of the Marine Corps's own *Small-Unit Leaders' Guide to Counterinsurgency (SULG)* in early 2005.[90] The prescriptions the *SULG* recommends were drawn from a wide swath of experience, including that of Marines returning from Iraq and that of allied forces across history: British, French, and Australian. The summary judgments of these experts reflect many key lessons drawn from the Banana Wars and recorded in the Caribbean-era *Small Wars Manual*, as well as many practiced in the CAP program. Tactical approaches that constitute familiar ground for the Corps—empowering initiative across decentralized junior leadership, engaging in constant patrols, training locals as force multipliers, and maintaining productive media relations—receive detailed attention within the *SULG* for their utility to the counterinsurgent fight.[91] Principles drawn from the CAP program are referenced in both the larger *FM-3-24* and the Marines' small-unit guide, with primary emphasis on building successful relationships with local defense forces.[92]

The *SULG* demonstrates far more caution in several areas than has been part of traditional American hubris regarding nation-building, including clear-eyed recognition that counterinsurgency enterprises are typically "measured in years or even decades." Despite Marine pride in perceived state-building successes in Caribbean states, the "likely role of the military" is defined within the *SULG* as "a supporting role to the political and economic initiatives designed to enhance the effectiveness and legitimacy of the government." Marines are to establish "a secure environment for these initiatives."[93] Genuinely winning hearts and minds is regarded as a typically "unachievable endstate." The manual states that a more realistic and strategically viable goal is to convince the population that their "interests are best served by the COIN force's success" and that the COIN force *will* succeed.

Despite all aforementioned cautions on the nation-building front, the manual does makes clear that Marines are expected to "own" their AO and take responsibility for it. In a section referencing the involvement of other agencies and their participation in the unit's AO, it states: "Regardless of the agencies involved, this is your AO and you must stay involved with all upcoming and ongoing efforts. Remember, you are the one that will have to live with whatever happens in your AO, everyone else is just a tourist."[94] Though intended to buoy Marine fighting spirit and commitment to mission, such verbiage also reinforces an essential blind spot in the American perspective: an unwillingness to fully appreciate the limits of American power and to recognize that in a counterinsurgency struggle the most essential component is not the tactical approach of a foreign force, but rather the character of the at-once indispensable yet largely uncontrollable host government. It is this governing body, not US forces, that must attain legitimate "ownership" of the respective territory. Political and strategic success is achieved when *Marines* are relegated to the "tourist" role.

One of the most impressive insights in the *SULG* doctrine is a healthy skepticism toward the utility of large-scale civic action. Although the CAP program is not specifically cited as the source of this wisdom, lessons reminiscent of that program are embedded in the manual's logic: "Populace mobilization is an incremental, gradual process. . . . Large, spectacular, 'quick fix' activities rarely succeed in winning over the populace. A steady stream of incremental measures to build trusted networks normally works better."[95]

Toward this end, the manual acknowledges the strategically deleterious impacts of prejudice and maltreatment of locals. Marines are admonished to bridge cultural gaps and are warned against being sucked into tactics employed by the enemy to get them to hate members of the indigenous population.[96] In line with this thinking, the manual's pages beat a steady theme of treating locals with dignity and respect and investing in a serious understanding of their culture.[97] It reminds the infantry officer that this is not an undermining of his Devil Dog–ness nor a new or "soft" approach. It is necessary, and it is quintessentially Marine. Referencing the most highly regarded Marine of all time, the manual sums up: "Marines like Chesty Puller have successfully done this in our history and it is vital to successful COIN operations."[98]

Reinforcing the gravity of this imperative, Marine leadership created the Center for Advanced Operational Culture and Learning (CAOCL) in May 2005. The onus for its creation came both from the top and the ground up: Hundreds of officers and NCOs returning from Iraq and Afghanistan pushed for the development of courses, language training, and a network of contacts to enhance cultural awareness. Citing celebrity forebears Smedley Butler, "Red Mike" Edson, and "Pete" Ellis, CAOCL's founders recruited interest by reminding Marines that cultural savvy featured prominently in some of the Marines' legendary success stories across time.[99] In addition to predeployment briefs, CAOCL experts provided Marines with a useful textbook for navigating cultural terrain, *Operational Culture for the Warfighter*, and supplied input for the Marine's signature predeployment training feature, the exercise Mojave Viper.[100]

For grunts, Mojave Viper was perhaps the most recognized and appreciated of the Marines' stateside counterinsurgency innovations. It was situated at the Marine Corps Air Ground Combat Center in Twentynine Palms, California, whose desertscape supplied the right topography for simulating operations in Iraq. The thirty-day exercise provided Marines training across all aspects of Krulak's three-block war: live fire, force-on-force training, and practice with stability operations enhanced by Arab role-players. Exercises emphasized the skill set necessary in a counterinsurgency environment: appropriate use of force, dealing with angry crowds, interfacing with Iraqi soldiers and civilians, running checkpoints, responding to incendiary press reporting, mediating tensions between the Iraqi army and police, and pursuing the enemy in a way that preserves normalcy and develops trust with the population. As the training exercise became more advanced, its designers worked to duplicate the demographic divisions on the ground in Marine AOs and add more lessons drawn from the *SULG*.[101] Marines writing to the *Gazette* about the utility of this exercise emphasized its value and advocated for more of it, along with earlier exposure in the predeployment cycle.[102] The existence of such counterinsurgency-specific training, augmented by a dose of cultural education, represents a significant step forward from the two weeks of CAP school offered during the Vietnam War or the ill-attended classes set up in the Caribbean.

Gen. John Allen attributes much of the success Marines had in their outreach to the tribes in 2006 to the enhanced military education being supplied stateside. Officers who internalized and applied the education on offer aimed for a deeper understanding of tribalism and Iraqi codes of conduct in order to recognize the opportunities in front of them. "We learned from Iraqis, we brought in sociologists, and we went over. This was an historic means of preparation, and we hit the ground running and immediately were able to capitalize on the great work that had been done . . . ahead of us."[103]

## Patient, Persistent Presence and Establishing the Moral High Ground

The "great work" referenced by General Allen during 2004–6 period comprised two basic elements: the persistent presence of US forces and their much higher standard of moral conduct vis-à-vis the core enemy, al-Qaeda. General Kelly acknowledges that al-Qaeda's outrageous brutality likely "caused" the Sunni Awakening and tipped the tribes toward partnering with US forces, but he emphasizes that Marine behavior enabled the Awakening's success: "The sheikhs would tell me that in spite of the fact that we were killing you guys ... in spite of the fact that we were rocketing you all the time, you were still trying to force us to work with you." These sheikhs acknowledged the Marines' use of limited force, efforts to reach out to the governor, and consistent efforts to repair infrastructure "even in the bad days" as actions that kept the door open for later cooperation.[104]

Key to keeping that door open was incessant dismounted patrolling, the feature of Marine practice that came of age in Nicaragua and was the signature activity of the CAP program. Marines were critical of their Army counterparts for not doing the same. Army patrols tended to be conducted from inside a mounted ride, keeping "troops who are desperately needed to interact with locals cocooned in vehicles."[105]

Writing some fifteen years after Vietnam, Larry Cable referenced the Marine "gospel of the patrol" as a firm "lesson learned" for the Corps, one including recognition that patrols needed to be small and independently led in order to be effective: "The marines eschewed large search and clear operations, noting that large operations invariably failed."[106] In interviews and memoirs, Marines do indeed express consistent comfort with and an expectation toward operating in small units, in austere environments, and far from the flagpole. Although the intent was to carry this lesson forward, Marines in Iraq often defaulted to large sweep operations in the years preceding the Sunni Awakening. Even when patrols were conducted in small units and on foot, the strategic yield could be difficult to discern.[107] A number of factors affected the utility of patrols, including varied access to a native linguist, the Marines' hurried pace as a response to overwhelming task loads, the sheer size and population density of their AOs, and rotation schedules that often interrupted the establishment of long-term relationships with locals.

Despite the limited immediate effects of these efforts, Marine officers have identified persistent patrolling as a reinforced "lesson learned," given the key role it played in the eventual success against insurgents in Anbar. General Kelly claims, "Consistency counts, and persistent presence on your feet puts you in more danger, no doubt, but also stacks the deck in your favor as you see more, hear more, know more, and engage more."[108] After visiting multiple sites around Anbar Province, Lt. Col. Kurt Wheeler concluded in 2007, "One of the key components for success has been effective dismounted operations; there is no substitute for 'boots on the ground.'"[109] Col. Michael M. Walker, commander of a civil affairs group, believes the consistency of Marine presence starting as early as 2004 sowed the seeds that later bloomed into productive tribal engagement.[110]

In addition to a persistent patrol presence, consistent acts of civic action, while sometimes inadvertently swelling the funds of the insurgency, demonstrated in no uncertain terms a higher moral standard and concern for the population than was on offer from the al-Qaeda side. Although civic action in the absence of the ability to provide security would yield little by way of productive relationships with the population, it did offer the opportunity to collect intelligence and to educate a sometimes aggressive chain of command on the impact their kinetic action was having on the people.[111] It also provided locals with a mounting collection of stark comparisons between the behavior of al-Qaeda insurgents and the US forces pursuing them.

Although America's Devil Dogs had rained havoc on insurgents in the city of Fallujah, they acted as honorable combatants in burying the dead. Kael Weston recounts the grim, even horrific jobs Marines took on in removing the fallen from Fallujah streets, identifying the remains, and burying them nearby. Heroic efforts were made to work with local government officials to reassure residents that their dead had been treated respectfully.[112] This behavior posed a stark contrast to the methods of al-Qaeda, whose members increased their lethality and barbarity after 2004, committing atrocities against residents unwilling to submit to their dominance, refusing to return bodies in time for proper Islamic burials, and purposely defiling corpses. General Mattis observes:

> It is the forbearance of the troops, the self-discipline of the NCOs and junior officers, that almost always keeps us on the side of the angels here, and the people are watching this. And as the enemy cuts off the heads of young boys, as they kill a sheikh and leave his body to sit out there in the August sun for four days, as they continue this sort of behavior, these forced marriages, what you and I would call rape, . . . these are all telling. . . . And so eventually these mistakes, and our forbearance, pay off, and in a very short period of time, all of a sudden the tribes realize whose side they're really on, and it all shifts.[113]

Kael Weston notes that some junior Marines undermined their own positive narrative by engaging in juvenile actions that angered locals, such as confiscating Iraqi vehicles and using them for entertainment until they were damaged. On the whole, however, he maintains high praise for those Marines who trained their mission-centric sights on civil affairs. He claims that the some of the best Marines could easily have filled roles as diplomats or US Agency for International Development workers. "Iraqis used to tell me that what made U.S. Marines so fearsome in fighting, more than any other U.S. military branch in their view, also made them so effective in rebuilding." Weston applauded their locally coordinated rebuilding efforts in the aftermath of Fallujah, which included reconstructing sewers and roads and providing electricity, water, schools, and soccer fields. The collaboration worked.[114]

Imperfect but remarkably restrained ROE, persistent presence, and constant outreach established American forces as a more attractive partner to the local population than al-Qaeda insurgents. When al-Qaeda atrocities and attacks against civilian populations began to stack up, Marines were standing ready to take advantage of their enemies' missteps and ally with locals against them. Mattis noted, "The tipping point [came] probably due as much to our own restraint as . . . the enemy's mistakes. And the enemy, they were so stupid. They made mistake after mistake. And eventually we, by maintaining our ethical stance, our moral stance, the people there—watching the reality of us versus enemy—shift[ed]."[115]

One incident recounted in particularly moving detail by journalist Bill Ardolino began with an al-Qaeda chlorine attack in March of 2007. Sick and burning from the gas explosion, civilians of this town—Albu Aifan—were near the Fallujah General Hospital but did not trust the doctors and nurses there to protect them from insurgent retribution. Instead, they leaned on a local leader who had begun to form a cooperative alliance with the Marines. Marines responded to his call and did so without the benefit of protective chemical gear. Prizing their alliance above their own safety, Marines drove into the haze at ground zero and worked with the local sheikhs to triage patients and transport the wounded to American compounds. Even Marines who had allowed the harshness of combat and previous failures at outreach to sour them on the Iraq experience soon found themselves swept up in the opportunity to supply medical aid. Coughing and sometimes vomiting from the gas themselves, Marines and corpsmen treated nearly one hundred Iraqis. Both their selfless act of rescue and the cultural sensitivity with which they administered it—separating wounded women from men for treatment and responding with "*afwan*" (you're welcome) to the villagers' expressions of gratitude—solidified the Marine bond with the town and demonstrated, from the Iraqi perspective, that "the American was 'a man of honor.'"[116]

Observing the switch from "hostile" to "open" among citizens of the Anbar region, Ardolino notes that the eventual turn of the Sunni tribes to the Americans was not so much a significant change in tactics on the American side as it was "Anbari fatigue after three years of bloody conflict," as well as "the rise of a more dangerous, common enemy."[117] In short, "the Americans were not particularly liked, but they were rational." Al-Qaeda crimes made the occupation forces look "merciful and humane" by comparison.[118] Iraqis concur with this assessment. In their oral histories, Iraqis cite the horrors wreaked by al-Qaeda as the catalyst that prompted their reach toward Americans.[119]

To the extent that Marine practice in Anbar may be used as a template for future counterinsurgency success, it is important to consider a counterfactual: If the barbaric al-Qaeda element of the insurgency had been absent and Marines had been fighting on behalf of a Shi'ite-led government against a homegrown Sunni insurgency continually fueled by the corrupt and discriminatory practices of its country's leadership, when, and under what conditions, would progress against insurgent forces have been made?[120]

## LESSONS REWARDED: ENABLING THE ANBAR AWAKENING, 2005–9

The set of counterinsurgency principles US forces pursued in order to take advantage of al-Qaeda's missteps and co-opt the Sunni Awakening movement were not innovative in the sense of being brand new. They are readily found both within the *Small Wars Manual* and the practices of the CAP program. In several cases, however, these lessons were advanced and improved on to an "innovative" degree, providing an opportunity for enhanced lessons learned for the Corps.

Marines attempted a formal reinstitution of the CAP program during their 2004 redeployment to Iraq, but the experiment was limited in scope and short-lived.[121] Several structural features of both the Iraq War and the modern Marine Corps made the original CAP program difficult to replicate. Vietnamese Popular Forces (PFs) represented a preexisting security element within a larger national military structure, which Marines co-opted and trained as a force multiplier. Iraq's security forces, on the other hand, were being recruited by the US military from scratch. Given the need to reconstruct a full-fledged national military force, CAP teams in Iraq were partnered with an overwhelming number of recruits. In its few short months in operation, the Task Force 2/7 CAP platoon put over seven hundred Iraqi National Guardsman through one week of training.[122] With such lopsided ratios, Marines were unable to engage in the "shared hardship, joint operations, and close personal relationships" noted as essential to success in the *SULG* and characteristic of the Vietnam CAP program.[123] The sheer numbers of local forces recruited for training, alongside disruptions precipitated by the larger operations in nearby Fallujah, meant that the nascent CAP experiment did not have much of a chance to succeed.

In addition, structural features of the modern Marine Corps disrupted many of the key advantages of the original CAP experiment in Vietnam. From a force structure perspective, the primary impediment was rotation schedule. Marines in a Vietnam CAP unit were not rotated in and out as squads; they rotated their ranks typically one or two individual Marines at a time. Tours in Vietnam were assigned individually, and high casualty rates meant that new members were refreshed on a fairly consistent basis. The upside of this brutal reality was that the relationships formed between villagers and their CAP squad could be maintained across consecutive years. New members of the CAP squad were introduced in ones and twos and could be socialized and introduced to villagers by Marines who had been there a while. This, combined with the willingness of CAP Marines to extend their tours, meant that relationships in the village had the quality of genuine continuity to a much higher degree than relationships established in Iraq.

Although attempts were made to establish continuity in Marine AOs and to return units to areas where they had previously served, the result was still disruptive to relationships between Iraqi civilians and US troops. If detailed and ongoing familiarity with both terrain and village residents were key to the CAP program's successes, these were lessons unavoidably interrupted by the wholesale rotation schedules of the modern US military. That said, the operations template eventually adopted by US forces, including the Army, which emphasized getting out of forward operating bases (FOBs) and into Iraq's neighborhoods, partnering with local security forces, initiating positive interaction with residents as a means of diminishing insurgent influence, and accepting a higher degree of risk to US troops while doing so, represented significant steps toward a CAP-like approach across the force. For the Marine Corps as a service, it is significant that these CAP-like duties became widely accepted as behavior expected of all Marines, not relegated to a side program populated by those who were "a breed apart." The "doing windows" mentality consciously cultivated in the post-Vietnam era, alongside a general appreciation of the CAP program and commandant-championed concepts such as three-block warfare, all culminated to provide for wider receptivity toward this approach. The "normalization" of these lessons learned must be noted as a remarkable step in the Marines' institutional march forward.

In 2005–6, Anbar Province could not have looked less promising. Comprising one-third of Iraq's territory and less than 10 percent of the population, Anbar was nonetheless producing 34 percent of Coalition causalities.[124] In an attempt to halt the downward spiral, a selection of officers across both the Army and Marine Corps took a new tack, spearheading an effective combination of counterinsurgency practices that departed from the default settings then cycling for US forces. These were put into play in advance of both the publication of counterinsurgency doctrine and the "surge" of US forces to the region. The later introduction of *FM 3-24*, therefore, alongside a modest infusion of surge troops to the area, built on momentum already under way and tipped nascent successes "over the top."[125]

The clear match between the new and highly publicized counterinsurgency doctrine forged by the Army and Marine Corps and the "innovative" practices emerging from Anbar helped validate the "new" methods and persuade a critical mass of US forces operating across Iraq to accept and implement changes to their approach. This occurred early enough in the counterinsurgency timeline to make a real difference—a success story that eluded the majority of US forces in Vietnam. Weston, alongside others, claims that this process, often attributed primarily to the US Army, ought to be credited in large part to the Marines. While much of the literature on the turnaround in Iraq justifiably credits the Army for new doctrine and for co-opting the Sunni Awakening in Ramadi,

it was US Marines who had most effectively and most persistently engaged Anbar tribes throughout the war in Iraq's Sunni west. Everyone knew the United States Marine Corps comprised the strongest tribe—especially Iraqis, not just other US military branches. The USMC's olive-branch outreach and strategic shift toward Anbar tribes had started in 2004, when US civilian leaders in Baghdad and Washington showed little to no interest. I had been around since then, so I knew the details well beyond the Power Point slides.[126]

Weston concurs that a constellation of factors were required in making the timing right for the set of counterinsurgency practices that Marines eventually applied. Primary in that constellation was a pragmatism born of a bruising and fruitless cycle of violence that neither the US nor Sunni side could break without conceding in important ways. Weston described the dynamic that dominated Anbar from 2004 to 2007 as "USMC versus IED."[127] To extract themselves from this cycle, Americans had to rethink cherished notions concerning the "right" structures in Iraqi society to amplify with coercive power, and tribal sheikhs had to make peace with a lineup of missteps and humiliations suffered at American hands. A willingness to do so on both sides took some bloody years in the making.

Marine notions concerning "right" and "legitimate" structures of power were informed by long-standing Western and American perceptions concerning just governance and assumptions about the natural progression of human civilizations toward Western structures of democracy. Tribes in the Anbar region tried a number of times to reach out to Marines, asking for their support in reclaiming weapons and ammunition and in acquiring vehicles in order to defend their territory and engage in a serious fight against al-Qaeda. These initial overtures were rebuffed by both American civilian leaders and the Marines carrying out their political mandate. The overwhelming priority for American civil and military forces in Iraq was to support the legitimacy and empowerment of the newly constructed government in Baghdad.[128] Arming and supporting the tribes was perceived as a primitive and antidemocratic move, one that would undermine efforts to stabilize Iraq as a functioning, modernizing democracy. During the early years in Iraq, Marines urged the tribes to support the national government by sending their sons to the Iraqi Army.[129] Only after two years of costly stalemate were Marines willing to break with what they continued to believe was a "right" and superior strategy: supporting an elected, Western-style government, effectual or not. Even after allying with the tribes in a successful partnership that made real and measurable gains against insurgents, Marine officers were careful to admonish caution about the practice:

> Don't forget the big picture. When it comes to dealing with the tribes, you can't sell yourself all the way on them. You have to remember that there's an elected government, there's a legitimate

government, and however the two sides may fight over joint forces, you, at the end of the day, need to remember that you're on the side of Iraqi government, so they may or may not be as effective at leading the people. But the tribes have to be subordinate to the governor and the mayor.[130]

Given the dissonance in values that their military partnership with the tribes caused, Marines felt compelled to rationalize their joint operations as a "short term" move, necessary because "there really wasn't a government functioning," a preliminary, forced-by-necessity step in a longer process that would eventually facilitate bridges between the tribes and elected government and act as a stabilizing factor in a democratizing Iraq.[131] This perceptual lens and value structure reveals that future American counterinsurgency practice, whether carried out by the US Army or Marines, will likely continue to privilege "properly processed"—that is, elected—leaders over unelected but indigenously legitimate ones in counterinsurgency fights. This value is strategically sound when the elected host-nation government acts in ways that earn it legitimacy with the population. It becomes a strategic millstone when, as is often the case, the propped-up, albeit elected, government is disastrously culpable in its own demise.

US strengths in resources, willpower, and good intentions are most effectively employed in the role of "the great amplifier" rather than "the creator" when applied abroad. When US forces amplify indigenous efforts already under way, as they did when supporting the selection of PFs who were earnest in their fight against the Viet Cong or Anbar's Sunni tribes in their push against al-Qaeda, the effect is often a dramatic turn to success. When, instead, US forces in foreign lands pour their willpower, resources, and fighting strength into propping up new institutions of their own making, the result has very often been strategic failure.

The Sunni tribes in Anbar had to undergo their own sorting-out process in order to be organized for and inclined toward effective partnering with Marines. Marines were not entirely unsympathetic to the Sunni position: They acknowledged that Sunnis had been pushed from their pedestal by the invasion, subsequent de-Ba'athification, and disbanding of the military. The tribes had then suffered the humiliation of an American "occupation." Colonel Wheeler notes, "As our presence dragged on, their desire to inflict pain on us and drive us from their lands intersected with what they saw as similar goals among AQI [al-Qaeda in Iraq], foreign fighters, and other radicals. A marriage of convenience was formed."[132] That marriage lasted until al-Qaeda proved itself a fatally abusive partner.

On the basis of his deep study of the tribes and his experience as foreign area officer specializing in the Middle East, Maj. Alfred B. "Ben" Connable argues that the social and political factors present in Iraq meant that "even if we had done all the right things," the tribes would not have been internally organized nor internally disposed to partnering with Marines much earlier on than they did. They too had to mature into the fight, get sick of the violence, make efforts toward internal coordination, and fail when fighting al-Qaeda on their own.[133] Analysis provided by other close observers to the conflict, military and civilian alike, concurs.[134] Weston notes that the increasingly sectarian government in Baghdad likely hastened rapprochement between the "Marine tribe" and Anbari tribes. Sunnis in Anbar had shifted from a fear of Marines never leaving the province to one of the Marines leaving too soon. American leathernecks had become a buffer for Sunnis fearful of their own Shi'ite-dominated government.[135]

Once a selection of key leaders within both the US military and influential, albeit sometimes junior, Sunni tribes in Anbar arrived at a position of mutual compromise, the joint moves made toward effective counterinsurgency were, for the most part, familiar practices in counterinsurgency history, including the Marines' own. The scholarship that thoughtfully, and in great detail, documents the emergence of these practices in Anbar focuses on three case studies in particular: the pioneering efforts of Marine colonel Dale Alford in Al Qa'im in 2005, of Army colonel Sean MacFarland in Ramadi in 2006, and Marine lieutenant colonel Bill Jurney, operating under MacFarland in Ramadi's city center.[136]

Although the wider literature on the Iraq War tends to focus on MacFarland's success in Ramadi as the critical case in co-opting the burgeoning Sunni Awakening movement, Marines, perhaps unsurprisingly, tend to focus primary attention on one of their own. Alford's earlier initiative in Al Qa'im is celebrated within the *Gazette* as the first successful and enduring partnership with Iraqi tribes and as a "textbook example" of how counterinsurgency success is achieved.[137] His experience in Al Qa'im is given more attention than other Anbar case studies in the *Gazette*, including a twice-printed first-person account (2006 and 2007) of his approach and lessons learned.[138] When written about by others, Alford's successes are attributed to Marine-brand innovation and adaption.[139] It is somewhat unfortunate that the few detailed write-ups examining this case tend to treat it as an admirable exemplar of the Marine value of "innovation" rather than mark its easily discernable parallels with counterinsurgency lessons of the past (despite the fact that Alford notes his explicit emulation of CAP principles in his own recorded accounts). Rooting the Al Qa'im experience in successful practices within the Marine counterinsurgency past would reinforce the virtue of serious study of the Corps's small-wars history in order to *build on* and *advance* lessons learned. By motivating future Marines through the "innovation" value instead, the Corps is reinforcing a forward-looking optic, one that may not be deeply informed by the past and risks a repeat of the trial-and-error learning cycle: a process that will produce less "innovation" in the counterinsurgency future than a re-creation of lessons learned in earlier eras, wasting time in which these lessons could have been implemented and advanced.

Alford's approach was informed by his familiarity with the CAP program, multiple experiences across "operations other than war," and recent deployment to Afghanistan. He captured the ethos of his approach in an overarching mantra—"It's the People, Stupid"—a prime directive that privileged the population as the center of gravity.[140] Even under that mantra, Alford began his endeavor by repeating the large sweep operations that Marines had already been pursuing to little effect, but with two important changes in practice. First, Alford and his team engaged in a detailed survey of the area to be swept in order to construct an extensive "no target" list that included sacred sites such as mosques, as well as important infrastructure features such as water towers and hospitals. Second, he prepared to consolidate the gains made through clearing operations by following up immediately with the establishment of "battlefield positions."[141]

Alford's battlefield positions, later dubbed "combat outposts" by the Marines and "security stations" by others across the region who pursued a similar strategy, were manned by both Marines and Iraqi security forces in advance of substantive engagement with the local tribes. The placement of battlefield positions was carefully considered in consultation with a specialist on Arabic culture and Middle Eastern tribes, Maj. Ed Rueda, who was able to provide advice on leveraging the internal dynamics of Al Qa'im's tribes and shaping operations according to tribal territory. Each outpost was situated to reflect tribal AOs and therefore maximize cooperation with the respective tribe.[142] Recognizing the invaluable nature of this sort of cultural understanding, Alford advises that future counterinsurgency efforts be supported by "language training and significant regional, cultural, and religious immersion" within the predeployment curriculum.[143]

Alford consciously emulated the CAP concept of his Vietnam forebears, insisting that his Marines train, eat, and live with their indigenous counterparts in order to reap the benefits of local familiarity and bonds of trust.[144] Alford made clear to the local population that his Marines and their Iraqi security counterparts were not going back to the FOBs—they were here to stay. Fellow Marine Capt. William Birdzell quotes Alford directly in his admiring account of the success achieved by Alford's population-centric methods:

> Live amongst the people, eat off the local economy and the people will tell you where the bad guys are, where they're hiding their weapons and where the IEDs are. . . . Get out of these damn FOBs that have . . . a nice gym and showers and internet and telephones. . . . The way you get force protection is you live amongst the people. Not with more armor, not with more bases. . . . We should be taking off armor. . . . When I walked into a village the people would deal with me a lot quicker than if you came in all armored up looking like a robot.[145]

That this approach is more risky sits fine with a Devil Dog organization that identifies with being in harm's way as a matter of course. Across all scholarly and military accounts not one Marine unit, in contrast to some within the Army, listed "protect the force" as a top mission objective.[146] Birdzell explains: "Fighting irregulars at their level may result in our taking higher short-term casualties in certain circumstances. However, we are an organization whose mission is to win, not just survive."[147]

Alford's dispersed battle positions and the constant patrolling of joint Marine and Iraqi Army units facilitated outreach to sheikhs, imams, and city councilmen.[148] Building on a lesson learned the hard way in Vietnam, Alford rejected the typical military measurements of success—insurgents dead, weapons found, and dollars spent—in favor of a metric more illuminating of Marine advances in winning the support of key sectors within the population. Dubbed "eats on streets," Alford required his Marines to report the number of meals they had been invited to eat in households.[149] Gradually, increased security and efforts at making inroads with local leaders produced results: The battalion's officers recruited over a thousand local men to join the police force. This augmented and locally constructed security presence meant a significant uptick in intelligence from the population. Alford's battalion skillfully pooled these inputs to create a "fused and nuanced" intelligence picture of their AO. The net result was a locally supported security situation that led to a dramatic decline in sniping and IED attacks and created a context stable enough to sustain civil affairs and reconstruction.[150]

Many of the practices employed by Alford have parallels with lessons successfully learned and implemented in the past. These include organizing Marines into dispersed small-unit outposts that are manned by combined US and indigenous security forces that engage in continual patrolling and outreach to the community. These units avoid large-sweep and heavy-handed kinetic operations and work to win allies within the population by protecting collaborators, acting quickly on local intelligence tips, empowering local partners in their own efforts to achieve security, and providing valuable civic action.

Alford advanced a number of these familiar principles through particularly effective implementation. A few lessons that had been recognized as important in past counterinsurgency experiences but may not have been effectively implemented were given new life by Alford and others in the Anbar experience and honed to fine degree. For instance, advances in intelligence included a system for coordinating and fusing the inputs received from both technological and human sources. These were pooled in a way that effectively enabled more precise targeting of insurgents. In addition, the cooperation of locally based allies was shored up through weapons supply, training, and strategically channeled civic action. Alford masterfully leveraged his use of civic action resources to create unity of effort across key leaders within his AO. On the sound advice of his cultural adviser, Alford held reconstruction funds in check until those local leaders with whom he had been working were able to get two recalcitrant tribes on board. Alford made it clear that all relevant regional tribes needed to be vested in the joint effort to oust extremists in order for infrastructural investment to begin. It worked.[151]

Units that followed Alford's added to his success by implementing effective measures to separate civilians from active insurgents. These included using combined units in small outposts as "bait" to lure out insurgents (a tactic reminiscent of the fight against Haitian *cacos*) and house-to-house visits, which built up census databases identifying both persons and vehicles.[152] The practices initiated by Alford and duplicated or advanced by others fit neatly within the overarching operating paradigm eventually adopted by US civilian and military leadership: "clear, hold, and build."[153] Application of similar methods by both Marine and US Army forces across the region resulted in a dramatic turnaround of US military fortunes. By the end of December 2007, "attacks on Coalition forces had dropped to the lowest levels since the conception of Multi-National Force-West in 2004."[154]

## LESSONS THREATENED: TAKING EARLY LEAVE OF IRAQ

The Marines' application of and improvements to prior counterinsurgency lessons achieved operational, if not strategic, success. US forces became perceived as a better friend to Sunni tribes than their own government. Iraqi sheikhs offered opinions representative of Sunni sentiment: "To tell you the truth, if you look at the Americans' role, and what they did in here, they were more interested in the welfare of the Iraqi people than the government of Anbar was."[155] In the fight against al-Qaeda, "the government of Iraq didn't help us with anything. It was all help from the Coalition."[156] For some, the warmth that resulted between US and Iraqi forces ran deep: "The relationship that developed here between the American forces and the Iraqis was unlike any other relationship in the world. During meals, we offered the Americans spoons to eat with, but they refused. They ate just like Middle Easterners, with their own hands. Everybody supported our movement. The Army and the Marines—I can't say one supported us more than the other."[157]

Operational success against insurgents had been achieved, but the political end state required to declare strategic success remained elusive. By late 2008, Emma Sky, a political adviser to US forces, observed that "the greatest threat to Iraq's stability had become the legitimacy and capability of the government, rather than insurgents."[158] Sunnis continued to regard the Baghdad government as "a Shi'a-led, Iranian-backed government" and warned that a drawdown of US presence would exacerbate internal problems, creating a situation "much more dangerous than in 2005."[159]

The US military leadership recognized that gains made against insurgents in Iraq were fragile. The strides forward in stability and normalization of civilian life would be fleeting without an ongoing advisory and support presence. They, alongside Sunni counterparts, advised a gradual drawdown in Iraq in order to maintain long-term stability. Washington chose instead to bow to the pressures of American impatience with the protracted nature of irregular war and bring the troops home. The tumbling of Iraq back into a bloody state occurred in fairly short order. This reversal of Marine "wins" in Iraq threatens to devalue the lessons hard forged there. As it was after the Vietnam War, the strong temptation will be to wash hands of an ugly and ultimately unsuccessful enterprise. The concluding chapter of this volume examines the lessons Marines continue to identify as worth learning from their Iraq experience, as well as those in jeopardy of being lost.

## NOTES

1. Ardolino, *Fallujah Awakens*, 209. For frustrations on this point, see Groen and Contributors, *With the 1st Marine Division*, 370–71.
2. Gen. Jim Mattis, correspondence with the author, October 5, 2016; Maj. Gen. John R. Allen, interview in McWilliams and Wheeler, *Al-Anbar Awakening*, 1:232.
3. Maj. Alfred B. Connable, interview, ibid., 124.
4. Col. George P. Garrett, correspondence with the author, July 18, 2014; Maj. Alfred B. Connable, correspondence with the author, August 25, 2014.
5. Gen. Charles C. Krulak, "Commandant's Planning Guidance (CPG)," *Marine Corps Gazette* (August 1995): A-3. See also "The Commandant's Warfighting Laboratory," *Marine Corps Gazette* (September 1995); Gen. Charles C. Krulak, "Embracing Innovation," *Marine Corps Gazette* (January 1996); and Maj. Kenneth R. Bergman, "A Ticket to Ride the Dragon," *Marine Corps Gazette* (February 1996).
6. Frank Hoffman, correspondence with the author, July 17, 2014; Col. George P. Garrett, correspondence with the author, July 18, 2014; Terriff, "Warriors and Innovators."
7. Gen. Charles C. Krulak, "Building a Corps for the 21st Century," *Leatherneck* (April 1998): 28.
8. Gen. Charles C. Krulak, "The Strategic Corporal: Leadership in the Three Block War," *Marine Corps Gazette* (January 1999): 21–22.
9. Brig. Gen. John F. Kelly, "Tikrit, South to Babylon," *Marine Corps Gazette* (February 2004): 18.
10. 1st Lt. Christopher S. Tsirlis, "The MAGTF Officer in Iraq," *Marine Corps Gazette* (December 2004): 16–18.
11. Ricks, *Generals*, 631–32.
12. Gen. Jim Mattis, correspondence with the author, October 23, 2013.

13. Groen and Contributors, *With the 1st Marine Division*, 133 (italics in original).
14. Col. James A. "Al" Pace, "Civil-Military Operations Center," *Marine Corps Gazette* (June 2005), cited 10, 10–13. See also Staff of the Marine Corps Center for Lessons Learned, "Operation IRAQI FREEDOM Lessons Learned," *Marine Corps Gazette* (May 2005): 78–81.
15. Reynolds, *Basrah, Baghdad, and Beyond*, 145, 147.
16. Quoted in West and Smith, *March Up*, 265–66.
17. Kelly, "Tikrit, South to Babylon"; Brig. Gen. John F. Kelly, "Part II: Tikrit, South to Babylon," *Marine Corps Gazette* (March 2004): 37–41; Brig. Gen. John F. Kelly, "Part III: Tikrit, South to Babylon," *Marine Corp Gazette* (April 2004): 43–47; Col. Christopher C. Conlin, "What Do You Do for an Encore?," *Marine Corps Gazette* (September 2004): 74–80.
18. Pamela Hess, "Feature: In Najaf, U.S. Battles Clerics," United Press International (hereafter UPI), July 28, 2003; West and Smith, *March Up*, 261; Groen and Contributors, *With the 1st Marine Division*, 376–97.
19. West and Smith, *March Up*, 265.
20. Kelly, "Part III: Tikrit, South to Babylon," 45.
21. Ibid.
22. Quoted in Shultz, *Marines Take Anbar*, 62.
23. The Estes account claims zero combat deaths, a claim later corrected by Marine Corps leadership according to Frank Hoffman, correspondence with the author, December 17, 2016; Estes, *U.S. Marines in Iraq*, 1.
24. West, *No True Glory*, 50.
25. Hoffman, *Learning while under Fire*, 177.
26. Ibid., 48, 64.
27. PFC Rich Mattingly, "'America's Battalion' Trains to Win Small Wars," *Leatherneck* (December 2004), 34.
28. Gen. Jim Mattis, correspondence with the author, December 2015; West, *No True Glory*, 3–7.
29. West, *No True Glory*, 12; Shultz, *Marines Take Anbar*, 64–65.
30. West, *Strongest Tribe*, 29.
31. Ross W. Simpson, "Fallujah: A Four Letter Word," *Leatherneck* (February 2005): 16–21.
32. Enlisted Marine Adam Keliipaakaua, correspondence with the author, July 16, 2014; Simpson, "Fallujah: A Four Letter Word," 16–21.
33. Ardolino, *Fallujah Awakens*, 57.
34. West, *No True Glory*, xx.
35. Recorded in Estes, *U.S. Marines in Iraq*, 31.
36. Gen. James N. Mattis, correspondence with the author, December 2015; Gen. James T. Conway, interview in McWilliams and Wheeler, *Al-Anbar Awakening*, 1:49–51.
37. Robert D. Kaplan, "Five Days in Fallujah," *Atlantic*, July/August 2004, https://www.theatlantic.com/magazine/archive/2004/07/five-days-in-fallujah/303450/.

38. Col. Gary W. Anderson, "Fallujah and the Future of Urban Operations," *Marine Corps Gazette* (November 2004): 52–58; Shultz, *Marines Take Anbar*, 76–77.

39. West, *No True Glory*, 91; Gen. Jim Mattis, correspondence with the author, December 2015; Weston, *Mirror Test*, 32.

40. Gen. Jim Mattis, correspondence with the author, December 2015; Gen. James T. Conway, interview in McWilliams and Wheeler, *Al-Anbar Awakening*, 1:57; Hoffman, *Learning while under Fire*, 181.

41. Ricks, *Fiasco*, 343.

42. McWilliams, *U.S. Marines in Battle*, 2. See also Estes, *U.S. Marines in Iraq*, 38–39.

43. Recorded in West, *No True Glory*, as "kicked our butts," 322. Repeated by Marines in its likely original form as "kicked our ass": Col. John Keenan, "Editorial: 'Al Jazeera Kicked Our Ass,'" *Marine Corps Gazette* (September 2007).

44. Lt. Col. Stephen G. Brozak, "The Marine Corps, the Media, and the 21st Century," *Marine Corps Gazette* (January 2002): 44.

45. Ibid., 45.

46. Gen. Jim Mattis, correspondence with the author, February 7, 2015.

47. Capt. Joseph M. Plenzler, "Conducting Expeditionary Public Affairs," *Marine Corps Gazette* (February 2004): 26–27.

48. Groen and Contributors, *With the 1st Marine Division*, 37.

49. West and Smith, *March Up*, 253.

50. Plenzler, "Conducting Expeditionary Public Affairs," 27.

51. Pamela Hess, "Media New Boogeyman of Iraq," UPI, September 26, 2003. See also Erin Solaro, "Ideas for Marines: The Care and Feeding of Journalistic Orphans," *Marine Corps Gazette* (September 2005): 74–75; Richard Tomkins, "War Reflection: With the Marines in Iraq," UPI, April 21, 2003.

52. Col. Glenn T. Starnes, "Leveraging the Media," *Marine Corps Gazette* (February 2005): 53.

53. Lt. Gen. John F. Sattler, interview in McWilliams and Wheeler, *Al-Anbar Awakening*, 1:77–82.

54. Hoffman, *Learning while under Fire*, 183; McWilliams, *U.S. Marines in Battle*, 6.

55. Shultz, *Marines Take Anbar*, 93–94.

56. McWilliams, *U.S. Marines in Battle*, 1, 6.

57. Hoffman, *Learning while under Fire*, 183.

58. Shultz, *Marines Take Anbar*, 93–94.

59. Hoffman, *Learning while under Fire*, 183–84.

60. McWilliams, *U.S. Marines in Battle*, 6–7.

61. Sattler, interview in McWilliams and Wheeler, *Al-Anbar Awakening*, 1:77–82.

62. West reports that President George W. Bush's approval rating in the United States rebounded from 40 percent to 50 percent because of "American bravery during the Fallujah fight." West, *Strongest Tribe*, 64.

63. Sheikh Aifan Sadun al-Issawi, oral history in Montgomery and McWilliams, *Al-Anbar Awakening*, 2:92.

64. Themes repeated in the oral histories of Sheikh Aifan Sadun al-Issawi, Sheikh Sabah al-Sattam Effan Fahran al-Shurji al-Aziz, Governor Mamoun Sami Rashid al-Alwani, Mr. Kamis Ahmad Abban al-Alwani, Maj. Gen. Tariq Yusif Mohammad al-Thiyabi, Staff Brig. Gen. (Pilot) Nuri al-Din Abd al-Karim Mukhlif al-Fahadawi, Staff Maj. Gen. Abdullah Mohammad Badir al-Jaburi, Staff Brig. Gen. Haqi Isma'eel Ali Hameed, and Staff Maj. Gen. Khadim Muhammad Faris al-Fahadawi al-Dulaymi, collected in Montgomery and McWilliams, *Al-Anbar Awakening*, vol. 2.

65. Gov. Mamoun Sami Rashid al-Alwani, ibid., 153.

66. Ardolino, *Fallujah Awakens*, 37.

67. Ibid., 116–23; West, *Strongest Tribe*, 156, 269.

68. 1st Sgt. Paul A. Berry, "From the Warlords," *Marine Corps Gazette* (February 2004): 36.

69. Kelly, "Part III: Tikrit, South to Babylon," 45.

70. Campbell, *Joker One*, 188–89, 194–201, 271.

71. Maj. Clint J. Nussberger, "Engagement in the 21st Century and the Need for 'Operational' Marine Linguists," *Marine Corps Gazette* (October 2003): 39–40; Cpl. Roger D. Huffstetler, Jr., "Translate This," *Marine Corps Gazette* (December 2005).

72. Boudreau, *Packing Inferno*; West, *Strongest Tribe*, 11.

73. Estes, *U.S. Marines in Iraq*. See also Russell, *Innovation, Transformation, and War*, 55.

74. Hoffman, *Learning while under Fire*, 204. See also West, *Strongest Tribe*, and Shultz, *Marines Take Anbar*, 120–43.

75. Russell, *Innovation, Transformation, and War*, 63.

76. West, *Strongest Tribe*, 107, 150–51.

77. J. Kael Weston, correspondence with the author, September 12, 2016; Weston, *Mirror Test*.

78. Hoffman, *Learning while under Fire*, 200, 206, 192; West, *Strongest Tribe*, 50; J. Kael Weston, correspondence with the author, December 10, 2016.

79. Maj. Alfred B. Connable, interview in McWilliams and Wheeler, *Al-Anbar Awakening*, 1:121–24; Ardolino, *Fallujah Awakens*, 52; Weston, *Mirror Test*, 112, 121.

80. Estes, *U.S. Marines in Iraq*, 101.

81. Ibid.; West, *Strongest Tribe*, 101; Russell, *Innovation, Transformation, and War*, 62. This American propensity was true across the force: Success was measured in numbers, primarily involving kinetic operations against insurgents. Kilcullen, *Accidental Guerrilla*, 121.

82. Ardolino, *Fallujah Awakens*, 27.

83. James Joyner, "Why We Should Be Glad the Haditha Massacre Marine Got No Jail Time," *Atlantic*, January 25, 2012; Hoffman, *Learning while under Fire*, 195.

84. Tim McGirk, "Collateral Damage or Civilian Massacre in Haditha?" *Time*, March 19, 2006.

85. Sgt. Samuel J. Stevens, "Psychology of the Good Guys," *Marine Corps Gazette* (July 2008): 21; Sgt. Benjamin T. Upton, "View through a Sniper Scope," *Marine Corps Gazette* (June 2007); Capt. Jose R. Hernandez, "Ethics for Juniors," *Marine Corps Gazette* (September 2009); 1st Lt. Matthew H. Peterson, "Parallels between Iraq and Vietnam," *Marine Corps Gazette* (October 2006): 10; Capt. Erik C. C. Quist, "The Decisionmaking Quandary," *Marine Corps Gazette* (October 2011); S.Sgt. Lance Minor, "Conflicting Loyalties and the Marine NCO," *Marine Corps Gazette* (July 2008): 39–41; Maj. David B. Ashe, "The Law of War," *Marine Corps Gazette* (February 2009); Capt. Michael DeSa (Ret.), "The Fray in Our Institutional Fabric," *Marine Corps Gazette* (December 2014): 14.

86. Peterson, "Parallels between Iraq and Vietnam," 10.

87. United States Marine Corps (hereafter USMC), *Small Wars Manual*, section I, "General Characteristics," 8.

88. Moyar, *Question of Command*, 243.

89. Ibid., 248.

90. Gen. Jim Mattis, correspondence with the author, January 7, 2015; Maj. Jeffrey Davis, correspondence with the author, February 8, 2015. The primary authors of the *SULG* included Maj. Jeffrey Davis under Col. Doug King, along with David Kilcullen and Capt. Timothy Maas.

91. USMC, *Small-Unit Leaders' Guide to Counterinsurgency*, 25, 27, 34, 41, 56–58, 60, 78, 90–133, 148–52.

92. US Army / Marine Corps, *Counterinsurgency Field Manual*, 184–87; USMC, *Small-Unit Leaders' Guide to Counterinsurgency*, 31.

93. USMC, *Small-Unit Leaders' Guide to Counterinsurgency*, 3.

94. Ibid., 134.

95. Ibid., 41–42.

96. Ibid., 40.

97. Gen. James N. Mattis, foreword to USMC, *Small-Unit Leaders' Guide to Counterinsurgency*. See also pages 16–17, 24, 39–42, 73, and 136.

98. USMC, *Small-Unit Leaders' Guide to Counterinsurgency*, 39.

99. Lt. Col. James L. Higgins, Maj. Michelle L. Trusso, and Maj. Alfred B. Connable, "Marine Corps Intelligence," *Marine Corps Gazette* (December 2005): 23–24.

100. Salmoni and Holmes-Eber, *Operational Culture*.

101. "Exercise Mojave Viper," *Marine Corps Gazette* (December 2006): 48–52; Capt. Scott A. Cuomo and Capt. Brian J. Donlon, "Training a 'Hybrid' Warrior," *Marine Corps Gazette* (February 2008): 50–55.

102. Capt. Scott A. Cuomo, "Will We Be Prepared for What's Next?," *Marine Corps Gazette* (July 2007): 9–12; Capt. Matthew Van Echo, "Good Decisionmakers Are Not Enough," *Marine Corps Gazette* (May 2009): 36–40.

103. Allen, interview in McWilliams and Wheeler, *Al-Anbar Awakening*, 1:237.

104. Maj. Gen. John F. Kelly, interview, ibid., 244. See also Lt. Col. Kurt Wheeler, "Good News in Al Anbar?," *Marine Corps Gazette* (April 2007), and "II MEF Marines Depart Anbar Province: Security Remains Stable," *Leatherneck* (March 2008).

105. Maj. Adam T. Strickland, "MCDP 1, *Warfighting*, Revisited," *Marine Corps Gazette* (August 2005): 53. See also Gordon Dillow, "Building Karmah: Fighting Terrorism with Handshakes and Smiles," *Leatherneck* (August 2004): 14.

106. Cable, *Conflict of Myths*, 168, 108.

107. Lt. Col. Lance A. McDaniel, "Transitioning from Conventional Combat," *Marine Corps Gazette* (November 2005): 53; Reynolds, *Basrah, Baghdad, and Beyond*, 118–19. See also USMC, *Small-Unit Leaders' Guide to Counterinsurgency*, 25, 54, 119; Campbell, *Joker One*, 86; and Ardolino, *Fallujah Awakens*, 22–23.

108. Lt. Gen. John F. Kelly, foreword to Montgomery and McWilliams, *Al-Anbar Awakening*, 2:x.

109. Lt. Col. Kurt Wheeler, "Counterinsurgency Success in Al Anbar," *Leatherneck* (October 2007): 21.

110. Col. Michael M. Walker, interview in McWilliams and Wheeler, *Al-Anbar Awakening*, 1:74.

111. Ardolino, *Fallujah Awakens*, 104–5.

112. Ibid., 63–78.

113. Maj. Gen. James N. Mattis, interview in McWilliams and Wheeler, *Al-Anbar Awakening*, 1:33.

114. Weston, *Mirror Test*, 133, 122.

115. Mattis, interview in McWilliams and Wheeler, *Al-Anbar Awakening*, 1:32.

116. Ardolino, *Fallujah Awakens*, 180–203.

117. Ibid., 109.

118. Ibid., 110, 208.

119. Noted within oral histories from Sheikh Aifan Sadun al-Issawi, Sheikh Sabah al-Sattam Effan Fahran al-Shurji al-Aziz, Mr. Kamis Ahmad Abban al-Alwani, and Maj. Gen. Tariq Yusif Mohammad al-Thiyabi, available in Montgomery and McWilliams, *Al-Anbar Awakening*, 2:92.

120. Matthew T. Penny examines the particulars within the Anbar context that contributed to success there and argues that they may not be easily duplicated. Penny, "Anbar Awakening in Context," 111. See also Kahl, "Walk before Running."

121. 1st Lt. Jason Goodale and 1st Lt. Jon Webre, "The Combined Action Platoon in Iraq," *Marine Corps Gazette* (April 2005): 40–42; Lt. Col. Philip C. Skuta, "Introduction to 2/7 CAP Platoon Actions in Iraq," *Marine Corps Gazette* (April 2005): 35; Lt. Col. Philip Skuta, "Partnering with the Iraqi Security Forces," *Marine Corps Gazette* (April 2005).

122. Goodale and Webre, "Combined Action Platoon," 40–42.

123. USMC, *Small-Unit Leaders' Guide to Counterinsurgency*, 3.

124. Wheeler, "Good News in Al Anbar?," 36.

125. Wheeler, "Counterinsurgency Success in Al Anbar," 23.

126. Weston, *Mirror Test*, 143–44.

127. J. Kael Weston, correspondence with the author, September 12, 2016.

128. Kilcullen, *Accidental Guerrilla*, 122.

129. West, *Strongest Tribe*, 23–25, 41, 75; Hoffman, *Learning while under Fire*, 202; Penny, "Anbar Awakening in Context," 109; Capt. Michael C. Vasquez, "Tribalism under Fire," *Marine Corps Gazette* (January 2008): 62–67.

130. Maj. Daniel R. Zappa, interview in McWilliams and Wheeler, *Al-Anbar Awakening*, 1:221. See also Maj. Gen. Walter E. Gaskin Sr., interview, ibid., 210.

131. Allen, interview, ibid., 230.

132. Wheeler, "Good News in Al Anbar?," 37.

133. Connable, interview in McWilliams and Wheeler, *Al-Anbar Awakening*, 1:125–36.

134. Smith and MacFarland, "Anbar Awakens."

135. J. Kael Weston, correspondence with the author, December 10, 2016.

136. Russell, *Innovation, Transformation, and War*; Hoffman, *Learning while under Fire;* Shultz, *Marines Take Anbar*; West, *Strongest Tribe*; Kilcullen, *Accidental Guerrilla*; Moyar, *Question of Command.*

137. Wheeler, "Good News in Al Anbar?," 38.

138. Lt. Col. Julian D. Alford and Maj. Edwin O. Rueda, "Winning in Iraq," *Marine Corps Gazette* (June 2006). See also Andrew Lubin, "Counterinsurgency and Leadership," *Marine Corps Gazette* (October 2009).

139. Wheeler, "Good News in Al Anbar?," 38; Savanna J. Buckner, "Unlocking the Insurgency: The Al Qa'im Campaign," *Leatherneck* (March 2015); Shultz, *Marines Take Anbar*; Russell, *Innovation, Transformation, and War*; Hoffman, *Learning while under Fire.*

140. Russell, *Innovation, Transformation, and War*, 66. See also Buckner, "Unlocking the Insurgency," 37.

141. Russell, *Innovation, Transformation, and War,* 64–67; Hoffman, *Learning while under Fire*, 193.

142. Capt. Scott Cuomo, "The 'Wild, Wild West': Iraqi Lessons for Afghanistan," *Marine Corps Gazette* (October 2009): 25.

143. Alford and Rueda, "Winning in Iraq," 30.

144. Ibid.; Russell, *Innovation, Transformation, and War*, 64–67.

145. Capt. William Birdzell, "For What Are We Ready?," *Marine Corps Gazette* (April 2007): 52.

146. Russell, *Innovation, Transformation, and War*, 99.

147. Birdzell, "For What Are We Ready?," 53.

148. Moyar, *Question of Command*, 236.

149. Russell, *Innovation, Transformation, and War*, 65–67.

150. Ibid.; Moyar, *Question of Command*, 236.

151. Cuomo, "'Wild, Wild West,'" 27–28; Russell, *Innovation, Transformation, and War*, 65–67.

152. Russell, *Innovation, Transformation, and War.*

153. Wheeler, "Good News in Al Anbar?," 38.

154. "II MEF Marines Depart Anbar Province," 19.

155. Sheikh Ali Hatim Abd al-Razzaq Ali al-Sulayman Al-Assafi, oral history in Montgomery and McWilliams, *Al-Anbar Awakening*, 2:116. See also Staff Maj. Gen. Jasim Muhammad Salih Habib, oral history, ibid., 253.

156. Staff Maj. Gen. Khadim Muhammad Faris al-Fahadawi al-Dulaymi, oral history, ibid., 272.

157. Maj. Gen. Tariq Yusif Mohammad al-Thiyabi, oral history, ibid., 193.

158. Sky, "Iraq, from Surge to Sovereignty," 120.

159. Sheikh Ali Hatim Abd al-Razzaq Ali al-Sulayman Al-Assafi, oral history in Montgomery and McWilliams, *Al-Anbar Awakening*, 2:119; Brig. Gen. David G. Reist, interview in McWilliams and Wheeler, *Al-Anbar Awakening*, 1:154; Zappa, interview, ibid., 223; Sheikh Sabah al-Sattam Effan Fahran al-Shurji al-Aziz, oral history in Montgomery and McWilliams, *Al-Anbar Awakening*, 2:146.

# CONCLUSION

## Lessons Learned and Lessons Lost

Marine counterinsurgency practice across one hundred years of fighting time is characterized by both marked continuities and some impressive innovations. The operational cultural narratives that shaped Marine behavior in each counterinsurgency round were influenced by US national and military cultures situated within the times, as well as by the internal identity, norms, values, and aspects of perceptual lens that continued to evolve within the Corps.

The experience of the Iraq War has added variety and depth to the collection of counterinsurgency lessons Marines can claim. How these will translate into future practice will depend on which lessons Marines themselves extract from their recent experience and institutionalize into training. The vast assembly of potential lessons learned accumulated over the last decade and a half are present but analytically unaccounted for in a Marine "lessons learned" data repository. Attempts to identify the "right" lessons from Iraq and Afghanistan have met with internal friction and have, for the most part, fallen flat. Much like during the post–Banana Wars experience, the preservation of lessons learned has taken place largely through informal channels and through the voices of authors within the *Marine Corps Gazette*. Its articles that referenced both "lessons" and "Iraq" since the Marine pullout in 2009 are evaluated here alongside other source material (including memoirs, scholarly accounts, reports by embedded journalists, and interviews of those overseeing Marine Corps programs) in order to understand the way in which Marines have ingested their Iraqi counterinsurgency experience and to identify the lessons most likely to be learned through reinforcement in training and doctrine, as well as those in jeopardy of being lost.

## LESSONS LEARNED

In assessing its own lessons learned, America's First to Fight force is most at home when commenting on conventional capabilities that fared well in Operation Iraqi Freedom (OIF) and Operation Enduring Freedom (OEF). These include the performance of the Marine air-ground task force

(MAGTF) as well as the empowerment of small-unit leaders in decentralized decision making. Both are well-established Marine modes of fighting that represent sources of pride. Another is logistical excellence. It is important to note that while all three are celebrated as having been tested and honed in recent counterinsurgency fights, their additional appeal is the obvious applicability to conventional conflict.

## Training Indigenous Security Forces

Of those lessons particularly important to irregular warfare, training indigenous forces garnered the most attention within Marine journals. A long-standing and well-known tradition for the Corps, including during peacetime, the Marine role in training and advising continues to be scrutinized for areas where Marines can improve on performance. Today's leathernecks clearly "own" the training role, as indicated both by the earnest tone of the articles and the consistent references to Marine heroes such as Pete Ellis and Chesty Puller as iconic trainers.[1] Marines addressing the topic emphasize that strides forward in effective advising are not only important for counterinsurgency theaters, but are also immediately applicable to ongoing partnering and training operations with allies.[2]

Nearly two decades of counterinsurgency have moved this century's Devil Dogs well beyond their CAP program predecessors in imagining which Marines can fill the advising and training role. Duty that involves living together with indigenous forces—eating, sleeping, and training beside them—has become a mentoring formula that is integral to the Marine approach, albeit one requiring a high degree of maturity and discernment. The widespread Marine Corps interest in this topic, identity ownership of the role, and continued involvement in advisory tasks mean that Marines are likely to absorb and improve on many of the lessons learned in this category.

Despite the positive attention circulating around the training topic, an important blind spot remains. American forces across time have focused on the *proper processing and training* of locals as the key to an effective indigenous security force rather than the existence of *local will to fight* in the direction Americans are pointing. In Marine assessments of the Iraq experience, disappointing performance on the part of indigenous forces is attributed to *insufficient training*—a situation fixable through the talents, hard work, and determination of their trainers—rather than *insufficient will to fight*. Leatherneck-penned articles do not acknowledge or explore the cultural or contextual incentives of indigenous recruits as variables that must be considered when forecasting their readiness and likely fighting form. Instead, Marines placed all responsibility to transform local recruits into capable warriors—ready *and willing* to fight—on their own shoulders.

Bing West observed this mind-set in action in 2005, noting that the US military's "can-do spirit" created immense pressure for positive reporting on the state of training provided for indigenous troops. Thus, a country-wide review of progress made during that period received only positive reports. The prevailing feedback was that training Iraqi forces to self-sufficiency could be accomplished within twelve months—an estimate West categorized as "dizzying optimism."[3] The US military's approach is a reflection of an admirable trait and one the Marines prize above all else: taking responsibility for the mission and seeing it through. That same trait, however, creates a perennial blind spot by eclipsing from serious consideration those factors that are outside Marine control. Rather than assume that the will to fight can be inspired through training, military planners are better served by a hard-nosed evaluation of the incentives present for locals to fight alongside them and an equally rigorous evaluation of which incentives the United States is in a position to alter.

West's one-on-one conversations with commanders yielded more candid assessments than the reports they made to "higher." Officers were frustrated with the caliber of recruits they were given, the lack of discipline, motivation, and capacity for leadership on the part of Iraqi officers, and insufficient material support from Baghdad.[4] Many of these concerns melted away once tribes, motivated on their own terms, began sending recruits to join the fight. With a common enemy in their sights and strong incentives on both sides to coordinate efforts, frustration on the American side eased, and partnership with the increased number of higher-caliber recruits produced rapid successes.

The will to fight alongside American forces, more so than the high quality of training offered by US Marines, determines the existence of an effective and reliable indigenous partner for counterinsurgency operations. Pecuniary rewards are inadequate, as shown by the low quality of recruits who responded to this incentive during the Banana Wars, and so is the opportunity for excellent martial training, as evidenced in Iraq. The efforts of local recruits can be amplified exponentially by US training and resources when the American cause is one that they, of their own accord, judge worth fighting for. Only when this essential factor is in play do the counterinsurgency best practices of living, eating, sleeping beside, and training with indigenous partners make a real difference.

## Intelligence

Intelligence was relatively weak during the Banana Wars, significantly improved on during the CAP program, and advanced further during the Corps's time in Iraq. Marines never remedied serious intelligence deficits while operating in Haiti, the Dominican Republic, or Nicaragua. Bad relations between infantry and the local populations kept Marines largely in the dark concerning the whereabouts of their adversary. Marines in the CAP program fared considerably better, owing in part to voluntary contributions from sympathetic locals but predominantly because of their intense familiarity with their villages. CAP intelligence was absorbed by the CAP squad but was not taken seriously by officers, so it was not incorporated by headquarters in ways that could be looped back and made useful to other Marines.

Marines in Iraq struggled during the initial years to gain traction with the population. Their own often bluntly applied operations, their inability to provide security to collaborators, and the discriminatory practices of the central government they were fighting for inhibited the volunteering of intelligence from locals. When Marines became the partner of choice for Sunni tribes, accurate and useful intelligence grew from a trickle to a torrent.[5] Innovators in both the US Army and Marine Corps made good use of the increased information flow by pioneering practices that effectively fused and redistributed intelligence.[6] Their efforts, often improved by others who rotated in, significantly increased the accuracy of insurgent targeting and produced an uptick in operational tempo for going after them. While scholars trumpet the success of US forces in this regard, Marines themselves are more critical. Evaluating their own experience, Marines find plenty of room for improvement.[7] Still, their efforts represent a significant step forward from leatherneck progenitors. The critical attention the subject has received in the *Gazette* represents ardent interest in incorporating lessons learned and improving on them.

## Culture Matters

Devil Dog default settings are not dialed to welcome what many grunts tend to regard as "sensitivity training": schooling on the cultural mores of other lands. Marines come by this honestly through an American heritage that downplays the relevance of culture to almost any problem and a Marine service culture built on a death-and-destruction combat image. In the early stages of the Iraq War, a fair number of Marine warriors expressed less-than-enthusiastic attitudes about the cultural training on offer. When deployed, enlisted Marines tended toward neutral or pejorative terms when referencing the sea of unfamiliar Arab faces around them. One is hard pressed to find a memoir penned by an infantry Marine that does not somewhere refer to the locals as "hajjis."[8] A captain writing for the *Gazette* lamented the refusal of some Marines to rid themselves of negative mental constructs when dealing with the Iraqi population. He claimed in 2005 that many Marines in Iraq were "uncomfortable with a foreign culture and still blinded by anger from 11 September 2001" and therefore continued to "seethe at hajjis and avoid all contact." He referenced one sergeant who refused to invest in understanding Iraqi culture and almost never left the base, rationalizing, "Sir, it's not important for me to learn that hajji s—t. I'm never going to use it anyway."⁹

An appreciation for the value of cultural knowledge developed over time, however, as both officers and enlisted experienced more years in a population-driven war. By 2007 Maj. Gen. Richard C. Zilmer claimed that most Marines recognized "that dealing in a counterinsurgency in the Middle East, or in the Arab world, requires a fundamental understanding of the culture." He went on to point out that the Corps had already institutionalized this priority to an unprecedented degree by identifying an increased number of officers for training as cultural experts, standing up the Marine Corps University's Center for Advanced Operational Culture and Learning (CAOCL), and institutionalizing cultural training through Mojave Viper.¹⁰ The counterinsurgency progress made in Anbar Province continued to reinforce "culture matters" as a "lesson recognized." Both Col. Dale Alford and Col. Sean MacFarland were aided in no small part by cultural experts whom they sought out and leaned on for advice in navigating the complex tribal networks within their areas of operations (AOs). Capt. Travis Patriquin, a former US Army Special Forces Arabic speaker, provided a major assist to MacFarland in forging links with local tribes, and Maj. Ed Rueda, an expert on Middle Eastern culture, proved indispensable in the same way for Alford in Al Qa'im.¹¹

A review of *Gazette* and *Leatherneck* articles on the topic of cultural education offers a more encouraging trend line than that which followed past irregular conflicts. The first item of note is that the US military services have created their own vocabulary for considering the range of social and cultural influences on operations, including such labels as "cross-cultural competence," "human terrain," and "operational culture."¹² Although social science experts employed by the US military find some of the labels controversial owing to the uneven performance of the programs in which they originated and the historical baggage they accrued, and some may cringe at the obsolete notions of "culture" often packaged into their definitions, the martial flavor of the emergent jargon does signal a level of military "ownership" of cultural study and creates a common lexicon for discussion.

A review of *Gazette* and *Leatherneck* articles containing both "human terrain" and "cultural" within their text reveals that today's Marines have achieved stronger consensus than their predecessors concerning the value of cultural training and education programs, which advance their ability to effectively engage with foreign populations. The Banana Wars–era discussants who churned out the *Small Wars Manual* repeatedly voiced the utility of understanding "the people, their temperament, customs, activities and the everyday working of the average native mind,"¹³ but they were a bounded camp within the Corps and focused almost exclusively on the application of this knowledge to small wars. As their Corps turned to an amphibious role involving landing operations and the securing of advanced bases, "lessons recognized" identified by this group concerning the utility of investing in cultural knowledge faded along with the *Small Wars Manual* itself.

Interest in culture resurged during the Vietnam War era, and the investment by US military institutions in conducting social science analysis was impressive but fraught with controversy, staining both the effort and those scholars associated with it.[14] Ironically, CAP Marines—a group particularly well positioned to profit from the insights derived from this US investment— saw none of it. Cultural education, even within the CAP school curriculum, was minimal: It focused on bits of advice regarding day-to-day interactions and a smattering of Vietnamese lingo. CAP Marines, like Capt. Merritt Edson on Nicaragua's Coco River before them, hit the ground culturally naive and "figured it out." Their initially steep and sometimes deadly learning curve was gradually overcome as these Marines adapted to their new environment. The testimonials of CAP Marines regarding the advantages that could have been theirs through predeployment culture and language training were lost in the howl of voices raging over the loss of Vietnam. CAP Marines, even had they tried to press the issue, made up too tiny a number of the overall Marine force to have significant impact on institutional attitudes concerning cultural training going forward.

In contrast, today's Marines operate in an era in which cultural education and training has been grown across more than a decade of time and institutionalized to a much higher degree. As a consequence of this exposure, Marine authors are quick to point out the indispensable role cultural competence plays in a counterinsurgency fight.[15] They also highlight its relevance across a much wider range of Marine missions and tasks, including many held dear within the Corps, such as the future composition of the MAGTAF,[16] excellence within Recon units,[17] improvement to the Marine Corps Planning Process,[18] information operations,[19] the placement of patrol outposts and solicitation of intelligence,[20] and relationships with allies.[21] Some have advocated analysis of human terrain as the seventh warfighting skill.[22] One somewhat humorous article suggests using cultural analytics honed in Iraq and Afghanistan to decode the increasingly strange (to military men and women) ways of American civilian counterparts when posted to recruitment duty.[23]

Human terrain and other more sophisticated sociocultural concepts have remained part of the conversation across mission sets and across the years since the Marines departed Iraq. Their *Marine Corps Vision and Strategy 2025* document declares that Marines of the future will "go to greater lengths to understand our enemies and the range of cultural, societal, and political factors affecting all with whom we interact."[24] An important note, however, is that wherever the advocacy of cultural knowledge is found, it is almost universally alongside a warning that not enough is being done to encourage and reward this skill: "If these so-called soft sciences [sociology, anthropology, ethnography, and psychology] are the art that complements the science in 'military science,' the Department of Defense's (DoD's) 50-pound brain is lopsided, with 49 pounds in the left hemisphere of the brain and focused on the sciences of kinetic warfare (ballistics, hydro- and aerospace engineering, etc.) and 1 pound in the other hemisphere genuinely focused on civil populations and the indices of instability."[25] The reward system and clear hierarchy of the Corps means that aptitude in dissecting the sociocultural aspects of war will remain an undercelebrated aspect of the warfighter personality. The persistent result is that a number of current officers ignore available culture-related education and make needless mistakes as a consequence.[26]

While a recalcitrant bunch will likely always be in the mix across US services and cross-cultural competence is not likely to displace combat valor any time soon on the Corps's altar of worship, it would be wrong to discount the unmatched steps forward made in cultural education within the most recent counterinsurgency era.[27] They represent an integration level that moves beyond that of a simple lesson recognized. Sustaining forward momentum toward refinement and institutionalization is the challenge ahead. Scholars involved with this effort worry that the aspects of cultural education and training likely to persist will be those of least utility to the Corps. The Department of Defense is most comfortable with a regional studies approach to cultural education—one that will fall short for all wars outside the regions selected. A superior educational method, found in modest form within the current Corps's officer curricula, emphasizes universal decoding skills. Called a "culture-general" approach, this method focuses on the concepts and skills that help Marines identify and understand the information necessary to navigate diverse cultures wherever they are deployed. Without the expansion of culture-general education, future Marines will find themselves ill-prepared for fights in unexpected theaters. Anticipating that likely end, experts hope to keep little pieces of the culture-general capability tucked away—a set of "tiny pilot lights" burning in corners of the military services over the next ten years. They predict that these will either receive a burst of fuel from another round of population-centric conflicts or eventually burn out. If the latter, the Corps will once again be left to rely on its signature norm of adaptability in place of appropriately focused education regimens.[28]

## LESSONS NOT TO LOSE

Not all lessons that might be learned from the experience in Iraq have received the attention they merit. The staying power of counterinsurgency itself, as a particular war discipline, does not seem to be faring well within Marine Corps classrooms. Some officers who earned their stripes in counterinsurgency fights across the last decades worry that the lessons from these wars are not being addressed with the serious attention they deserve. One points out that updated inclusion of these lessons in doctrine would be the right first step but that real institutionalization is found in "a general dynamic in which the tactical lessons of a decade's worth of COIN becomes ingrained in the living, rather than textual, institutional memory of the Marine Corps."[29] This would include significant emphasis in curriculum at the Basic School (TBS), an emphasis that remains absent and is protested by a number of concerned first lieutenants:

> If TBS is to serve as the foundation of every Marine Corps officer's basic warfighting education, then why do we completely exclude from that education the type of battles we fought for the last decade and are likely to fight again in the future? Despite having spent the last 13 years conducting counterinsurgency and stability operations, TBS students receive only 3 hours of instruction and a dense, lengthy handout on the topics. The counterinsurgency lecture does little to discuss the strategies and tactics the Marine Corps and Army used during OIF and OEF and, instead, simplifies stability operations into a dated case study on Marines in Haiti or the French in Algeria.[30]

Lack of curriculum notwithstanding, future Marines will benefit from established counterinsurgency doctrine, doctrine that was both produced and applied during the course of the Iraq and Afghanistan wars and that provided the foundation for a more general acceptance of new practices across US services. Both the Army and the Marine Corps vested their institutional support in seeing it through. The serious crafting of combined-service "COIN" doctrine in a manner timely enough to see it applied is an event unprecedented across prior Marine Corps small-wars experience. Also unprecedented is the amount of public attention the doctrine received. These "artifacts" of this century's counterinsurgency experience will make it harder for its doctrine to fade from memory.

## No One COIN Formula

One lesson that future Marines might glean from the Iraq experience is that despite helpful new doctrine offering time-tested best practices, there is no one formula for creating counterinsurgency success across diverse AOs. The successes of varied units across the Anbar Province demonstrates that while many core principles are consistent across cases, these were applied with an eye toward a local area's specific operational context—a point Alford himself makes in an article assessing the transferability of methods from Iraq to Afghanistan.[31] Thus, one takeaway for sound pedagogy in service schoolhouses is the utility of studying counterinsurgency success stories *in context*. Although leaders within Anbar pursued a somewhat similar repertoire of counterinsurgency best practices, these were not prioritized in the same way across cases or implemented in the same chronological order. In some cases, Marines worked to forge key local relationships first and then jointly pursued robust security operations alongside indigenous partners. In other cases, Marines had to establish themselves as an effective security presence by chalking up significant wins against al-Qaeda insurgents before attempting meaningful relations with tribal leadership. In a few areas Marines used multiple large-sweep operations in advance of setting up combat outposts. In others, the strategy focused on using small combined teams as "bait" in order to draw insurgents into the open. The larger lesson drawn from these cases, then, is that best counterinsurgency practices must be contextually assessed and determined through intimate familiarity with one's AO. An effective education of counterinsurgency practice, therefore, will focus on close study of particular cases in order to understand the decision-making process: how leaders decided which operational approach to prioritize and pursue and why. This learning method will help reinforce Marine values of adaptability and will validate their regard for doctrine as a general source of guidance—a suggested repertoire of best practices—rather than a set formula that restricts and overdirects small-unit action.

Thus, investing in the compilation and serious study of cases beyond Alford's in both Iraq and Afghanistan would go some distance in encouraging flexible thinking and diminishing the temptation to draw the false "lesson learned" of a universal formula for counterinsurgency. Marines do little more than note Col. Sean MacFarland's success in Ramadi in their journals, for instance, and fail to analytically dissect the practices he and Marine lieutenant colonel William Jurney, who served under him, put to good use. A deep study of First Battalion, Sixth Marine Regiment's tour in Ramadi under Jurney would offer Marines proud ownership of innovation practiced by one of their own, as well as make plain the diversity in successful methods practiced across AOs.[32]

## Measuring Counterinsurgency Success

Despite the academic congratulations Alford received for his innovative and sensible measure of stability in his area—the "eats on streets" count of how many meals his Marines shared with local families—there is little indication that this approach moved beyond a few pockets of operation in Iraq or is likely to displace traditional, albeit often less useful, quantitative assessment data. Across its history, the activities pursued by the Marine Corps in irregular conflict have been largely shaped by American metrics valuing countable and tangible achievements. The result has often been detrimental to desired strategic effect. Marines of the Banana Wars era pursued impressive physical and quantifiable ends over cultivating democratic means. Marines of the Vietnam era, initially from national habit and later against their better judgment, continued to report their successes largely by counting American inputs rather than critically assessing the strategic effect that these produced. Commandant Leonard Chapman, in a "State of the Corps" write-up intended for political consumption, outlined the basic goal in Vietnam: "The Marine Corps has consistently advocated the principle that the war in South Vietnam can be conclusively won only through convincing the South Vietnamese people in the villages and hamlets that their hope lies with freedom, not with communism." He then went on to offer up progress toward this ideological goal by way of countable combat actions: enemy dead, major operations of battalion size or larger, amphibious landings, enemy caches uncovered, sorties flown, troops lifted, supplies delivered, and finally, a countable perhaps worth counting—enemy defected.[33]

The CAP program suffered particularly in this regard. As Deborah Avant points out, the metrics used to measure success were devised by the Army and were a poor fit for the CAP program's ambitions.[34] If CAP units were successful in their mission, VC elements would disappear from their neighborhood and cease to inflict themselves in material and ideological ways on the villagers. Therefore, a measure of CAP success would be a decrease in VC engagements (a drop in contacts and therefore kills) and a consequent blooming of political and economic life in the village (perhaps measured in number of officials who moved back, upticks in intelligence, renewed economic activity, resettlement of refugees, friendly attitudes expressed toward CAP Marines, etc.).[35] Instead, all reports assessing the CAP program, even those written by sources intimately familiar with it, applied exactly the same sort of measuring stick that a line unit at the time was using: number of kinetic contacts, number of VC dead, and comparative number of Marines and PFs wounded and killed in action.[36] Captain Williamson articulated his frustration with this seemingly inescapable misfit of measurement:

> If one measures success in terms of the number of V.C. captured and killed, the amount of ammunition and funds expended, or the quantity of soap and candy distributed, then one may realize a statistical triumph and a practical disaster. But if the criteria of accomplishment involved more subjective judgments, like the development of an esprit de Corps among men of totally alien cultures, a reciprocity of confidence and respect, the construction of a communication system that is open, honest and frank, and the ability to work effectively as a team despite the impediments of language or the dichotomy inherent between the part-time amateur and the full-time professional, then evaluation will at least have validity.[37]

Marines in Iraq defaulted to many of the same patterns of measurement that had been employed in prior engagements, with a primary focus on insurgents killed and weapons found. As real progress began to be made in Anbar, additional metrics were offered up, including the number of willing recruits headed to American training and the volume of intelligence coming from the population—both more reliable indicators of strategic progress. A turn toward genuinely innovative metrics that can reliably measure strategic progress will require an investment in creative qualitative analysis, which can provide context for and extract meaning from the traditional pile of quantitative data. The qualitative skill set required for this sort of analysis remains underdeveloped across the force and runs counter to strong American preferences for facts in the form of numbers-driven "hard data."[38] Counting American inputs to the fight as achievements in their own right, regardless of positive strategic impact, is a trend likely to continue. Assessments that attempt to capture less tangible but more meaningful progress indicators toward political goals will be the product of innovators insistent on more sensible metrics but will often be overridden by deeply entrenched American measuring and reporting instincts.[39]

## CONTINUING BLIND SPOTS: HUBRIS IN NATION-BUILDING

The evidence assembled across three eras of American counterinsurgency experience reveals that although roundly abused in the Banana Wars and Vietnam cases, the American can-do mentality—which perceives struggling nations as a problem to be "fixed" and the American polity and its military arm as the means to do so—did not suffer permanent and lasting harm and was reasserted in the run-up to the invasion of Iraq in 2003.[40] Thomas Ricks makes the point that not all US institutions were equally naive to the possible complications endemic to regime change in Iraq.[41] Nevertheless, the dominating perception among civilian overseers was that military intervention in Iraq would achieve quick results and would not require a lengthy stay on the part of US military forces.[42] Given the military's reluctance to think in terms of occupation duty, neither the Department of Defense nor Central Command provided a serious counterweight to civilian assessments of a quick transition to Iraqi self-rule.[43] Marine leadership engaged in a measure of postwar planning on their own but were prohibited from accessing the State Department's comprehensive "Future of Iraq" study, which had laid out many of the challenges likely to be faced. Referencing the study was considered taboo for military planners since its long-range and complex approach was not compatible with the Pentagon's vision of a quick turnaround in postwar Iraq.[44] American hubris regarding nation-building is a product of a perceptual lens that regards humans as problem-solving agents and the American nation as a possessor of "exceptional" keys to success. This, combined with a strong penchant for ahistoricism and national ignorance of foreign cultures, is a consistent cultural recipe that has led, and is likely to continue to lead, to the United States shaping nation-building and counterinsurgency tasks in improbable, if not impossible, terms for the service members sent to execute them.

Although Banana Wars–era officers openly acknowledged that changing indigenous culture was exactly what they were about, modern American sensibilities have rendered it no longer acceptable to cast nation-building in those terms. Therefore, contemporary Marines (and other service members) are asked to transform fundamental aspects of foreign cultures but are prohibited from thinking of it that way. Rather, Marines, alongside their civilian and military service counterparts, operate within an ideological milieu in which nation-building is a path-clearing exercise advanced on behalf of an indigenous population seeking expedited movement toward self-governance.

Serious reservations concerning the transportability of the American experiment are habitually lost to history. Because these views are not chronicled, codified, and studied, the memory of many lessons recognized dies with the veterans who lived them. In their place, the ardent problem-solving and optimism-as-power themes of American culture, which are consistently validated in the social, economic, and technical arenas of national life, position another generation for naiveté and optimistic overstretch in the foreign realm. Naysayers to this process are cast in disfavor along the lines of an oft-referenced American slogan: "The man who says it can't be done is generally interrupted by someone doing it."[45]

The resurgent can-do American mentality is habitually teamed with a premium on expediency, dual values that have sometimes led nation-building Marines to create the inverse of what was strategically intended. As chronicled in this research, Marines of the Caribbean era unintentionally set the stage for legacies of dictatorship. It is a painful nation-building irony that Marines generated this unfortunate strategic end by attempting to do as much good as possible in the shortest amount of time. The hard-wired valuing of efficiency is perhaps the most deleterious of the American cultural inclinations when applied to nation-building tasks. This value is found in robust form in American public and commercial culture and is only amplified by the internal cultures of the US military—especially so with US Marines. Marines pride themselves on the quickest tempo of the services— speediest to the scene and soonest to mission accomplishment. They are willing to pursue this "lane" at great cost to themselves and others.

As has been demonstrated in repeated fashion, the nation-building that prospers, not just during the counterinsurgency engagement but beyond, is that in which locals have personally invested and that is sustainable through local resources after foreign mentors leave. Involving local input in a meaningful way will almost universally be a process that taxes the limits of a Marine's patience and often exceeds his ability to watch a project founder rather than step in and get it done. The Marine values of efficiency in action and mission accomplishment do not easily endure the sorts of convoluted local processes or much slower cultural tempos an indigenous theater may impose.

To dispatch government services more efficiently, the US military, with American political support, gravitates toward centralizing structures that may have the effect of disenfranchising local sources of power. This tendency is inappropriately assigned to American forces alone. Military cultures across the globe are more likely to value security and order above the pluralism of contending voices. When combined with vast American resources, however, and US determination to build large-scale national forces and substantially improved infrastructure, the results can be the dramatic inverse of what was intended. The authoritarian outcomes of this particular formula, despite their display in repeated fashion, remain obscured by a perceptive lens that focuses on American *intentions* in the nation-building process to the exclusion of a thorough analysis of *unintended* but consistent *after effects*. The failure to critically analyze the legacies of Marine nation-building efforts is a serious one and has resulted in a perennial blind spot concerning the ways in which good intentions can go awry when the United States reaches to assist other nations.

The local empowerment provided by CAP Marines represents an approach that might safeguard against inadvertently stage-setting for a future dictatorship, although it was not with this in mind that CAP Marines pursued their mission. In this sense, local empowerment remains a positive blind spot: a useful but underappreciated and underanalyzed practice. CAP Marines protected local officials and supported the village security forces and in so doing provided a check on the potentially exploitive reach of South Vietnam's central government. The architects of the CAP program did not design their force-multiplying program with this particular nation-building goal in mind—it was simply the fortunate by-product of the CAP squad's mandate to serve within a geographically bounded village and the protective instinct that developed as they did so. On the broader scale, the American instinct to build up the government of Saigon and vest considerable coercive power in its national security forces (which were fighting their countrymen in a counterinsurgency) was in full form.

Marines in Iraq took a different path but arrived at the same positive blind spot. There is no evidence to indicate that Marines making decisions in Iraq were aware of, and therefore consciously avoiding, the authoritarian groundwork thrice produced by their Caribbean predecessors. The American focus on empowering and legitimizing the government in Baghdad and raising up a national security force for its defense acted as the steering mechanism for most all decisions and operations in Iraq. By at least 2006, observers of the fight were noting the deleterious impact of the Coalition's obsession with supporting top-down governance from Baghdad.[46] Bing West claims that Marines were "deprived of local allies" by the Coalition's determination to build a modern Iraq.[47] Only after years of bloody stalemate did Marines break with this pattern and provide a measure of empowerment to the tribes, a decision that had the effect of providing a check on Baghdad's power by keeping local power brokers in the game.

In their nation-building efforts, US policymakers and their military services fall victim to a second consistent blind spot: a fixation on their own efforts as the primary determinant of counterinsurgency victory and a concomitant undervaluing of the critical role of the host government. Colin Gray notes the futility in remaining blind on this score: "Even if the armed forces of a polity are organized, commanded, and led in battle by a general blessed in good measure with competent strategic sense that advantageous fact will prove of little value should the country's political leadership not be capable of exercising political sense."[48] Given what may seem an obvious fact—that the character and practices of the host government are the most critical factors in establishing its political legitimacy and thereby energizing citizens to fight on its behalf—it is somewhat alarming that this determinative feature of counterinsurgency success is a subject of only passing mention within Marine journals. Instead, Marines remain dedicated to a no-excuses approach to their mission sets, leading them to shoulder responsibility for the whole of counterinsurgency success. In addressing the problem of garnering support for the host government, one of the Corps's brightest lights continues to see this as a Marine problem to be fixed: Marines, alongside their indigenous security force counterparts, "should force the local leadership, both formal and informal power structures, along with the average local person, to make a conscious choice of which side to support, the government's or the insurgent's." It is the Marine's job to "ultimately persuad[e] all players involved to side with the host-nation government."[49]

US forces justify their ownership of this problem through a fiction embraced in Vietnam and pursued again in Iraq and Afghanistan: that the goodwill US military forces establish with host populations, whether through the provision of security, the construction of infrastructure, the distribution of humanitarian aid, or the offer of education or medical services, can somehow be "gifted" to an unpopular host government in order to enhance its legitimacy. It cannot. Local populations are not typically naive to the source of help provided. As noted in the last chapter, Iraqis who had already soured on the Shi'a bent of their Baghdad government did not afford it new credit as a result of Marine efforts: "The government of Iraq didn't help us with anything. It was all help from the Coalition."[50] As a foreign force, Marines can work to provide a strategic pause in violence and can use their resources to amplify the efforts of indigenous governing structures, but it cannot earn political legitimacy for them.

A lesson that might be drawn from the success of the Anbar Awakening is that governance structures created by a foreign occupying force are unlikely to attain the credibility and loyalty base necessary to win popular support in the near, and critical, term. The United States will have more success working with existing social and political structures that, whether on the right side of history by US standards or not, already draw the loyalty and support of the resident population. In Iraq, structures of this sort were somewhat limited after the US decisions to ban Ba'ath bureaucratic institutions and personnel and disband the national military. By doing so, the Coalition reduced itself to the remaining forms of social and political organization that operated at a regional and sometimes local level. Lt. Col. Kurt Wheeler, a reservist Marine whose perspective benefited from recording oral histories in Iraq, observed that in Anbar Province "tribal leaders . . . still had far more 'wasta' (respect status) than any elected leader."[51]

Expanding the power and reach of existing organizations in a nondemocratic society will come at a cost to American democratizing ambitions in the near term but will likely prove more effective in defeating insurgents. This operational approach would also require that the United States come to grips with its support role in counterinsurgency and nation-building efforts. US energies and resources have been most effectively spent when in the service of indigenously motivated trajectories already under way. In this sense, it is the US that becomes the force multiplier instead of the other way around.[52]

## LESSONS FOR THE FUTURE

Compared to the overwhelming task set of Marine nation-builders in Iraq, CAP Marines in Vietnam pursued a largely uncomplicated affair. In theory, CAP Marines were charged with enhancing the social and economic life of villagers, but in practice they focused almost solely on protecting them from enemies—both foreign and domestic—and helping out in useful, neighborly ways. The economics and politics of village life operated largely of its own accord. Villagers lived at a subsistence level in very humble circumstances, and Marine civic action was, for the most part, of an equally humble sort. Marines rarely tried to step into governing roles, act as legal arbitrator, or provide municipal utilities. When employing the CAP program as a template for action, it is worth considering whether this lighter footprint—a security-oriented posture in a context of limited civic expectations—was a factor in the locals' acceptance of an enduring Marine presence.

Perhaps with this principle in mind, the *Small-Unit Leaders' Guide to Counterinsurgency* (*SULG*) aims for an operational world in which the military's role is appropriately bounded to the role of security: providing a protected space for others—including US diplomats and, most essentially, representatives of the indigenous government—to pursue political and economic initiatives. Its authors harbor serious reserve about the ability of a foreign force to remain welcome as occupiers and to successfully implement political and social change. Caution notwithstanding, this is not a lesson any branch of the military can independently champion and implement. The military serves as an executor of civilian policy, not the crafter of it. Whatever reservations may be harbored by the Corps's leadership regarding the sensibility of their nation-building orders from a civilian administration, they will be beholden to American national perceptions regarding what is possible and appropriate for the military services to achieve.

## Savvy Civic Action

National pattern suggests that in some perhaps not-so-distant future Marines will again be assigned nation-building tasks. Given this eventuality, it is worth examining the positive lessons that can be drawn from eras in which Marines pursued nation-building efforts and steered investments of civic action to good effect. As already discussed, nation-building efforts of a civic-action sort may not achieve the intended strategic effect of boosting the popular fortunes of self-destructive host governments, but there are other tactical and operational advantages to be had by appropriately applied civic action that are worth considering.

The frugal sort of civic action offered by CAP squads and practiced in a number of places across Iraq served to enhance unit intelligence by providing increased access into an AO and exposure to the voices within it. Familiarization with both territory and persons yielded indispensable tactical and operational knowledge. In addition, CAP squads reported a degree of force protection that resulted from their simple acts of service among the population. Villagers took risks to protect "their" Marines. Civic action also served as a morale enhancer. CAP Marines perceive themselves to have significantly more pride in their tours and peace of soul regarding their service than many of their Marine counterparts. Their personal acts of service to the Vietnamese provided salve on emotional war wounds but also a boost to the image of the Corps. Americans at home responded with enthusiasm to popularized photos of CAPpers "making friends" with smiling Vietnamese villagers. The cover of the August 25, 1967, *Life* magazine captures the heartwarming scene of a CAP Marine, M16 in one hand and two fishing poles in the other, accompanying a young Vietnamese boy on crutches down a dirt lane. The image is a direct reflection (likely intentional) of the opening sequence of the 1960s' *The Andy Griffith Show*. Americans responded warmly and enthusiastically to such scenes, and not without reason. The war in Vietnam represented an ideological contest, and evidence in photos such as these seemed to suggest to the American public that CAP Marines were having some success in bringing the Vietnamese into the American fold.

Large-scale, infrastructure-based civic action, while often derided for its excesses, provides some hope for the economic advancement of the host nation and supplies the very real short-term benefit of military operational utility. Improvements to national roadways and communication links have often proved essential to the military proficiency of the US force. These might be pursued in the future for the military maneuvering they allow and the general health of the troops that they preserve, but they should not be assumed as a device for incurring strategic gratitude from the local population.

The primary lesson drawn from the last years of civic engagement in Iraq is an important one. Alford, Jurney, MacFarland, and other savvy officers leading the turn toward tribal engagement were strategic rather than even-handed in their disbursement of "civic action." US funds and contracts rewarded security cooperation and acted as an incentive for previously reluctant tribes to come on board. Sheikhs were allowed to build up their personal power base through control over the distribution of lucrative US contracts.[53] The result was dramatic. Cooperation between US forces and the tribes "broke the back" of al-Qaeda in Anbar.[54]

## The Matter of Time

US military advice, alongside the pleas of Sunni partners, did not dissuade US political leadership from the decision to withdraw troops quickly and completely from Iraq. The sharp departure of US forces raises an issue that must be considered across the US joint force in future counterinsurgency planning. The force must consider, and account for, aspects of future counterinsurgency over which they will have limited control. One of these is staying power. Marines in Iraq reaped the benefits of convincing Iraqi residents that they would stay until the job was done. As noted by a Marine lance corporal, "we just needed to finally convince them that we were going to be there for the duration, that we were in it to win it" in order to seal the deal on joint counterinsurgent cooperation.[55] Historian Richard Shultz notes that "once the sheikhs were convinced that I MEF intended to stay the course in Anbar, they opened the doors to the support of the population. And that population, in turn, swelled the ranks of the Anbar security forces and delivered a wealth of local intelligence on the whereabouts of the AQI network in the province."[56] Colonel Jurney reinforces the criticality of "staying power" from his own experience in Ramadi: "The first question the people are going to ask you is, 'When are you leaving?' You've got to show them you're not going to leave. I mean, if they tell you things and then you leave, they're going to be dead. So it's got to be based on permanent presence."[57]

The problem with Marine assurances of this sort is that no matter how sincerely intended, Marines don't get to make this call. US political leaders determine whether US military personnel stay or depart, and those locals who risk their lives on well-intended promises may be left hanging. The primary asset of the CAP program—the Marines' assurance that they would be a permanent feature in the village until the security situation was well in hand—encouraged trust from the villagers "knowing we are going to stay."[58] This trust, however, was misplaced. Looking back, one CAP Marine stated bitterly, "Do you want to know the worst thing I did in Vietnam? . . . Winning hearts and minds. Winning hearts and minds was the ultimate betrayal. Those are the folks who were hanging on to the helicopters and embassy walls. It's really sad that we won some of them over."[59] CAP Marines believed that they would stay in their village, or at least their replacements would, until Americans had worked themselves out of a job—until PFs were ably trained and they, alongside legitimated South Vietnamese regulars, could handle VC and North Vietnamese Army incursions. In reality, however, the Marines had no control over how long they stayed. Decisions from "higher" and the political climate at home were intervening variables. The trust from villagers that became strategically helpful in the CAP program by yielding a measure of intelligence on the enemy and protection for the Marines, and which later cemented success in Anbar, will be difficult to replicate in future operations. The US national record of departing a theater with an insurgency still in swing—in Vietnam, Iraq, and very likely in Afghanistan—will in all probability be well understood by foreign populations in tomorrow's counterinsurgency scenarios. It will, and should, act as an impediment to their willingness to establish relationships of reliance and trust with US forces.

Perhaps owing to acknowledgment of this operational reality, the *SULG* strikes a lesson-recognized cautionary note: "Be very wary of training, operating alongside, and establishing publicly visible relationships with indigenous forces if you cannot commit to the effort on a long-term basis. Abandoning a young and inexperienced indigenous force before it is ready to fight on its own will almost guarantee insurgent exploitation."[60] This counsel is issued not because Marines have real control over the timing of their departure, but as a nudge toward thoughtful analysis concerning the appropriate relationship with locals once US departure is on the horizon.

## AMERICANS, MARINES, AND THE PROBLEM OF FUTURE COUNTERINSURGENCY

The operational cultural narratives that have shaped Marine thinking and activity in small wars have been drawn from multiple sources. The outlook of the Corps on its future role, however, is powerfully shaped by an internal service instinct protective of hard-won identity goods and the Corps's place of distinction in the lineup of US armed services. The heart of Marine Corps service culture is at odds with efforts to improve on and invest in future full-spectrum counterinsurgency operations, especially those emphasizing nation-building and civic action. A pervasive Marine perception is that a strong focus on training for nation-building operations threatens to diminish the core feature of Devil Dog identity as an elite fighting force and that counterinsurgency professionalism may compromise Marine core competencies in the area of amphibious operations.

A Vietnam-era essay that the *Gazette* honored with an award highlighted these sorts of identity worries and organizational paranoia about pursuing civic action. Its Marine author acknowledged the likely strategic advantages of civic action but worried about the impact on the identity image of the nation's premier fighting force. His striking and historically inaccurate perceptual lens was that past Marine practices regarding civic action were of a limited and temporary nature. Entirely eclipsing the decades of nation-building engineered in the Caribbean, he argued that the sort of civic action demanded in Vietnam would represent a "significant departure" from Marine Corps practice and "trespass into an area generally accepted as the domain of the US Army and civilian governmental agencies." More worrying than service territoriality was the impact that pursuing such soft tactics would have on the Marine Corps's blood-makes-the-green-grass-grow image and recruitment: "Excessive attention to humanitarian programs will ultimately result in a change in the service image beyond that which is conducive to the procurement of fighting men. Under these circumstances the Marine Corps could be attracting men who would be of greater service to the Peace Corps." Based in instincts to protect Marine warrior identity and fueled by the organizational paranoia endemic to the Corps, his comments reflect an internal conflict between preservation of the core identity of his service and the "soft tactics" that seem to be aiding in mission accomplishment. His summary statement on the matter is to try it out carefully but withdraw "from civic action involvement if such steps are determined to be in the best interest of the nation and the Marine Corps."[61] Marines will do civic action "windows" if it is assigned to them but will prefer to keep it on the down low.

Marines in Iraq pursued civic action and "key leader engagements" on a regular basis but were not immune to worries about the impact on image. Devil Dogs prize the reputation of aggressive violence that precedes them and see it, appropriately, as a force multiplier in its own right. Consequently, enlisted Marines in Iraq obeyed orders to distribute humanitarian aid but were often keen to note for the record that they were not the "soccer ball force." It is not without solid rationale that Marines instinctively protect their warfighter image: Establishing identity credentials as the "best fighting force in the world" is no mean feat. Marines ultimately lent their support to civil-military operations in the 2006–7 turnaround era because their leadership demanded it, and it was producing mission success. Maj. Daniel Zappa, who headed the civil-military operations campaign under Colonel Jurney in Ramadi, noted that the civic action emphasis "temper[ed] a lot of things that Marines are trained to do and that you can't just do wantonly in this town. You can't just be all about kinetics and killing and shooting people and talking about it, which is what we, as a culture, value."[62]

Adam Keliipaakaua served four tours in enlisted ranks, two in Afghanistan and two in Iraq, and sums up the grunt mentality with signature Marine candor. When asked if his tours reflected "what Marines do," he provided contrasting assessments of his deployments. Stationed in Haditha in the immediate aftermath of the 2005 massacre, his mission was to "redeem the Marines [sic] reputation and destroy the enemy as soon as possible." By the time he departed, "there was still plenty of enemy left," but his unit had maintained an aggressive fight. In his assessment, this is "exactly what Marines do." He compares that tour to the follow-on deployment two years later in Karma, Iraq. His mission there was to "create a solid relationship with the village elder, and encourage as well as support the [Iraqi Civilian Watch]." In his colorful assessment, "this was the only deployment that wasn't exactly 'what Marines do.' I was a squadleader at the time and it was difficult to teach the new Marines restraint instead of bayonetting everyone we could to death. . . . Not an ideal deployment for Marines, but legitimate relative to Iraq's situation at the time." His final tour landed him in Sangin, Afghanistan, where "the mission from my perspective as squadleader was to fight past every inch of land and kill as many of them as we could." With a bow to the Marines' veneration of suffering in all-out combat, Keliipaakaua sums up: "Sangin came to be the deadliest campaign for Marines in the Afghan war suffering 25 dead and approximately 200 wounded." For him, "this deployment was the definition of 'What Marines do.'"[63] Michael Blalock, who enlisted in 2004 and itched to get out of Iraq and into Afghanistan because that was "where warriors really test their skills," put it more bluntly: "Peacekeeping drives Marines crazy because Marines are built to fight."[64]

Content analysis of the *Gazette* demonstrates that the enlisted are not alone in this attitude. Despite Al Qa'im being the "model" for future counterinsurgency, the attention it is paid in the *Gazette* pales in comparison to enthusiastic recounts of the battles of Fallujah. From 2004 through the end of 2016, the *Gazette* boasted no fewer than 460 articles that referenced one of the two battles in some form and 25 that featured Fallujah in the title. By contrast, Al Qa'im—where Marines launched the formula that moved them toward real counterinsurgency success—is referenced in just 60 articles from the time it occurred in 2005 through late 2016 and is showcased in the title of only one.

In fairness to Marines' fighting bias, their institution has never signaled that any other sort of duty compares. Tyler Boudreau reminds readers who may be critical of his bloody memoir, *Packing Inferno*, that the entirety of the Marine rank and career advancement system privileges raw combat experience:

> To get command—the really big commands—to reach the stars in a profession of arms, to develop his credibility and his mystique, an officer needs, above all, corporate knowledge. He's got to have combat experience. That's the goose that lays the golden eggs. And with respect to combat, I think it's fair to say that there is an unspoken hierarchy of experiences. The bloodiest battle is up at the top of the pyramid and it just goes downhill from there. So being *in* a fight is always better than being *near* one, and being near a fight is most certainly preferable to handing out soccer balls and attending town-council meetings.[65]

Marine warfighters will engage in the population-centric tasks they are given because they expect to "do windows." Flexibility and an acceptance of an "all roles" lane in the duty lineup means that Marines will follow non-traditional orders. It does not, however, change Marine default preferences.

Despite the population-centric bent of today's counterinsurgencies, there are a number of reasons why America's Devil Dogs should find small-wars fights attractive. It can certainly be plenty bloody enough. Warriors are offered a chance to test their skills across more than enough deadly (and even horrific) encounters in irregular combat. It also plays to Marine grunt-based strengths. The Marine valuing of the human rather than technical elements of war and the showcasing of the individual Marine as weapon are nowhere better staged than in the small-unit, low-tech, marksmanship-intensive combat outposts of counterinsurgency warfare. In addition, the austere environment, away from large bases and masses of supporting flanks, requires individual Marines to exercise the full range of their "adapt, improvise, and overcome" training in a semiautonomous environment.[66]

The "intangibles" on which Marines pride themselves—challenge, leadership, and self-reliance—hold more promise for application in a dispersed and decentralized irregular war than a conventional one. And whether Marines are ready to admit it or not, the CAP program demonstrates that a healthy mix of neighborly civic action in the stew of active combat can yield strong emotional benefits for the Marines who participate. This combination, especially in fights of dubious national necessity, provides a balm to some of the disillusionment that might otherwise beset forces sent to counterinsurgency scenes.

In addition, Marines can no longer argue, as did their Caribbean predecessors, that irregular fights mean an inevitable stain on their service. To date, Marine conduct in the Iraq War (with the exception of the Haditha incident discussed in the previous chapter) remains largely celebrated by the American domestic public. It is a mark of improved discipline and restraint since the Vietnam days, as well as the Corps's intentional and increasingly sophisticated handling of the media, that an open invitation for members of the press to observe and record unit activities in theater has had the effect of enhancing the status and reputation of the Marine Corps with Americans at home. A decade of immersion in counterinsurgency conflict did nothing but improve the Corps's image in the public eye—a significant turn of the tide from previous counterinsurgency eras.[67]

This combination of potential "good fits" of small-wars practice may find traction with some aspects of Marine Corps culture but are bested by values and an identity that leathernecks hold yet more dear. Marines instinctively resist engagements in which their ability to bring violence to bear cannot be the variable that is decisive in victory. The Corps will continue to keep population-centric counterinsurgency on its roster as an ancillary task but is eager to return to what is perceived as its traditional competencies, primary among them, amphibious operations. Defending this stance, Maj. Gen. Larry Nicholson notes the tension created by dividing time between counterinsurgency training and preparations for conventional war. His summary thought: "I don't know if they are completely incompatible, but if you have a Marine Corps that is not talking about amphibious operations, . . . then you are in great peril."[68] Convinced that Marines will retain key lessons from their last two theaters and will keep a spot in the Marine curriculum for future counterinsurgency operations, Gen. Jim Mattis concurs with Nicholson on the imperative of getting back to the sea: "[Marines] must be able to land from ships. While such landings seem commonplace to some folks, they are the most complex ops . . . in which I've ever engaged, to include ground combat in COIN or conventional/mech[anized] fights. So amphibious ops do not well reward dabblers; one must master them or failure, even in peacetime, can be catastrophic." He argues further that the Marine Corps is a general-purpose force that must demonstrate ready agility to engage wily foes across the full spectrum of military operations and points to Colin Gray's logic that strategic adversaries tracking the training and preparation of US forces do so in order to strike where warfighting practices are weak. Given this perspective, Marines must restore focus on conventional preparations in order to deliver for their nation the fewest big regrets.[69]

Yet where regrets are concerned, the history of US involvement in counterinsurgencies indicates a track record of naiveté with regard to what military and treasury resources can fix and what they cannot, nearly ensuring that interventions will be saddled with varying weights of regretful baggage. It is hubris born out of this American perceptual lens more than the distinctive attributes of service culture that most significantly determines whether Marines can be successful in a counterinsurgency theater. If American administrations continue to employ a perceptual lens that underrates the critical role played by the indigenous host government and overrates the

US ability to shape it, then they will continue to place Marines in counterinsurgency environments in which they may make significant headway against belligerents, may build an impressive array of infrastructure, and may succeed in providing a security perimeter around elections but cannot transfer whatever legitimacy they earn to a failing host government and therefore cannot, despite the host of lessons learned, achieve a true strategic victory.

As a military force, Marines are well trained to do what foreign forces *can do* in a host theater: provide a measure of security space for the host government to effectively engage its own population. The lessons leathernecks have adopted and cultivated over time have created a Marine Corps that is prepared to implement counterinsurgency best practices toward that end. The primary insight derived for students of counterinsurgency, however, is that it is not doctrinal formulas or effective tactical execution of counterinsurgency tasks that are in need of primary attention. Much of this has arguably been mastered. The lessons lost and perennial blind spots that continue to plague American counterinsurgency efforts abroad are those born out of fundamentally misplaced notions regarding what one nation can do on behalf of another.

## NOTES

1. Lt. Col. Patrick Carroll (Ret.) and CWO5 Terry Walker (Ret.), "A Legacy Pete Ellis Would Embrace," *Marine Corps Gazette* (February 2015); Lt. Col. David Brown (Ret.), "Marine Corps Advisors: Past and Present," *Marine Corps Gazette* (August 2011).
2. Capt. Dilan Swift, "A Picture Is Worth a Thousand Rounds," *Marine Corps Gazette* (February 2016).
3. West, *Strongest Tribe*, 83.
4. Ibid., 78, 185.
5. Ardolino, *Fallujah Awakens*, 84–85, 204; Staff Brig. Gen. Haqi Isma'eel Ali Hameed, oral history in Montgomery & McWilliams, *Al-Anbar Awakening*, 2:231.
6. Russell, *Innovation, Transformation, and War*; Lt. Col. Timothy Oliver, "A Blueprint for Success," *Marine Corps Gazette* (July 2010): 78–83.
7. Capt. Duane A. Durant, "(Re)Shaping the Battlespace," *Marine Corps Gazette* (December 2007): 41–43; Capt. Jeffrey S. Dinsmore, "Intelligence Support to Counterinsurgency Operations," *Marine Corps Gazette* (July 2007): 13–16; Maj. Eugene P. Wittkopf, "Catching More IED Emplacers," *Marine Corps Gazette* (May 2007): 58–60; Capt. Matthew T. Kralovec, "Intelligence Information Management," *Marine Corps Gazette* (July 2009): 35–42.
8. Across enlisted Marines interviewed for this project, this term was regarded as neutral or pejorative but represented a general dismissiveness toward the mixed Arab population of Iraq.

9. Capt. David J. Danelo, "The Linguistic Tipping Point," *Marine Corps Gazette* (October 2005): 30. On continuing deficits to understand culture, see Maj. Alfred B. Connable, "The Expeditionary FAO," *Marine Corps Gazette* (March 2005): 51–53; Lt. Col. George W. Smith Jr., "Genesis of an Ulcer," *Marine Corps Gazette* (April 2005): 29–34; and Lt. Col. James L. Higgins, Maj. Michelle L.Trusso, and Maj. Alfred B. Connable, "Marine Corps Intelligence," *Marine Corps Gazette* (December 2005): 23–24.

10. Maj. Gen. Richard Zilmer, interview in McWilliams and Wheeler, *Al-Anbar Awakening*, 1:147–49.

11. Smith and MacFarland, "Anbar Awakens," 47; Moyar, *Question of Command*, 239; Russell, *Innovation, Transformation, and War*, 116; Capt. Scott Cuomo, "The 'Wild, Wild West,'" *Marine Corps Gazette* (October 2009): 25.

12. Capt. Michael Ulmer, "Stability Operations," *Marine Corps Gazette* (June 2015); CWO4 Timothy S. McWilliams, USMCR (Ret.), "Leading Across Cultures," *Marine Corps Gazette* (April 2015).

13. United States Marine Corps (hereafter USMC), *Small Wars Manual*, ch. 2, "Organization," section II, "The Staff in Small Wars," 17.

14. Deitchman, *Best-Laid Schemes*.

15. Cuomo, "Wild, Wild West," 30.

16. Capt. Brian Kerg, "Drones, Hackers, Anthropologists, Marines," *Marine Corps Gazette* (November 2016).

17. Lt. Col. Jordan D. Walzer, Capt. Jordan Jones, and Capt. Matthew Eamhardt, "Marine Reconnaissance," *Marine Corps Gazette* (October 2012).

18. Paula Holmes-Eber and Maj. Brian Kane, "Incorporating Culture into the MCPP," *Marine Corps Gazette* (October 2009).

19. "Religious Cultural Engagement," *Marine Corps Gazette* (January 2013).

20. Capt. Luis R. Perez, "Patrol Base Outcast," *Marine Corps Gazette* (April 2011).

21. Maj. Giuseppe A. Stavale, "Living with Ghosts: Japan's Human Terrain and the U.S.-Japan Alliance," *Marine Corps Gazette* (November 2014).

22. Isaac D. Pacheco, "The 7th Warfighting Skill: How Culture Is Changing the Face of Today's Battlefield," *Leatherneck* (October 2009), reprinted in the *Marine Corps Gazette* (April 2010).

23. Maj. Bryan Eovito and Capt. Brandon A. Salter, "Leading Diversity: Mapping Our Human Terrain," *Marine Corps Gazette* (November 2013).

24. USMC, *Marine Corps Vision and Strategy 2025*, 6.

25. Capt. Karl D. Klicker, "Social Sciences: A Tool for COIN," *Marine Corps Gazette* (April 2012): 59.

26. Maj. Andrés H. Cáceres-Solari, "Engagement for Southeast Asia," *Marine Corps Gazette* (December 2013).

27. Capt. Amelia J. Griffith, "Operational Culture: Got SCRAT? Stressing the Importance of Operational Culture," *Marine Corps Gazette* (August 2012).

28. Fosher, foreword in *Cross-Cultural Competence*; Kerry Fosher, director of research, CAOCL, Marine Corps University, interview with the author, January 13, 2017 (Note: The views provided by Kerry Fosher are her own and do

not necessarily reflect the position of the US Marine Corps.); Ben Connable, interview with the author, January 12, 2017.

29. 1st Lt. Michael E. Orzetti, "Ownership of Lessons Learned," *Marine Corps Gazette* (August 2013): 73–74. See also Carroll and Walker, "Legacy Pete Ellis Would Embrace," DE8; Maj. Arlon Smith, Maj. Devin Myler, and Capt. Adam McLaurin, "Institutionalizing Security Force Assistance in the USMC," *Marine Corps Gazette* (September 2015): 84–85; Maj. Trevor Howell, "Traditional Amphibious Warfare," *Marine Corps Gazette* (September 2014): 20; and Maj. Francisco X. Zavala, "Victory in Counterinsurgency," *Marine Corps Gazette* (November 2016).

30. 1st Lt. Jameson Clem, 1st Lt. Emily Elledge, 1st Lt. Michael Wellock, and 1st Lt. Matthew Williams, "What Happens after 'the War'?," *Marine Corps Gazette* (August 2015): 81.

31. Col. Norman Cooling, Col. Dale Alford, Col. Chip Bierman, and Lt. Col. James Donnellan, "Retooling for Afghanistan," *Marine Corps Gazette* (October 2009).

32. Moyar, *Question of Command*, 241; Russell, *Innovation, Transformation, and War*, 125–33; West, *Strongest Tribe*, 208–9; Hoffman, *Learning while under Fire*, 204; Maj. Daniel Zappa, interview in McWilliams and Wheeler, *Al-Anbar Awakening*, 1:204–9; Lt. Col. William M. Jurney, interview, ibid., 198–99.

33. Chapman, "State of the Corps," 29–30.

34. Avant, "Institutional Sources," 420.

35. For examples of CAP reports of these sorts of indicators, see Warren V. Smith, oral history in Hemingway, *Our War Was Different*, 140; Klyman, "Combined Action Program."

36. Allnutt, *Marine Combined Action Capabilities*, 11–12. See *Fact Sheet on the Combined Action Force*, enclosures 8–12.

37. Capt. R. E. Williamson, "A Briefing for Combined Action," *Marine Corps Gazette* (March 1968): 43.

38. Connable, *Embracing the Fog of War*.

39. See Klicker, "Social Sciences," and Connable, *Embracing the Fog of War*.

40. Rhodes, "America's Crusade."

41. Ricks, *Fiasco*.

42. MacDonald, *Overreach*.

43. Reynolds, *Basrah, Baghdad, and Beyond*, 41–42; Ricks, *Generals*, 589–91.

44. Moyar, *Question of Command*, 220–21; Brig. Gen. John F. Kelly, "Tikrit, South to Babylon," *Marine Corps Gazette* (February 2004):18; Reynolds, *Basrah, Baghdad, and Beyond*, 145.

45. Attributed to writer, artist, and libertarian Elbert Hubbard. For a quick reference, see https://en.wikiquote.org/wiki/Elbert_Hubbard.

46. Kilcullen, *Accidental Guerrilla*, 122, 126.

47. West, *Strongest Tribe*, 41.

48. Gray, "Strategic Sense," 6.

49. Cuomo, "Wild, Wild West," 30. West, *Strongest Tribe*, 87, notes this mentality in action in Iraq.

50. Staff Maj. Gen. Khadim Muhammad Faris al-Fahadawi al-Dulaymi, oral history in Montgomery and McWilliams, *Al-Anbar Awakening*, 2:272.
51. Lt. Col. Kurt Wheeler, "Good News in Al Anbar?," *Marine Corps Gazette* (April 2007): 37.
52. Russell, *Innovation, Transformation, and War*, 116.
53. Smith and MacFarland, "Anbar Awakens"; Maj. Gen. John R. Allen, interview in McWilliams and Wheeler, *Al-Anbar Awakening*, 1:230; Maj. Gen. Walter E. Gaskin Sr., interview, ibid., 210; Moyar, *Question of Command*, 239–40; Russell, *Innovation, Transformation, and War*, 130.
54. Russell, *Innovation, Transformation, and War*, 133.
55. Ardolino, *Fallujah Awakens*, 217
56. Shultz, *Marines Take Anbar*, 183.
57. Lt. Col. William M. Jurney, interview in McWilliams and Wheeler, *Al-Anbar Awakening*, 1:194–95.
58. Oral history file 2304-6, USMC Vietnam War Oral History Collection, Marine Corps Archives and Special Collections, Gray Research Center, Quantico, VA, transcription by Victoria Cattanach, February 21, 2012.
59. Mike Patton, correspondence with the author, January 17, 2012. See also John Balanco, oral history in Hemingway, *Our War Was Different*, 69.
60. USMC, *Small-Unit Leaders' Guide to Counterinsurgency*, 31.
61. Maj. William C. Holmberg, "Civic Action," *Marine Corps Gazette* (June 1966): 23–28.
62. Maj. Daniel R. Zappa, interview in McWilliams and Wheeler, *Al-Anbar Awakening*, 1:206.
63. Adam Keliipaakaua, correspondence with the author, July 16, 2014.
64. Michael Blalock, correspondence with the author, May 14, 2014.
65. Boudreau, *Packing Inferno*, 64–65.
66. For a particularly inventive example of Marine improvisation tactics, see Brig. Gen. John F. Kelly, "Part III: Tikrit, South to Babylon," *Marine Corps Gazette* (April 2004): 44.
67. Data retrieved November 23, 2012, at http://www.gallup.com/poll/148127/americans-army-marines-important-defense.aspx.
68. Maj. Gen. Larry Nicholson, conversation with the author, January 11, 2012.
69. Gen. Jim Mattis, correspondence with the author, October 23, 2013, and March 12, 2015.

# BIBLIOGRAPHY

Adamsky, Dima. *The Culture of Military Innovation.* Stanford, CA: Stanford University Press, 2010.

Art, Robert J., and Robert Jervis, eds. *International Politics: Enduring Concepts and Contemporary Issues.* 8th ed. New York: Pearson, 2007.

Allen, Maj. Gen. John R. Interview in McWilliams and Wheeler, *Al-Anbar Awakening,* Vol. 1.

Allnutt, Bruce C. *Marine Combined Action Capabilities: The Vietnam Experience.* Interim Technical Report commissioned by the Office of Naval Research Group Psychology Programs, December 1969.

Althen, Gary. *American Ways: A Guide for Foreigners in the United States.* Yarmouth, ME: Intercultural Press, 1988.

Anderson, Ben. *No Worse Enemy.* Oxford, UK: Oneworld Publications, 2012.

Ardolino, Bill. *Fallujah Awakens: Marines, Sheikhs, and the Battle against Al Qaeda.* Annapolis, MD: Naval Institute Press, 2013.

Avant, Deborah D. "The Institutional Sources of Military Doctrine: Hegemons in Peripheral Wars." *International Studies Quarterly* 37, no. 4 (December 1993).

Avruch, Kevin. *Culture and Conflict Resolution.* Washington, DC: United States Institute of Peace Press, 2006.

Aylwin-Foster, Brig. Nigel R. F. "Changing the Army for Counterinsurgency Operations." *Military Review* (November/December 2005).

Barnett, Roger W. *Navy Strategic Culture: Why the Navy Thinks Differently.* Annapolis, MD: Naval Institute Press, 2009.

Beckett, Ian F. W., ed. *The Roots of Counterinsurgency.* New York: Blandford, 1988.

Berger, Thomas. *Cultures of Antimilitarism: National Security in Germany and Japan.* Baltimore: Johns Hopkins University Press, 1998.

———. "Norms, Identity, and National Security in Germany and Japan." In Katzenstein, *Culture of National Security.*

Bernard, H. Russell. *Research Methods in Anthropology: Qualitative and Quantitative Approaches.* 3rd ed. Walnut Creek, CA: AltaMira, 2002.

Bickel, Keith B. *Mars Learning: The Marine Corps' Development of Small Wars Doctrine, 1915–1940.* Boulder, CO: Westview, 2001.

Blackman, R. R., Jr. Foreword to United States Marine Corps, *Marine Corps Values and Leadership.*

Bloomfield, Alan. "Time to Move On: Reconceptualizing the Strategic Culture Debate." *Contemporary Security Policy* 33, no. 3 (October 2012). doi: 10.1080/13523260.2012.727679.

Boot, Max. *The Savage Wars of Peace: Small Wars and the Rise of American Power.* New York: Basic Books, 2002.

Booth, Ken. "The Concept of Strategic Culture Affirmed." In Jacobsen, *Strategic Power.*

Boudreau, Tyler E. *Packing Inferno: The Unmaking of a Marine.* Port Townsend, WA: Feral House, 2008.

Bradley, James. *Flags of Our Fathers.* New York: Bantam Books, 2000.

Brogan, D. W. *The American Character.* New York: Alfred A. Knopf, Borzoi Books, 1944.

Brooks, David C. "U.S. Marines and Miskito Indians: The Rio Coco Patrol of 1928." In Evans, *U.S. Marines and Irregular Warfare.*

Builder, Carl H. *The Masks of War: American Military Styles in Strategy and Analysis.* Baltimore: Johns Hopkins University Press, 1989.

Burk, James. "Military Culture." *Encyclopedia of Violence, Peace, and Conflict.* Vol. 2. San Diego, CA: Academic Press, 1999.

Cable, Larry E. *Conflict of Myths: The Development of American Counterinsurgency Doctrine and the Vietnam War.* New York: New York University Press, 1986.

Calder, Bruce J. "Caudillos and *Gavilleros* versus the United States Marines: Guerrilla Insurgency during the Dominican Intervention, 1916–1924." In Evans, *U.S. Marines and Irregular Warfare.*

———. *The Impact of Intervention: The Dominican Republic during the U.S. Occupation of 1916–1924.* Princeton, NJ: Markus Wiener, 2006.

Caldwell, William B., and Steven M. Leonard. "Field Manual 3-07, Stability Operations: Upshifting the Engine of Change." *Military Review* (July/August 2008).

Campbell, Donovan. *Joker One: A Marine Platoon's Story of Courage, Leadership, and Brotherhood.* New York: Random House, 2010.

Cameron, Craig M. *American Samurai: Myth, Imagination, and the Conduct of Battle in the First Marine Division, 1941–1951.* Cambridge: Cambridge University Press, 1994.

Cassidy, Robert M. "Back to the Street without Joy: Counterinsurgency Lessons from Vietnam and Other Small Wars." In Evans, *U.S. Marines and Irregular Warfare.*

———. *Counterinsurgency and the Global War on Terror: Military Culture and Irregular War.* Stanford, CA: Stanford University Press, 2008.

———. *Peacekeeping in the Abyss: British and American Peacekeeping Doctrine and Practice after the Cold War.* Westport, CT: Praeger, 2004.

Cohen, Eliot. "Constraints on America's Conduct of Small Wars." *International Security* 9, no. 2 (Autumn 1984).

Collins, John M. *America's Small Wars: Lessons for the Future.* McLean, VA: Brassey's, 1991.

Connable, Ben. "Culture Warriors: Marine Corps Organizational Culture and Adaption to Cultural Terrain." *Small Wars Journal*. http://smallwarsjournal.com/blog/journal/docs-temp/4-connable.pdf.

———. *Embracing the Fog of War: Assessment and Metrics in Counterinsurgency*. Santa Monica, CA: Rand, 2012.

———. Interview in McWilliams and Wheeler, *Al-Anbar Awakening*, Vol. 1.

Conway, Gen. James T. Interview in McWilliams and Wheeler, *Al-Anbar Awakening*, Vol. 1.

Cooling, Col. Norman L., and Lt. Col. Roger B. Turner. "Understanding the Few Good Men: An Analysis of Marine Corps Service Culture." Supplied to the Ed Darack website accessed at http://www.darack.com/sawtalosar/USMC-SERVICE-CULTURE.pdf.

Corson, William R. *The Betrayal*. New York: W. W. Norton, 1968.

Cunliffe, Marcus. "Formative Events from Columbus to World War I." In *American Character and Foreign Policy*, edited by Michael P. Hamilton. Grand Rapids, MI: William B. Eerdmans, 1986.

Dalgaard-Nielsen, Anja. "The Test of Strategic Culture: Germany, Pacifism and Preemptive Strikes." *Security Dialogue* 36 (2005).

Datesman, Maryanne Kearney, Joann Crandall, and Edward N. Kearny. *American Ways: An Introduction to American Culture*. 4th ed. White Plains, NY: Pearson Education, 2014.

Deitchman, Seymour J. *The Best-Laid Schemes: A Tale of Social Research and Bureaucracy*. Quantico, VA: Marine Corps University Press, 2014. First published 1976 by MIT Press.

Du Bois, Cora. "The Dominant Value Profile of American Culture." *American Anthropologist* 57 (December 1955).

Dye, Julia. *Backbone: History, Traditions, and Leadership Lessons of Marine Corps NCOs*. Oxford, UK: Osprey, 2011.

Echevarria, Antulio J., II. *Toward an American Way of War*. Strategic Studies Institute monograph (March 2004). https://ssi.armywarcollege.edu/pubs/display.cfm?pubID=374.

Eisenstadt, Michael, and Kenneth M. Pollack. "Armies of Snow and Armies of Sand: The Impact of Soviet Military Doctrine on Arab Militaries." *Middle East Journal 55*, no. 4 (Autumn 2001).

Eliason, William T. "An Interview with James F. Amos." *Joint Force Quarterly* 64, no. 1 (2012).

Eriksen, Thomas Hylland. *Small Places, Large Issues: An Introduction to Social and Cultural Anthropology*. 2nd ed. Sterling, VA: Pluto Press, 2001.

Estes, Lt. Col. Kenneth W. *Handbook for Marine NCOs*. 4th ed. Annapolis, MD: Naval Institute Press, 1996.

———. *U.S. Marines in Iraq, 2004–2005: Into the Fray*. Washington, DC: United States Marine Corps History Division, 2011.

Evans, Col. Stephen S., ed. *U.S. Marines and Irregular Warfare, 1898–2007: Anthology and Selected Bibliography*. Quantico, VA: Marine Corps University Press, 2008.

Farrell, Theo. "America's Misguided Mission." Review of *Democracy by Force: US Military Intervention in the Post-Cold War World*, by Karin von Hippel. *International Affairs* 76, no. 3 (2000).

———. "Constructivist Security Studies: Portrait of a Research Program." *International Studies Review* 4, no. 1 (2002).

———. "Culture and Military Power." *Review of International Studies* 24, no. 3 (July 1998).

———. *The Norms of War: Cultural Beliefs and Modern Conflict*. London: Lynne Rienner, 2005.

———. "Strategic Culture and American Empire." *SAIS Review* 25, no. 2 (Summer/Fall 2005).

Fehrenbach, T. R. *U.S. Marines in Action: Two Hundred Years of Guts and Glory*. New York: E-reads, 2003. First published 1962 by Monarch Books.

Feng, Huiyun. "A Dragon on Defense: Explaining China's Strategic Culture." In Johnson, Kartchner, and Larsen, *Strategic Culture and Weapons of Mass Destruction*.

Fick, Nathanial. *One Bullet Away: The Making of a Marine Officer*. New York: Houghton Mifflin, 2005.

Fischer, Claude S. *Made in America: A Social History of American Culture and Character*. Chicago: University of Chicago Press, 2010.

Fisher, Glen. *Mindsets: The Role of Culture and Perception in International Relations*. 2nd ed. Yarmouth, ME: Intercultural Press, 1997.

Flynn, G. J. Foreword to United States Marine Corps, *Marine Corps Operating Concepts, Assuring Littoral Access . . . Winning Small Wars*. 3rd ed. (June 2010). http://www.hqmc.marines.mil/Portals/142/Docs/MOC%20July%2013%20update%202010_Final%5B1%5D.pdf.

Fosher, Kerry. Foreword in *Cross-Cultural Competence for a 21st Century Military*, edited by Allison Greene and Robert Sands. Lanham, MD: Lexington Books, 2014.

Freedman, David H. *Corps Business*. New York: Harper Business, 2000.

Fuller, Stephen M., and Graham A. Cosmas. *Marines in the Dominican Republic 1916–1924*. Washington, DC: History and Museums Division Headquarters, US Marine Corps, 1974.

Gaskin, Maj. Gen. Walter E., Jr. Interview in McWilliams and Wheeler, *Al-Anbar Awakening*, Vol. 1.

Geertz, Clifford. *The Interpretation of Cultures*. New York: Basic Books, 1973.

Gentry, John A. "Norms as Weapons of War." *Defense & Security Analysis* 26, no. 1 (March 2010).

Giles, Greg. "Continuity and Change in Israel's Strategic Culture." In Johnson, Kartchner, and Larsen, *Strategic Culture and Weapons of Mass Destruction*.

Glaser, Barney G., and Anselm L. Strauss. *The Discovery of Grounded Theory: Strategies for Qualitative Research*. Chicago: Aldine Publishing, 1967.

Glenn, John. "Realism versus Strategic Culture: Competition and Collaboration?" *International Studies Review* 11 (2009).

Glenn, John, Darryl Howlett, and Stuart Poore, eds. *Neorealism versus Strategic Culture*. Burlington, VT: Ashgate Publishing, 2004.

Gobat, Michel. *Confronting the American Dream: Nicaragua under U.S. Imperial Rule*. Durham, NC: Duke University Press, 2005.

Goodson, Barry L. *CAP Mot: The Story of a Marine Special Forces Unit in Vietnam, 1968–1969*. Denton: University of North Texas Press, 1997.

Gray, Colin S. "British and American Strategic Cultures." Paper prepared for the symposium "Democracies in Partnership: 400 Years of Transatlantic Engagement," Williamsburg, VA, April 18–19, 2007.

———. "Irregular Enemies and the Essence of Strategy: Can the American Way of War Adapt?" Strategic Studies Institute monograph (March 2006). https://ssi .armywarcollege.edu/pubs/display.cfm?pubID=650.

———. *Modern Strategy*. Oxford: Oxford University Press, 1999.

———. "National Style in Strategy: The American Example." *International Security* 6, no. 2 (Fall 1981).

———. "Out of the Wilderness: Prime Time for Strategic Culture." In Johnson, Kartchner, and Larsen, *Strategic Culture and Weapons of Mass Destruction*.

———. *Perspectives on Strategy*. Oxford: Oxford University Press, 2013.

———. "Strategic Sense: Missing from Action." *Infinity Journal* 5, no. 3 (Fall 2016).

Greathouse, Craig B. "Examining the Role and Methodology of Strategic Culture." *Risk, Hazards & Crisis in Public Policy* 1, no. 1 (2010). doi: 10.2202/ 1944-4079.1020.

Groen, Lt. Col. Michael S., and Contributors. *With the 1st Marine Division in Iraq, 2003*. Occasional Paper. Quantico, VA: Marine Corps University (2006).

Grondona, Mariano. "A Cultural Typology of Economic Development." In *Culture Matters: How Values Shape Human Progress*, edited by Lawrence E. Harrison and Samuel P. Huntington. New York: Basic Books, 2000.

Haglund, David. "What Good Is Strategic Culture?" In Johnson, Kartchner, and Larsen, *Strategic Culture and Weapons of Mass Destruction*.

Hall, Edward T. *Beyond Culture*. New York: Anchor Books, 1989.

———. *The Silent Language*. New York: Premier Books, 1963.

Hall, Edward T., and Mildred Reed Hall. *Understanding Cultural Differences: Germans, French, and Americans*. Yarmouth, ME: Intercultural Press, 1990.

Hanson, Victor Davis. *Carnage and Culture: Landmark Battles in the Rise of Western Power*. New York: Anchor Books, 2001.

Haycock, Ronald, ed. *Regular Armies and Insurgency*. London: Croom Helm, 1979.

Heald, Morell. "Foreign Relations, American Style." In *American Character and Culture in a Changing World: Some Twentieth Century Perspectives*, edited by John A. Hague. Westport, CT: Greenwood, 1979.

Heinlein, Robert A. *Starship Troopers*. New York: Ace Books, 1987.

Hemingway, Al. *Our War Was Different: Marine Combined Action Platoons in Vietnam*. Annapolis, MD: Naval Institute Press, 1994.

Heuser, Beatrice. *The Evolution of Strategy: Thinking War from Antiquity to the Present*. Cambridge: Cambridge University Press, 2010.

———. *NATO, Britain, France and the FRG: Nuclear Strategies and Forces for Europe, 1949–2000.* London: Macmillan, 1997.

———. *Nuclear Mentalities? Strategies and Beliefs in Britain, France and the FRG.* London: Macmillan, 1998.

Hillen, John. "Must U.S. Military Culture Reform?," *Orbis* 43, no. 1 (Winter 1999).

Hoffman, Lt. Col. (Ret.) Frank G. "Learning while under Fire: Military Change in Wartime." Unpublished dissertation, King's College London, War Studies Department, March 2015.

———. "The Marine Mask of War." *Foreign Policy Research Institute E-Notes,* November 10, 2011.

Hoffman, Stanley. *Gulliver's Troubles or the Setting of American Foreign Policy.* New York: McGraw Hill, 1968.

Holmes-Eber, Paula. *Culture in Conflict.* Stanford, CA: Stanford University Press, 2014.

Hudson, Valerie. "Cultural Expectations of One's Own and Other Nations' Foreign Policy Action Templates." *Political Psychology* 20, no. 4 (December 1999).

Huntington, Samuel. *The Soldier and the State.* Cambridge, MA: Belknap Press of Harvard University Press, 1957.

"An Interview with James T. Conway." *Joint Force Quarterly* 59, no. 4 (2010).

Jacobsen, Carl G., ed. *Strategic Power: USA/USSR.* London: Macmillan, 1990.

Johnson, Dominic D. P., and Dominic Tierney. *Failing to Win: Perceptions of Victory and Defeat in International Politics.* Cambridge, MA: Harvard University Press, 2006.

Johnson, Jeannie L. "Conclusion: Toward a Standard Methodological Approach." In Johnson, Kartchner, and Larsen, *Strategic Culture and Weapons of Mass Destruction.*

Johnson, Jeannie L., and Matthew T. Berrett. "Cultural Topography: A New Research Tool for Intelligence." *Studies in Intelligence* 55, no. 2 (June 2011).

Johnson, Jeannie L., Kerry M. Kartchner, and Jeffrey A. Larsen, eds. *Strategic Culture and Weapons of Mass Destruction: Culturally Based Insights into Comparative National Security Policymaking.* New York: Palgrave Macmillan, 2009.

Johnson, Wray R. "Airpower and Restraint in Small Wars: Marine Corps Aviation in the Second Nicaraguan Campaign, 1927–33." In Evans, *U.S. Marines and Irregular Warfare.*

Johnston, Alastair Iain. *Cultural Realism: Strategic Culture and Grand Strategy in Chinese History.* Princeton, NJ: Princeton University Press, 1995.

———. "Thinking about Strategic Culture." *International Security* 19, no. 4 (Spring 1995).

Johnston, Andrew M. "Does America Have a Strategic Culture?" *Journal of Conflict Studies* 18, no. 2 (Fall 1998). https://journals.lib.unb.ca/index.php/JCS/article/view/11700/12457.

Jones, Rodney W. "India's Strategic Culture and the Origins of Omniscient Paternalism." In Johnson, Kartchner, and Larsen, *Strategic Culture and Weapons of Mass Destruction.*

Joyner, James. "Why We Should Be Glad the Haditha Massacre Marine Got No Jail Time." *Atlantic*, January 25, 2012.

Jurney, Lt. Col. William M. Interview in McWilliams and Wheeler, *Al-Anbar Awakening*, Vol. 1.

Kahl, Colin H. "Walk before Running." *Foreign Affairs* 87, no. 4 (July/August 2008).

Katzenstein, Peter J., ed. *The Culture of National Security: Norms and Identity in World Politics*. New York: Columbia University Press, 1996.

Keesing, Roger M., and Andrew J. Strathern. *Cultural Anthropology: A Contemporary Perspective*. 3rd ed. Fort Worth, TX: Harcourt Brace, 1998.

Kelly, Lt. Gen. John F. Foreword to Montgomery and McWilliams, *Al-Anbar Awakening*, Vol. 2.

Kelly, Maj. Gen. John F. Interview in McWilliams and Wheeler, *Al-Anbar Awakening*, Vol. 1.

Kier, Elizabeth. "Culture and Military Doctrine: France between the Wars." *International Security* 19, no. 4 (Spring 1995).

Kilcullen, David. *The Accidental Guerrilla: Fighting Small Wars in the Midst of a Big One*. New York: Oxford University Press, 2009.

Kincade, William. "American National Style and Strategic Culture." In Jacobsen, *Strategic Power*.

Klein, Yitzhak. "Theory of Strategic Culture." *Comparative Strategy* 10, no. 1 (1991).

Klyman, Robert A. "The Combined Action Program: An Alternative Not Taken." Honors thesis, Department of History, University of Michigan, 1986. http://www.capmarine.com/cap/thesis-klyman.htm.

Kowert, Paul, and Jeffrey Legro. "Norms, Identity and Their Limits." In Katzenstein, *Culture of National Security*.

Krulak, Victor H. *First to Fight: An Inside View of the U.S. Marine Corps*. Annapolis, MD: Naval Institute Press, 1999.

Kurth, James. "Iraq: Losing the American Way." *American Conservative*, March 15, 2004. http://www.theamericanconservative.com/articles/iraq-losing-the-american-way/.

Lam, Kent, Roger Buehler, Cathy McFarland, Michael Ross, and Irene Cheung. "Cultural Differences in Affective Forecasting: The Role of Focalism." *Personality and Social Psychology Bulletin* 31, no. 9 (2005).

Langley, Lester D. *The Banana Wars: United States Intervention in the Caribbean, 1898–1934*. Wilmington, DE: Scholarly Resources, 1985.

Lee, Oliver M. "The Geopolitics of America's Strategic Culture." *Comparative Strategy* 27, no. 3 (2008).

Legro, Jeffrey W. *Cooperation under Fire: Anglo-German Restraint during World War II*. New York: Cornell University Press, 1995.

———. "Whence American Internationalism." *International Organization* 54, no. 2 (2000).

———. "Which Norms Matter? Revisiting the 'Failure' of Internationalism." *International Organization* 51, no. 1 (Winter 1997).

Linn, Brian M., and Russell F. Weigley. "The American Way of War Revisited." *Journal of Military History* 66, no. 2 (April 2002).

Long, Jerry Mark. "Does Al Qaeda Have a Strategic Culture?" In Johnson, Kartchner, and Larsen, *Strategic Culture and Weapons of Mass Destruction*.

Longhurst, Kerry. "Why Aren't the Germans Debating the Draft? Path Dependency and the Persistence of Conscription." *German Politics* 12, no. 2 (August 2003).

Lotz, Hellmut. "Myth and NAFTA: The Use of Core Values in U.S. Politics." In *Culture and Foreign Policy*, edited by Valerie Hudson. Boulder, CO: Lynne Rienner, 1997.

Lynn, John A. *Battle: A History of Combat and Culture from Ancient Greece to Modern America, Revised and Updated Edition*. New York: Basic Books, 2008.

MacDonald, Michael. *Overreach: Delusions of Regime Change in Iraq*. Cambridge, MA: Harvard University Press, 2014.

Mahnken, Thomas G. "U.S. Strategic and Organizational Subcultures." In Johnson, Kartchner, and Larsen, *Strategic Culture and Weapons of Mass Destruction*.

Marston, Daniel, and Carter Malkasian, eds. *Counterinsurgency in Modern Warfare*. Oxford, UK: Osprey, 2010.

Mason, Leonard. "The Characterization of American Culture in Studies of Acculturation." *American Anthropologist* 57 (December 1955).

Mattis, Gen. James N. Foreword to *Small-Unit Leader's Guide to Counterinsurgency*. US Marine Corps, MCIP 3-33.01 (2006).

———. Interview in McWilliams and Wheeler, *Al-Anbar Awakening*, Vol. 1.

McWilliams, CWO4 Timothy S. *U.S. Marines in Battle: Fallujah, November–December 2004*. Quantico, VA: History Division, United States Marine Corps, 2014.

McWilliams, CWO4 Timothy S., and Lt. Col. Kurtis P. Wheeler. *Al-Anbar Awakening*. Vol. 1, *American Perspectives*. Quantico, VA: Marine Corps University Press, 2009.

Mead, Walter Russell. *Special Providence: American Foreign Policy and How It Changed the World*. New York: Century Foundation, 2001.

Mearsheimer, John J. "Anarchy and the Struggle for Power." In Art and Jervis, *International Politics*.

Meilinger, Phillip S. "American Military Culture and Strategy." *Joint Force Quarterly* 46, no. 3 (2007).

———. "Book Review: *The Icarus Syndrome: The Role of Air Power Theory in the Evolution and Fate of the U.S. Air Force*." *Armed Forces and Society* 22, no. 1 (Fall 1995).

Melton, Stephen L. "Conceptualizing Victory Anew: Revisiting U.S. Law, Doctrine, and Policy for War and Its Aftermath." *Joint Force Quarterly* 60, no. 1 (2011).

Meyer, Christoph. "Convergence towards a European Strategic Culture? A Constructivist Framework for Explaining Changing Norms." *European Journal of International Relations* 11, no. 4 (December 2005).

———. "The Purpose and Pitfalls of Constructivist Forecasting: Insights from Strategic Culture Research for the European Union's Evolution as Military Power." *International Studies Quarterly* 55, no. 3 (September 2011).

Millett, Allan R. *Semper Fidelis: The History of the United States Marine Corps.* New York: Free Press, 1991.

Millett, Richard, and G. Dale Gaddy. "Administering the Protectorates: The U.S. Occupation of Haiti and the Dominican Republic." In Evans, *U.S. Marines and Irregular Warfare.*

Molavi, Afshin. *The Soul of Iran: A Nation's Journey to Freedom.* New York: W. W. Norton, 2002.

Montgomery, Col. Gary W., and CWO4 Timothy S. McWilliams, eds. *Al-Anbar Awakening.* Vol. 2, *Iraqi Perspectives.* Quantico, VA: Marine Corps University, 2009.

Moon, J. Donald. "The Logic of Political Inquiry: A Synthesis of Opposed Perspectives." In *Political Science: Scope and Theory, Handbook of Political Science.* Vol. 1. Edited by Fred I. Greenstein and Nelson W. Polsby. Reading, MA: Addison-Wesley, 1975.

Moore, Maj. Russell A. "Strategic Culture: How It Affects Strategic 'Outputs.'" Marine Corps College, Marine Corps University, Marine Corps Combat Development Command, 1998.

Morgan, Matthew J. "An Evolving View of Warfare: War and Peace and the American Military Profession." *Small Wars and Insurgencies* 16, no. 2 (June 2005).

Morgenthau, Hans J. "Six Principles of Political Realism." In Art and Jervis, *International Politics.*

Moyar, Mark. *A Question of Command: Counterinsurgency from the Civil War to Iraq.* New Haven, CT: Yale University Press, 2009.

Murray, Williamson. "An Anglo-American Strategic Culture?" Paper prepared for the symposium "Democracies in Partnership: 400 Years of Transatlantic Engagement," Williamsburg, VA, April 18–19, 2007.

———. "Does Military Culture Matter?" In *America the Vulnerable: Our Military Problems and How to Fix Them,* edited by John F. Lehman and Harvey Sicherman. Philadelphia: Foreign Policy Research Institute, 2002.

Nagl, John A. *Learning to Eat Soup with a Knife: Counterinsurgency Lessons from Malaya and Vietnam.* Chicago: University of Chicago Press, 2005.

O'Connell, Aaron B. *Underdogs: The Making of the Modern Marine Corps.* Cambridge, MA: Harvard University Press, 2012.

Pei, Minxin, Samia Amin, and Seth Garz, "Building Nations: The American Experience." In *Nation-Building: Beyond Afghanistan and Iraq,* edited by Francis Fukuyama. Baltimore: Johns Hopkins University Press, 2006.

Penny, Matthew T. "The Anbar Awakening in Context . . . and Why It Is So Hard to Replicate." *Military Review* 95, no. 2 (March/April 2015).

Peterson, Michael E. *The Combined Action Platoons: The U.S. Marines' Other War in Vietnam.* New York: Praeger, 1989.

Porter, Patrick. *Military Orientalism: Eastern War through Western Eyes.* London: Hurst, 2009.

Price, William. *Devil Dog Diary: A Day-by-Day Account of U.S. Marine Corps Basic Training.* Denver: Outskirts, 2008.

Record, Jeffrey. "The American Way of War: Cultural Barriers to Successful Counterinsurgency." CATO Institute, Policy Analysis No. 577 (September 1, 2006). http://www.cato.org/pub_display.php?pub_id=6640.

Reist, Brig. Gen. (Ret.) David G. Interview in McWilliams and Wheeler, *Al-Anbar Awakening*, Vol. 1.

Renda, Mary A. *Taking Haiti: Military Occupation and the Culture of U.S. Imperialism, 1915–1940*. Chapel Hill: University of North Carolina Press, 2001.

Reynolds, Col. (Ret.) Nicholas E. *Basrah, Baghdad, and Beyond: The U.S. Marine Corps in the Second Iraq War*. Annapolis, MD: Naval Institute Press, 2005.

Rhodes, Edward. "America's Crusade." In *Global Politics in a Changing World: A Reader*. 4th ed. Edited by Richard W. Mansbach and Edward Rhodes. Boston: Houghton Mifflin, 2009.

Ricks, Thomas E. *Fiasco*. New York: Penguin, 2006.

———. *The Generals*. Detroit: Thorndike Press (large-print edition), 2012.

———. *Making the Corps*. New York: Scribner, 2007.

Russell, James A. *Innovation, Transformation, and War: Counterinsurgency Operations in Anbar and Ninewa Provinces, Iraq, 2005–2007*. Stanford, CA: Stanford University Press, 2011.

Salmoni, Barak A., and Paula Holmes-Eber. *Operational Culture for the Warfighter: Principles and Applications*. Quantico, VA: Marine Corps University Press, 2008.

Sarkesian, Sam C. *America's Forgotten Wars: The Counterrevolutionary Past and Lessons for the Future*. Westport, CT: Greenwood, 1984.

Sattler, Lt. Gen. John F. Interview in McWilliams and Wheeler, *Al-Anbar Awakening*, Vol. 1.

Schaffer, Ronald. "The 1940 Small Wars Manual and the 'Lessons of History.'" *Military Affairs* 36, no. 2 (April 1972).

Schivelbusch, Wolfgang. *The Culture of Defeat: On National Trauma, Mourning, and Recovery*. London: Granta Books, 2001.

Schmidt, Hans. *Maverick Marine: General Smedley D. Butler and the Contradictions of American History*. Lexington: University Press of Kentucky, 1987.

———. *The United States Occupation of Haiti, 1915–1934*. New Brunswick, NJ: Rutgers University Press, 1971.

Shultz, Richard H. *The Marines Take Anbar: The Four-Year Fight against Al Qaeda*. Annapolis, MD: Naval Institute Press, 2013.

Siegl, Michael B. "Military Culture and Transformation." *Joint Force Quarterly* 49, no. 2 (2008).

Simmons, Brig. Gen. (Ret.) Edwin H. Foreword to *A Fellowship of Valor: The Battle History of the United States Marines*, by Col. Joseph H. Alexander. New York: HarperCollins, 1997.

———. *The United States Marines: A History*. 4th ed. Annapolis, MD: Naval Institute Press, 2003.

Sky, Emma. "Iraq, from Surge to Sovereignty: Winding Down the War in Iraq." *Foreign Affairs* 90, no. 2 (March/April 2011).

Sledge, E. B. *With the Old Breed: At Peleliu and Okinawa*. Novato, CA: Presido Press, 1981.

Smith, James M. *USAF Culture and Cohesion: Building an Air and Space Force for the 21st Century*. INSS Occasional Paper 19, Air Force Planning Series. Colorado Springs, CO: USAF Academy, USAF Institute for National Security Studies, June 1998. http://www.au.af.mil/au/awc/awcgate/usafa/ocp19.pdf.

Smith, Larry. *The Few and the Proud: Marine Corps Drill Instructors in Their Own Words*. New York: W. W. Norton, 2006.

Smith, Maj. Niel, and Col. Sean MacFarland. "Anbar Awakens: The Tipping Point." *Military Review* 88, no. 2 (March/April 2008).

Snyder, Jack. "The Concept of Strategic Culture: Caveat Emptor." In Jacobsen, *Strategic Power*.

———. *The Soviet Strategic Culture: Implications for Limited Nuclear Operations*. Santa Monica, CA: Rand, 1977.

Sondhaus, Lawrence. *Strategic Culture and Ways of War*. London: Routledge, 2006.

Southard, John. *Defend and Befriend: The U.S. Marine Corps and Combined Action Platoons in Vietnam*. Lexington: University Press of Kentucky, 2014.

Spooner, Richard. *A Marine Anthology: In the Spirit of Semper Fidelis*. Williamstown, NJ: Phillips Publications, 2010.

Stewart, Edward C., and Milton Bennett. *American Cultural Patterns: A Cross-Cultural Perspective*. Rev. ed. Boston: Intercultural Press, 1991.

Sturkey, Marion F. *Warrior Culture of the U.S. Marines*. Plum Branch, SC: Heritage Press International, 2010.

Sun Tzu Wu. *The Art of War*. Translated by Lionel Giles. Harrisburg, PA: Military Service Publishing, 1949.

Swidler, Ann. "Culture in Action: Symbols and Strategies." *American Sociological Review* 51, no. 2 (April 1986).

Terriff, Terry. "'Innovate or Die': Organizational Culture and the Origins of Maneuver Warfare in the United States Marine Corps." *Journal of Strategic Studies* 29, no. 3 (June 2006).

———. "Warriors and Innovators: Military Change and Organizational Culture in the US Marine Corps." *Defence Studies* 6, no. 2 (June 2006).

Thomason, Capt. John W., Jr. "The Marine Brigade." U.S. Naval Institute *Proceedings* (November 1928). In *On the Corps: USMC Wisdom from the Pages of Leatherneck, Marine Corps Gazette, and Proceedings*, edited by Lt. Col. Charles P. Neimeyer. Annapolis, MD: Naval Institute Press, 2008.

Twomey, Christopher P. "Lacunae in the Study of Culture in International Security." *Contemporary Security Policy* 29, no. 2 (August 2008).

Ulbrich, David J. *Preparing for Victory: Thomas Holcomb and the Making of the Modern Marine Corps, 1936–1943*. Annapolis, MD: Naval Institute Press, 2011.

United States Army. *Field Manual on Stability Operations: FM 3-07*. Headquarters, Department of the Army, October 2008.

United States Army / Marine Corps. *Counterinsurgency Field Manual: FM 3-24*. Chicago: University of Chicago Press, 2007.

United States Marine Corps. *Fact Sheet on the Combined Action Force*. III Marine Amphibious Force. March 31, 1970. Declassified document provided on the U.S. Marines Combined Action Platoons website. http://capmarine.com/cap /data.htm.

———. *Marine Corps Operating Concepts: Assuring Littoral Access ... Winning Small Wars* [changed to *Proven Crisis Response*]. 3rd ed. (June 2010). https://www.defensetech.org/2010/06/29/marine-corps-releases-new-operating -concept/.

———. *Marine Corps Values and Leadership: User's Guide for Discussion Leaders*. Quantico, VA: Marine Corps University, 1996.

———. *Marine Corps Vision and Strategy 2025*. Quantico, VA: Marine Corps Combat Development Command, June 2008. https://search.usa.gov/search?affiliate =mdm&query=2025.

———. *Small-Unit Leaders' Guide to Counterinsurgency*. MCIP 3-33.01 (2006).

———. *Small Wars Manual*. New York: Skyhorse, 2009. Originally published 1940.

———. *Sustaining the Transformation*. US Marine Corps MCRP 6-11D.

———. *United States Marine Guidebook of Essential Subjects*. Arlington, VA: Marine Corps Institute, 1983.

———. *Warfighting*. MCDP 1. US Marine Corps, 1997.

Walker, Col. Michael M. Interview in McWilliams and Wheeler, *Al-Anbar Awakening*, Vol. 1.

Waltz, Kenneth N. "The Anarchic Structure of World Politics." In Art and Jervis, *International Politics*.

Warren, James. "Small Wars and Military Culture." *Culture and Society* 36, no. 6 (September/October 1999).

Weigley, Russell F. *The American Way of War: A History of United States Military Strategy and Policy*. Bloomington: Indiana University Press, 1973.

West, Bing. *No True Glory: A Frontline Account of the Battle of Fallujah*. New York: Bantam Dell, 2005.

———. *The Strongest Tribe: War, Politics, and the Endgame in Iraq*. New York: Random House, 2008.

———. *The Village*. New York: Pocket Books, 2003.

West, Bing, and Maj. Gen. Ray L. Smith. *The March Up: Taking Baghdad with the United States Marines*. New York: Bantam Dell, 2003.

Weston, J. Kael. *The Mirror Test: America at War in Iraq and Afghanistan*. New York: Alfred A. Knopf, 2016.

Williams, Robin. "Values and Modern Education in the United States." In *Values in America*, edited by Donald Barrett. Notre Dame, IN: University of Notre Dame Press, 1961.

Wilson, Peter. "The English School Meets the Chicago School: The Case for a Grounded Theory of International Institutions." *International Studies Review* 14 (2012).

Woulfe, James B. *Into the Crucible: Making Marines for the 21st Century*. Novato, CA: Presidio Press, 1998.

Yates, Lawrence A. *The US Military's Experience in Stability Operations, 1789–2005*. Global War on Terrorism Occasional Paper 15. Fort Leavenworth, KS: Combat Studies Institute Press, 2006.

Zappa, Maj. Daniel R. Interview in McWilliams and Wheeler, *Al-Anbar Awakening*, Vol. 1.

Zilmer, Maj. Gen. Richard C. Interview in McWilliams and Wheeler, *Al-Anbar Awakening*, Vol. 1.

# INDEX

# ABOUT THE AUTHOR

Jeannie L. Johnson is an assistant professor in the Political Science Department of Utah State University. She worked as an intelligence analyst from 1998 to 1999 and pioneered the Cultural Topography Framework with Matt Berrett, then the Central Intelligence Agency's assistant director for global issues. Dr. Johnson's primary research interest, strategic culture, examines the impact of national and organizational cultures on the formation of security policy.

Milton Keynes UK
Ingram Content Group UK Ltd.
UKHW040027030224
437022UK00003B/73

9 781626 165564